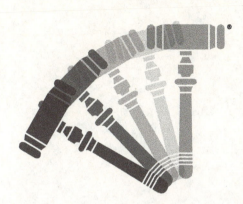

Casenote® *Legal Briefs*

TORTS

Keyed to Courses Using

Epstein and Sharkey's
Cases and Materials on Torts
Eleventh Edition

Wolters Kluwer

Copyright © 2016 CCH Incorporated. All Rights Reserved.

Published by Wolters Kluwer in New York.

Wolters Kluwer Legal & Regulatory US serves customers worldwide with CCH, Aspen Publishers, and Kluwer Law International products. (www.WKLegaledu.com)

No part of this publication may be reproduced or transmitted in any form or by any means, electronic or mechanical, including photocopy, recording, or utilized by any information storage and retrieval system, without written permission from the publisher. For information about permissions or to request permissions online, visit us at www.WKLegaledu.com, or a written request may be faxed to our permissions department at 212-771-0803.

To contact Customer Service, e-mail customer.service@wolterskluwer.com, call 1-800-234-1660, fax 1-800-901-9075, or mail correspondence to:

Wolters Kluwer
Attn: Order Department
P.O. Box 990
Frederick, MD 21705

Printed in the United States of America.

1 2 3 4 5 6 7 8 9 0

ISBN 978-1-4548-7319-8

SUSTAINABLE FORESTRY INITIATIVE   Certified Sourcing
www.sfiprogram.org
SFI-00756

About Wolters Kluwer Legal & Regulatory US

Wolters Kluwer Legal & Regulatory US delivers expert content and solutions in the areas of law, corporate compliance, health compliance, reimbursement, and legal education. Its practical solutions help customers successfully navigate the demands of a changing environment to drive their daily activities, enhance decision quality and inspire confident outcomes.

Serving customers worldwide, its legal and regulatory portfolio includes products under the Aspen Publishers, CCH Incorporated, Kluwer Law International, ftwilliam.com and MediRegs names. They are regarded as exceptional and trusted resources for general legal and practice-specific knowledge, compliance and risk management, dynamic workflow solutions, and expert commentary.

Format for the Casenote® Legal Brief

Nature of Case: This section identifies the form of action (e.g., breach of contract, negligence, battery), the type of proceeding (e.g., demurrer, appeal from trial court's jury instructions), or the relief sought (e.g., damages, injunction, criminal sanctions).

Palsgraf v. Long Island R.R. Co.

Injured bystander (P) v. Railroad company (D)

N.Y. Ct. App., 248 N.Y. 339, 162 N.E. 99 (1928).

Party ID: Quick identification of the relationship between the parties.

Fact Summary: This is included to refresh your memory and can be used as a quick reminder of the facts.

NATURE OF CASE: Appeal from judgment affirming verdict for plaintiff seeking damages for personal injury.

FACT SUMMARY: Helen Palsgraf (P) was injured on R.R.'s (D) train platform when R.R.'s (D) guard helped a passenger aboard a moving train, causing his package to fall on the tracks. The package contained fireworks which exploded, creating a shock that tipped a scale onto Palsgraf (P).

Rule of Law: Summarizes the general principle of law that the case illustrates. It may be used for instant recall of the court's holding and for classroom discussion or home review.

🏛 **RULE OF LAW**
The risk reasonably to be perceived defines the duty to be obeyed.

FACTS: Helen Palsgraf (P) purchased a ticket to Rockaway Beach from R.R. (D) and was waiting on the train platform. As she waited, two men ran to catch a train that was pulling out from the platform. The first man jumped aboard, but the second man, who appeared as if he might fall, was helped aboard by the guard on the train who had kept the door open so they could jump aboard. A guard on the platform also helped by pushing him onto the train. The man was carrying a package wrapped in newspaper. In the process, the man dropped his package, which fell on the tracks. The package contained fireworks and exploded. The shock of the explosion was apparently of great enough strength to tip over some scales at the other end of the platform, which fell on Palsgraf (P) and injured her. A jury awarded her damages, and R.R. (D) appealed.

Facts: This section contains all relevant facts of the case, including the contentions of the parties and the lower court holdings. It is written in a logical order to give the student a clear understanding of the case. The plaintiff and defendant are identified by their proper names throughout and are always labeled with a (P) or (D).

ISSUE: Does the risk reasonably to be perceived define the duty to be obeyed?

HOLDING AND DECISION: (Cardozo, C.J.) Yes. The risk reasonably to be perceived defines the duty to be obeyed. If there is no foreseeable hazard to the injured party as the result of a seemingly innocent act, the act does not become a tort because it happened to be a wrong as to another. If the wrong was not willful, the plaintiff must show that the act as to her had such great and apparent possibilities of danger as to entitle her to protection. Negligence in the abstract is not enough upon which to base liability. Negligence is a relative concept, evolving out of the common law doctrine of trespass on the case. To establish liability, the defendant must owe a legal duty of reasonable care to the injured party. A cause of action in tort will lie where harm,

though unintended, could have been averted or avoided by observance of such a duty. The scope of the duty is limited by the range of danger that a reasonable person could foresee. In this case, there was nothing to suggest from the appearance of the parcel or otherwise that the parcel contained fireworks. The guard could not reasonably have had any warning of a threat to Palsgraf (P), and R.R. (D) therefore cannot be held liable. Judgment is reversed in favor of R.R. (D).

DISSENT: (Andrews, J.) The concept that there is no negligence unless R.R. (D) owes a legal duty to take care as to Palsgraf (P) herself is too narrow. Everyone owes to the world at large the duty of refraining from those acts that may unreasonably threaten the safety of others. If the guard's action was negligent as to those nearby, it was also negligent as to those outside what might be termed the "danger zone." For Palsgraf (P) to recover, R.R.'s (D) negligence must have been the proximate cause of her injury, a question of fact for the jury.

Concurrence/Dissent: All concurrences and dissents are briefed whenever they are included by the casebook editor.

▶ *ANALYSIS*

The majority defined the limit of the defendant's liability in terms of the danger that a reasonable person in defendant's situation would have perceived. The dissent argued that the limitation should not be placed on liability, but rather on damages. Judge Andrews suggested that only injuries that would not have happened but for R.R.'s (D) negligence should be compensable. Both the majority and dissent recognized the policy-driven need to limit liability for negligent acts, seeking, in the words of Judge Andrews, to define a framework "that will be practical and in keeping with the general understanding of mankind." The Restatement (Second) of Torts has accepted Judge Cardozo's view.

Analysis: This last paragraph gives you a broad understanding of where the case "fits in" with other cases in the section of the book and with the entire course. It is a hornbook-style discussion indicating whether the case is a majority or minority opinion and comparing the principal case with other cases in the casebook. It may also provide analysis from restatements, uniform codes, and law review articles. The analysis will prove to be invaluable to classroom discussion.

Quicknotes

FORESEEABILITY A reasonable expectation that change is the probable result of certain acts or omissions.

NEGLIGENCE Conduct falling below the standard of care that a reasonable person would demonstrate under similar conditions.

PROXIMATE CAUSE The natural sequence of events without which an injury would not have been sustained.

Issue: The issue is a concise question that brings out the essence of the opinion as it relates to the section of the casebook in which the case appears. Both substantive and procedural issues are included if relevant to the decision.

Holding and Decision: This section offers a clear and in-depth discussion of the rule of the case and the court's rationale. It is written in easy-to-understand language and answers the issue presented by applying the law to the facts of the case. When relevant, it includes a thorough discussion of the exceptions to the case as listed by the court, any major cites to the other cases on point, and the names of the judges who wrote the decisions.

Quicknotes: Conveniently defines legal terms found in the case and summarizes the nature of any statutes, codes, or rules referred to in the text.

Wolters Kluwer Legal & Regulatory US is proud to offer *Casenote*® *Legal Briefs*—continuing thirty years of publishing America's best-selling legal briefs.

Casenote® *Legal Briefs* are designed to help you save time when briefing assigned cases. Organized under convenient headings, they show you how to abstract the basic facts and holdings from the text of the actual opinions handed down by the courts. Used as part of a rigorous study regimen, they can help you spend more time analyzing and critiquing points of law than on copying bits and pieces of judicial opinions into your notebook or outline.

Casenote® *Legal Briefs* should never be used as a substitute for assigned casebook readings. They work best when read as a follow-up to reviewing the underlying opinions themselves. Students who try to avoid reading and digesting the judicial opinions in their casebooks or online sources will end up shortchanging themselves in the long run. The ability to absorb, critique, and restate the dynamic and complex elements of case law decisions is crucial to your success in law school and beyond. It cannot be developed vicariously.

Casenote® *Legal Briefs* represents but one of the many offerings in Legal Education's Study Aid Timeline, which includes:

- *Casenote*® *Legal Briefs*
- *Emanuel*® *Law Outlines*
- Emanuel® *Law in a Flash* Flash Cards
- Emanuel® *CrunchTime*® Series

Each of these series is designed to provide you with easy-to-understand explanations of complex points of law. Each volume offers guidance on the principles of legal analysis and, consulted regularly, will hone your ability to spot relevant issues. We have titles that will help you prepare for class, prepare for your exams, and enhance your general comprehension of the law along the way.

To find out more about our law school tools for success, visit us at *www.WKLegaledu.com* or email us at *legaledu@wolterskluwer.com*. We'll be happy to assist you.

A. Decide on a Format and Stick to It

Structure is essential to a good brief. It enables you to arrange systematically the related parts that are scattered throughout most cases, thus making manageable and understandable what might otherwise seem to be an endless and unfathomable sea of information. There are, of course, an unlimited number of formats that can be utilized. However, it is best to find one that suits your needs and stick to it. Consistency breeds both efficiency and the security that when called upon you will know where to look in your brief for the information you are asked to give.

Any format, as long as it presents the essential elements of a case in an organized fashion, can be used. Experience, however, has led *Casenote® Legal Briefs* to develop and utilize the following format because of its logical flow and universal applicability.

NATURE OF CASE: This is a brief statement of the legal character and procedural status of the case (e.g., "Appeal of a burglary conviction").

There are many different alternatives open to a litigant dissatisfied with a court ruling. The key to determining which one has been used is to discover *who is asking this court for what.*

This first entry in the brief should be kept as *short as possible.* Use the court's terminology if you understand it. But since jurisdictions vary as to the titles of pleadings, the best entry is the one that addresses who wants what in this proceeding, not the one that sounds most like the court's language.

RULE OF LAW: A statement of the general principle of law that the case illustrates (e.g., "An acceptance that varies any term of the offer is considered a rejection and counteroffer").

Determining the rule of law of a case is a procedure similar to determining the issue of the case. Avoid being fooled by red herrings; there may be a few rules of law mentioned in the case excerpt, but usually only one is *the* rule with which the casebook editor is concerned. The techniques used to locate the issue, described below, may also be utilized to find the rule of law. Generally, your best guide is simply the chapter heading. It is a clue to the point the casebook editor seeks to make and should be kept in mind when reading every case in the respective section.

FACTS: A synopsis of only the essential facts of the case, i.e., those bearing upon or leading up to the issue.

The facts entry should be a short statement of the events and transactions that led one party to initiate legal proceedings against another in the first place. While some cases conveniently state the salient facts at the beginning of the decision, in other instances they will have to be culled from hiding places throughout the text, even from concurring and dissenting opinions. Some of the "facts" will often be in dispute and should be so noted. Conflicting evidence may be briefly pointed up. "Hard" facts must be included. Both must be *relevant* in order to be listed in the facts entry. It is impossible to tell what is relevant until the entire case is read, as the ultimate determination of the rights and liabilities of the parties may turn on something buried deep in the opinion.

Generally, the facts entry should not be longer than three to five *short* sentences.

It is often helpful to identify the role played by a party in a given context. For example, in a construction contract case the identification of a party as the "contractor" or "builder" alleviates the need to tell that that party was the one who was supposed to have built the house.

It is always helpful, and a good general practice, to identify the "plaintiff" and the "defendant." This may seem elementary and uncomplicated, but, especially in view of the creative editing practiced by some casebook editors, it is sometimes a difficult or even impossible task. Bear in mind that the *party presently* seeking something from this court may not be the plaintiff, and that sometimes only the cross-claim of a defendant is treated in the excerpt. Confusing or misaligning the parties can ruin your analysis and understanding of the case.

ISSUE: A statement of the general legal question answered by or illustrated in the case. For clarity, the issue is best put in the form of a question capable of a "yes" or "no" answer. In reality, the issue is simply the Rule of Law put in the form of a question (e.g., "May an offer be accepted by performance?").

The major problem presented in discerning what is *the* issue in the case is that an opinion usually purports to raise and answer several questions. However, except for rare cases, only one such question is really the issue in the case. Collateral issues not necessary to the resolution of the matter in controversy are handled by the court by language known as *"obiter dictum"* or merely *"dictum."* While dicta may be included later in the brief, they have no place under the issue heading.

To find the issue, ask *who wants what* and then go on to ask *why did that party succeed or fail in getting it.* Once this is determined, the "why" should be turned into a question.

The complexity of the issues in the cases will vary, but in all cases a single-sentence question should sum up the issue. *In a few cases,* there will be two, or even more rarely, three issues of equal importance to the resolution of the case. Each should be expressed in a single-sentence question.

Since many issues are resolved by a court in coming to a final disposition of a case, the casebook editor will reproduce the portion of the opinion containing the issue or issues most relevant to the area of law under scrutiny. A noted law professor gave this advice: "Close the book; look at the title on the cover." Chances are, if it is Property, you need not concern yourself with whether, for example, the federal government's treatment of the plaintiff's land really raises a federal question sufficient to support jurisdiction on this ground in federal court.

The same rule applies to chapter headings designating sub-areas within the subjects. They tip you off as to what the text is designed to teach. The cases are arranged in a casebook to show a progression or development of the law, so that the preceding cases may also help.

It is also most important to remember to *read the notes and questions* at the end of a case to determine what the editors wanted you to have gleaned from it.

HOLDING AND DECISION: This section should succinctly explain the rationale of the court in arriving at its decision. In capsulizing the "reasoning" of the court, it should always include an application of the general rule or rules of law to the specific facts of the case. Hidden justifications come to light in this entry: the reasons for the state of the law, the public policies, the biases and prejudices, those considerations that influence the justices' thinking and, ultimately, the outcome of the case. At the end, there should be a short indication of the disposition or procedural resolution of the case (e.g., "Decision of the trial court for Mr. Smith (P) reversed").

The foregoing format is designed to help you "digest" the reams of case material with which you will be faced in your law school career. Once mastered by practice, it will place at your fingertips the information the authors of your casebooks have sought to impart to you in case-by-case illustration and analysis.

B. Be as Economical as Possible in Briefing Cases

Once armed with a format that encourages succinctness, it is as important to be economical with regard to the time spent on the actual reading of the case as it is to be economical in the writing of the brief itself. This does not mean "skimming" a case. Rather, it means reading the case with an "eye" trained to recognize into which "section" of your brief a particular passage or line fits and having a system for quickly and precisely marking the case so that the passages fitting any one particular part of the brief can be easily identified and brought together in a concise and accurate manner when the brief is actually written.

It is of no use to simply repeat everything in the opinion of the court; record only enough information to trigger your recollection of what the court said. Nevertheless, an accurate statement of the "law of the case," i.e., the legal principle applied to the facts, is absolutely essential to class preparation and to learning the law under the case method.

To that end, it is important to develop a "shorthand" that you can use to make marginal notations. These notations will tell you at a glance in which section of the brief you will be placing that particular passage or portion of the opinion.

Some students prefer to underline all the salient portions of the opinion (with a pencil or colored underliner marker), making marginal notations as they go along. Others prefer the color-coded method of underlining, utilizing different colors of markers to underline the salient portions of the case, each separate color being used to represent a different section of the brief. For example, blue underlining could be used for passages relating to the rule of law, yellow for those relating to the issue, and green for those relating to the holding and decision, etc. While it has its advocates, the color-coded method can be confusing and time-consuming (all that time spent on changing colored markers). Furthermore, it can interfere with the continuity and concentration many students deem essential to the reading of a case for maximum comprehension. In the end, however, it is a matter of personal preference and style. Just remember, whatever method you use, underlining must be used sparingly or its value is lost.

If you take the marginal notation route, an efficient and easy method is to go along underlining the key portions of the case and placing in the margin alongside them the following "markers" to indicate where a particular passage or line "belongs" in the brief you will write:

N   (NATURE OF CASE)
RL   (RULE OF LAW)
I   (ISSUE)
HL   (HOLDING AND DECISION, relates to
      the RULE OF LAW behind the decision)
HR   (HOLDING AND DECISION, gives the
      RATIONALE or reasoning behind the
      decision)
HA   (HOLDING AND DECISION, applies the
      general principle(s) of law to the facts of
      the case to arrive at the decision)

Remember that a particular passage may well contain information necessary to more than one part of your brief, in which case you simply note that in the margin. If you are using the color-coded underlining method instead of marginal notation, simply make asterisks or checks in the margin next to the passage in question in the colors that indicate the additional sections of the brief where it might be utilized.

The economy of utilizing "shorthand" in marking cases for briefing can be maintained in the actual brief writing process itself by utilizing "law student shorthand" within the brief. There are many commonly used words and phrases for which abbreviations can be substituted in your briefs (and in your class notes also). You can develop abbreviations that are personal to you and which will save you a lot of time. A reference list of briefing abbreviations can be found on page x of this book.

C. Use Both the Briefing Process and the Brief as a Learning Tool

Now that you have a format and the tools for briefing cases efficiently, the most important thing is to make the time spent in briefing profitable to you and to make the most advantageous use of the briefs you create. Of course, the briefs are invaluable for classroom reference when you are called upon to explain or analyze a particular case. However, they are also useful in reviewing for exams. A quick glance at the fact summary should bring the case to mind, and a rereading of the rule of law should enable you to go over the underlying legal concept in your mind, how it was applied in that particular case, and how it might apply in other factual settings.

As to the value to be derived from engaging in the briefing process itself, there is an immediate benefit that arises from being forced to sift through the essential facts and reasoning from the court's opinion and to succinctly express them in your own words in your brief. The process ensures that you understand the case and the point that it illustrates, and that means you will be ready to absorb further analysis and information brought forth in class. It also ensures you will have something to say when called upon in class. The briefing process helps develop a mental agility for getting to the *gist* of a case and for identifying, expounding on, and applying the legal concepts and issues found there. The briefing process is the mental process on which you must rely in taking law school examinations; it is also the mental process upon which a lawyer relies in serving his clients and in making his living.

Abbreviations for Briefs

acceptance	acp	offer	O
affirmed	aff	offeree	OE
answer	ans	offeror	OR
assumption of risk	a/r	ordinance	ord
attorney	atty	pain and suffering	p/s
beyond a reasonable doubt	b/r/d	parol evidence	p/e
bona fide purchaser	BFP	plaintiff	P
breach of contract	br/k	prima facie	p/f
cause of action	c/a	probable cause	p/c
common law	c/l	proximate cause	px/c
Constitution	Con	real property	r/p
constitutional	con	reasonable doubt	r/d
contract	K	reasonable man	r/m
contributory negligence	c/n	rebuttable presumption	rb/p
cross	x	remanded	rem
cross-complaint	x/c	res ipsa loquitur	RIL
cross-examination	x/ex	respondeat superior	r/s
cruel and unusual punishment	c/u/p	Restatement	RS
defendant	D	reversed	rev
dismissed	dis	Rule Against Perpetuities	RAP
double jeopardy	d/j	search and seizure	s/s
due process	d/p	search warrant	s/w
equal protection	e/p	self-defense	s/d
equity	eq	specific performance	s/p
evidence	ev	statute	S
exclude	exc	statute of frauds	S/F
exclusionary rule	exc/r	statute of limitations	S/L
felony	f/n	summary judgment	s/j
freedom of speech	f/s	tenancy at will	t/w
good faith	g/f	tenancy in common	t/c
habeas corpus	h/c	tenant	t
hearsay	hr	third party	TP
husband	H	third party beneficiary	TPB
injunction	inj	transferred intent	TI
in loco parentis	ILP	unconscionable	uncon
inter vivos	I/v	unconstitutional	unconst
joint tenancy	j/t	undue influence	u/e
judgment	judgt	Uniform Commercial Code	UCC
jurisdiction	jur	unilateral	uni
last clear chance	LCC	vendee	VE
long-arm statute	LAS	vendor	VR
majority view	maj	versus	v
meeting of minds	MOM	void for vagueness	VFV
minority view	min	weight of authority	w/a
Miranda rule	Mir/r	weight of the evidence	w/e
Miranda warnings	Mir/w	wife	W
negligence	neg	with	w/
notice	ntc	within	w/i
nuisance	nus	without	w/o
obligation	ob	without prejudice	w/o/p
obscene	obs	wrongful death	wr/d

Table of Cases

A Alcorn v. Mitchell 13
American Motorcycle Association v.
    Superior Court 78
Andrews v. United Airlines 43
Anon 52
Anonymous 126
Asahi Kasei Pharma Corp. v. Actelion Ltd. 225
Auvil v. CBS 60 Minutes 188

B Baltimore and Ohio R.R. v. Goodman 56
Barker v. Lull Engineering Co. 141
Beems v. Chicago, Rock Island &
    Peoria R.R. 63
Berkovitz v. United States 238
Berry v. Sugar Notch Borough 87
Bird v. Holbrook 8
Blumenthal v. Drudge 176
Blyth v. Birmingham Water Works 39
Bolton v. Stone 28
Boomer v. Atlantic Cement Co. 125
Boring v. Google Inc. 201
Breunig v. American Family Insurance Co. 36
Brower v. New York Central & H.R.R. 88
Brown v. Collins 25
Brown v. Kendall 21
Brown & Williamson Tobacco Corp. v.
    Jacobson 191
Buch v. Amory Manufacturing Co. 100
Butterfield v. Forrester 62
Byrne v. Boadle 58

C Campo v. Scofield 139
Canterbury v. Spence 51
Carroll Towing Co., United States v. 42
Casa Clara Condominium Association, Inc. v.
    Charley Toppino & Sons, Inc. 136
Clinton v. Jones 239
Clodgo v. Rentavision, Inc. 167
Coblyn v. Kennedy's, Inc. 14
Coggs v. Bernard 105
Colmenares Vivas v. Sun Alliance
    Insurance Co. 59
Cooley v. Public Service Co. 41
Courvoisier v. Raymond 7
Cox Broadcasting Corp. v. Cohn 205
Crisci v. Security Insurance Co. 164
Curtis Publishing Co. v. Butts 194

D Dalury v. S-K-I, Ltd. 70
Daly v. General Motors Corp. 146
Daniels v. Evans 35
Denver & Rio Grande R.R. v. Peterson 38
Derheim v. N. Fiorito Co. 66
Desnick v. American Broadcasting Co., Inc. 203
Dillon v. Legg 98

Dimmitt Chevrolet, Inc. v. Southeastern Fidelity
    Insurance Corp. 165
Dougherty v. Stepp 3
Duncan v. Kansas City Southern Railway 157

E Edgington v. Fitzmaurice 219
E. Hulton & Co. v. Jones 183
Ellsworth v. Martindale-Hubbell Law Directory,
    Inc. 185
Ely-Norris Safe Co. v. Mosler Safe Co. 235
Ensign v. Walls 124
Erie Railroad Co. v. Stewart 106
Escola v. Coca Cola Bottling Co. of Fresno 134

F Factors Etc., Inc. v. Pro Arts, Inc. 211
Faulk v. Aware, Inc. (1962) 186
Faulk v. Aware, Inc. (1963) 187
Firth v. State of New York 175
532 Madison Avenue Gourmet Foods, Inc. v.
    Finlandia Center, Inc. 229
Fletcher v. City of Aberdeen 37
Fletcher v. Rylands (1865) 22
Fletcher v. Rylands (1866) 23
Fontainebleau Hotel Corp. v. Forty-Five
    Twenty-Five, Inc. 122
Fuller v. Illinois Central R.R. 67

G Gehrts v. Batteen 117
Geier v. American Honda Motor Co. 147
General Electric Co. v. Joiner 85
Gertz v. Robert Welch, Inc. 195
Gyerman v. United States Lines Co. 64

H Hammontree v. Jenner 29
Harding v. Town of Townshend 161
Haynes v. Alfred A. Knopf, Inc. 206
Hebert v. Enos 96
Herskovits v. Group Health Cooperative 84
Hood v. Ryobi America Corp. 145
Hudson v. Craft 5
Hull v. Orange, *see* The Thorns Case 18
Hurley v. Eddingfield 101

I I. de S. and Wife v. W. de S. 11
Indiana Harbor Belt R.R. v. American
    Cyanamid Co. 119
Intel Corp. v. Hamidi 113
International News Service v. Associated
    Press 232
Ira S. Bushey & Sons, Inc. v. United States 127

K Kemezy v. Peters 158
Kennedy v. Cannon 190
Kingston v. Chicago & N.W. Ry. 79
Kline v. 1500 Massachusetts Avenue
    Apartment Corp. 108

L Laborers Local 17 Health and Benefit Fund v.
Philip Morris, Inc. *220*
Laidlaw v. Organ................................ *218*
Lama v. Borras.................................. *48*
Lamson v. American Axe & Tool Co. *68*
LeRoy Fibre Co. v. Chicago, Milwaukee and
St. Paul Ry. *65*
Li v. Yellow Cab Co. of California *71*
Lumley v. Gye.................................. *224*

M MacDonald v. Ortho Pharmaceutical Corp. *142*
MacPherson v. Buick Motor Co. *133*
Marshall v. Nugent *94*
Martin v. Herzog. *54*
Mayhew v. Sullivan Mining Co. *45*
McDougald v. Garber *154*
McGuire v. Almy................................ *6*
Michalson v. Nutting.......................... *121*
Mims v. Metropolitan Life Insurance Co. *173*
Mitchell v. Rochester Railway *97*
Moch Co. v. Rensselaer Water Co. *107*
Mogul Steamship Co. v. McGregor, Gow &
Co. *231*
Mohr v. Williams *4*
Montgomery v. National Convoy & Trucking
Co. *102*
Moore v. Regents of the University of
California *115*
Mosler Safe Co. v. Ely-Norris Safe Co. *236*
Murphy v. Steeplechase Amusement Co. *69*
Murray v. UNMC Physicians *49*
Muzikowski v. Paramount Pictures Corp. *178*

N Nader v. General Motors Corp. *200*
National Basketball Association, The v.
Motorola, Inc. *233*
NCAA Student-Athlete Name & Likeness
Licensing Litig., In re *208*
New York Central R.R v. Grimstad *75*
New York Times Co. v. Sullivan *192*

O Obsidian Finance Group, LLC v. Cox............ *196*
Osborne v. McMasters *53*
Osborne v. Montgomery....................... *40*
O'Shea v. Riverway Towing Co. *156*
Overseas Tankship (U.K.) Ltd. v. Morts Dock &
Engineering Co., Ltd. (Wagon Mound
No. [1]) *91*

P Palsgraf v. Long Island R.R. *92*
Parmiter v. Coupland *177*
Pasley v. Freeman............................ *214*
People Express Airlines, Inc. v. Consolidated
Rail Corp. *228*
Petrovich v. Share Health Plan of Illinois,
Inc. *128*
Ploof v. Putnam *9*
Poggi v. Scott *114*

Pokora v. Wabash Ry. *57*
Polemis & Furness, Withy & Co., In re *90*
Powell v. Fall................................ *26*

R Rainer v. Union Carbide Corporation.............. *169*
Robert Addie & Sons (Collieries), Ltd. v.
Dumbreck.................................... *103*
Roberts v. Ring *34*
Rogers v. Elliott *123*
Rowland v. Christian *104*
Ryan v. New York Central R.R. *86*
Rylands v. Fletcher........................... *24*

S Scott v. Shepherd............................ *20*
Sidis v. F-R Publishing Corp. *204*
Sindell v. Abbott Laboratories *81*
Spano v. Perini Corp. *118*
Speller v. Sears, Roebuck and Co. *138*
State Farm Mutual Automobile Insurance Co. v.
Campbell.................................... *159*
Stone v. Bolton *27*
Sullivan v. Old Colony Street Railway............ *152*
Summers v. Tice *80*
Swinton v. Whitinsville Savings Bank.............. *217*

T Tarasoff v. Regents of University of California..... *109*
Tarleton v. M'Gawley *227*
Terwilliger v. Wands *184*
The Thorns Case (Hull v. Orange) *18*
Time, Inc. v. Hill............................. *207*
Titus v. Bradford, B. & K. R. Co. *44*
The T.J. Hooper (1931)......................... *46*
The T.J. Hooper (1932)......................... *47*
Tuberville v. Savage.......................... *12*

U Uhr v. East Greenbush Cent. Sch. Dist. *55*
Ultramares Corporation v. Touche............... *221*
Union Stock Yards Co. of Omaha v. Chicago,
Burlington, & Quincy R.R. *77*

V Varian Medical Systems, Inc. v. Delfino *181*
Vassallo v. Baxter Healthcare Corp. *143*
Vaughan v. Menlove........................... *33*
Vincent v. Lake Erie Transportation Co. *10*
Virden v. Betts and Beer Construction
Company.................................... *95*
Vogel v. Grant-Lafayette Electric
Cooperative................................. *120*
Volkswagen of America, Inc. v. Young.......... *140*
Vosburg v. Putney *2*
Vulcan Metals Co. v. Simmons Manufacturing
Co. *216*

W Wagner v. International Railway *89*
Wagon Mound (No. 1), *see* Overseas
Tankship (U.K.) Ltd. v. Morts Dock &
Engineering Co., Ltd. *91*
Watt v. Longsdon.............................. *189*
Weaver v. Ward............................... *19*

Wilkinson v. Downton 15
Wilkow v. Forbes, Inc. 180
Wilson v. Workers' Compensation Appeals
   Board 168
Winterbottom v. Wright.......................... 132

Wyeth v. Levine.................................... 148
Y Ybarra v. Spangard 60
Z Zibbell v. Southern Pacific Co. 153
Zuchowicz v. United States......................... 76

CHAPTER 1

Intentional Harms: The Prima Facie Case and Defenses

Quick Reference Rules of Law

PAGE

1. *Vosburg v. Putney.* In an action to recover damages for an alleged assault and battery, the victim must only show either that the alleged wrongdoer had an unlawful intention to produce harm (i.e., an unlawful intention in committing the act which occurred) or that he committed an unlawful act. — 2

2. *Dougherty v. Stepp.* Every unprivileged entry onto the land of another is a trespass regardless of the amount of actual damages. — 3

3. *Mohr v. Williams.* If defendant's actions exceed the consent given and defendant does a substantially different act than the one authorized, defendant is liable. — 4

4. *Hudson v. Craft.* A promoter is liable where he conducts boxing matches or prize fights without a license and in violation of the statutory provisions regardless of the rights as between the contestants. The consent of the combatants does not relieve him of that liability. — 5

5. *McGuire v. Almy.* An insane person may be capable of entertaining the intent to commit a battery. — 6

6. *Courvoisier v. Raymond.* An action of force is justified by self-defense whenever the circumstances are such as to cause a reasonable man to believe that his life is in danger or that he is in danger of receiving great bodily harm and that it is necessary to use such force for protection. — 7

7. *Bird v. Holbrook.* Unless adequate notices are posted, a spring gun cannot be used to protect property. — 8

8. *Ploof v. Putnam.* Necessity justifies the entry upon the land of another. — 9

9. *Vincent v. Lake Erie Transportation Co.* Public necessity may require the taking of private property for public purposes, but our system of jurisprudence requires that compensation be made. — 10

10. *I. de S. and Wife v. W. de S.* An act that causes another to be fearful of a harmful or offensive contact is known as an assault, and the plaintiff may recover damages, even though there is no actual physical contact or physical harm. — 11

11. *Tuberville v. Savage.* A threatening gesture will not constitute an assault when there are accompanying words that clearly negate the gesture's threat. — 12

12. *Alcorn v. Mitchell.* Punitive damages may be assessed for highly offensive conduct to provide an alternative redress to physical retribution. — 13

13. *Coblyn v. Kennedy's, Inc.* (1) If a person is restrained in his or her personal liberty by fear of a personal difficulty, it amounts to false imprisonment. (2) If a shopkeeper has reasonable grounds to believe a person has committed or is attempting to commit larceny of goods for sale on the premises, the shopkeeper may detain that person in a reasonable manner for a reasonable length of time. — 14

14. *Wilkinson v. Downton.* Extreme and outrageous conduct which causes physical harm or mental distress creates a valid cause of action. — 15

Vosburg v. Putney

Student (P) v. Student (D)

Wis. Sup. Ct., 50 N.W. 403 (1891).

NATURE OF CASE: Appeal from award of damages for a battery.

FACT SUMMARY: While at school, 11-year-old Putney (D) kicked 14-year-old Vosburg (P) in the leg, and, as a result, Vosburg (P) later lost the use of that leg.

🏛 RULE OF LAW
In an action to recover damages for an alleged assault and battery, the victim must only show either that the alleged wrongdoer had an unlawful intention to produce harm (i.e., an unlawful intention in committing the act which occurred) or that he committed an unlawful act.

FACTS: Vosburg (P), 14 years old, and Putney (D), 11 years old, were both students at the high school in Waukesha. On February 20, 1889, while school was in session, Putney (D) lightly kicked Vosburg (P) in the leg. Since Vosburg's (P) leg was in a weakened condition from a previous injury which was still healing, the kick caused Vosburg (P) to permanently lose the use of that leg (i.e., infection destroyed the bone). Thereafter, Vosburg (P) sued Putney (D) for damages resulting from the kick. The jury found the kick was the exciting cause of Vosburg's (P) injury, Putney (D) did not intend harm, and Vosburg (P) was entitled to $2,500 damages. Thereupon, judgment was entered for Vosburg (P) and this appeal followed.

ISSUE: In an action to recover damages for an alleged assault and battery, must the victim prove that the alleged wrongdoer intended to do him harm?

HOLDING AND DECISION: (Lyon, J.) No. In an action to recover damages for an alleged assault and battery, the victim must only show either that the alleged wrongdoer had an unlawful intention to produce harm (i.e., an unlawful intention in committing the act which occurred) or that he committed an unlawful act. This rule is based upon the rationale that "if the intended act is unlawful, the intention to commit it must necessarily be unlawful." Of course, once it is established that the wrongdoer committed an assault and battery, he is liable for all injuries resulting directly from the wrongful act, whether or not the injuries could have been foreseen by him. Here, since the kick occurred after regular school exercises had commenced (i.e., when there was no "implied license of the playgrounds" allowing for boyish sports, etc.), it was unlawful. As such, Putney (D) committed an assault and battery and he is liable for all damages that resulted, even though Vosburg's (P) leg was in a weakened condition from a previous injury. Since certain testimony, though,

was erroneously admitted at trial, the judgment is reversed and the case remanded.

▶ ANALYSIS
Any intent to do an act that is wrong is sufficient. Malice is not necessary. Note that the intent may be to "do" the wrongful act or to do an act which is "substantially certain" to cause a result which is wrongful. Note, also, that this case demonstrates the well-settled proposition that "the tortfeasor must take his victim as he finds him." Referred to in negligence as the "thin skull" doctrine, it essentially means the fact that a plaintiff, such as Vosburg (P), is particularly susceptible to serious injury, will not mitigate the tortfeasor's liability whatsoever.

■■■

Quicknotes
ASSAULT The intentional placing of another in fear of immediate bodily injury.

BATTERY Unlawful contact with the body of another person.

INTENT The state of mind that exists when one's purpose is to commit an act.

THIN SKULL DOCTRINE Doctrine holding the defendant is liable in tort for the aggravation of a plaintiff's existing injury or condition, regardless of whether the magnitude of the injury was foreseeable.

■■■

Dougherty v. Stepp

Landowner (P) v. Adverse possession claimant (D)

N.C. Sup. Ct., 18 N.C. 371 (1835).

NATURE OF CASE: Appeal from judgment for defendant in action to recover damages for trespass.

FACT SUMMARY: Stepp (D) entered the unenclosed property of Dougherty (P) without permission for the purpose of surveying Dougherty's (P) property and claiming a portion of it as his own.

🏛 RULE OF LAW
Every unprivileged entry onto the land of another is a trespass regardless of the amount of actual damages.

FACTS: Stepp (D) entered the unenclosed property of Dougherty (P) without consent. While on the property, Stepp (D) surveyed the land and claimed part of it as his own. However, the surveying techniques involved no marking of trees or cutting of bushes. The jury found for Stepp (D), and Dougherty (P) appealed. The state's highest court granted review.

ISSUE: Is every unprivileged entry onto the land of another a trespass regardless of the amount of actual damages?

HOLDING AND DECISION: (Ruffin, C.J.) Yes. Every unprivileged entry onto the land of another is a trespass regardless of the amount of actual damages. An action for trespass can be maintained without proof of any actual damage. From every entry against the will of the landowner, the law implies some damage; "if nothing more, the treading down the grass or herbage." Reversed.

▶ ANALYSIS

The purpose of this decision is that at common law the trespass action was a safeguard against the repeated trespasser. Without the deterrent of legal liability for mere entry on the land without damage, the trespasser could after numerous entries onto the land claim an easement by prescription. The case also presents the old rule that a person is strictly liable for trespass, i.e., if he enters the land of another without permission, he is liable regardless of his intent or negligence in doing so. The present rule is that liability for trespass exists only if there is intentional or negligent intrusion.

Quicknotes

PRESCRIPTIVE EASEMENT A manner of acquiring an easement in another's property by continuous and uninterrupted use in satisfaction of the statutory requirements of adverse possession.

TRESPASS QUARE CLAUSUM FREGIT Action for damages sustained as a result of the defendant's illegal entry onto plaintiff's property.

Mohr v. Williams

Patient (P) v. Surgeon (D)

Minn. Sup. Ct., 104 N.W. 12 (1905).

NATURE OF CASE: Action to recover damages for battery.

FACT SUMMARY: Without permission, either in writing or orally, the defendant operated on plaintiff's ear.

🏛 RULE OF LAW
If defendant's actions exceed the consent given and defendant does a substantially different act than the one authorized, defendant is liable.

FACTS: Plaintiff was admitted to surgery so that defendant could operate on her right. When plaintiff was unconscious, defendant discovered the issue with the right ear was not that serious, but that the left ear was infected. Thus, without awakening the plaintiff, defendant operated on the left ear. Defendant did this despite only having permission to operate on the right ear. The operation was successful, but plaintiff nevertheless brought an action for battery.

ISSUE: If no emergency condition is found during the course of the operation to which plaintiff has consented, is there valid consent to perform a different operation?

HOLDING AND DECISION: (Brown, J.) No. If defendant's actions exceed the consent given and defendant does a substantially different act than the one authorized, defendant is liable. Unless the defendant discovers a condition that endangers the life of the plaintiff patient during the operation to which the plaintiff consented, there is no consent to a different operation. In this case, the diseased condition was not discovered in the course of the authorized operation but by independent examination before the operation, and, further, it was not an imminently dangerous condition. Affirmed.

▶ ANALYSIS

The case falls into the majority view. However, doctors have circumvented the problem of this decision by requiring the patient to give blanket consent to any remedy the physician thinks best.

◼▬◼

Quicknotes

BATTERY Unlawful contact with the body of another person.

◼▬◼

Hudson v. Craft

Boxer (P) v. Fight organizer (D)

Cal. Sup. Ct., 204 P.2d 1 (1949).

NATURE OF CASE: Appeal from dismissal of an action for damages for assault and battery.

FACT SUMMARY: Hudson (P) was injured in an unlicensed carnival boxing match for which he was promised $5, but his complaint for damages against Craft (D), the concessionaire, was dismissed on the ground that he consented to his injury.

> ## 🏛 RULE OF LAW
> A promoter is liable where he conducts boxing matches or prize fights without a license and in violation of the statutory provisions regardless of the rights as between the contestants. The consent of the combatants does not relieve him of that liability.

FACTS: Hudson (P), an 18-year-old boy, attended a carnival where he paid a separate admission to enter a boxing concession. Craft (D), the operator of the concession, had no license from the state athletic commission to stage prize fights. Hudson (P) was promised $5 prize money to participate in a boxing match. Hudson (P) fought and was struck, suffering injuries for which he sought damages. Hudson's (P) complaint was dismissed on the ground that he had consented to risk of injury. Hudson (P) appealed, arguing that his consent was ineffective as a matter of policy.

ISSUE: Is a promoter liable where he conducts boxing matches or prize fights without a license and in violation of the statutory provisions regardless of the rights as between the contestants?

HOLDING AND DECISION: (Carter, J.) Yes. A promoter is liable where he conducts boxing matches or prize fights without a license and in violation of the statutory provisions regardless of the rights as between the contestants. Reversed.

▶ ANALYSIS

The minority rule stated in the decision is followed by Restatement (Second) of Torts § 60, while the exception (the concise rule) is found in § 61. The majority rule holds that where persons consent to fight, each may sue the other for his injuries. This being contrary to the maxim, "one is not legally injured if he has consented to the act complained of or was willing that it should occur," the courts have attempted to rationalize the majority rule on the basis of the state being a party to a breach of the peace to which breach no one may consent.

Quicknotes

BATTERY Unlawful contact with the body of another person.

PROMOTER LIABILITY A finding of liability on the part of a promoter where the corporation has not expressly assumed the acts of the promoter.

McGuire v. Almy

Nurse (P) v. Insane patient (D)

Mass. Sup. Jud. Ct., 8 N.E.2d 760 (1937).

NATURE OF CASE: Action for damages for assault and battery.

FACT SUMMARY: Almy (D), an insane ward, injured her nurse, McGuire (P), during a rage.

 **RULE OF LAW**
An insane person may be capable of entertaining the intent to commit a battery.

FACTS: McGuire (P), a registered nurse, had been hired to give 24-hour care to Almy (D), an insane person. Almy (D) had a violent attack during which she broke furniture and warned McGuire (P) not to enter her room or she would be killed. After entering, McGuire (P) approached Almy (D) who stood in striking position with a piece of furniture raised above her head. When McGuire (P) grabbed for the hand with the weapon, Almy (D) struck her. There was a jury verdict for McGuire (P). Almy (D) appealed the denial of her motion for a directed verdict.

ISSUE: May an insane person be liable for a battery?

HOLDING AND DECISION: (Qua, J.) Yes. An insane person is to be judged by the same standards as a normal person. Intent to do the act is the key to a battery, not the intent to harm. If an insane person can entertain that intent then he can be liable for battery. The standard applies even though an insane person's act may be uncontrollable. The loss is placed on the insane actor rather than on the innocent victim. Judgment for the plaintiff on the verdict.

▌ *ANALYSIS*

This case represents a basic policy decision that is generally accepted. The policy reasons are: (1) the loss is better borne by the actor than the victim; (2) liability will encourage closer surveillance by custodians; and, (3) insanity is easily feigned. The counter argument is that one should not be liable for acts not within his control. This is not generally accepted.

Quicknotes

BATTERY Unlawful contact with the body of another person.

INSANITY DEFENSE A defense which negates liability or culpability by alleging that the defendant is inflicted with a psychological condition preventing him from controlling his actions or comprehending the nature and consequences of his conduct.

INTENT The existence of a particular state of mind whereby an individual seeks to achieve a particular result by his action.

Courvoisier v. Raymond

Shop owner (D) v. Sheriff (P)

Colo. Sup. Ct., 47 P. 284 (1896).

NATURE OF CASE: Appeal from award of damages.

FACT SUMMARY: Courvoisier (D) believed that Raymond (P), a policeman, was one of the rioters outside of his home and shot him as he approached.

🏛 RULE OF LAW

An action of force is justified by self-defense whenever the circumstances are such as to cause a reasonable man to believe that his life is in danger or that he is in danger of receiving great bodily harm and that it is necessary to use such force for protection.

FACTS: On June 12, 1892, Courvoisier (D) was asleep in a room he occupied over his jewelry store when two men invaded his house. Presuming these men to be burglars, Courvoisier (D) took his revolver and ejected them. Once outside, the men were joined by others who assaulted Courvoisier (D) with stones. In order to frighten the men away, Courvoisier (D) fired several shots in the air. The shots attracted the attention of deputy sheriff Raymond (P) and two other deputy sheriffs. As the other two officers approached the men in the street, Raymond (P) approached Courvoisier (D) from the direction of the rioting men. As Raymond (P) approached, Courvoisier (D) shot him. Thereafter, Raymond (P) sued Courvoisier (D) for damages. As a defense, Courvoisier (D) claimed that he believed his life was in danger, that Raymond (P) was one of the rioters, and that the shooting was necessary for his self-defense. After a verdict for Raymond (P), this appeal followed.

ISSUE: Can a person justify the use of force as self-defense only if he was "actually" in danger of being killed or seriously injured?

HOLDING AND DECISION: (Hayt, C.J.) No. An act of force is justified by self-defense whenever the circumstances are such as to cause a reasonable man to believe that his life is in danger or that he is in danger of receiving great bodily harm and that it is necessary to use such force for protection. Under this rule, a person using force does not actually have to be in danger as long as he reasonably believes that he is and that force is necessary for his self-defense. Here, though, the trial court instructed the jury that the shooting was only justified if Raymond (P) was actually attacking Courvoisier (D). Since this instruction was in error, the judgment must be reversed.

▶ ANALYSIS

This case illustrates the general view. Note, also, that under the general rule there is no duty to retreat, rather than use force, whenever a person reasonably believes that he is in danger and that force is necessary for self-defense. Under the minority view, though, a person must retreat rather than use deadly force, unless (1) retreating would be dangerous to oneself or a third person, or (2) he is in his own home, or (3) he is attempting a "valid arrest." Note, finally, that there is no privilege of self-defense when the danger has passed or when excessive force is used.

▬■▬

Quicknotes

SELF-DEFENSE A justification doctrine that permits one to respond to a threatened injury with a corresponding degree of physical force, while negating any corresponding legal consequence for the results of his defensive act.

▬■▬

Bird v. Holbrook

Trespasser (P) v. Landowner (D)

C.P., 130 Eng. Rep. 911 (1825).

NATURE OF CASE: Action for damages resulting from an assault.

FACT SUMMARY: Bird (P) was injured by a spring gun on Holbrook's (D) property.

🏛 **RULE OF LAW**
Unless adequate notices are posted, a spring gun cannot be used to protect property.

FACTS: Holbrook's (D) garden had been robbed of valuable flowers. Holbrook (D) set a spring gun to injure the thief if he tried to steal more flowers. No notices were posted. Bird (P) entered Holbrook's (D) property to recover a peafowl that had flown onto the property. Bird (P) did not see the wires to the spring gun and was shot. Holbrook (D) alleged self-defense and that a party should not profit from his own wrongs (trespass). Damages were awarded Bird (P) on the grounds the force used was excessive and was designed to injure rather than deter.

ISSUE: May deadly force in the nature of traps be used without notice to protect property?

HOLDING AND DECISION: (Best, C.J.) No. Deadly force in the nature of traps may not be used without notice to protect property. Here, Holbrook's (D) sole purpose was to injure the thief. Barbed wire or glass on a wall is meant to deter. It is noticeable and is not calculated to cause severe injury. A spring gun is for the purpose of killing or maiming. Its use is not privileged. If notices are posted all around the property that deadly traps are present, and with knowledge of this fact a party enters, no suit may be maintained. However, where no notice of such traps is present, liability is predicated on the assumption that human life is more important than property. Even a thief could recover. Affirmed.

CONCURRENCE: (Burrough, J.) Not only should Holbrook (D) have given notice of the spring guns, but had he (D) just wanted to protect his property from thieves, he would have set the guns only at night. Furthermore, if Holbrook (D) had been present when Bird (P) intruded, Holbrook (D) could not have lawfully taken Bird (P) into custody.

▶ *ANALYSIS*

One is not privileged to spread poison on land for the purpose of killing trespassing animals. Cases have split over whether a felon can recover for injury caused to him by traps. The use of dangerous animals is also prohibited unless their presence is well posted. If injury occurs to those who rightfully enter on to the land of another, posting of notices will not normally save a defendant from liability unless contributory negligence or assumption of the risk can be established.

■=■

Quicknotes

DEADLY FORCE Physical force used in the defense of oneself or others that carries with it the potential for causing death.

■=■

Ploof v. Putnam

Sailor (P) v. Dock owner (D)

Vt. Sup. Ct., 71 A. 188 (1908).

NATURE OF CASE: Damages for battery.

FACT SUMMARY: Ploof (P) sued for damages caused when Putnam (D) denied him the use of a safe mooring for his boat during a storm.

 RULE OF LAW
Necessity justifies the entry upon the land of another.

FACTS: Ploof (P) was sailing upon a lake with his wife and children. A storm arose and Ploof (P) attempted to moor his boat to Putnam's (D) dock. Putnam's servant unmoored the boat, causing the storm to drive the boat into the shore. Ploof (P), his wife, and children were injured and the boat was destroyed. Ploof (P) sued Putnam (D) in trespass and also for not permitting the boat to be anchored to the dock during the storm. The lower court held for Ploof (P).

ISSUE: Does necessity justify an entry upon the land of another?

HOLDING AND DECISION: (Munson, J.) Yes. Entry upon the land of another may be justified by necessity. Many cases have established the rule that necessity, and an inability to control movements inaugurated in the proper exercise of a strict right, will justify entries upon land and interferences with personal property that would otherwise have been trespasses. The doctrine of necessity applies with special force to the preservation of human life. One may sacrifice the personal property of another to save his life or the lives of his fellows. The evidence showed that there was a necessity to preserve human life. However, the allegations of Ploof (P) do not show that there were no natural objects to which he could have moored the boat with equal safety. The lower court judgment, finding a necessity, is affirmed and the cause remanded.

▶ **ANALYSIS**

This rule follows the great weight of authority which gives a private individual a privilege to enter another's land if the emergency is sufficiently great, if one enters to save his own life, the life of another, or his own property. The scope of this privilege is narrower than the privilege that allows an individual to act for a public goal. For example, an individual who dynamites a house to prevent the spread of fire or who destroys property that during wartime should not reach enemy hands is not liable to the true owner. The rule is found in Restatement (Second) of Torts § 197. Note that one acting under the private privilege must reimburse the true owner for the cost of repairing any damage that he has caused.

■◼■

Quicknotes

BATTERY Unlawful contact with the body of another person.

NECESSITY A defense to liability for unlawful activity where the conduct is unavoidable and is justified by preventing the injury to life or health.

■◼■

Vincent v. Lake Erie Transportation Co.

Wharf owner (P) v. Transportation company (D)

Minn. Sup. Ct., 124 N.W. 221 (1910).

NATURE OF CASE: Damages for injury to property.

FACT SUMMARY: Vincent (P) sued for damages to its wharf, caused by Lake Erie Transportation Co. (D) negligently keeping its boat tied to the wharf.

🏛 RULE OF LAW
Public necessity may require the taking of private property for public purposes, but our system of jurisprudence requires that compensation be made.

FACTS: Lake Erie Transportation Co. (D) moored their boat to Vincent's (P) wharf at the place and in the manner designated by Vincent (P). Cargo consigned to Vincent (P) was unloaded. By the time the cargo was unloaded a storm had arisen which prevented the boat from leaving the wharf. Vincent (P) sued for damages caused to the wharf by the boat's hitting it during the storm. The trial court rendered a judgment for Vincent (P). The defendant appealed.

ISSUE: May public necessity require the taking of private property for public purposes?

HOLDING AND DECISION: (O'Brien, J.) Yes. Public necessity may require the taking of private property for public purposes, but our system of jurisprudence requires that compensation be made. The ship's master was required to use ordinary prudence and care. The evidence showed that it would have been imprudent for the ship's master to have attempted to leave the dock. However, this was not a case in which, because of an act of God or an unavoidable accident, the infliction of injury was beyond the control of the defendant. Here, the defendant prudently and advisedly availed itself of the plaintiff's property for the purpose of preserving its own more valuable property. Having thus preserved the ship at the expense of the dock, the defendant must compensate the owner of the dock for the injury inflicted. The judgment for the plaintiff is affirmed.

DISSENT: (Lewis, J.) The damage was caused by an unavoidable accident. Therefore, the defendant is not liable for damages.

▶ ANALYSIS

The few cases in this area appear to agree with *Vincent*. The same liability apparently attaches to the infliction of personal injury in cases of private necessity. The Restatement (Second) of Torts combines the principles of *Ploof v. Putnam*, 71 A. 188 (1908), and *Vincent* in § 197, and creates a privilege in favor of an actor to enter the land of another in order to avoid serious harm, coupled with an obligation on the part of the actor to pay for whatever he damages.

Quicknotes

PUBLIC NECESSITY The defense of necessity, alleging that the harm caused by the defendant was less than the harm sought to be prevented against the public; since the public interest is involved, defendant is not required to pay for any damage caused.

I. de S. and Wife v. W. de S.

Tavern owner (P) v. Patron (D)

At the Assizes, 1348 [or 1349] Year Book, Liber Assisarum, f. 99, pl. 60.

NATURE OF CASE: Action to recover damages for trespass, because of an assault made upon the plaintiff.

FACT SUMMARY: W (D) struck at I's wife M (P) with a hatchet, but missed her.

🏛 RULE OF LAW
An act that causes another to be fearful of a harmful or offensive contact is known as an assault, and the plaintiff may recover damages, even though there is no actual physical contact or physical harm.

FACTS: W (D) was beating with a hatchet upon the door of I's tavern, which was closed for the night. When I's wife M (P) put her head out the window and ordered W (D) to stop, he struck at her with the hatchet. W (D) claimed there was no trespass for which the woman (P) could recover, since he did not actually harm her.

ISSUE: Is there a wrong and a trespass for which a plaintiff may recover damages, when the plaintiff is caused to fear for her safety, but is not actually harmed?

HOLDING AND DECISION: (Thorpe, C.J.) Yes. An assault—making another fearful of a harmful contact—is a harm for which a plaintiff may recover. In this case, W (D) struck at I's wife M (P) with a hatchet, thereby frightening her. The harm was in the assault itself, and she is entitled to recover damages from W (D).

▶ ANALYSIS

This case was one of the earliest decisions to recognize a mental, as opposed to physical injury, and the need to compensate the plaintiff for such an injury. Thus, the law of assault developed to protect a person's interest in freedom from being fearful of a harmful or offensive contact upon his person, as opposed to battery, which protected a person from the injury itself.

■■■

Quicknotes

ASSAULT The intentional placing of another in fear of immediate bodily injury.

■■■

Tuberville v. Savage

[Parties not identified.]

K.B., 86 Eng. Rep. 684 (1669).

NATURE OF CASE: Action for damages for assault and battery.

FACT SUMMARY: Savage (D) struck at Tuberville (P), claiming Tuberville (P) had assaulted him first.

🏛 RULE OF LAW

A threatening gesture will not constitute an assault when there are accompanying words that clearly negate the gesture's threat.

FACTS: Savage's (D) evidence of an assault committed upon him was that Tuberville (P) put his hand on his sword and said, "If it were not assize-time, I would not take such language from you."

ISSUE: Is there an assault when a threatening gesture is made but is accompanied by words that indicate that no attempt at violence will be made?

HOLDING AND DECISION: [Judge not stated in casebook excerpt.] No. There can be no assault even when a threatening gesture is made, when accompanying words negate the threat of the gesture. This is because there can be no assault, without an intent to cause apprehension of a harmful contact. In this case, Tuberville (P), although he put his hand on his sword, clearly indicated by his words that he had no intent to harm Savage (D). Savage's (D) claim that he was acting in self-defense to Tuberville's (P) assault therefore failed because there was no assault.

▶ ANALYSIS

The holding of this case represents the current view that for an assault, there must be an overt act, together with an apparent ability and intent to carry out the threat immediately. When there is an overt act that is threatening but is accompanied by words that clearly negate its threat, a reasonable person would not be fearful of any immediate harm. On the other hand, it is possible for the words to make an assault out of an act that is itself not sufficient for an assault, as where the defendant has been making verbal threats and then suddenly reaches into his pocket. Where the words state a conditional threat, so that the plaintiff reasonably believes no harm will occur if he meets that condition, there may still be an assault. A robber holding a gun who says, "Your money or your life," has committed an assault even if it is clear he will not harm the victim if he is given the money.

Quicknotes

ASSAULT The intentional placing of another in fear of immediate bodily injury.

Alcorn v. Mitchell

Trespass victim (D) v. Trespasser (P)

Ill. Sup. Ct., 63 Ill. 553 (1872).

NATURE OF CASE: Action in damages for insult and emotional distress.

FACT SUMMARY: At the conclusion of a trial, Alcorn (D) spit in Mitchell's face.

RULE OF LAW

Punitive damages may be assessed for highly offensive conduct to provide an alternative redress to physical retribution.

FACTS: After the conclusion of an action for trespass, Alcorn (D) spit in Mitchell's (P) face. Mitchell (P) recovered punitive damages of $1,000 for the offensive battery. Alcorn (D) appealed, alleging the award was excessive.

ISSUE: May punitive damages be awarded for an offensive battery where the only other redress would be physical retribution?

HOLDING AND DECISION: (Sheldon, J.) Yes. Highly egregious antisocial conduct may be subjected to awards of punitive damages. Such actions provoke physical retribution, and an alternative method of redress/satisfaction must be provided by the law in order to discourage future misconduct of this nature. Spitting in the face of another in courtroom is such an action. Severe punitive awards are encouraged by the law to give a party an adequate redress and to punish the other for his misconduct. Affirmed.

▶ ANALYSIS

Any offensive touching of clothes or a cane may be prosecuted as a battery and/or the intentional infliction of emotional distress, *Republica v. De Longchamps*, 1 U.S. 111 (Pa. 1784). An offensive kiss will also be deemed a battery for which damages may be recovered for injured feelings, *Craker v. Chicago & N.W. Ry.*, 36 Wis. 657 (1875). Seizing an object from a person' hand will also be deemed a battery because of its close connection to the plaintiff's body and the concomitant shock/embarrassment, *Morgan v. Loyacomo*, 1 So.2d 510 (Miss. 1941).

Quicknotes

PUNITIVE DAMAGES Damages exceeding the actual injury suffered for the purposes of punishment, deterrence and comfort to plaintiff.

Coblyn v. Kennedy's, Inc.

Shopper (P) v. Store (D)

Mass. Sup. Jud. Ct., 268 N.E. 2d 860 (1971).

NATURE OF CASE: Action for false imprisonment.

FACT SUMMARY: An employee of Kennedy's, Inc. (D) detained Coblyn (P) on suspicion of shoplifting.

RULES OF LAW

(1) If a person is restrained in his or her personal liberty by fear of a personal difficulty, it amounts to false imprisonment.

(2) If a shopkeeper has reasonable grounds to believe a person has committed or is attempting to commit larceny of goods for sale on the premises, the shopkeeper may detain that person in a reasonable manner for a reasonable length of time.

FACTS: Coblyn (P), a small, elderly man, was leaving Kennedy's, Inc. (D) store when an employee stopped him, grasped his arm, and accused him of shoplifting. Coblyn (P) went inside where another clerk confirmed that the item in question belonged to Coblyn (P). Coblyn (P) became sick from the excitement and was hospitalized with a "myocardial infraction." Coblyn brought suit for false imprisonment and Kennedy's (D) asserted that no imprisonment had taken place and that it was protected by the "shopkeeper's privilege" to detain suspected shoplifters.

ISSUE:

(1) Does submitting to restraint on one's personal liberty for fear of personal difficulty amount to false imprisonment?

(2) Can a shopkeeper detain a person who the shopkeeper "honestly suspects" of being a shoplifter?

HOLDING AND DECISION: (Spiegel, J.)

(1) Yes. If a person is restrained of his or her personal liberty by fear of a personal difficulty it is false imprisonment. A genuine restraint is sufficient to be imprisonment; and any demonstration of physical power which, it appears, can be avoided only by submission, operates to constitute imprisonment. Considering Coblyn's (P) age and health, Kennedy's (D) employee's grasp on Coblyn's (P) arm gave Coblyn (P) no choice other than to comply with their request.

(2) No. A shopkeeper must have "reasonable" grounds to believe that a person has shoplifted before the shopkeeper may detain that person in a reasonable manner for a reasonable length of time. The court held that there were no reasonable grounds to believe that Coblyn (P) was shoplifting. Exceptions overruled.

ANALYSIS

The "shopkeeper's privilege" allows the storeowner to retain the suspect for an investigation only. There is no privilege to arrest or to demand that the suspect sign a confession.

Quicknotes

FALSE IMPRISONMENT Intentional confinement to a bounded area from which one cannot reasonably leave, for an appreciable length of time, however short.

PROBABLE CAUSE A reasonable basis for believing that a crime has been committed.

Wilkinson v. Downton

Wife of supposed accident victim (P) v. Storyteller (D)

Q.B., 2 Q.B. 57 (1897).

NATURE OF CASE: Appeal by Downton (D) from judgment for Wilkinson (P) for injuries caused by nervous shock.

FACT SUMMARY: As part of a practical joke, Downton (D) told Wilkinson (P) that her husband had been severely injured in an accident.

🏛 RULE OF LAW
Extreme and outrageous conduct which causes physical harm or mental distress creates a valid cause of action.

FACTS: Downton (D) represented to Wilkinson (P) that Wilkinson's (P) husband had been seriously injured in an accident and was lying at The Elms in Leytonstone with two broken legs. Downton (D) requested that she get a cab and two pillows, and go to her husband. All of this was untrue. The effect of the statement was a severe mental shock that threatened Wilkinson's (P) reason and entailed weeks of suffering. There was no evidence that Wilkinson (P) was predisposed to ill health or weakness of constitution. Downton (D) contended that damage caused by nervous shock is not actionable.

ISSUE: Is extreme and outrageous conduct that caused physical harm a valid cause of action?

HOLDING AND DECISION: (Wright, J.) Yes. Extreme and outrageous conduct that causes physical harm is a valid cause of action. Where a person willfully does an act that is calculated to cause physical harm and in fact does cause physical harm, there is a good cause of action. Here, Downton (D) suddenly appeared before Wilkinson (P) and with apparent seriousness advised that her husband had been injured. This is an act that could not fail to produce grave effects under the circumstances, and therefore an intention to produce such an effect must be imputed. Affirmed.

▶ ANALYSIS

This case set the precedent on which the new tort of intentional infliction of emotional distress was founded. In it, the court recognized that there are some special situations where recovery must be allowed even though the established rule of law held otherwise. Justice Wright imposed liability simply because he believed that Downton's (D) conduct was beyond the realm of common decency. The rule that has since evolved is that there is liability for conduct that is calculated to cause, and does cause, severe mental distress.

■━■

Quicknotes

INTENTIONAL INFLICTION OF EMOTIONAL DISTRESS Intentional and extreme behavior on the part of the wrongdoer with the intent to cause the victim to suffer severe emotional distress, or with reckless indifference, resulting in the victim's suffering severe emotional distress.

■━■

Strict Liability and Negligence: Historic and Analytic Foundations

Quick Reference Rules of Law

PAGE

1. *The Thorns Case (Hull v. Orange)*. Even an innocent trespass on land is actionable.   18

2. *Weaver v. Ward*. An actor is liable for injury directly caused by his act unless he can prove   19
himself utterly without fault.

3. *Scott v. Shepherd*. A party will be liable for setting forces in motion that are likely to cause   20
injury of a sort and do cause injury even though the force is diverted by another.

4. *Brown v. Kendall*. If in the prosecution of a lawful act, a casualty purely accidental arises, i.e.,   21
the injury was unavoidable, and the conduct of the defendant was free from blame, no action
can be supported for an injury arising therefrom.

5. *Fletcher v. Rylands*. Where a party's actions unwittingly cause damage to the land of another,   22
he is liable regardless of negligence.

6. *Fletcher v. Rylands*. If a person brings anything onto his property that, if it escapes, might   23
damage his neighbor's property, he is responsible for all the damage that is the natural
consequence of the escape.

7. *Rylands v. Fletcher*. A person using his land for a dangerous, nonnatural use is strictly liable   24
for damage to another's property resulting from such nonnatural use.

8. *Brown v. Collins*. Property owners should not be held strictly liable for the natural   25
consequences of the escape of things they bring on their land.

9. *Powell v. Fall*. A person who operates a potentially dangerous machine is liable for injuries   26
resulting therefrom even if the operator is not negligent.

10. *Stone v. Bolton*. A known risk, even if extremely slight, is actionable if it occurs and leads to a   27
foreseeable injury.

11. *Bolton v. Stone*. If a party takes reasonable care to prevent a known risk, or its chance of   28
occurrence is extremely slight, no negligence exists.

12. *Hammontree v. Jenner*. A sudden illness that renders a driver unconscious will not be   29
grounds for an action in negligence or strict liability.

The Thorns Case (Hull v. Orange)

[Parties not identified.]

Y.B. Mich. 6 Ed.4, f. 7, pl. 18 (1466).

NATURE OF CASE: Action for damages due to a trespass.

FACT SUMMARY: Defendant alleged that the injury done to plaintiff's land was caused while recovering thorn bushes that had inadvertently fallen on the land.

 RULE OF LAW
Even an innocent trespass on land is actionable.

FACTS: Defendant had land adjacent to plaintiff. Defendant cut some thorn bushes on his land that, through no fault of his own, fell on plaintiff's land. Defendant entered plaintiff's land to recover the thorn bushes. Plaintiff brought suit for the trespass, alleging damage to crops. Defendant alleged that his actions were privileged, since the loss occurred without any fault on his part and the entry was to recover his property.

ISSUE: Is every trespass that causes damage actionable?

HOLDING AND DECISION: (Littleton, J.) Yes. Fault is not required for liability. If the land or person of another is invaded to his detriment, it is actionable regardless of whether the defendant acted legally or was totally without fault. The defendant's actions caused the loss. Defendant will be deemed liable.

CONCURRENCE: (Choke, C.J.) The falling of the thorn bushes onto the plaintiff's land was not lawful and the coming to take them away was thus unlawful. If on the other hand, the wind had caused the thorns to fall, then the defendant could have lawfully gone onto the plaintiff's land to recover them.

CONCURRENCE: (Pigot, J.) Where there is damage to the plaintiff's land, an action in trespass will lie, notwithstanding that the defendant's action was lawful and the result of that action was not intentional, as where a defendant cuts willows and they stop water from flowing to the plaintiff's mill, or where a defendant's draining of a pond to take the fish therein floods the plaintiff's land.

CONCURRENCE: (Brian, J.) Where a person acts, he is bound to act so as not to injure others, and, even if the act is lawful (as it was here), and the consequence of his act is against his will (as it was here), a party injured by the act will have an action against the person committing the act. For example, if a defendant is building a house and a timber falls and damages the defendant's neighbor's house, the neighbor has an action in trespass against the defendant, notwithstanding that the building of the house was lawful and the falling of the timber was against the defendant's will. This is also the case where a defendant, acting in self-defense, harms a third party. The defendant's self-defense is lawful, and the harm to the third party is unintended. Nevertheless, the third party will have an action against the defendant.

DISSENT: (Yonge, J.) Where the plaintiff suffers no legal injury, no action for trespass will lie. Here, the defendant's entry onto the plaintiff's land to recover his thorns, which were his property, was not tortious, so even if the plaintiff suffered damages, he did not suffer a tort, and, therefore, he has no action against defendant.

ANALYSIS

It has been held that, without justification, the trampling of a single blade of grass is actionable in trespass, i.e., nominal damages may be awarded for every unjustified trespass. Every unwarranted invasion of property is actionable. Nominal damages are generally not awarded where no injury was caused and the entry was to recover property. The entry must be intentional or caused by the defendant's actions. One who is pushed onto the property of another is not liable. However, the pusher would be liable, since he caused the entry.

Quicknotes

TRESPASS Unlawful interference with, or damage to, the real or personal property of another.

Weaver v. Ward

Injured soldier (P) v. Soldier whose weapon accidentally discharged (D)

K.B., 80 Eng. Rep. 284 (1616).

NATURE OF CASE: Action to recover damages for assault and battery.

FACT SUMMARY: During a military exercise Ward's (D) musket accidentally discharged injuring Weaver (P).

🏛 RULE OF LAW
An actor is liable for injury directly caused by his act unless he can prove himself utterly without fault.

FACTS: Ward (D) and Weaver (P) were participants in a military exercise. During the exercise, Ward's (D) musket accidentally discharged, injuring Weaver (P). Ward (D) contended that the accidental nature of his action should be a defense. The lower court held, as a matter of law, that a showing of accident alone is not a defense to an injury caused by Ward (D). The court gave judgment for Weaver (P) by sustaining his demurrer to the answer.

ISSUE: Is an actor excused from liability for the consequence of his act if he can prove that the injury occurred utterly without his fault?

HOLDING AND DECISION: [Judge not stated in casebook excerpt.] Yes. An actor will be excused from liability if he can show the lack of any fault. Ward (D), however, voluntarily fired the musket and therefore was at fault. Affirmed.

▶ ANALYSIS

This is one of the first cases clearly recognizing that some form of fault may be necessary for imposition of liability upon an actor. Modernly, the test for imposition of liability under a fault-based negligence theory is whether a reasonable man might have taken the defendant's (Ward's) action. If so, then there is no negligence, no fault, and consequently no liability.

▬■▬

Quicknotes

ASSAULT AND BATTERY Illegal bodily contact.

NEGLIGENCE Conduct falling below the standard of care that a reasonable person would demonstrate under similar conditions.

TRESPASS Unlawful interference with, or damage to, the real or personal property of another.

▬■▬

Scott v. Shepherd

Blinded stall owner (P) v. Squib thrower (D)

K.B., 96 Eng. Rep. 525 (1773).

NATURE OF CASE: Action in damages for trespass.

FACT SUMMARY: Shepherd (D) threw a lighted squib into a marketplace where, to avoid injury, it was thrown by others until it finally burned Scott (P).

🏛 RULE OF LAW
A party will be liable for setting forces in motion that are likely to cause injury of a sort and do cause injury even though the force is diverted by another.

FACTS: Shepherd (D) threw a lighted squib (made of gunpowder, etc.) into a marketplace. The squib landed on Yates's stall. Willis threw it away to prevent injury to Yates's stall and person. It landed on Ryal's stall and he threw it away for the same reason. It then landed on Scott (P) and blinded him in one eye. Scott (P) sued Shepherd (D) for trespass. The jury found for Scott (P) subject to this court's opinion.

ISSUE: Is one liable for setting in motion a force which is liable to cause injury even though it is misdirected and injures another?

HOLDING AND DECISION: (Nares, J.) The action of trespass is maintainable. The natural and probable consequence of the act done by the defendant was injury to somebody and therefore was unlawful. The defendant must answer for his actions whether the injury caused is immediate or not. Judgment for Scott (P).

CONCURRENCE: (De Grey, C.J.) Yes. Throwing a lighted squib into a crowded marketplace can obviously cause injury to someone. The force unleashed was designed to indiscriminately cause injury. The injury is a direct and immediate act of Shepherd (D). The throwing of the squib was an unlawful act, and whatever follows from it Shepherd (D) is responsible for. Everything done after the original throwing was a continuation of the first throw. Any innocent person removing the danger from oneself to another is justifiable and the blame lies upon the first thrower.

DISSENT: (Blackstone, J.) Trespass only lies for immediate actions. Consequential damages of the sort herein are not actionable as a trespass, but must be brought as a trespass on the case. The intervention of third parties destroys the immediate nature of the force. The original act was, as against Yates, a trespass not as against Ryal, or Scott (P). The tortuous act was complete when the squib lay at rest upon Yates's stall. Shepherd (D) is not responsible for what Willis or Ryal did with the squib.

▶ ANALYSIS

A trespass will lie where one throws a stone at another and inadvertently hits a third party. An action will also lie where one throws a bomb into a crowded area killing and injuring a number of people including the person against whom it was directed. Where a specific injury was intended or was likely to occur, intent to injure a specific party or property is not required. The general intent to cause injury is sufficient to establish the trespass or assault.

◼▬◼

Quicknotes

TRESPASS Unlawful interference with, or damage to, the real or personal property of another.

TRESPASS ON THE CASE Action at common law in early England granting a remedy to a person who sustains injury to his person or property as a result of the defendant's conduct.

Brown v. Kendall

Injured dog owner (P) v. Stick-wielding dog owner (D)

Mass. Sup. Jud. Ct., 60 Mass. 292 (1850).

NATURE OF CASE: Trespass for assault and battery.

FACT SUMMARY: Kendall (D), while attempting to separate his dog from Brown's (P) dog when the two dogs were fighting, accidentally struck Brown (P) with a stick.

🏛 RULE OF LAW
If in the prosecution of a lawful act, a casualty purely accidental arises, i.e., the injury was unavoidable, and the conduct of the defendant was free from blame, no action can be supported for an injury arising therefrom.

FACTS: Two dogs, owned by Brown (P) and Kendall (D), respectively, were fighting. Kendall (D) attempted to separate the dogs with a stick. When he raised the stick to strike the dogs, Kendall (D) stepped back to avoid the dogs as they approached him, and he accidentally struck Brown (P), who was behind him, in the eye, inflicting a serious injury. Brown (P) brought an action in trespass for assault and battery. The trial court instructed the jury that if it was not a necessary act, and Kendall (D) was not in duty bound to part the dogs, he was responsible for the consequences of the blow, unless it appeared he exercised extraordinary care, so the accident was inevitable. It further instructed that if Kendall (D) had no duty to separate the dogs, then the burden of proving extraordinary care was on him, as well as showing alternatively lack of ordinary care on the part of Brown (P). Following Kendall's (D) death, his executrix (D) was summoned in.

ISSUE: If in the prosecution of a lawful act, a casualty purely accidental arises, can an action be supported for an injury arising therefrom?

HOLDING AND DECISION: (Shaw, C.J.) No. If in the prosecution of a lawful act, a casualty purely accidental arises, i.e., the injury was unavoidable, and the conduct of the defendant was free from blame, no action can be supposed for an injury arising therefrom. The instructions that should have been given are to the effect that Brown (P) could not recover: (1) if at the time of the accident both Kendall (D) and Brown (P) were using ordinary care; (2) if Kendall (D) was using ordinary care and Brown (P) was not; or (3) if neither were using ordinary care. What constitutes ordinary care will vary with the circumstances, but generally, it means that kind and degree of care which prudent and cautious people would use. Such is required under the circumstances and is necessary to guard against probable danger. An inevitable accident is one the defendant could not avoid by the use of the kind and degree of care necessary under the circumstances. Because the instructions to the jury placed the burden on Kendall (D) to show that he used extraordinary care or that Brown (P) failed to use ordinary care, rather than having placed the burden of proof on Brown (P) to prove his case, a new trial must be ordered.

▌ANALYSIS

This case established that some form of fault, negligent or intentional, must form the basis of liability. Consequently, the loss from an unavoidable accident will stay where it falls. This case is also interesting because its discussion includes the concept of contributory negligence, which was fully accepted by the Massachusetts court, but which is losing favor to the concept of comparative negligence today.

Quicknotes

ASSAULT The intentional placing of another in fear of immediate bodily injury.

BATTERY Unlawful contact with the body of another person.

NEGLIGENCE Conduct falling below the standard of care that a reasonable person would demonstrate under similar conditions.

ORDINARY CARE The degree of care exercised by a reasonable person when conducting everyday activities or under similar circumstances; synonymous with due care.

TRESPASS Unlawful interference with, or damage to, the real or personal property of another.

Fletcher v. Rylands

Flooded landowner (P) v. Reservoir owner (D)

Ex., 159 Eng. Rep. 737 (1865).

NATURE OF CASE: Action in strict liability for damages.

FACT SUMMARY: Fletcher's (P) land was flooded when Rylands's (D) reservoir leaked through an unknown, abandoned mine.

🏛 RULE OF LAW
Where a party's actions unwittingly cause damage to the land of another, he is liable regardless of negligence.

FACTS: Rylands (D) constructed a dam on his property. Fletcher's (P) land and mines were flooded when water seeped through old abandoned mine shafts on Rylands's (D) property. Rylands (D) did not know of these shafts and the reservoir had been competently built. Fletcher (P) sued for damages. Rylands (D) defended on the ground that he was totally without negligence.

ISSUE: Is a party liable for damage to the land of another where he was not negligent?

HOLDING AND DECISION: (Bramwell, B.) Yes. If Rylands (D) had intentionally caused the flooding he would be liable. We perceive no difference where the injury was unintentional. The damage was the same. When a party, by his acts, causes injury to the land of another, he will be liable regardless of negligence. Rylands's (D) acts caused the flooding and, regardless of fault, Fletcher (P) should be compensated.

DISSENT: (Martin, B.) Injury to personal property is not actionable without fault/negligence. There is no difference between damage to personal or real property.

▶ *ANALYSIS*

Most modern jurisdictions would not follow the above decision. Injuries sustained through no one's fault must be borne by the injured party as a cost of living in our modern society. Neither injury to real nor personal property is actionable without fault except where the particular activity is deemed "hazardous." These activities are subject to a strict liability in tort theory and no negligence need be shown.

Quicknotes

NEGLIGENCE Conduct falling below the standard of care that a reasonable person would demonstrate under similar conditions.

TRESPASS Unlawful interference with, or damage to, the real or personal property of another.

Fletcher v. Rylands

Flooded landowner (P) v. Reservoir owner (D)

Ex., L.R. 1 Ex. 265 (1866).

NATURE OF CASE: Appeal from decision in an action for damages to property.

FACT SUMMARY: Fletcher (P) contended that Rylands (D) was responsible for damage to Fletcher's (P) mining property caused by the breakage of Rylands's (D) reservoir, which flooded Fletcher's (P) property.

🏛 RULE OF LAW
If a person brings anything onto his property that, if it escapes, might damage his neighbor's property, the person is responsible for all the damage that is the natural consequence of the escape.

FACTS: Fletcher (P) sued Rylands (D) after Rylands (D) built a reservoir on his own property, the reservoir leaked, and Fletcher's (P) mining property was flooded and damaged. The lower court held that Rylands (D) was responsible for causing the damage to Fletcher's (P) mines. Rylands (D) appealed on the basis that his duty was to take all reasonable and prudent precautions to keep the reservoir from damaging a neighbor's property but no more.

ISSUE: If a person brings anything onto his property that, if it escapes, might damage his neighbor's property, is the person responsible for all the damage that is the natural consequence of the escape?

HOLDING AND DECISION: (Blackburn, J.) Yes. If a person brings anything onto his property that, if it escapes, might damage his neighbor's property, the person is responsible for all the damage that is the natural consequence of the escape. Someone who has brought something on his property that was not naturally there and that is harmless to others as long as it is confined to his own property but which he knows will be damaging if it should escape to his neighbor's property, should be responsible for any damage caused his neighbor if it escapes. There is no ground here for saying that Fletcher (P) took upon himself any risk arising from uses to which Rylands (D) chose to apply to his land. Fletcher (P) neither knew nor could stop Rylands (D) from building his reservoir and storing water, so long as that water remained on Rylands's (D) property and did not escape onto Fletcher's (P) property. Affirmed.

▶ ANALYSIS

Dam failures in England in the 1800s were frequent and considered great disasters. Before the landmark case of *Fletcher v. Rylands* was tried, several dam failures had already occurred with great loss of life and property. The

decision in *Fletcher* no doubt was meant to be a cure for what had become extremely costly events. However, the rule of strict liability set forth in *Fletcher* was rarely, if ever, followed, and later decisions instead applied a standard that was somewhere between negligence and strict liability.

▄▄▄

Quicknotes

STRICT LIABILITY Liability for all injuries proximately caused by a party's conducting of certain inherently dangerous activities without regard to negligence or fault.

▄▄▄

Rylands v. Fletcher

Reservoir owner (D) v. Flooded landowner (P)

H.L., L.R. 3 H.L. 330 (1868).

NATURE OF CASE: Appeal from an award of damages for injury to land.

FACT SUMMARY: Rylands (D) built a reservoir on his land, but the water escaped through an abandoned mine shaft and flooded an adjoining mine owned by Fletcher (P).

🏛 RULE OF LAW
A person using his land for a dangerous, nonnatural use is strictly liable for damage to another's property resulting from such nonnatural use.

FACTS: Rylands (D) built a water reservoir on his land. The water escaped through an abandoned coal mine shaft and flooded an adjoining coal mine owned by Fletcher (P). Fletcher (P) sued for damages to his land caused by the water.

ISSUE: Is a person who uses his land for a dangerous, nonnatural use, strictly liable for damage to another's property resulting from such nonnatural use?

HOLDING AND DECISION: (Lord Cairns, C.) Yes. A person using his land for a dangerous, nonnatural use is strictly liable for damage to another's property resulting from such nonnatural use. If water had naturally accumulated upon the land and, by the laws of nature had run off on to adjoining land, there would be no liability. But if water, not being a natural condition of the land, is introduced upon it, any water that escapes does so at the landowner's peril; for which any damage to adjoining land he is strictly liable. Judgment of the Court of Exchequer Chamber affirmed.

CONCURRENCE: (Lord Cranworth, C.) No matter how cautious a person is, he will be liable if he brings upon his land something that causes damage to his neighbor's land. The determinative factor is not whether the defendant has acted with due care but rather if his actions caused the damage. Rylands (D) brought onto his land water and stored it in a reservoir that ended up harming Fletcher (P) and, therefore, Rylands (D) is liable.

▶ ANALYSIS

This is the leading case from which was developed the doctrine of strict liability for abnormally dangerous activities or conditions. In determining whether a certain activity is a nonnatural use, the court looks to the place where the activity occurs, the customs of the community, and the natural fitness or adaptation of the premises for the purpose. The restatement, while accepting the principle of the case, has limited it to ultrahazardous activities.

◼◼◼

Quicknotes

DUE CARE The degree of care that can be expected from a reasonably prudent person under similar circumstances; synonymous with ordinary care.

STRICT LIABILITY Liability for all injuries proximately caused by a party's conducting of certain inherently dangerous activities without regard to negligence or fault.

◼◼◼

Brown v. Collins

Landowner (P) v. Runaway horse owner (D)

N.H. Sup. Ct., 53 N.H. 442 (1873).

NATURE OF CASE: Action for damages to property.

FACT SUMMARY: Brown (P) sued Collins (D) on strict liability grounds after Collins's (D) horses were frightened, became unmanageable, broke from Collins's (D) control, went onto Brown's (P) land, and broke a post there.

RULE OF LAW
Property owners should not be held strictly liable for the natural consequences of the escape of things they bring on their land.

FACTS: Collins (D), who generally exercised ordinary care and skill in managing his horses, lost that control when the horses became frightened. The horses then became unmanageable and ran against and broke a post on Brown's (P) land. Brown (P) sued Collins (D) for the damage caused by the runaway horses, arguing that Collins (D) should be held strictly liable pursuant to *Rylands v. Fletcher*, L.R. 3 H.L. 330 (1868).

ISSUE: Should property owners be held strictly liable for the natural consequences of the escape of things they bring on their land?

HOLDING AND DECISION: (Doe, J.) No. Property owners should not be held strictly liable for the natural consequences of the escape of things they bring on their land. Most of the rights of property, as well as of person, in the social state are not absolute but relative. Everything that a person can bring upon his land is capable of escaping against his will, without his fault, with or without his assistance, in some form, solid, liquid, or gaseous—and of doing damage after its escape. Even if an arbitrary test were applied only to the things a man brings on his land, it would still recognize the peculiar rights of savage life in a wilderness, ignore the rights growing out of a civilized state of society, and make a distinction not warranted by the enlightened spirit of common law. It would impose a penalty upon efforts, made in a reasonable, skillful, and careful manner, to rise above a condition of barbarism. Legal principles should not throw so serious an obstacle in the way of progress and improvement. Judgment for Collins (D).

ANALYSIS

As reflected in the above case, the standard of strict liability set forth in *Rylands v. Fletcher*, L.R. 3 H.L. 330 (1868), was not initially popular in courts. Current cases have adhered to the *Rylands* standard more closely, and in 1984, it was reported that thirty of the states accepted *Rylands's* strict liability principles while only seven rejected them. Other state courts continue to move in support of the *Rylands* standard.

■■■■

Quicknotes

STRICT LIABILITY Liability for all injuries proximately caused by a party's conducting of certain inherently dangerous activities without regard to negligence or fault.

■■■

Powell v. Fall

Farmer (P) v. Tractor driver (D)

Q.B., 5 Q.B. 597 (1880).

NATURE OF CASE: Appeal of strict liability judgment.

FACT SUMMARY: Fall (D) contended he was not liable for damages to Powell's (P) haystack caused by a spark from Fall's (D) tractor because the tractor complied with all laws regulating its construction and use.

🏛 RULE OF LAW
A person who operates a potentially dangerous machine is liable for injuries resulting therefrom even if the operator is not negligent.

FACTS: Powell (P) owned a farm adjoining a public highway. Fall (D) drove his steam propelled tractor in a reasonably prudent manner on the highway, and a spark from the engine escaped, igniting Powell's (P) haystack. Powell (P) sued for damages. The lower court found for Powell (P) reasoning that a person who operates a potentially dangerous machine is liable for injuries resulting therefrom even if the operator is not negligent. It also found that the statutes, while authorizing the use of tractors, did not abrogate any cause of action against the operator for damages caused by their use. Fall (D) appealed.

ISSUE: Is a person who operates a potentially dangerous machine strictly liable for injuries resulting from such operation?

HOLDING AND DECISION: (Mellor, J.) Yes. A person who operates a potentially dangerous machine is liable for injuries resulting therefrom even if the operator is not negligent. The statutes, while authorizing the use of tractors, did not abrogate any cause of action against the operator for damages caused by their use. Therefore despite the fact there was no negligence, responsibility for the damage to the hay must rest with Fall (D). Judgment for Powell (P).

CONCURRENCE: (Lord Bramwell, J.) Yes. A person who operates a potentially dangerous machine is liable for injuries resulting therefrom even if the operator is not negligent because one who keeps a dangerous thing on his property is strictly liable if it escapes and injures his neighbor. The statutes have no effect on the common law rule.

▶ ANALYSIS

The lower court specifically relied upon *Rylands v. Fletcher*, L.R. 3H.L. 330 (1868). This case was appealed and affirmed, and specifically overruled *Vaughn v. Taff Vale Ry. Co.*, 5 H & N. 679, 29 L.J. (Ex.) 247 (1860), which held that the operator of a railroad was not to be held liable for injuries without proof of negligence.

━━━

Quicknotes

ABNORMALLY DANGEROUS ACTIVITY An activity, as set forth in Restatement (Second) of Torts § 520, giving rise to strict liability on the part of the actor for damages caused thereby.

NEGLIGENCE Conduct falling below the standard of care that a reasonable person would demonstrate under similar conditions.

STRICT LIABILITY Liability for all injuries proximately caused by a party's conducting of certain inherently dangerous activities without regard to negligence or fault.

━━━

Stone v. Bolton

Injured woman (P) v. Cricket club (D)

Ct. App., 1 K.B. 201 (1950).

NATURE OF CASE: Action for damages for personal injury caused by negligence.

FACT SUMMARY: Stone (P) was injured when a cricket ball was hit over a fence and struck her.

🏛 **RULE OF LAW**
A known risk, even if extremely slight, is actionable if it occurs and leads to a foreseeable injury.

FACTS: Stone (P) was struck and injured by a cricket ball that was hit over a high wall onto a public street. Stone (P) brought suit for negligence against the home cricket club (D), but not against the batsman or the batsman's club. The cricket club (D) defended on the ground that over the last 30 years only six balls had been hit over the wall. The cricket club (D) alleged that the risk was so slight that injury was unforeseeable.

ISSUE: Is a known risk, regardless of how slight, actionable if it occurs and leads to a foreseeable injury?

HOLDING AND DECISION: (Lord Jenkins, J.) Yes. A known risk, even if extremely slight, is actionable if it occurs and leads to a foreseeable injury. The cricket club (D) knew that balls could be hit over the wall. The cricket club (D) knew that if the ball cleared the wall it could strike and injure a passerby. Regardless of how unlikely the possibility of injury, the cricket club (D) owed a duty to protect the public against a known risk. The wall was never made higher and the cricket field was never moved even though the risk was known. This was negligence and Stone (P) may recover.

▶ *ANALYSIS*

The decision herein is akin to a theory of strict liability, i.e., any risk, however slight, must be guarded against to avoid a finding of negligence. The law of negligence elaborated in *Bolton v. Stone*, A.C. 850 (1951), is not quite so strict. However, where the activity is inherently dangerous to life or property, e.g., blasting, strict liability rules generally apply and negligence need not be established. A policy decision has been made that while the activity is socially acceptable, the risk of harm is so potentially great that people and property must be protected.

Quicknotes

FORESEEABILITY A reasonable expectation that an act or omission would result in injury.

NEGLIGENCE Conduct falling below the standard of care that a reasonable person would demonstrate under similar conditions.

Bolton v. Stone

Cricket club (D) v. Injured woman (P)

H.L., A.C. 850 (1951).

NATURE OF CASE: Appeal of damages award for negligence.

FACT SUMMARY: Stone (P) was struck by a cricket ball. Defendant, the cricket club (D), appealed the lower courts finding of negligence.

🏛 RULE OF LAW
If a party takes reasonable care to prevent a known risk, or its chance of occurrence is extremely slight, no negligence exists.

FACTS: Stone (P) was struck and injured by a cricket ball that was hit over a wall onto a public street. Only six balls in 30 years had cleared that wall. The cricket club (D) was held guilty of negligence in not protecting passersby from a known risk. The cricket club (D) maintained that the chance of injury was so slight that it was not negligent in failing to protect against a recurrence.

ISSUE: Is the occurrence of an extremely rare known risk actionable?

HOLDING AND DECISION: (Lord Reid, J.) No. If a party takes reasonable care to prevent a known risk, or its chance of occurrence is extremely slight, no negligence exists. In a modern society it is virtually impossible to guard against the creation of all risks. People must expect to be exposed to occasional risks. Property owners may use their premises in any reasonable manner even if it creates a slight risk to passersby. Only the creation of substantial risks is actionable. Here, only six balls had been hit over the wall in 30 years. The court of appeals held that if such a risk of injury could not be guarded against, the use of the property should have been discontinued. This is an application of a strict liability theory. Once the risk occurs it is foreseeable and must be guarded against. Negligence law, which is applicable herein, is less strict. Reasonable risks of a slight nature are permitted where one uses one's property in a reasonable manner. While I personally feel sorry for Stone (P), the law of negligence will not permit recovery for the occurrence of such a slight risk of injury. Reversed.

CONCURRENCE: (Lord Radcliffe, J.) The cricket club (D) is not guilty of any culpable act or omission. The cricket club's (D) actions did not fall below the standard of conduct that a reasonable person would set for himself. A reasonable person would not have abandoned the use of the ground for cricket or increased the height of the surrounding fences.

▌ANALYSIS

Many courts might disagree with the decision herein if the known risk could have easily and inexpensively been prevented. Strict liability is normally imposed against antisocial activities such as nuisances on the grounds that a person should not have to suffer known risks associated with such conduct. Occasionally, certain conduct is made unlawful and private damage actions are allowed for previously acceptable risks, e.g. modern pollution laws.

Quicknotes

FORESEEABILITY A reasonable expectation that an act or omission would result in injury.

NEGLIGENCE Conduct falling below the standard of care that a reasonable person would demonstrate under similar conditions.

REASONABLE CARE The degree of care observed by a reasonably prudent person under similar circumstances; synonymous with due care or ordinary care.

Hammontree v. Jenner

Car accident victim (P) v. Epileptic driver (D)

Cal. Ct. App., 97 Cal. Rptr. 739 (1971).

NATURE OF CASE: Action for damages based on negligence and strict liability.

FACT SUMMARY: Jenner (D) had an epileptic seizure while driving and injured Hammontree (P).

🏛 RULE OF LAW
A sudden illness that renders a driver unconscious will not be grounds for an action in negligence or strict liability.

FACTS: Jenner (D) had a history of epileptic seizures. Jenner (D) had been under a doctor's care and medication since 1951. Jenner's (D) last seizure was in 1953. In 1967, Jenner (D) apparently had a seizure while driving and while unconscious he crashed into Hammontree's (P) store causing personal injuries and property damage. Hammontree (P) brought suit for negligence and strict liability in tort. The judge refused to instruct the jury on strict liability on the ground that the theory was not applicable to sudden illnesses that strike a driver rendering him unconscious. The jury found no negligence.

ISSUE: Is strict liability in tort a proper theory to apply to sudden illnesses that render a driver unconscious?

HOLDING AND DECISION: (Lillie, J.) No. A sudden illness that renders a driver unconscious will not be grounds for an action in negligence or strict liability. The court declined to superimpose absolute liability in such situations. This was not akin to a products liability case where a manufacturer put out a defective product. Here, Jenner (D) had not had a seizure for 14 years, was under a doctor's care, and was receiving medication to control his condition. The jury properly found Jenner (D) had no notice of the onset of the seizure or any grounds to suspect it was likely to occur. Since there were no grounds for a finding of negligence, Hammontree (P) could not recover. Affirmed.

▶ ANALYSIS

Where the driver has constructive or actual notice of the onset of a serious illness that might make driving dangerous, negligence may be found. Where an outside force beyond the driver's control, e.g., a swarm of bees enters the car and causes the accident, no liability will normally be found. These cases are all decided on a fault/negligence issue. Sudden heart attack is not grounds for liability. *Tannyhill v. Pacific Motor Transport Co.*, 227 Cal. App. 2d 512 (1964).

Quicknotes

FORESEEABILITY A reasonable expectation that an act or omission would result in injury.

NEGLIGENCE Conduct falling below the standard of care that a reasonable person would demonstrate under similar conditions.

STRICT LIABILITY Liability for all injuries proximately caused by a party's conducting of certain inherently dangerous activities without regard to negligence or fault.

Cal. Ct. App. 20 Cal. App. 3d 528 (1971)

RULE OF LAW

ANALYSIS

Negligence

Quick Reference Rules of Law

PAGE

1. *Vaughan v. Menlove.* The level of care is determined by what a reasonably prudent man would do in similar circumstances. — 33

2. *Roberts v. Ring.* If one, by his acts or omissions, causes injury to others, his negligence is judged by the standard of care usually exercised by the ordinary prudent normal man. — 34

3. *Daniels v. Evans.* When a minor undertakes an adult activity that can result in grave danger to himself and to others, he is held to the same standard of care as the average prudent adult. — 35

4. *Breunig v. American Family Insurance Co.* A person seized with a sudden mental disability for which he had no warning will be excused from the general rule holding an insane person liable for his negligence. — 36

5. *Fletcher v. City of Aberdeen.* A person who is infirm is held to that degree of care as would be exhibited by a reasonably prudent man suffering the same infirmity in the same situation. — 37

6. *Denver & Rio Grande R.R. v. Peterson.* Once a party assumes a duty he must act in a reasonable manner no matter what his station in life. — 38

7. *Blyth v. Birmingham Water Works.* Negligence involves the creation of an "unreasonable" risk, by act or omission, which a reasonable and prudent man would not create. — 39

8. *Osborne v. Montgomery.* To determine whether a risk is acceptable, the value of the social interest involved should be balanced against the risk created. — 40

9. *Cooley v. Public Service Co.* Where danger to two classes of persons cannot be simultaneously guarded against, only the most immediate and injurious risk need be protected. — 41

10. *United States v. Carroll Towing Co.* There is a duty of care to protect others from harm when the burden of taking adequate precautions is less than the product of the probability of the resulting harm and the magnitude of the harm. — 42

11. *Andrews v. United Airlines.* Even a small risk of serious injury to passengers may form the basis of a common carrier's liability if that risk could be eliminated consistent with the practical operation of airline travel. — 43

12. *Titus v. Bradford, B. & K. R. Co.* The unbending test of negligence in methods, machinery, and appliances is the ordinary usage of the business. — 44

13. *Mayhew v. Sullivan Mining Co.* "Custom" has no proper place in the definition of what constitutes ordinary care. — 45

14. *The T.J. Hooper.* The standard of care in a negligence case changes with advances, knowledge, and new devices of demonstrated worth. — 46

15. *The T.J. Hooper.* Regardless of the custom of an industry or trade, a defendant will be held liable if his actions fall beneath the standard of the average prudent man. — 47

16. *Lama v. Borras.* In a medical malpractice case, the plaintiff must show that the physician's treatment fell below the standard of care applicable to the general practitioner, resulting in the plaintiff's injury. — 48

CHAPTER 3

17. *Murray v. UNMC Physicians.* In a medical malpractice action involving an issue of failure to provide medical treatment, the standard of care is a question for the jury where the medical treatment is extremely expensive, its abrupt discontinuance would be devastating for the patient, and physicians waited for confirmation of insurance coverage of the treatment prior to administering it..   49

18. *Canterbury v. Spence.* A physician owes a duty to reasonably disclose to a patient all information concerning an operation that a reasonable physician in the community would disclose based on sound medical considerations.   51

19. *Anon.* Laws are meant to give a remedy.   52

20. *Osborne v. McMasters.* The breach of a statutory duty to a member of the protected class is negligence per se.   53

21. *Martin v. Herzog.* The unexcused omission to perform a statutory duty is negligence per se.   54

22. *Uhr v. East Greenbush Cent. Sch. Dist.* A private right of action cannot be fairly implied where it would be inconsistent with the statute's legislative scheme.   55

23. *Baltimore and Ohio R.R. v. Goodman.* When a plaintiff perceives a risk and fails to adequately take precautions to guard against it, no recovery will be allowed, and the judge must direct a verdict in favor of the defendant.   56

24. *Pokora v. Wabash Ry.* A plaintiff is not required to get out of his vehicle to see if a train is approaching to avoid contributory negligence.   57

25. *Byrne v. Boadle.* When it is highly probable that an injury is due to the negligence of the defendant, and the defendant has better access to the evidence concerning the injury, the doctrine of res ipsa loquitur creates an inference that the defendant was negligent, and puts the burden on defendant to introduce contrary evidence.   58

26. *Colmenares Vivas v. Sun Alliance Insurance Co.* The control requirement of the doctrine of res ipsa loquitur is satisfied where the defendant is ultimately responsible for the agent or instrument causing the injury.   59

27. *Ybarra v. Spangard.* Where an unexplained injury occurs during a medical procedure to a part of the body not under treatment, res ipsa loquitur applies against all of the doctors and medical employees who take part in caring for the patient.   60

Vaughan v. Menlove

Neighboring cottage owner (P) v. Farmer (D)

C.P., 132 Eng. Rep. 490 (1837).

NATURE OF CASE: Action for damages for negligence.

FACT SUMMARY: Menlove's (D) hayrick burst into flames and the fire spread to Vaughan's (P) cottages.

RULE OF LAW
The level of care is determined by what a reasonably prudent man would do in similar circumstances.

FACTS: Menlove (D) stored a hayrick on his land near Vaughan's (P) land. The rick was very dry and Menlove (D) was repeatedly warned that it should be moved or unloaded. The rick burst into flames by spontaneous combustion. The fire spread and burned Vaughan's (P) cottages. The trial judge (Patteson, J.) charged the jury that it should decide if Menlove (D) was grossly negligent by applying a standard of care owed by a reasonably prudent man in similar circumstances. From an adverse verdict, Menlove (D) appealed on the grounds that he owed no duty of care to Vaughan (P) and the proper standard of care should be whether, in his eyes, his conduct was proper. The lawyers for Vaughan (P) (Talfourd and Whately) argued that even if this was a case of first impression, the principles to be applied to it were well established, and that the correct standard to be applied was that of the reasonably prudent man. They also argued that applying any other standard would create greater uncertainties and difficulties. Arguing for Menlove (D), his lawyer (Richards) contended that Menlove's (D) actions were lawful, as he had the right to place his hayrick wherever he wanted on his own property, and that his actions should be judged against his own best judgment under the circumstances, since different people have different levels of judgment and faculties. Thus, Richards argued that a determination of gross negligence should be judged against Menlove's (D) faculties, and not those of others, since the measure of prudence varies with the variation in people's faculties.

ISSUE: Is the standard of care determined by that of the reasonably prudent man?

HOLDING AND DECISION: (Tindal, C.J.) Yes. While the reasonable, prudent man standard is inexact, attempting to determine the standard of care based on the thoughts of an individual is more difficult. Menlove (D) may use his property in any manner he wishes. However, he owes a general duty to do so in a manner that will not endanger the property of another. The proper standard of care is determined by deciding what a reasonably prudent man would do in similar circumstances. The jury may more easily determine this than attempting to determine a defendant's subjective belief. Rule discharged.

CONCURRENCE: (Park, J.) A man must so use his own property as not to injure that of others. It was proper to let the jury decide if Menlove (D) acted like a reasonably prudent man.

CONCURRENCE: (Vaughan, J.) Every one takes upon himself the duty of so dealing with his own property as not to injure the property of others. It is clear that Menlove (D) was grossly negligent and it should not have been left to the jury to decide.

ANALYSIS

Other activities which have been deemed unreasonable are burning weeds near the land of another; cutting trees near a sidewalk or the land of another; and engaging in hazardous activities on one's land. For these and similar activities the owner of property owes a duty of care to others. All of these activities may cause damage to others if not properly performed. The less likely the activity is to cause others damage, the lower the standard of care.

Quicknotes

NEGLIGENCE Conduct falling below the standard of care that a reasonable person would demonstrate under similar conditions.

REASONABLY PRUDENT PERSON A hypothetical person whose judgment represents the standard to which society requires its members to act in their private affairs and in their dealings with others.

STANDARD OF CARE A uniform degree of behavior against which a person's conduct can be measured when determining liability in negligence cases.

Roberts v. Ring

Father of 7-year-old (P) v. Elderly driver (D)

Minn. Sup. Ct., 173 N.W. 437 (1919).

NATURE OF CASE: Appeal from denial of damages for negligence.

FACT SUMMARY: Roberts's (P) son ran in front of Ring's (D) car and was injured.

RULE OF LAW

If one, by his acts or omissions, causes injury to others, his negligence is judged by the standard of care usually exercised by the ordinary prudent normal man.

FACTS: Ring (D), an infirm, 70-year-old man, was driving four or five miles per hour in blocked traffic. Roberts's (P) son, a seven-year-old, ran from behind a buggy in front of Ring's (D) car and was struck and injured. Roberts (P) sued Ring (D) for damages based on negligence. The jury instruction told the jury to take into account Ring's (D) age and infirmities. The jury found for Ring (D). Roberts (P) appealed.

ISSUE: If one, by his acts or omissions, causes injury to others, should his negligence be judged by the standard of care usually exercised by the ordinary prudent normal man?

HOLDING AND DECISION: (Hallam, J.) Yes. If one, by his acts or omissions, causes injury to others his negligence is judged by the standard of care usually exercised by the ordinary prudent normal man. Ring (D) was driving only four or five miles per hour when he saw the boy. It is common knowledge that an auto traveling at that speed can be stopped in a very few feet. Yet, Ring's (D) car knocked the boy down and ran over him. The evidence shows Ring's (D) lack of alertness in stopping his car. Therefore, Ring (D) was negligent. Ring's (D) advanced age does not relieve him from the charge of negligence. Such infirmity, to the extent it should be considered at all, presents a reason why Ring (D) should refrain from operating an auto in a crowded street. Reversed.

ANALYSIS

A related issue concerns the proper standard of care to which to hold beginners. The general rule has been to hold the beginner to the standard of care expected of those who are reasonably skilled and practiced in the art. However, an exception arises in cases in which the plaintiff has assumed the risk that defendant will exercise a lower standard of care, such as where an experienced driver agrees to teach a beginning driver how to drive.

Quicknotes

NEGLIGENCE Conduct falling below the standard of care that a reasonable person would demonstrate under similar conditions.

REASONABLY PRUDENT PERSON A hypothetical person whose judgment represents the standard to which society requires its members to act in their private affairs and in their dealings with others.

STANDARD OF CARE A uniform degree of behavior against which a person's conduct can be measured when determining liability in negligence cases.

Daniels v. Evans

Administrator of estate of deceased motorcycle driver (P) v. Car driver (D)

N.H. Sup. Ct., 224 A.2d 63 (1966).

NATURE OF CASE: Negligence of a minor.

FACT SUMMARY: Daniels, age 19, was killed when his motorcycle collided with Evans's (D) car. Evans (D) objected to the court's instruction to the jury that Daniel was not to be held to the same degree of care as an adult.

🏛 RULE OF LAW
When a minor undertakes an adult activity that can result in grave danger to himself and to others, he is held to the same standard of care as the average prudent adult.

FACTS: Daniel, 19 years of age, was killed when his motorcycle collided with Evans's (D) car. The trial court, instructing the jury as to the standard of care to be applied to Daniels stated, "he is not held to the same degree of care as an adult." The jury gave a verdict for the administrator of the estate of Daniels (P). Evans (D) objected to the jury instructions, arguing that a minor operating a motor vehicle must be judged by the same standard of care as an adult.

ISSUE: Is a minor operating a motor vehicle, or engaging in any other potentially dangerous adult activity, held to an adult standard of care?

HOLDING AND DECISION: (Lampron, J.) Yes. Although the trial court's instructions to the jury reflect this court's traditional yardstick for judging the standard of care for minors, most of the cases applying that standard dealt with minors engaged in activities commensurate with their age (e.g., riding a bicycle or horse, walking). But many recent cases hold that—especially in the operation of motor vehicles—a minor undertaking any adult activity, which can result in grave danger to himself or others, must be judged by the care a reasonable and prudent adult would use. It would be unfair to the public to require a lesser standard. Although one, observing a typical child's activity, may anticipate conduct that does not reach adult standards of care and prudence, one cannot always determine that the driver of an approaching automobile is an adult or a minor, and often could not protect himself even if warned. Further, the state statute regarding obedience to traffic laws applies to "any person." This would indicate the intent of the legislature that all drivers have a right to expect that others—regardless of age and experience—will obey traffic laws and thus exercise the adult standard of ordinary care. The same legislative intent is evident in the state's excluding application of its *parens patriae* power over minors in cases where they are charged with violations of laws regard-

ing motor vehicles, airplanes, boating, and hunting. To apply to minors a lower standard than adults in the operation of motor vehicles, is unrealistic, contrary to the intent of the legislature and harmful to public policy. Exception sustained.

▶ ANALYSIS

The rule is now quite generally accepted that whenever a child, whether as plaintiff or as defendant, engages in an activity which is normally one for adults only, such as driving an auto or flying an airplane, the public interest and public safety require that any consequences stemming from his incapacity shall fall on him rather than on the innocent victim, and that he must be held to an adult standard without allowance for his age.

■■━■■

Quicknotes

ORDINARY CARE The degree of care exercised by a reasonable person when conducting everyday activities or under similar circumstances; synonymous with due care.

PARENS PATRIAE Maxim the government as sovereign is conferred with the duty to act as guardian on behalf of those citizens under legal disability.

STANDARD OF CARE A uniform degree of behavior against which a person's conduct can be measured when determining liability in negligence cases.

■■━■■

Breunig v. American Family Insurance Co.

Truck driver (P) v. Insurance company (D)

Wis. Sup. Ct., 173 N.W.2d 619 (1970).

NATURE OF CASE: Action for damages for personal injury from negligence.

FACT SUMMARY: While overcome by a sudden state of insanity, Erma Veith, insured by American Family Ins. Co. (D), drove her automobile into Breunig's (P) truck.

🏛 RULE OF LAW
A person seized with a sudden mental disability for which he had no warning will be excused from the general rule holding an insane person liable for his negligence.

FACTS: A psychiatrist testified that Ms. Veith, insured by American Family Ins. Co. (D), told him that while she was driving she believed God was directing her car. She saw a truck coming and stepped on the accelerator in order to become airborne, because she knew she could fly. Instead of flying, she collided with Breunig's (P) truck. At the time of the collision, Ms. Veith's automobile was on the left side of the road. The jury found her causally negligent on the theory she "had knowledge or forewarning of her mental delusions or disability."

ISSUE: Is a sudden, unforeseen state of insanity a defense to liability for negligence?

HOLDING AND DECISION: (Hallows, C.J.) Yes. Sudden mental incapacity that strikes without warning is an exception to the general rule that an insane person will be held liable for negligence. Cases supporting the general rule generally involve preexisting or permanent insanity. The general rule is supported by the following policies: (1) where one of two innocent persons must suffer a loss it should be borne by the one who occasioned it; (2) to induce those interested in the insane person's estate to restrain and control him/her; and (3) the fear an insanity defense would lead to false claims of insanity to avoid liability. Sudden mental disability is equivalent to sudden physical disability such as heart attack, stroke, fainting, and epileptic seizure and should be treated alike and not under the general rule. Here, unless it is shown that Ms. Veith, insured by American Family Ins. Co. (D), had warning or knowledge that the mental disability would occur, she will not be held liable for acts she committed while suddenly mentally disabled. Affirmed.

▌ANALYSIS

In nearly all cases, an insane person is held liable for negligence without reference to his insanity. However, this rule has been criticized, as, in this case, a transitory, sudden mental disability is commonly regarded as a circumstances depriving the actor of control over his conduct and relieving him of liability.

■■■

Quicknotes

FORESEEABILITY A reasonable expectation that an act or omission would result in injury.

MENTAL CAPACITY The ability to comprehend the nature, terms, and effect of the act in which one is engaged.

■■■

Fletcher v. City of Aberdeen

Blind man (P) v. City (D)

Wash. Sup. Ct., 338 P.2d 743 (1959).

NATURE OF CASE: Action for damages for negligence.

FACT SUMMARY: A workman negligently removed a barrier around a ditch and Fletcher (P), who was blind, fell into it.

🏛 RULE OF LAW
A person who is infirm is held to that degree of care as would be exhibited by a reasonably prudent man suffering the same infirmity in the same situation.

FACTS: The City of Aberdeen (D) dug a ditch near a sidewalk to affect repairs. A barricade was erected. One of the workmen removed the barricade to do some work and negligently failed to replace it. Fletcher (P), who was blind, fell into it. Testimony indicated that Fletcher's (P) cane would have warned him of the ditch if the barrier were in place. The judge instructed the jury that the City (D) was not an insurer and it must find negligence on its part. The judge refused to instruct the jury that the City (D) owed no greater duty to the blind than to the sighted and that the blind should be held to the same standard of care as the sighted. The City (D) appealed from a verdict for Fletcher (P).

ISSUE: Are the blind held to the same standard of care as the sighted?

HOLDING AND DECISION: (Foster, J.) No. The City (D) is obligated to safeguard all who travel the streets. This obligation applies to the rich and the poor, the physically well, and those who are infirm. While the City (D) is not an insurer, it is liable for its negligence or that of its employees. While a sighted person would probably not have fallen into the ditch, a blind person is not held to that standard of care. If one suffering a physical infirmity is injured, he is not held to be contributorily negligent unless he has failed to act with the same degree of care that a prudent man with similar disability would have exhibited under similar circumstances. Affirmed.

▌ *ANALYSIS*

A private citizen does not owe the same duty to the infirm (normally). In such situations, the plaintiff who is infirm will normally be held to a higher standard of care in determining whether the private defendant was negligent. Cases dealing with private parties who hold themselves open to the public have caused a great deal of problems in this area. To what standard of care should the private party be held in such situations? Courts have split over the ques-tion, with most decisions being based on the factual nature of the injury.

Quicknotes

STANDARD OF CARE A uniform degree of behavior against which a person's conduct can be measured when determining liability in negligence cases.

Denver & Rio Grande R.R. v. Peterson

[Parties not identified.]

Colo. Sup. Ct., 69 P. 578 (1902).

NATURE OF CASE: [Nature of case not stated in casebook excerpt.]

FACT SUMMARY: [Facts not stated in casebook excerpt.]

🏛 **RULE OF LAW**
Once a party assumes a duty he must act in a reasonable manner no matter what his station in life.

FACTS: [Facts not stated in casebook excerpt.]

ISSUE: Once a party assumes a duty, must he act in a reasonable manner no matter what his station in life?

HOLDING AND DECISION: (Campbell, C.J.) Yes. Wealth is not a factor in determining whether a party has fulfilled his duty of due care and reasonable conduct. Once a party assumes a duty he must act in a reasonable manner. Poverty will not excuse the duty and wealth will not increase it. A warehouseman owes the same duty to those storing goods whether he is rich or poor.

▶ *ANALYSIS*

An infirmity will not normally excuse a duty of care. This is especially true where it is in a commercial setting. The standard of care to be met is that of a normally prudent person under similar circumstances. Beginners are generally held to the same standard of care as more experienced people. An exception is sometimes made where the party engaging the beginner is alerted to the fact that he is a beginner. The standard then becomes the reasonable care of a prudent beginner.

Quicknotes

DUTY OF CARE A principal of negligence requiring an individual to act in such a manner as to avoid injury to a person to whom he or she owes an obligatory duty.

Blyth v. Birmingham Water Works

Landowner (P) v. Water works company (D)

Ex., 156 Eng. Rep. 1047 (1856).

NATURE OF CASE: Action to recover damages for negligence on appeal.

FACT SUMMARY: An extraordinarily severe frost caused a fireplug owned by Birmingham Water Works (D) to flood the property of Blyth (P).

🏛 RULE OF LAW
Negligence involves the creation of an "unreasonable" risk, by act or omission, which a reasonable and prudent man would not create.

FACTS: Birmingham Water Works Co. (D) operated the water pipes in the county of Birmingham. By statute they were also required to maintain fireplugs for the pipes in a certain manner (18" below the surface, etc.) At all times, Water Works (D) maintained the fireplugs according to the law and had for 25 years. During an extraordinarily cold frost one winter, however, one of the plugs got stopped up by ice, which caused water from the pipes to flood the property of Blyth (P), causing damage. (Note, moving water does not freeze.) Blyth (P) sued for damages charging negligence of Water Works (D) in not taking adequate precautions to prepare for the contingency of this frost. Upon judgment for Blyth (P), Water Works (D) appealed contending that the frost was so extraordinary and unforeseeable as to make damage resulting from it a mere accident.

ISSUE: May negligence liability be imposed where damage results from a mere accident, the contingency of which was wholly extraordinary?

HOLDING AND DECISION: (Alderson, B.) No. Negligence liability may not be imposed where damage results from a mere accident, the contingency of which was wholly extraordinary. Negligence involves the creation of an "unreasonable" risk, by act or omission, which a reasonable and prudent man, guided upon those considerations that ordinarily regulate the conduct of human affairs, would not create. A reasonable man acts with reference to the average circumstances of ordinary times. He cannot be held, therefore, for extraordinary occurrences. Here, Water Works (D) took all necessary precautions for ordinary frost. They cannot equitably be held responsible for a frost such as the one involved here as such a frost is seldom seen south of the polar region. The judgment must be reversed. The rationale here is that making Water Works (D) responsible for all harm caused, even inadvertently, would be to make them the insurers of all people with whom they deal.

CONCURRENCE: (Bromwell, B.) The defendants were not bound to keep the plugs clear. It appears to me that the plaintiff was under quite as much obligation to remove the accumulated ice and snow as the defendants. However that may be, it appears to me that it would be monstrous to hold the defendants responsible because they did not foresee and prevent an accident, the cause of which was so obscure, that it was not discovered until many months after the accident had happened.

▶ ANALYSIS

This case points out the general rule for the negligence standard of care that all people owe. Basically, it is the objective "reasonable man under similar circumstances" test. Notes that simply following the statutory duties required above did not determine whether this standard had been met, however. Though compliance with a statute is evidence of meeting the standard, it is not conclusive. If the conduct involved nevertheless creates an "unreasonable risk" of harm, negligence will be found. On the other hand, failure to meet a statutory standard where (1) statutory duty is clear and (2) it is designed to prevent the type of injury suffered or protect the class of persons of which the victim is a member, may be negligence per se. Caution must be taken, however, to avoid confusion between the foreseeability standard for standard of care (above) and the absence of this standard for proximate cause.

Quicknotes

FORESEEABILITY A reasonable expectation that an act or omission would result in injury.

NEGLIGENCE Conduct falling below the standard of care that a reasonable person would demonstrate under similar conditions.

PROXIMATE CAUSE The natural sequence of events without which an injury would not have been sustained.

REASONABLE PERSON STANDARD The standard of care exercised by a hypothetical person who possesses the intelligence, education, knowledge, attention, and judgment required by society of its members when governing behavior; the standard applied to a person's judgment when determining breach of duty under the theory of negligence.

STANDARD OF CARE A uniform degree of behavior against which a person's conduct can be measured when determining liability in negligence cases.

Osborne v. Montgomery

Bicycle errand runner (P) v. Auto owner (D)

Wis. Sup. Ct., 234 N.W. 372 (1931).

NATURE OF CASE: Action for negligence.

FACT SUMMARY: A jury instruction that gave no definition of how to determine whether a risk was reasonable was challenged.

RULE OF LAW

To determine whether a risk is acceptable, the value of the social interest involved should be balanced against the risk created.

FACTS: Osborne (P), a 13-year-old youth, was riding his bicycle when the right handle bar of his bicycle came in contact with the outside edge of an opened door of Montgomery's (D) stopped car. The bicycle subsequently tipped and Osborne (P) was thrown to the ground and injured. The jury was instructed that negligence is the want of ordinary care and ordinary care is the degree of care that the great mass of mankind exercises under similar circumstances. The jury found Montgomery (D) negligent and Montgomery (D) appealed.

ISSUE: to determine whether a risk is acceptable, should the value of the social interest involved be balanced against the risk created.

HOLDING AND DECISION: (Rosenberry, C.J.) Yes. To determine whether a risk is acceptable, the value of the social interest involved should be balanced against the risk created. Human beings are constantly creating situations that lead to the injury of another. To determine whether the conduct is justified based on societal demands there must be a balancing of the social interest involved against the risk created by the conduct. If the interest justifies the risk, then the jury must be instructed to determine whether the defendant conducted himself under the situation with the same degree of care that a majority of people would exhibit under similar circumstances. Reversed and remanded on the question of damages.

ANALYSIS

Driving, even under hazardous conditions, is a socially justified risk. However, the driver must be handling his car in a reasonable, prudent manner consonant with the conditions. Observance of the speed limit where the streets are icy might not be deemed compliance with ordinary care under the above-announced rule of law. However, a fire engine speeding to a fire could justify a higher rate of speed so long as it was warranted and the driver handled the truck with the same degree of skill other drivers would exhibit in similar circumstances.

Quicknotes

CONTRIBUTORY NEGLIGENCE Behavior on the part of an injured plaintiff falling below the standard of ordinary care that contributes to the defendant's negligence, resulting in the plaintiff's injury.

ORDINARY CARE The degree of care exercised by a reasonable person when conducting everyday activities or under similar circumstances; synonymous with due care.

Cooley v. Public Service Co.

Injured telephone user (P) v. Power company (D)

N.H. Sup. Ct., 10 A.2d 673 (1940).

NATURE OF CASE: Action for damages resulting from negligence.

FACT SUMMARY: Public Service Co. (D) hung its electrical wires over telephone lines at a right angle.

RULE OF LAW
Where danger to two classes of persons cannot be simultaneously guarded against, only the most immediate and injurious risk need be protected.

FACTS: Public Service Co. (D) hung its uninsulated power lines at right angles above telephone company (D) lines. A severe storm downed one of Public Service's (D) lines. It fell across a telephone company line, burned through it and caused a loud screech on the line that injured Cooley (P) who was making a call. Cooley (P) sued both the telephone company (D) and Public Service (D) for negligence. The telephone company (D) was dismissed from the suit, and the jury found against Public Service (D) on the basis that certain safety devices could have been installed to protect against such an occurrence. Public Service (D) appealed a judgment against it on the ground that these devices would have caused a greater risk of electrocution to those on the streets below the lines. Public Service (D) alleged that its primary duty was to protect this class of people rather than telephone subscribers.

ISSUE: Where two classes cannot be protected simultaneously, is it negligence to only protect the class that is in the most serious and immediate danger?

HOLDING AND DECISION: (Page, J.) No. Public Service (D) owed its primary duty to pedestrians who could be electrocuted. Its safety devices were sufficient to protect that class. The safety devices suggested by Cooley (P) would have increased the risk to this class at the expense of protecting telephone subscribers from a reasonably remote and less dangerous risk. Where two or more classes are subjected to potential risk by the same socially permissible conduct, and both cannot be simultaneously protected, the duty is to protect the class that is in the most serious and immediate danger. Reversed.

ANALYSIS

Where there is a danger to property versus a risk to human life, the latter is always given preference. This is one of the major justifications for burying cables, power lines, etc. Certain risks carry with them a danger to both life and property that, because of the nature of the activity, cannot be reasonably safeguarded. These activities, e.g., blasting, are subjected to a strict liability theory for any class of injury.

Quicknotes

NEGLIGENCE Conduct falling below the standard of care that a reasonable person would demonstrate under similar conditions.

STRICT LIABILITY Liability for all injuries proximately caused by a party's conducting of certain inherently dangerous activities without regard to negligence or fault.

United States v. Carroll Towing Co.

Federal government (D) v. Tugboat company (D)

159 F.2d 169 (2d Cir. 1947).

NATURE OF CASE: Action to recover damages in admiralty for the sinking of a barge.

FACT SUMMARY: The attendant of defendant's barge abandoned it for twenty-one hours; during this period the barge broke loose and while it was adrift struck the plaintiff's barge causing it to sink.

🏛 RULE OF LAW
There is a duty of care to protect others from harm when the burden of taking adequate precautions is less than the product of the probability of the resulting harm and the magnitude of the harm.

FACTS: The attendant of defendant's barge left that barge unwatched for more than twenty-one hours during a period when the harbor was full of vessels. During the period when the attendant of defendant's barge was absent, the barge became untied and drifted away from the dock, running into another barge, sinking it.

ISSUE: Is the duty of care breached when defendant's conduct incurred a risk which could be avoided with very few precautions and which if it inflicts injury will cause a great amount of damage?

HOLDING AND DECISION: (Hand, J.) Yes. If the burden of preventing the injury is lower than the product of the probability of its occurring and the amount of harm that it will cause, then there is a breach of the duty of care and liability for negligence. In this case, the burden of preventing the accident was low; it only involved the watchmen staying in the vicinity of the barge or recruiting someone else to stand by and watch it. The probability of the barge getting untied and striking another barge is undoubtedly a variable that changes with conditions, as is the amount of injury that will result. The existing conditions, the crowded harbor with barges constantly being moved about, made the probability of injury more than a negligible factor and made the magnitude of resulting injury an enormous figure. Thus, since the burden of preventing the collision was low and the product of the probability and the amount of injury projected is high, the fact that it occurred was a breach of duty.

▶ ANALYSIS

This effort to formulate negligence, this "calculus of the risk," is an acceptable method of determining negligence. Behind this formula however, is always the recognition that the measure of the reasonableness of the risk revolves around the specific circumstances of the situation. Conduct is relative to the particular occasion and need.

■=■

Quicknotes

CONTRIBUTORY NEGLIGENCE Behavior on the part of an injured plaintiff falling below the standard of ordinary care that contributes to the defendant's negligence, resulting in the plaintiff's injury.

■=■

Andrews v. United Airlines

Injured passenger (P) v. Airline company (D)

24 F.3d 39 (9th Cir. 1994).

NATURE OF CASE: Appeal from summary judgment dismissing action in negligence.

FACT SUMMARY: Andrews (P), a passenger injured on a United Airlines (United) (D) flight when a briefcase fell out of an overhead compartment and hit her, alleged that United (D) was liable for negligence because it breached its duty of care to her.

🏛 RULE OF LAW
Even a small risk of serious injury to passengers may form the basis of a common carrier's liability if that risk could be eliminated consistent with the practical operation of airline travel.

FACTS: Andrews (P) was a passenger aboard a United Airlines (United) (D) flight when a briefcase fell out of an overhead compartment and hit her in the head, causing serious injuries. Andrews (P) alleged that United (D), as a common carrier, owed Andrews (P) an utmost duty of care and that United (D) breached that duty by not doing more to prevent objects from falling out of overhead compartments. United (D) moved for summary judgment, arguing that Andrews (P) showed too little proof of United's (D) breach to be allowed to go to a jury on the issue. The district court granted summary judgment for United (D) and Andrews (P) appealed.

ISSUE: May even a small risk of serious injury form the basis of a common carrier's liability if that risk could be eliminated consistent with the practical operation of airline travel?

HOLDING AND DECISION: (Kozinski, J.) Yes. Even a small risk of serious injury to passengers may form the basis of a common carrier's liability if that risk could be eliminated consistent with the practical operation of airline travel. Andrews (P) demonstrated that United (D) was aware of the problem of items falling out of overhead bins; however, its solution was to merely warn passengers of the danger. Here, United (D) as a common carrier owed an utmost duty of care to passenger Andrews (P). Andrews (P) presented enough proof that United (D) breached its duty to defeat summary judgment and have a jury decide the issue of breach. A reasonable jury might find that United (D) should have done more to prevent items from falling out of the overhead compartments, or it might find that United (D) did do enough. The district court, therefore, incorrectly granted summary judgment for United (D). Reversed and remanded.

▶ ANALYSIS
Common carriers owe a higher duty to passengers than the ordinary standard of care. The ordinary standard is that of reasonable care under the circumstances. Common carriers, as this case demonstrates, are responsible for even the slightest negligence. Regardless of the standard applied, the issues of duty and breach are ones to be decided by the jury, if a reasonable jury could decide the issues either way.

Quicknotes
COMMON CARRIER An entity whose business is the transport of persons or property.

DUTY OF CARE A principal of negligence requiring an individual to act in such a manner as to avoid injury to a person to whom he or she owes an obligatory duty.

NEGLIGENCE Conduct falling below the standard of care that a reasonable person would demonstrate under similar conditions.

SUMMARY JUDGMENT Judgment rendered by a court in response to a motion by one of the parties, claiming that the lack of a question of material fact in respect to an issue warrants disposition of the issue without consideration by the jury.

Titus v. Bradford, B. & K. R. Co.

Railroad brakeman (P) v. Railroad (D)

Pa. Sup. Ct., 20 A. 517 (1890).

NATURE OF CASE: Action for negligence.

FACT SUMMARY: Titus (P) was killed when a broad-gauge boxcar that Bradford, B. & K. R. Co. (D) had set on its narrow-gauge tracks tipped off its truck when a securing block became loose.

RULE OF LAW
The unbending test of negligence in methods, machinery, and appliances is the ordinary usage of the business.

FACTS: Bradford, B. & K. R. Co. (D) (the Railroad) customarily took the broad-gauge cars used by the other carrier having standard-gauge lines and set them on its narrow-gauge tracks by means of trucks, utilizing securing blocks to eliminate the undue rocking that otherwise occurred. One of these securing blocks became loose, and Titus (P), a brakeman riding the car, was killed. In defending a suit based on negligence seeking to recover damages for his death, the Railroad (D) offered testimony that the shifting of broad-gauge or standard car bodies onto narrow-gauge trucks for transportation was a regular part and common practice of the business of narrow-gauge railroads.

ISSUE: Is an employer free from negligence as long as his methods, machinery, and appliances comport with the ordinary usage of the business in which he is engaged?

HOLDING AND DECISION: (Mitchell, J.) Yes. An employer is free from negligence as long as his methods, machinery, and appliances comport with the ordinary usage of the business in which he is engaged. An employer is not bound to use the best and newest devices to avoid a claim that he is negligent. Rather, he performs his duty when he furnishes those of ordinary character and reasonable safety. In regard to the style of implement or nature of the mode of performance of any work, "reasonably safe" means safe according to the usage, habits, and ordinary risks of the business. Absolute safety is unattainable, and employers are not insurers. Furthermore, some jobs are essentially dangerous. The employer is liable not for the consequences of danger but for the consequences of negligence; the unbending test of negligence in methods, machinery and appliances is the ordinary usage of the business. No jury can be permitted to say that the usual and ordinary way, commonly adopted by those in the same business, is a negligent way for which liability shall be imposed. As the Railroad (D) acted in accord with his standard of care, it was not negligent. Furthermore, this was a perfectly plain case of acceptance of an employment with full knowledge of the risks. Reversed.

ANALYSIS

The use of safety codes, manuals, etc. as "pertinent and valuable aids in the resolution of the issue of negligence" was affirmed in *McComish v. DeSoi*, 42 N.J. 274, 200 LA.2d 116 (1964). While warning that prevailing safety practices were not "of themselves the absolute measure of due care," the court made it clear that they have "probative force as evidence" of what would constitute reasonable care in a particular area or situation.

Quicknotes

STANDARD OF CARE A uniform degree of behavior against which a person's conduct can be measured when determining liability in negligence cases.

Mayhew v. Sullivan Mining Co.

Mineworker (P) v. Mining company (D)

Me. Sup. Jud. Ct., 76 Me. 100 (1884).

NATURE OF CASE: Appeal from verdict for plaintiff in a negligence action.

FACT SUMMARY: Sullivan Mining Co. (D) argued that it should be allowed to present evidence regarding customary industry practices in defending against Mayhew's (P) negligence suit.

RULE OF LAW

"Custom" has no proper place in the definition of what constitutes ordinary care.

FACTS: Mayhew (P), an independent contractor, was hired by Sullivan Mining Co. (Sullivan) (D) to trace new veins of ore. While working on a platform 270 feet below ground, which contained a "bucket hole" that Mayhew (P) used in his work, Mayhew (P) was injured when he fell thirty-five feet down the mineshaft. Mayhew (P) fell through a hole about three feet by twenty-six inches in size, which had been cut by one of Sullivan's (D) employees as a "ladder hole." No railing or barrier had been put around this ladder hole or any light or other warning of its existence. At trial, the court refused to allow evidence regarding whether ladder holes in mines ever had railings. The jury found Sullivan (D) negligent and awarded Mayhew (P) $2,500. Sullivan (D) appealed.

ISSUE: Does "custom" have a proper place in the definition of what constitutes ordinary care?

HOLDING AND DECISION: (Barrows, J.) No. "Custom" has no proper place in the definition of what constitutes ordinary care. Here, Sullivan (D) contends that it should have been allowed by the trial court to question its mining superintendent, who had supervised the cutting of the ladder hole, regarding whether there was any lack of "average ordinary care" on Sullivan's (D) part. These questions related to whether it was customary or feasible in the mining business to fence or put a railing around a ladder hole. These questions were properly excluded. No matter what custom or practice in the mining industry could prove, it would have no tendency to show that the act was consistent with ordinary prudence or due regard for the safety of those who were using Sullivan's (D) premises by its invitation. The gross carelessness of the act appears conclusively upon its recital. Sullivan (D) argues that if one conforms to custom, he is so far exercising ordinary care. This argument proceeds upon an erroneous idea of what constitutes ordinary care. It is no excuse that carelessness is universal. Affirmed.

ANALYSIS

In the history of negligence decisions, the *Mayhew v. Sullivan Mining Co.* case has not been frequently followed. A more recent case states a more current view. This case is *Bimberg v. Northern Pacific Ry.*, 14 N.W. 410 (Minn. 1944). In *Bimberg*, the court stated that local usage and custom, either singly or in combination, will not justify or excuse negligence. Plans of construction or uses commonly followed by years of successful operation may be evidence of due care but cannot establish as safe in law what is dangerous in fact.

Quicknotes

ORDINARY CARE The degree of care exercised by a reasonable person when conducting everyday activities or under similar circumstances; synonymous with due care.

The T.J. Hooper

Owner of cargo (P) v. Tugboat (D)

53 F.2d 107 (S.D.N.Y 1931).

NATURE OF CASE: Appeal from award of damages for negligence.

FACT SUMMARY: *The T.J. Hooper* (D), a tugboat, lost its cargo after it failed to receive warnings of an approaching storm.

🏛 RULE OF LAW
The standard of care in a negligence case changes with advances, knowledge, and new devices of demonstrated worth.

FACTS: *The T.J. Hooper* (D) was one of six tugboats hauling coal barges from Virginia to New York. *Hooper's* (D) cargo was lost in a gale. Four of the other tugboats had received storm warnings on their radios and escaped the storm by moving to calmer waters. *Hooper* (D) was not equipped with a reliable radio and therefore failed to receive the storm warnings. Ninety percent of coast side tugboats had radios. The cargo owners (P) sued *Hooper* (D) for damages based on *Hooper's* (D) operator's negligence in failing to equip the boat with a reliable radio even though the use of such radios in coastal navigation was almost universally accepted. The trial court found for the cargo owners.

ISSUE: Does the standard of care in a negligence case change with advances, knowledge, and new devices of demonstrated worth?

HOLDING AND DECISION: (Coxe, J.) Yes. The standard of care in a negligence action changes with advances, knowledge, and new devices of demonstrated worth. Radio broadcasts were not new or untried in 1928. It was utilized by almost 90 percent of coastal tugboat operators and was regarded as necessary equipment on every reasonably equipped tugboat. The use of the radios was so extensive it became an almost universal practice in coastal navigation. *Hooper's* (D) owner had a duty to supply effective receiving sets. Affirmed.

▶ ANALYSIS

On appeal (60 F.2d 737 [2d Cir. 1932]), Judge Learned Hand affirmed the lower court's decision on a novel basis. Judge Hand disagreed with the trial court in its contention that the use of receiving sets was generally adopted by coastal tugboats operating in 1928. However, Judge Hand held that even though the use of such radios was not customary, the failure of the tugboat owner to obtain such necessary equipment still constituted negligence.

Quicknotes

JOINT LIABILITY Liability owed to an injured party by two or more parties where each party has the right to insist that the other tortfeasors be joined to the matter.

The T.J. Hooper (1932)

Owner of cargo (P) v. Tugboat (D)

60 F.2d 737 (2d Cir. 1932).

NATURE OF CASE: Appeal in action for exoneration from, or limitation of, liability.

FACT SUMMARY: Eastern Transportation Co. (D), the owner of two tugs, unsuccessfully appeals the refusal of the trial court to limit Eastern's (D) liability toward the owners of barges and their cargoes of coal that were lost in a storm the tugs could have avoided had they been equipped with radio receivers.

RULE OF LAW

Regardless of the custom of an industry or trade, a defendant will be held liable if his actions fall beneath the standard of the average prudent man.

FACTS: This is a petition by the Eastern Transportation Co. (Eastern) (D), as owner of the tugs *Mantrose* and *The T.J. Hooper*. The tugs were towing barges #17 and #30 belonging to the Northern Barge Co. (P). The barges carried coal owned by the New England Coal and Coke Co. and N.H. Hartwell & Son, Inc. The tugs sank in a storm, losing the barges and their cargo. The cargo owners sued the barge owners under contracts of carriage and Northern Barge (P) sued Eastern (D) under the towing contract—both for its own loss and as bailee of the cargo. The trial court found the tugs unseaworthy because they could have secured storm warnings. The trial court held Eastern (D) and Northern Barge (D) jointly liable to the cargo owners. Eastern (D) petitioned exoneration from, or limitation of, liability.

ISSUE: Is negligence in matters of business or industry to be determined by the customs common to the trade?

HOLDING AND DECISION: (Hand, J.) No. The fact that it was not a general custom for tugs to have radio receivers with which to receive weather warnings is not determinative. Reasonable prudence required the installation of such sets in the case of tugs towing heavily laden barges, strung out for half a mile and with little power to maneuver. A radio receiver would have given them necessary protection that would be available in no other way. The whole industry may have lagged in the installation of these sets, which is not to say that ordinary prudence would not regard them as necessary. Affirmed.

ANALYSIS

Professor and legal scholar William Prosser stated that, according to the majority of cases, it is the better view that not every custom is conclusive merely because it is a custom. A custom must meet the challenge of "learned reason" and be given only the evidentiary weight the situation deserves. Therefore, where common knowledge and ordinary judgment will recognize unreasonable danger, it may be that the whole trade or industry may be found negligent.

Quicknotes

CUSTOM AND USAGE A customary practice that is so widespread that it has become mandatory and has the force of law.

Lama v. Borras

Patient (P) v. Doctor (D)

16 F.3d 473 (1st Cir. 1994).

NATURE OF CASE: Appeal from jury verdict for plaintiff in medical malpractice suit.

FACT SUMMARY: Roberto Romero Lama (P) brought suit alleging medical malpractice against Borras (D) and Hospital del Maestro (D) on the basis that Borras (D) was negligent in failing to administer a conservative treatment program prior to resorting to surgery.

🏛 RULE OF LAW
In a medical malpractice case, the plaintiff must show that the physician's treatment fell below the standard of care applicable to the general practitioner, resulting in the plaintiff's injury.

FACTS: Roberto Romero Lama (Romero) (P) suffered from back pain. His physician, Alfonso, referred him to Borras (D), a neurosurgeon, who concluded that Romero had a herniated disc and scheduled him for surgery. During surgery, Borras (D) found that Romero had an "extruded" disc and attempted to remove the extruding material. Romero's symptoms remained in effect for several days after the operation and Borras (D) scheduled a second operation. Romero (P) suffered from discitis, an infection of the space between the discs. He filed suit against Borras (D) alleging negligence. The jury awarded Romero (P) $600,000 and the district court rejected Borras's (D) motion for judgment as a matter of law and for a new trial. Borras (D) appealed.

ISSUE: In a medical malpractice case, must the plaintiff show that the physician's treatment fell below the standard of care applicable to the general practitioner resulting in the plaintiff's injury?

HOLDING AND DECISION: (Stahl, J.) Yes. In a medical malpractice case, the plaintiff must show that the physician's treatment fell below the standard of care applicable to the general practitioner resulting in the plaintiff's injury. In order to establish a prima facie case of medical malpractice in Puerto Rico, the plaintiff must show: (1) the norms of medical care and knowledge applicable to the general practitioner; (2) proof the physician failed to follow such norms in the patient's treatment; and (3) a causal relationship between the physician's act or omission and the patient's injury. The plaintiff must establish the relevant national standard of care. This is usually accomplished by expert testimony. The plaintiff must also prove by a preponderance of the evidence that the physician's negligent conduct was the factor that "most probably" caused the plaintiff's injury. Expert testimony is generally required to establish this as well. Borras (D) claimed that Romero (P)

failed to establish a general medical standard governing the need for conservative treatment prior to the first operation. Here there was sufficient evidence for the jury to conclude Borras (D) failed to provide the proper conservative treatment program prior to surgery. When a physician exposes a patient to risk-prone surgery, he is liable for harm sustained that is associated with a foreseeable risk. Here discitis is a foreseeable risk of lumbar disc surgery. With respect to the issue of causation, nearly all of the expert testimony stated that conservative treatment would have eliminated the need for surgery in most cases. Romero (P) introduced legally sufficient evidence to support each element of negligence by Borras (D). Affirmed.

▌ANALYSIS

Note that the standard of care applicable in medical malpractice cases departs from the usual standard of the "reasonable person" normally applied by juries. Courts resort to the use of custom in order to provide more consistent results. The typical standard in medical malpractice suits is the physician use the degree of knowledge and skill possessed by physicians in good standing in the community and under similar circumstances.

■■■

Quicknotes

STANDARD OF CARE A uniform degree of behavior against which a person's conduct can be measured when determining liability in negligence cases.

■■■

Murray v. UNMC Physicians

Deceased patient's spouse (P) v. Physicians (D)

Neb. Sup. Ct., 806 N.W.2d 118 (2011).

NATURE OF CASE: Appeal from order of new trial in action for medical malpractice.

FACT SUMMARY: UNMC (D), Mrs. Murray's physicians, waited to give her an extremely expensive medicine (Flolan) until they had confirmation her insurance would cover the cost of the Flolan, because once Flolan was started, discontinuing it would have devastating consequences for the patient. Mrs. Murray died before the Flolan was administered, and her husband, Murray (P), brought suit for medical malpractice. A key issue was the appropriate standard of care and whether the standard could be tied to the need for insurance payments.

> ## RULE OF LAW
> In a medical malpractice action involving an issue of failure to provide medical treatment, the standard of care is a question for the jury where the medical treatment is extremely expensive, its abrupt discontinuance would be devastating for the patient, and physicians waited for confirmation of insurance coverage of the treatment prior to administering it.

FACTS: Mrs. Murray suffered from pulmonary arterial hypertension. Flolan, a medicine that can treat this condition, must be administered on a continuing basis for the rest of a patient's life once it is started, at a cost of around $100,000 per year. If it is discontinued, it can have devastating consequences for a patient, including death. Prior to administering Flolan to Mrs. Murray, her physicians UNMC (D) awaited insurance approval—because they wanted to be certain she would have a continuous, uninterrupted supply. Before insurance confirmation was received, Mrs. Murray died of cardiac arrest. Her husband, Murray (P), brought a medical malpractice action against UNMC (D). The cause of death was disputed. Murray (P) presented evidence it was arterial hypertension. UNMC (D) presented evidence it was myocarditis, an inflammation of the heart usually caused by viral or bacterial infection. Murray (P) also presented evidence earlier administration of Flolan would have prevented Mrs. Murray's death. Murray (P) moved for a directed verdict on the standard of care, arguing as a matter of law, insurance coverage cannot dictate what doctors do, but this motion was denied. Murray (P) also requested the jury be instructed if the standard of care requires prescription of a drug, it is not a defense to a claim the standard of care has been violated if the drug would not be provided until approved by an insurance carrier. That instruction was refused. The jury returned a general verdict for UNMC (D), but the trial court granted a new trial, explaining as a matter of law, a medical standard

of care cannot be tied to or controlled by an insurance company or the need for payment. UNMC (D) appealed the grant of a new trial, and the state's highest court granted review.

ISSUE: In a medical malpractice action involving an issue of failure to provide medical treatment, is the standard of care a question for the jury where the medical treatment is extremely expensive, its abrupt discontinuance would be devastating for the patient, and physicians waited for confirmation of insurance coverage of the treatment prior to administering it?

HOLDING AND DECISION: (Gerrard, J.) Yes. In a medical malpractice action involving an issue of failure to provide medical treatment, the standard of care is a question for the jury where the medical treatment is extremely expensive, its abrupt discontinuance would be devastating for the patient, and physicians waited for confirmation of insurance coverage of the treatment prior to administering it. The issue in this case is a narrow one, but it appears in the context of broader policy discussions of what the appropriate standard of care should be. In this state, the standard of reasonable and ordinary care is unitary and wealth-blind. Some argue this standard cannot be reconciled with today's healthcare marketplace, which is increasingly driven by cost and insurance concerns, and it leads to physicians declining altogether patients who cannot afford to pay or who are uninsured. On the other hand, some have argued permitting physicians to make medical decisions based on resource scarcity would compromise the fiduciary relationship between patient and physician, creating a conflict of interest because the patient's well-being would no longer be the physician's focus. Whether the legal standard of care should change to alleviate that conflict, and how it might change, has been the subject of considerable debate. It has been suggested the customary standard of care could evolve to permit the denial of marginally beneficial treatment, when high costs would not be justified by minor expected benefits. Another suggestion is the standard of care should evolve to consider two separate components: (1) a skill component, addressing the skill with which diagnoses are made and treatment is rendered, that would not vary by a patient's financial circumstances and (2) a resource component, addressing deliberate decisions about how much treatment to give a patient, that would vary so as to not demand more of physicians than is reasonable. Some have suggested physicians should be permitted to rebut the presumption of a unitary standard of

Continued on next page.

care when diminution of care arises by economic necessity instead of negligence, whereas many have suggested custom should no longer be the benchmark for the standard of care, and practice standards or guidelines could be promulgated that would settle issues of resource allocation. Although these policy considerations are serious and difficult, they are not presented by this case. Contrary to the trial court's belief, this is not a case in which an insurance company overrode the medical judgment of a patient's physicians or in which those physicians allowed their medical judgment to be subordinated to a patient's ability to pay for treatment. Nor is this a case in which the parties disputed the cost-effectiveness of the treatment at issue. Rather, UNMC's (D) evidence was its decision to wait to begin Flolan treatment was not economic—it was a medical decision, based on the health consequences to the patient if the treatment is interrupted. Thus, the trial court's concerns about health care policy were misplaced in a situation in which the patient's ability to continue to pay for treatment was still a medical consideration. In other words, even when the standard of care is limited to medical considerations relevant to the welfare of the patient, and not economic considerations relevant to the welfare of the health care provider, the standard of care used in this case was still consistent with a medical standard of care. The case did not implicate other policy concerns because it did not involve a conflict of interest between the physician and patient—there was no evidence, for instance, of a financial incentive for UNMC's (D) physicians to control costs. Instead, the physicians were weighing the risk to Mrs. Murray's health of delaying treatment against the risk to her health of potentially interrupted treatment. Accordingly, it was a jury question as to whether the Flolan should have been administered immediately, and, therefore, it was error for the trial court to have ordered a new trial. Reversed.

▶ ANALYSIS

A unitary, or wealth-blind, standard of care is defined as that which health care providers, in the same community or in similar communities and engaged in the same or similar lines of work, would ordinarily exercise and devote to the benefit of their patients under like circumstances. This standard developed in a world of fee-for-service medicine and persisted while health insurance still primarily provided first-dollar unlimited coverage. Today, however, health plans and self-insured corporations are placing increasingly stringent controls on health care resources, thereby limiting physicians' freedom to practice medicine as they see fit. As this case amply discusses, the appropriateness of this standard is increasingly being questioned in light of the realities of today's healthcare marketplace.

Quicknotes

DIRECTED VERDICT A verdict ordered by the court in a jury trial.

STANDARD OF CARE A uniform degree of behavior against which a person's conduct can be measured when determining liability in negligence cases.

Canterbury v. Spence

Patient (P) v. Surgeon (D)

464 F.2d 772 (D.C. Cir. 1972).

NATURE OF CASE: Action in negligence for damages.

FACT SUMMARY: Dr. Spence (D) performed an operation on Canterbury (P) without advising him of the risks associated with the surgery.

RULE OF LAW
A physician owes a duty to reasonably disclose to a patient all information concerning an operation that a reasonable physician in the community would disclose based on sound medical considerations.

FACTS: Canterbury (P), a minor, complained of back problems. Dr. Spence (D), after making an examination, recommended a laminectomy to correct what he thought was a ruptured disk. Spence (D) did not inform Canterbury (P) or his mother that in approximately one percent of the cases the operation resulted in paralysis. After the operation which revealed a swollen spinal cord in poor condition rather than a ruptured disk, Canterbury (P) was placed in a post-operative unit. Canterbury (P) was allowed to vacate while unattended, contrary to Spence's (D) orders. Canterbury (P) slipped and fell off the bed which had no safety rail. No nurses were in attendance. Paralysis resulted and an emergency operation was only partially successful. Some four years later, two years after Canterbury (P) reached his majority age, suit was brought against Spence (D) for negligence in performing the operation and for failure to disclose known risks. The hospital (D) was sued for failure to have nurses in attendance and to provide a safety rail for the bed. No medical testimony was adduced with respect to normal hospital post-operative procedures. Only Dr. Spence (D) was called as an adverse witness. Spence (D) testified that the information was withheld to prevent an adverse psychological condition and because the surgery was needed. This was the prevalent practice in the medical community. Some evidence was adduced that the operation could have been negligently performed and/or could have caused the paralysis. A non-suit was granted in favor of both Spence (D) and the hospital (D) on the ground that Canterbury (P) had failed to establish a prima facie case. The threshold question of the statute of limitations was not decided.

ISSUE: Must a physician disclose substantial known risks even though the custom was not to disclose them?

HOLDING AND DECISION: (Robinson, J.) Yes. A physician must disclose any substantial risks peculiarly associated with a particular operation if members of the medical community would reasonably expect that such information was relevant to an informed consent to the therapy. Exceptions are made where the patient is unconscious in an emergency situation; where the patient is emotionally unstable and the disclosure would affect his well-being; and where the risks (such as infection) are those normally associated with all operations. The mere fact that disclosure might prevent consent is immaterial. Only those facts the physician reasonably feels are relevant to an informed consent, based on his knowledge of the patient, the nature of the operation, and his experience, need be disclosed. The objective criteria against which disclosure will be measured is the reasonable medical practitioner in the community. Liability cannot be found for nondisclosure unless it was the proximate cause of the injury. If the patient would have consented anyway or the injury resulted from a preexisting or intervening condition, no liability will be found. Expert testimony is normally required to determine whether disclosure or nondisclosure was reasonable since it deals with the impact of the information on the patient. Dr. Spence's (D) testimony as to a one percent chance of paralysis and his failure to disclose are sufficient to submit the question to the jury. Reversed and remanded for new trial.

ANALYSIS

On remand the case was decided in favor of Spence (D) and the hospital (D), 509 F.2d 537 (D.C. Cir. 1975). The required disclosure should include the risk, the frequency of occurrence, alternative methods of treatment, and the medical prognosis from nontreatment. A one percent chance of loss of hearing was deemed to require disclosure in *Scott v. Wilson*, 396 S.W. 2d 532 (1965). However, a 1.5 percent chance of the loss of an eye was held not to require disclosure in *Yeates v. Harms*, 393 P.2d 982 (1964).

Quicknotes

DUTY TO DISCLOSE The duty owed by a fiduciary to reveal those facts that have a material effect on the interests of the party that must be informed.

REASONABLE CARE STANDARD The care exercised by a reasonably prudent person.

Anon.

[Parties not identified.]

K.B., 87 Eng. Rep. 791 (1703).

NATURE OF CASE: [Nature of case not stated in casebook excerpt.]

FACT SUMMARY: [Facts not stated in casebook excerpt.]

RULE OF LAW
Laws are meant to give a remedy.

FACTS: [Facts not stated in casebook excerpt.]

ISSUE: What, in part, are laws meant to do?

HOLDING AND DECISION: (Holt, C.J.) Laws are meant to give a remedy. If a law allows or prohibits something, an individual is entitled to use the law in order to obtain what is allowed by the law or to be compensated for his injuries when a violation of that law occurs.

ANALYSIS

Essentially, the court is saying that it would be counterintuitive for a law to give a right but not a remedy when one's rights are harmed.

■=■

Osborne v. McMasters

Poison victim (P) v. Drug store clerk (D)

Minn. Sup. Ct., 41 N.W. 543 (1889).

NATURE OF CASE: Action in negligence for damages.

FACT SUMMARY: Contrary to statutes, McMasters (D) sold an unlabeled poison to Osborne (P).

🏛 RULE OF LAW
The breach of a statutory duty to a member of the protected class is negligence per se.

FACTS: McMasters (D) sold an unlabeled poison to Osborne (P). Osborne (P) accidentally took it internally, evidently thinking it was something else, and died. Osborne's heirs (P) brought a wrongful death action alleging that the violation of the criminal statute prohibiting the sale of unlabeled poisons was negligence per se. Both McMasters (D) and storeowner were sued. Counsel argued that the violation of a statutory duty was not civilly actionable unless it was based on a common-law duty of due care.

ISSUE: Is the violation of a statutory duty to a member of the protected class negligence per se?

HOLDING AND DECISION: (Mitchell, J.) Yes. Negligence involves the breach of a duty of due care. At common law a duty must be found before alleged conduct is actionable. Where a statute imposes a duty, the breach thereof is negligence per se with respect to any member of the protected class. The statute sets the duty owed to class members. The owner of the shop is equally liable under the doctrine of respondeat superior even though he would not be liable criminally under the statute. Affirmed.

▶ ANALYSIS

Statutes are designed to protect specific classes of individuals. Here, the public in general was being protected. If a party outside the protected class is injured, no negligence per se is involved. For example, if a plaintiff is injured by one driving without a license it may not be negligence per se. The licensing statute has been deemed, in some courts, to be revenue-raising in nature and not enacted to protect the public in general.

◼▭

Quicknotes

NEGLIGENCE Conduct falling below the standard of care that a reasonable person would demonstrate under similar conditions.

NEGLIGENCE PER SE Conduct amounting to negligence as a matter of law because it is either so contrary to ordinary prudence or it is in violation of statute.

STANDARD OF CARE A uniform degree of behavior against which a person's conduct can be measured when determining liability in negligence cases.

Martin v. Herzog

Buggy driver (P) v. Car driver (D)

N.Y. Ct. App., 126 N.E. 814 (1920).

NATURE OF CASE: Action for damages for death of plaintiff's intestate.

FACT SUMMARY: Martin's (P) decedent was killed in a collision between the buggy he was driving and Herzog's (D) automobile. Martin (P) was driving the buggy without lights, in violation of a criminal statute requiring lights.

🏛 RULE OF LAW
The unexcused omission to perform a statutory duty is negligence per se.

FACTS: Martin (P) was driving his buggy without lights when he was killed in a collision between the buggy and Herzog's (D) car. It was after dark and there was a criminal statute requiring lights. The trial judge refused Herzog's (D) request for an instruction that the absence of lights on Martin's (P) vehicle was prima facie evidence of contributory negligence and instructed instead that the jury might consider the absence of lights as some evidence of negligence, but that it was not conclusive evidence. He granted Martin's (P) request for an instruction that the fact that Martin's intestate was driving without a light is not negligence in itself. The jury returned a verdict for the plaintiff. The appellate division reversed. Martin (P) appealed to the court of appeals.

ISSUE: Is the unexcused omission of a statutory duty contributory negligence per se?

HOLDING AND DECISION: (Cardozo, J.) Yes. The unexcused omission of the statutory signals is more than just evidence of negligence; it is negligence in itself. Jurors have no power to relax the duty that one traveler on the highway owes under a statute to another traveler. It is error to instruct them that they have. The omission of lights, since it was unexcused, was negligence. However, a causal connection between the negligence and the injury must also be shown. Evidence of a collision occurring after dark between a car and an unlighted buggy is evidence from which a causal connection may be inferred between the collision and the lack of signals. If nothing is shown to break the connection, there is prima facie evidence of negligence contributing to the result.

▶ ANALYSIS

This case states the position, followed by a great majority of the courts, that violation of a statute is negligence per se when a statute applies to the facts and the violation is unexcused. Note, however, that the court emphasizes that one must not confuse the question of negligence with that of the causal connection between the negligence and the injury, and that conduct that is negligent is not always contributory negligence.

■=■

Quicknotes

CONTRIBUTORY NEGLIGENCE Behavior on the part of an injured plaintiff falling below the standard of ordinary care that contributes to the defendant's negligence, resulting in the plaintiff's injury.

NEGLIGENCE PER SE Conduct amounting to negligence as a matter of law because it is either so contrary to ordinary prudence or it is in violation of statute.

PRIMA FACIE Action in which the plaintiff introduces sufficient evidence to submit an issue to the judge or jury for determination.

■=■

Uhr v. East Greenbush Cent. Sch. Dist.

Parents (P) v. School district (D)

N.Y. Ct. App., 720 N.E.2d 886 (1999).

NATURE OF CASE: Appeal from summary judgment for defendant in negligence case.

FACT SUMMARY: The Uhrs (P) alleged that East Greenbush Central School District (D) was negligent when it failed to test their daughter for scoliosis as required by state statute.

🏛 RULE OF LAW
A private right of action cannot be fairly implied where it would be inconsistent with the statute's legislative scheme.

FACTS: Education Law § 905(1) required testing of all students between the ages of eight and sixteen for scoliosis at least once each school year. The Uhrs (P) claimed that the East Greenbush Central School District (the District) (D) failed to test their daughter in the 1993–1994 school year, and as a result, the ailment was allowed to progress undetected, to her detriment. The court granted the District's (D) motion for summary judgment, holding that Education Law § 905(1) did not create a private cause of action, and that the Uhrs (P) had not stated a valid claim for common law negligence. The Uhrs (P) appealed, claiming a private cause of action may be fairly implied when the statute is silent.

ISSUE: May a private right of action be fairly implied where it would be inconsistent with the statute's legislative scheme?

HOLDING AND DECISION: (Rosenblatt, J.) No. A private right of action cannot be fairly implied where it would be inconsistent with the statute's legislative scheme. Here, the legislature has vested the Commissioner of Education with the duty to implement Education Law and to adopt rules and regulations for that purpose. Education Law § 905(1) provides that school authorities shall not suffer any liability that would not have existed in the absence of that section. When creating the statutory duty for school districts to test students for scoliosis, the legislature clearly precluded any private cause of action based on that statutory duty. Affirmed.

▶ ANALYSIS

The court found that the school district did have a statutory duty to test the students. It also found that the legislature had clearly contemplated administrative enforcement of the statute. The language of the statute clearly sought to immunize the school districts from any liability that might arise out of the scoliosis-screening program.

■▬■

Quicknotes

BREACH The violation of an obligation imposed pursuant to contract or law, by acting or failing to act.

DUTY An obligation owed by one individual to another.

IMMUNITY Exemption from a legal obligation.

NEGLIGENCE Conduct falling below the standard of care that a reasonable person would demonstrate under similar conditions.

■▬■

Baltimore and Ohio R.R. v. Goodman

Railroad company (D) v. Accident victim (P)

275 U.S. 66 (1927).

NATURE OF CASE: Action in damages for wrongful death.

FACT SUMMARY: Goodman (P) was killed when struck by a train at a blind railroad crossing.

RULE OF LAW

When a plaintiff perceives a risk and fails to adequately take precautions to guard against it, no recovery will be allowed, and the judge must direct a verdict in favor of the defendant.

FACTS: Goodman (P) was driving his truck when he approached a blind railroad crossing without signals or guardrails. Goodman (P) slowed to approximately 10 mph. However, as Goodman (P) approached the track he finally saw the train and could not stop in time. Goodman (P) was killed, and his heirs (P) filed a wrongful death action. Baltimore and Ohio Railroad (D) alleged that Goodman's (P) death resulted from his own negligence. The court refused to direct a verdict on the above evidence, and the jury found for the heirs (P).

ISSUE: Should the judge direct a verdict if the evidence indicates the plaintiff failed to take reasonable precautions to guard against a known risk?

HOLDING AND DECISION: (Holmes, J.) Yes. The judge should direct a verdict if the evidence indicates that the plaintiff failed to take reasonable precautions to guard against a known risk. Here, the risk was known. Goodman (P) was required to approach the tracks in a safe manner. If necessary he should have come to a complete stop, gotten out, and looked to see if a train was approaching. Goodman (P) knew that he, not the train, would have to stop. Driving at even 10 mph in a situation such as this is unsafe and negligent. Goodman's (P) negligence was the proximate cause of his death. In a clear-cut situation such as this one, the judge should have directed a verdict in favor of the Baltimore and Ohio Railroad (D). Reversed.

ANALYSIS

In *Torgeson v. Missouri K.T.R.R.*, 124 Kan. 798 (1928), someone took the advice offered above and got out and looked both ways. However, by the time he started his car again a train came by and struck it. Where the railroad crossing has warning devices, a plaintiff has the right to rely on them. *Toschi v. Christian*, 149 P.2d 848 (1944). Once the railroad has undertaken a duty to warn drivers of oncoming trains, the rule applied above is not utilized.

Quicknotes

DIRECTED VERDICT A verdict ordered by the court in a jury trial.

PROXIMATE CAUSE The natural sequence of events without which an injury would not have been sustained.

Pokora v. Wabash Ry.

Car driver (P) v. Railroad company (D)

292 U.S. 98 (1934).

NATURE OF CASE: Action for damages in negligence.

FACT SUMMARY: Pokora (P) was injured when his vehicle was struck by an oncoming train obscured by railroad cars that had been left at the crossing.

🏛 RULE OF LAW
A plaintiff is not required to get out of his vehicle to see if a train is approaching to avoid contributory negligence.

FACTS: Wabash Ry. (D) had a siding near a railroad crossing. Wabash left railroad cars at the siding. The cars obscured the view of oncoming trains. Pokora (P) approached the crossing, stopped, and heard nothing. Pokora (P) then crossed and was struck by a train. Based on *Baltimore and Ohio R.R. v. Goodman*, 275 U.S. 66 (1927), the court directed a verdict in favor of Wabash Ry. (D). It held that Pokora's (P) failure to get out of his car and look was contributory negligence.

ISSUE: Must a plaintiff get out of his vehicle and look for a train where his view of a crossing is obstructed?

HOLDING AND DECISION: (Cardozo, J.) No. A plaintiff is not required to get out of his vehicle to see if a train is approaching to avoid contributory negligence. That is an extremely unusual standard of behavior. Moreover, it is of doubtful benefit. By the time a party gets back to his car and attempts to cross, a train that could not have been seen at the time he looked could be upon him. Judges should refrain from framing standards of conduct that amount to rules of law. Extraordinary situations may not wisely or fairly be subjected to tests or regulations that are only fitting for the common place. Pokora (P) is not guilty of contributory negligence solely for failing to get out of his vehicle. Reversed.

▌ ANALYSIS

A judge should not set an abnormal standard of care. Again, the reasonable man standard should be applied in determining whether a plaintiff is contributorily negligent. Extraordinary situations must be decided on facts peculiar to the case since we have no experience with which to decide what a reasonable man might do under such circumstances. Such decisions are better left to the trier of fact who may decide on the basis of all of the evidence.

Quicknotes

CONTRIBUTORY NEGLIGENCE Behavior on the part of an injured plaintiff falling below the standard of ordinary care that contributes to the defendant's negligence, resulting in the plaintiff's injury.

Byrne v. Boadle

Pedestrian (P) v. Shop owner (D)

Ex., 159 Eng. Rep. 299 (1863).

NATURE OF CASE: Action to recover damages for negligence.

FACT SUMMARY: While Byrne (P) was walking along the street, passing Boadle's (D) shop, a barrel fell from the shop window and struck Byrne (P), injuring him.

🏛 RULE OF LAW
When it is highly probable that an injury is due to the negligence of the defendant, and the defendant has better access to the evidence concerning the injury, the doctrine of res ipsa loquitur creates an inference that the defendant was negligent, and puts the burden on defendant to introduce contrary evidence.

FACTS: Byrne (P) was walking in a public street past Boadle's (D) flour shop, when a barrel of flour rolled out of the window above Byrne (P), striking and injuring him. The trial court nonsuited Byrne (P), ruling that there was no evidence of any negligence.

ISSUE: Can a presumption of negligence arise solely from the fact that an accident occurred?

HOLDING AND DECISION: (Pollock, C.B.) Yes. According to the ancient doctrine of res ipsa loquitur, "the thing speaks for itself." The mere fact that a barrel of flour fell on a passerby outside of Boadle's (D) flour shop is prima facie evidence of the latter's negligence, and Byrne (P) cannot be expected to prove that it could not have happened without some negligence. If there are any facts inconsistent with a finding of negligence, it is for Boadle (D) to prove them. Reversed.

▶ ANALYSIS

This is one of the earliest cases applying the doctrine of res ipsa loquitur. In a later English case, the rule was stated as follows: "There must be reasonable evidence of negligence; but where the thing is shown to be under the management of the defendant or his servants, and the accident is such as in the ordinary course of things does not happen if those who have the management use proper care, it affords reasonable evidence, in the absence of explanation by the defendants, that the accident arose from want of care." To invoke the doctrine, the plaintiff need not explain away all possibilities, as long as he shows that such accidents do not occur without negligence; the burden of proof is then shifted to the defendant.

Quicknotes

PRIMA FACIE Action in which the plaintiff introduces sufficient evidence to submit an issue to the judge or jury for determination.

RES IPSA LOQUITUR A rule of law giving rise to an inference of negligence where the instrument inflicting the injury is in the exclusive control of the defendant and where such harm could not ordinarily result in the absence of negligence.

Colmenares Vivas v. Sun Alliance Insurance Co.

Tourists riding escalators (P) v. Insurance company (D)

807 F.2d 1102 (1st Cir. 1986).

NATURE OF CASE: Appeal from directed verdict denying damages for negligence.

FACT SUMMARY: Colmenares (P) suffered injuries while riding an escalator insured by Sun Alliance Insurance Co. (D).

🏛 RULE OF LAW
The control requirement of the doctrine of res ipsa loquitur is satisfied where the defendant is ultimately responsible for the agent or instrument causing the injury.

FACTS: Mr. and Mrs. Colmenares (P) were injured while riding an airport escalator in Puerto Rico. The Colmenares (P) sued Sun Alliance Insurance Co. (Sun) (D), the insurance carrier for the Port Authority, the airport owner, and the operator for negligence. Sun (D) brought a third-party action against Westinghouse Electric Corp. (Westinghouse) (D) based on a maintenance contract between the parties that required Westinghouse (D) to inspect, maintain, adjust, repair the escalator and handrail as needed, and to keep the escalator in a safe operating condition. The court ruled that there was no evidence that the Port Authority was negligent. The court also held that the case could not go to the jury based on the theory of res ipsa loquitur because the instrument causing the injury, the escalator, was not in the exclusive control of the Authority. The court then granted Sun's (D) motion for a directed verdict. The Colmenares (P) appealed.

ISSUE: Is the control requirement of the doctrine of res ipsa loquitur satisfied where the defendant is ultimately responsible for the agent or instrument causing the injury?

HOLDING AND DECISION: (Bownes, J.) Yes. The control requirement of the doctrine of res ipsa loquitur is satisfied where the defendant is ultimately responsible for the agent or instrument causing the injury. The injury-causing escalator was the property and under the exclusive control of the Port Authority. Even though such control was shared by Westinghouse (D), the Port Authority had a nondelegable duty of care to maintain the escalator in a safe condition. Therefore, the Port Authority effectively had exclusive control over the escalator for purposes of applying the res ipsa loquitur doctrine. The public is entitled to rely on the Port Authority, not its agents or contractors, for the safe condition of the escalator. Reversed.

DISSENT: (Torruella, J.) The malfunction of the escalator does not by itself raise an inference of negligence without additional proof of the cause of the malfunction.

The court has no basis of common knowledge to infer that the escalator's malfunction was the result of its operator's negligence.

▶ ANALYSIS

The exclusive control issue is often tricky in the case of multiple defendants. For example, in one case the court refused to apply the res ipsa loquitur doctrine to infer negligence in an airplane crash against a large number of the plane's manufacturers and repairs because the plaintiff failed to sue the company that had performed the most recent repairs. *Winns v. Rockwell International Corp.*, 705 F.2d 1449, 1454 (5th Cir. 1983).

Quicknotes

DUTY OF CARE A principal of negligence requiring an individual to act in such a manner as to avoid injury to a person to whom he or she owes an obligatory duty.

RES IPSA LOQUITUR A rule of law giving rise to an inference of negligence where the instrument inflicting the injury is in the exclusive control of the defendant and where such harm could not ordinarily result in the absence of negligence.

Ybarra v. Spangard

Surgery patient (P) v. Surgeon (D)

Cal. Sup. Ct., 154 P.2d 687 (1944).

NATURE OF CASE: Action to recover damages for personal injuries due to negligent malpractice.

FACT SUMMARY: Ybarra (P) suffered an injury to his right arm and shoulder while he was unconscious having his appendix removed under the care of six doctors and medical employees (D).

🏛 RULE OF LAW
Where an unexplained injury occurs during a medical procedure to a part of the body not under treatment, res ipsa loquitur applies against all of the doctors and medical employees who take part in caring for the patient.

FACTS: Ybarra (P) consulted Dr. Tilley (D), who diagnosed appendicitis. Dr. Tilley (D) arranged for an appendectomy to be performed by Dr. Spangard (D) at a hospital under the ownership and management of Dr. Swift (D). Ybarra (P) was wheeled into the operating room by nurse Gisler (D) and anesthetized by Dr. Reser (D). Dr. Reser (D) laid him back against two hard objects at the top of his shoulders. Ybarra (P) awoke the next morning in his hospital room attended by Thompson (D) and another nurse. When Ybarra (P) awakened he felt a sharp pain between his neck and his right shoulder. The pain spread down his arm, and after his release from the hospital he developed paralysis and atrophy of the muscles around the shoulder. Dr. Reser (D) and the nurses were employees of Dr. Swift (D); the other doctors (D) were independent contractors. The medical personnel (D) claimed that res ipsa loquitur should not apply against them because Ybarra (P) did not show an injury caused by an instrumentality under a defendant's control in that he did not show which of the several instrumentalities that he came in contact with in the hospital caused his injury, and did not show that any one particular defendant had exclusive control over any particular instrumentality.

ISSUE: Where an unexplained injury occurs during a medical procedure to a part of the body not under treatment, does res ipsa loquitur apply to permit negligence to be inferred against all of the doctors and medical employees who took part in caring for the injured patient?

HOLDING AND DECISION: (Gibson, C.J.) Yes. Where there has been an injury to a healthy part of the body not the subject of treatment, res ipsa loquitur applies to permit the inference of negligence against all doctors and medical employees who were entrusted with the patient's care. Every defendant in whose custody Ybarra (P) was placed for any period was under a duty to exercise ordinary care for his safety. The control at one time or another of one or more of the various agencies or instrumentalities that might have harmed Ybarra (P) was in the hands of every defendant or of his employees or temporary servants. Ybarra (P) was unconscious; it is unreasonable to require him to identify any one person as the one who did the negligent act in order to get his case before the jury. Reversed.

▶ ANALYSIS

This case is a prime example of the "smoking out the evidence" policy sometimes relied on by courts in invoking res ipsa loquitur. Obviously the medical personnel would keep silent to avoid implicating one of their number.

━━━

Quicknotes

ORDINARY CARE The degree of care exercised by a reasonable person when conducting everyday activities or under similar circumstances; synonymous with due care.

RES IPSA LOQUITUR A rule of law giving rise to an inference of negligence where the instrument inflicting the injury is in the exclusive control of the defendant and where such harm could not ordinarily result in the absence of negligence.

━━━

CHAPTER 4

Plaintiff's Conduct

Quick Reference Rules of Law

PAGE

1. *Butterfield v. Forrester.* A plaintiff will not be able to recover where his lack of due care contributed to the occurrence of the accident. — 62

2. *Beems v. Chicago, Rock Island & Peoria R.R.* The lack of contributory negligence on the part of the plaintiff renders the negligent defendant completely liable. — 63

3. *Gyerman v. United States Lines Co.* Contributory negligence is conduct on the part of the plaintiff that falls below the standard to which he should conform for his own protection, and that is a legally contributing causal connection with the negligence of the defendant in bringing about the plaintiff's harm. — 64

4. *LeRoy Fibre Co. v. Chicago, Milwaukee and St. Paul Ry.* The rights of one man in the use of his property cannot be limited by the wrongs of another. — 65

5. *Derheim v. N. Fiorito Co.* Failure to use a seatbelt is conduct that occurs before defendant's negligence, as opposed to contributory negligence, which customarily is thought of in terms of conduct contributing to the accident itself. — 66

6. *Fuller v. Illinois Central R.R.* The contributory negligence of a party injured will not defeat the action if it is shown that the defendant might, by the exercise of reasonable care and prudence, have avoided the consequence of the injured party's negligence. — 67

7. *Lamson v. American Axe & Tool Co.* A person cannot recover for negligently inflicted injuries when he has acted to assume the risk of such injuries. — 68

8. *Murphy v. Steeplechase Amusement Co.* One who takes part in a sport accepts the dangers that inhere in it insofar as they are obvious and necessary and they are not so serious as to justify the belief that precautions of some kind must have been taken to avert them. — 69

9. *Dalury v. S-K-I Ltd.* A standard signed liability waiver form may be held unenforceable if it violates public policy. — 70

10. *Li v. Yellow Cab Co. of California.* In California, contributory negligence is hereafter replaced with a system of "pure comparative negligence;" and, under this system, liability for negligently caused damage is assigned in direct proportion to the amount of negligence of the involved parties. — 71

Butterfield v. Forrester

Horseback rider (P) v. Landowner (D)

K.B., 103 Eng. Rep. 926 (1809).

NATURE OF CASE: Appeal of personal injury judgment in favor of defendant (D).

FACT SUMMARY: While riding very fast, Butterfield (P) ran into an obstruction that Forrester (D) had put in the road and was injured.

🏛 RULE OF LAW
A plaintiff will not be able to recover where his lack of due care contributed to the occurrence of the accident.

FACTS: Forrester (D) was making some repairs on his house and put up a pole across the road. However, passage was still possible. Butterfield (P) was riding very fast on the road, did not see the pole, and ran into it. He fell with his horse and was injured. There was no evidence of his being intoxicated. There was evidence that it was possible to see the obstruction from 100 yards away at the time of the accident and that, had Butterfield (P) not been riding so fast, he might have seen and avoided the pole. The jury found in favor of Forrester (D) and Butterfield (P) appealed.

ISSUE: Can a plaintiff who has not used reasonable care to avoid an accident recover for injury caused by the accident?

HOLDING AND DECISION: (Per curiam) No. A plaintiff who has not used reasonable care to avoid an accident cannot recover for injury caused by the accident. In order for Forrester (D) to have been liable not only would the pole have had to have been in the road, but Butterfield (P) would have had to have used ordinary care in navigating by it, which Butterfield (P) did not. Rule refused.

▶ ANALYSIS

This case states the defense of contributory negligence. The following theories have been used to support the theory: plaintiff is denied recovery to punish him for his own misconduct; plaintiff must come into court with "clean hands;" the defense is a deterrent to plaintiff's negligence; plaintiff's negligence is a superseding cause which makes the defendant's negligence no longer the proximate cause. The same standard is used as to determine negligence: the average reasonable person.

Quicknotes

CONTRIBUTORY NEGLIGENCE Behavior on the part of an injured plaintiff falling below the standard of ordinary care that contributes to the defendant's negligence, resulting in the plaintiff's injury.

PROXIMATE CAUSE The natural sequence of events without which an injury would not have been sustained.

Beems v. Chicago, Rock Island & Peoria R.R.

Railroad brakeman (P) v. Railroad company (D)

Iowa Sup. Ct., 12 N.W. 222 (1882).

NATURE OF CASE: Appeal from award granting damages for negligence.

FACT SUMMARY: The Railroad (D) contended that the fact Beems (P) attempted to uncouple the railroad cars while the train was moving at an unusual rate of speed constituted contributory negligence that barred his recovery for the injuries resulting therefrom.

RULE OF LAW
The lack of contributory negligence on the part of the plaintiff renders the negligent defendant completely liable.

FACTS: Beems (P), a brakeman for the Railroad (D), attempted to uncouple two railroad cars while the train was moving. Before Beems (P) attempted to do uncouple the cars, he signaled to other Railroad (D) employees to slow the speed of the train, but his signals were disregarded. His foot became caught between the rails, and he was killed by the train. His estate sued, contending the Railroad (D) employees were negligent in failing to slow the train on his order. The Railroad (D) defended, contending he was contributorily negligent in climbing between the cars while the train was proceeding at an unusual rate of speed, and therefore, even if the employees were negligent Beems (P) could not recover. The trial court instructed the jury that Beems (P) could not recover unless the employees were negligent. The jury found for Beems (P), and the Railroad (D) moved for a judgment notwithstanding the verdict, which was denied.

ISSUE: Does the lack of contributory negligence on the part of the plaintiff render the negligent defendant completely liable?

HOLDING AND DECISION: (Beck, J.) Yes. The lack of contributory negligence on the part of the plaintiff renders the negligent defendant completely liable for the consequences of his acts. In this case it was proper for the jury to conclude from the evidence that Beems (P) acted reasonably in relying on the employees to comply with his signals to slow the train down. Therefore, he was not negligent in boarding the train and attempting to uncouple the cars while the train was in motion. Lacking a finding of contributory negligence, the Railroad (D) was completely liable for the negligence of its employees. Affirmed.

ANALYSIS

Contributory negligence is a complete defense to liability for a defendant's negligence. It is believed a plaintiff should not recover if his own negligent actions contribute to the injury. Contributory negligence is not a defense to an intentional tort or where the defendant's conduct was shown to be wanton and reckless. Further, contributory negligence is not a defense where the defendant had the last clear chance to avoid the accident.

Quicknotes

CONTRIBUTORY NEGLIGENCE Behavior on the part of an injured plaintiff falling below the standard of ordinary care that contributes to the defendant's negligence, resulting in the plaintiff's injury.

WANTON AND RECKLESS Unlawful intentional or reckless conduct without regard to the consequences.

Gyerman v. United States Lines Co.

Longshoreman (P) v. Shipping company (D)

Cal. Sup. Ct., 498 P.2d 1043 (1972).

NATURE OF CASE: Appeal from a finding that plaintiff's contributory negligence barred his cause of action.

FACT SUMMARY: Gyerman (P), a longshoreman, was injured while unloading fishmeal sacks for United States Lines Co. (D), but the trial court held that Gyerman's (P) conduct was also negligent and barred his cause of action.

🏛 RULE OF LAW
Contributory negligence is conduct on the part of the plaintiff that falls below the standard to which he should conform for his own protection, and that is a legally contributing causal connection with the negligence of the defendant in bringing about the plaintiff's harm.

FACTS: Gyerman (P), a longshoreman, was injured while unloading fishmeal sacks in the warehouse of United States Lines Co. (D). Before he began work, Gyerman (P) noted that the packs were dangerously stacked. He complained to his supervisor that it was dangerous to proceed with the work, and was told that nothing could be done about the situation. Gyerman (P) proceeded with the work and was injured. The trial judge found United States Lines (D) was negligent in its failure to stack the sacks properly, but further found that Gyerman's (P) negligence in failing to stop work in the face of a known danger barred his cause of action. Gyerman (P) appealed.

ISSUE: Does the burden of proving all aspects of the affirmative defense of contributory negligence, including causation, rest on the defendant, unless the elements of the defense may be inferred from the plaintiff's evidence?

HOLDING AND DECISION: (Sullivan, J.) Yes. The burden of proving all aspects of the affirmative defense of contributory negligence, including causation, rests on the defendant, unless the elements of the defense may be inferred from the plaintiff's evidence. Merely because plaintiff asserts that his own negligence, if any, could not have caused his injury, does not shift to him the burden of proof on the issue. The fundamental question is whether the plaintiff, as "the negligent actor has so produced the harm to himself . . . for which he is sought to be held responsible . . . as to make the law regard his conduct as the cause of the harm." It is obvious here that Gyerman (P) did not create or maintain the dangerous conditions. The trial court found that United States Lines (D) had control of the cargo and directed its disposition and high stacking throughout the warehouse. United States Lines (D) alone created the risk of harm that materialized in the toppling of the stacks. Reversed and remanded.

▶ ANALYSIS

Courts have long held that contributory negligence is invalid as a defense for negligence where the defendant bases the claim on plaintiff's breach of a safety regulation. See *Koenig v. Patrick Construction Corp.*, 298 N.Y. 313, 83 N.E. 2d 133 (1948). In *Osborne v. Salvation Army*, 107 F.2d 929 (2d Cir. 1939), the court stated: "It is the general rule that a plaintiff may not waive a statute enacted for his protection and that he cannot do so because of assumption of risk is clear. To bar recovery in an action brought under the (workman's safety) statute because the plaintiff's acts contributed to his injuries would seem to render its enforcement entirely ineffective."

■━■

Quicknotes

AFFIRMATIVE DEFENSES An assertion raised by the defendant in the answer, permitting the introduction of additional evidence to address or refute a plaintiff's allegations; affirmative defenses shift the burden of proof to the defendant to establish all the elements of the defense.

CAUSATION The aggregate effect of preceding events that bring about a tortious result; the causal connection between the actions of a tortfeasor and the injury that follows.

CONTRIBUTORY NEGLIGENCE Behavior on the part of an injured plaintiff falling below the standard of ordinary care that contributes to the defendant's negligence, resulting in the plaintiff's injury.

PROXIMATE CAUSE The natural sequence of events without which an injury would not have been sustained.

■━■

LeRoy Fibre Co. v. Chicago, Milwaukee and St. Paul Ry.

Fiber company (P) v. Railroad (D)

232 U.S. 340 (1914).

NATURE OF CASE: Appeal from a finding of contributory negligence barring plaintiff's recovery.

FACT SUMMARY: LeRoy Fibre Co. (P) was found to be contributorily negligent in stacking straw on its property so near Chicago, Milwaukee and St. Paul Ry.'s (Chicago) (D) right of way as to allow sparks from Chicago's (D) railroad engine to ignite and destroy the straw.

RULE OF LAW
The rights of one man in the use of his property cannot be limited by the wrongs of another.

FACTS: LeRoy Fibre Co. (LeRoy) (P), makers of flax, brought suit against Chicago, Milwaukee and St. Paul Ry. (Chicago) (D) when straw on LeRoy's (P) property was ignited by Chicago's (D) railroad engine. The engine was on Chicago's (D) right of way, which passed near where the 700 tons of straw were stacked on LeRoy's (P) property. The jury, consistent with its instructions, found LeRoy (P) contributorily negligent by placing the straw within 100 feet of the right of way. LeRoy (P) appealed.

ISSUE: Does contributory negligence dictate that the rights of one man in the use of his property can be limited by the wrongs of another?

HOLDING AND DECISION: (McKenna, J.) No. The doctrine of contributory negligence does not dictate that the rights of one man in the use of his property can be limited by the wrongs of another. We concur with the simple requirement of the law, that everyone must use his property so as not to injure others. There is no exception to this rule merely because the defendant happens to be a railroad. Such operation is a legitimate use of property; other property in its vicinity may suffer inconveniences and be subject to risks by it, but a risk from wrongful operation is not one of them. Reversed.

CONCURRENCE: (Holmes, J.) If a man stacked his flax so near to a railroad that it obviously was likely to be set fire to by a well-managed train, I should say that he could not throw the loss upon the railroad by the oscillating result of an inquiry by the jury whether the railroad used due care. I should say that although of course he had a right to put his flax where he liked upon his own land, the liability of the railroad for a fire was absolutely conditioned upon the stacks being at a reasonably safe distance from the train.

ANALYSIS

Justice Holmes suggests a somewhat radical complication here in the theory of negligence, *i.e.*, a possibility that judgment of the negligence of the actor may depend on a judgment of the negligence of the victim, and vice versa. Compare this reasoning to the next case, *Derheim v. N. Fiorito*, 80 Wash. 2d 161, 492 P.2d 1030 (1972), a more recent case which espouses the modern view that "a defendant whose negligence proximately causes an injury to the plaintiff 'takes the plaintiff as he finds him.'"

Quicknotes

CONTRIBUTORY NEGLIGENCE Behavior on the part of an injured plaintiff falling below the standard of ordinary care that contributes to the defendant's negligence, resulting in the plaintiff's injury.

Derheim v. N. Fiorito Co.

Car accident victim (P) v. Truck driver (D)

Wash. Sup. Ct., 492 P.2d 1030 (1972).

NATURE OF CASE: Appeal from a verdict and judgment for plaintiff in a personal injury action.

FACT SUMMARY: N. Fiorito Co. (D), charged with negligence for injuries sustained by Derheim (P) in an auto accident between a Derheim (P) and an N. Fiorito Co. truck, claimed Derheim (P) was contributorily negligent for not using his car seatbelt.

RULE OF LAW
Failure to use a seatbelt is conduct that occurs before defendant's negligence, as opposed to contributory negligence, which customarily is thought of in terms of conduct contributing to the accident itself.

FACTS: Derheim (P) brought a personal injury action against N. Fiorito Co., (D) arising from the collision of Derheim's (P) car with a truck owned by N. Fiorito Co. (D) when the driver of the truck (D) made an illegal turn. When N. Fiorito Co. (D) was prevented from claiming contributory negligence by Derheim (P) because of Derheim's (D) failure to use his car seatbelt at the time of the accident, N. Fiorito Co. (D) appealed.

ISSUE: May a defendant claim contributory negligence by the plaintiff, where the plaintiff's injuries are increased by his failure to use his seatbelt?

HOLDING AND DECISION: (Hunter, J.) No. A defendant may not claim contributory negligence by the plaintiff, where the plaintiff's injuries are increased by his failure to use his seatbelt. Courts have traditionally said a defendant whose negligence proximately causes an injury to a plaintiff, "takes plaintiff as he finds him." We believe failure to use a seatbelt is conduct which occurs before defendant's negligence, as opposed to contributory negligence which customarily is thought of in terms of conduct contributing to the accident itself. It seems extremely unfair to mitigate the damages of one who sustains those damages in an accident for which he was in no way responsible, particularly where, as is the case here, there is no statutory duty to wear seatbelts. Affirmed.

▶ ANALYSIS

Contrast the opinion of the Washington court here with a later New York Court of Appeals decision in *Spier v. Barker*, 35 N.Y. 2d. 444, 323 N.E. 2d 164, 363 N.Y.S. 2d 916 (1974). In *Spier*, the court decided, "We today hold that nonuse of an available seatbelt, and expert testimony thereto, is a factor which the jury may consider, in light of all the other facts received in evidence, in arriving at its determination as to whether the plaintiff has exercised due care,

not only to avoid injury to himself, but to mitigate any injury he would likely sustain." See Kircher, "Seat Belt Defense–State of the Law," 53 *Marq. L. Rev.* 172, 186.

Quicknotes

ASSUMPTION OF RISK DOCTRINE An affirmative defense to a negligence suit by the defendant contending that the plaintiff knowingly and voluntarily subjected himself to the hazardous condition wholly absolving the defendant of liability for injuries incurred.

COMPARATIVE NEGLIGENCE Doctrine whereby the court in assessing the appropriate measure of damages compares the relative fault of the parties and reduces the amount of damages to be collected by the plaintiff in proportion to his degree of fault.

CONTRIBUTORY NEGLIGENCE Behavior on the part of an injured plaintiff falling below the standard of ordinary care that contributes to the defendant's negligence, resulting in the plaintiff's injury.

MITIGATION OF DAMAGES A plaintiff's implied obligation to reduce the damages incurred by taking reasonable steps to prevent additional injury.

Fuller v. Illinois Central R.R.

Wagon rider (P) v. Railroad (D)

Miss. Sup. Ct., 56 So. 783 (1911).

NATURE OF CASE: Appeal from judgment for the defendant in a negligence action.

FACT SUMMARY: After Fuller (P), who was riding in a one-horse wagon crossing a railroad track, was hit by an Illinois Central Railroad (D) train and killed, Fuller's (P) representative argued that the train's engineer had the last clear chance to avoid the accident.

RULE OF LAW

The contributory negligence of a party injured will not defeat the action if it is shown that the defendant might, by the exercise of reasonable care and prudence, have avoided the consequence of the injured party's negligence.

FACTS: Fuller (P), a man over seventy years old, was riding his one-horse wagon on a dirt road that crossed a stretch of the Illinois Central Railroad's (the Railroad) (D) track that ran perpendicular to it. Fuller (P) had his head down and did not observe the Railroad's (D) oncoming train. The train came down the tracks an hour late, faster than the usual 40 mph. The engineer could have stopped the train within 200 feet, but he did not slow the train at all. The only signal he gave was a routine whistle blast twenty seconds before the train hit the wagon and killed Fuller (P). Fuller's (P) representative sued the Railroad (D), and the Railroad (D) offered a defense of contributory negligence. Fuller's (P) representative argued that the Railroad's (D) engineer had the last clear chance to avoid injury either by braking or promptly sounding a warning-whistle. At trial, judgment was given for the Railroad (D), and Fuller's (P) representative appealed.

ISSUE: Will the contributory negligence of a party injured defeat the action if it is shown that the defendant might, by the exercise of reasonable care and prudence, have avoided the consequence of the injured party's negligence?

HOLDING AND DECISION: (McLain, J.) No. The contributory negligence of a party injured will not defeat the action if it is shown that the defendant might, by the exercise of reasonable care and prudence, have avoided the consequence of the injured party's negligence. This principle is known as the doctrine of "last clear chance" and has met with practically universal favor. The facts here show that for a distance of 660 feet west of the crossing where Fuller (P) was killed, the track was straight, and there were no obstructions; there was nothing to prevent those in charge of the Railroad's (D) train from seeing Fuller's (P) perilous position. No alarm was given.

Nothing was done to warn Fuller (P) of the approaching train, and he was unconscious of its approach. The only warning was too late to be of any benefit whatever. Fuller (P) was in a wagon, and the engineer could have seen that he was going to cross the track and could only with difficulty extricate himself from his perilous position. Reversed and remanded.

ANALYSIS

In the early cases, the contributory negligence defense worked to absolutely bar recovery by a negligent plaintiff. The last clear chance principle, as set forth in *Fuller*, allowed a plaintiff who was contributorily negligent to recover if he could prove that the defendant was also negligent by failing to use reasonable care to avoid the incident and he had the existing opportunity to avoid the harm. Thus, the last clear chance doctrine is really a method whereby responsibility is placed where it best reduces the likelihood of an accident.

■ ▬ ■

Quicknotes

CONTRIBUTORY NEGLIGENCE Behavior on the part of an injured plaintiff falling below the standard of ordinary care that contributes to the defendant's negligence, resulting in the plaintiff's injury.

LAST CLEAR CHANCE DOCTRINE An attempt by the courts to reduce the inherent unfairness of absolving the defendant of liability completely where the plaintiff has committed contributory negligence; the plaintiff is permitted to recover despite a finding of contributory negligence where the defendant was the last party capable of preventing the injury.

■ ▬ ■

Lamson v. American Axe & Tool Co.

Axe company employee (P) v. Axe company (D)

Mass. Sup. Jud. Ct., 58 N.E. 585 (1900).

NATURE OF CASE: Appeal from a directed verdict denying damages for negligence.

FACT SUMMARY: Lamson (P) was injured when a hatchet fell from an inadequate rack located above his workbench.

⚖ RULE OF LAW

A person cannot recover for negligently inflicted injuries when he has acted to assume the risk of such injuries.

FACTS: Lamson (P) was employed by American Axe Co. (D) to paint hatchets. He worked at a bench above which was a rack where he placed the hatchets to dry. The racks, which safely held the hatchets, were replaced by American Axe (D) with a rack that could not hold the hatchets when jarred sharply by nearby machinery. The jarring was a common occurrence. Lamson (P) complained to his supervisor about the danger and was told to use the racks or leave. Lamson (P) continued to work at the bench and was injured when a hatchet fell from the racks. Lamson (P) sued America Axe (D) for negligence. The trial court entered a directed verdict for American Axe (D) on the basis Lamson (P) assumed the risk of the injury. Lamson (P) appealed.

ISSUE: Can a person recover for negligently inflicted injuries when he has acted to assume the risk of such injury?

HOLDING AND DECISION: (Holmes, C.J.) No. A person cannot recover for negligently inflicted injuries when he has acted so as to assume the risk of such injury. Lamson (P) was well aware of the risk of injury presented by the rack and when given the choice of leaving or staying and working under those conditions, he chose to stay. As a result, he assumed the risk of such injury and cannot recover. Exceptions overruled.

▶ ANALYSIS

In order to assume a risk a person must be shown to have recognized and actually understood the risk of injury, and that he voluntarily chose to undertake it. The unreasonable assumption of a risk may also give rise to contributory negligence as an additional defense to liability. If a defendant is under a duty to make a condition safe, a plaintiff's reasonable assumption of risk will not bar recovery.

Quicknotes

ASSUMPTION OF RISK DOCTRINE An affirmative defense to a negligence suit by the defendant contending that the plaintiff knowingly and voluntarily subjected himself to the hazardous condition wholly absolving the defendant of liability for injuries incurred.

Murphy v. Steeplechase Amusement Co.

Injured rider (P) v. Amusement park (D)

N.Y. Ct. App., 166 N.E. 173 (1929).

NATURE OF CASE: Action to recover damages for personal injuries.

FACT SUMMARY: Murphy (P) was injured when he fell while riding an amusement ride—"The Flopper"—which was a moving belt that ran up an inclined plane and caused people to fall on padded walls and flooring.

🏛 RULE OF LAW
One who takes part in a sport accepts the dangers that inhere in it insofar as they are obvious and necessary and they are not so serious as to justify the belief that precautions of some kind must have been taken to avert them.

FACTS: While visiting the amusement park at Coney Island, New York (run by Steeplechase Amusement Co. [D]), Murphy (P), his wife, and their friends decided to ride "The Flopper" after watching others do so. "The Flopper" consists of a moving belt, running up an inclined plane, on which passengers sit or stand. There are four-foot high padded walls on either side of the groove in which the belt runs and padded flooring beyond those walls at the same angle as the belt (which is driven by a motor that runs on electrical current). The whole purpose of the ride was the laughter and merriment occasioned by the numerous spills the passengers took. In fact, Mrs. Murphy, who preceded her husband in boarding the ride, testified that she took a chance when she was asked if she thought a fall might be expected. When Murphy (P) fell on the ride, however, he blamed the fractured kneecap he suffered on a sudden start and stop of the belt. In a suit to recover for his injuries, Murphy (P) specifically charged that (1) the belt was dangerous to life and limb, (2) it was not properly equipped to prevent injuries to persons using it, (3) it was operated at a fast and dangerous rate of speed, and (4) there was no proper railing, guard, or other device to prevent a fall. At trial, Murphy (P) gave uncorroborated testimony (which was also contradicted by photographs and witnesses for Steeplechase [D]) that he fell on wood and not canvas padding. At the same trial, the president of Steeplechase (D) said such an accident had never occurred before, but a nurse in the emergency hospital serving the amusement park said there had been other injuries (she did not know how many), none of which involved broken bones or serious injuries. On this evidence, a verdict in favor of Murphy (P) was entered. Following an affirmation of that verdict on appeal, Steeplechase (D) brought the matter before this court on appeal.

ISSUE: Does one assume the risks that are inherent in a sport?

HOLDING AND DECISION: (Cardozo, C.J.) Yes. When one engages in a sport, he accepts the dangers that inhere in it insofar as they are obvious and necessary. The whole design of the ride in question was to illicit amusement and merriment from the spills taken by the riders. This was observed by Murphy (P) before he got on the ride. His injuries are no more than what common experience tells us could well happen at anytime as the consequence of a sudden fall. As to the allegation that an abnormal and extraordinary spasm in the machine's operation caused the fall, such a bare allegation is insufficient to provide the basis for a verdict absent some evidence firmer than a mere descriptive epithet (Murphy's [P] saying that he felt a jerk). All in all, the best advice is for the timorous to stay at home. Otherwise, they must accept the risks inherent in the actions and adventures they undertake. Thus, the judgment is reversed and a new trial granted.

▶ ANALYSIS

The legal maxim "volenti non fit injuria" (no wrong is done to one who is willing)—cited by the court—is the basis for the assumption of risk doctrine. Precisely what one has "willingly" chosen to risk is usually determined subjectively. However, there are certain risks all adults are held to appreciate.

Quicknotes

ASSUMPTION OF RISK DOCTRINE An affirmative defense to a negligence suit by the defendant contending that the plaintiff knowingly and voluntarily subjected himself to the hazardous condition wholly absolving the defendant of liability for injuries incurred.

Dalury v. S-K-I, Ltd.

Skier (P) v. Ski resort (D)

Vt. Sup. Ct., 670 A.2d 795 (1995).

NATURE OF CASE: Appeal from summary judgment for defendant in negligence action.

FACT SUMMARY: Dalury (P), who had signed a liability release form, was injured at S-K-I, Ltd. (D), a ski resort, after colliding with a metal pole that formed part of a control maze for a ski lift line.

RULE OF LAW

A standard signed liability waiver form may be held unenforceable if it violates public policy.

FACTS: Dalury (P) purchased a season pass at S-K-I, Ltd. (D) and signed a standard release-from-liability form and a photo identification card, which also contained the waiver language. The waiver stated that Dalury (P) acknowledged the risks inherent in skiing and that S-K-I (D) accepted no responsibility for "personal injury or property damage resulting from negligence, conditions of the premises, operations of the ski area, or actions or omissions of employees." Dalury (P) was badly injured when he collided with a metal pole used for directing the ski lift lines. Dalury (P) brought suit, and the trial judge granted summary judgment for S-K-I (D) on the basis of the waiver form. On appeal, Dalury (P) contended that the release was unenforceable as a matter of law because it violated public policy.

ISSUE: Can a standard signed liability waiver form be held unenforceable if it violates public policy?

HOLDING AND DECISION: (Johnson, J.) Yes. A standard signed liability waiver form may be held unenforceable if it violates public policy. Even a well-drafted liability release form may be void if enforcement would be contrary to public policy. In determining whether an exculpatory agreement violates public policy, the standard to be used is that found in *Wolf v. Ford*, 644 A.2d 522 (Md. 1994), which balanced the "totality of the circumstances of a given case against the backdrop of current societal expectations." Thousands of people buy lift tickets at S-K-I (D) every season; therefore a legitimate public interest is implicated. Under Vermont premises liability law, a business invitee has the right to assume that the premises are reasonably safe for the purposes for which they are being used. This standard applies to ski resorts too. S-K-I (D) is in the best position to insure against risks by properly maintaining their premises and training their employees. It would be illogical to put risks on skiers that S-K-I (D) is far better able to control and prevent. Dalury's (P) acknowledgment of the inherent risks of skiing, as expressed in the waiver form, should not allow S-K-I (D) to escape liability if they have been negligent. Reversed and remanded.

ANALYSIS

This was a case of first impression in Vermont and the holding reflects the majority approach for deciding whether public policy interests are implicated. However, the court declined to adopt a formulaic inquiry. A typical example of such an inquiry is the one developed in Colorado which balances: (1) the existence of a duty to the public, (2) the nature of the service performed, (3) whether the contract was fairly entered into, and (4) whether the intention of the parties is expressed in clear and unambiguous language. *Jones v. Dressel*, 623 P.2d 370 (Colo. 1981).

Quicknotes

ASSUMPTION OF RISK DOCTRINE An affirmative defense to a negligence suit by the defendant contending that the plaintiff knowingly and voluntarily subjected himself to the hazardous condition wholly absolving the defendant of liability for injuries incurred.

WAIVER The intentional or voluntary forfeiture of a recognized right.

Li v. Yellow Cab Co. of California

Auto accident victim (P) v. Cab company (D)

Cal. Sup. Ct., 532 P.2d 1226 (1975).

NATURE OF CASE: Appeal from denial of damages for negligence.

FACT SUMMARY: Nga Li (P) was injured in an automobile accident with a driver from the Yellow Cab Co. of California (D), but she was denied any compensation for her injuries because of her own contributory negligence.

🏛 RULE OF LAW
In California, contributory negligence is hereafter replaced with a system of "pure comparative negligence;" and, under this system, liability for negligently caused damage is assigned in direct proportion to the amount of negligence of the involved parties.

FACTS: Nga Li (P) made a left-hand turn into an intersection when a cab of the Yellow Cab Co. of California (D) was approaching from the opposite direction. This cab entered the intersection at an unsafe speed after the traffic signal had turned yellow. As a result, the cab struck Nga Li's (P) car, and she was injured. Thereafter, Nga Li (P) brought an action for damages against the Yellow Cab Co. of California (D) based upon the negligence of the cab driver. The trial court, though, held that Nga Li (P) was barred from any recovery because she was contributorily negligent. Thereupon, Nga Li (P) appealed on the ground that her contributory negligence should not have totally barred her recovery.

ISSUE: Must the doctrine of contributory negligence be followed in California today?

HOLDING AND DECISION: (Sullivan, J.) No. In California, contributory negligence is hereafter replaced with a system of "pure comparative negligence;" and, under this system, liability for negligently caused damage is assigned in direct proportion to the amount of negligence of the involved parties. This replacement is necessary in order to promote basic fairness, which demands that responsibility for damage be proportioned according to fault (i.e., that no one be allowed to escape liability for his or her negligence). As such, Nga Li (P) can recover from the Yellow Cab Co. of California (D) those damages that are proportionate to the cab company's amount of negligence. Reversed.

▌ ANALYSIS

This case illustrates a recent trend that attempts to avoid the harshness of the contributory negligence system (i.e., where any negligence by the injured party bars his recovery from the tortfeasor). Note that there are three forms of comparative negligence systems. First, there is the "pure" system discussed in this case. Second, there is the system in which the injured party can only recover if his negligence is "less than" the tortfeasor's. Third, there is the system in which the injured party can only recover if his negligence is "not greater than" the tortfeasor's.

■■■

Quicknotes

COMPARATIVE NEGLIGENCE Doctrine whereby the court in assessing the appropriate measure of damages compares the relative fault of the parties and reduces the amount of damages to be collected by the plaintiff in proportion to his degree of fault.

CONTRIBUTORY NEGLIGENCE Behavior on the part of an injured plaintiff falling below the standard of ordinary care that contributes to the defendant's negligence, resulting in the plaintiff's injury.

■■■

Causation

Quick Reference Rules of Law

PAGE

1. *New York Central R.R. v. Grimstad.* A negligent party is liable only for those damages that were actually caused by his negligence. — 75

2. *Zuchowicz v. United States.* Where a negligent act increases the chances that a particular type of accident would occur, and such an accident does in fact occur, a court may conclude that the negligent conduct was the cause of the injury. — 76

3. *Union Stock Yards Co. of Omaha v. Chicago, Burlington, & Quincy R.R.* When two parties commit a joint offense neither can seek indemnity or contribution from the other, unless the action of one party was primarily responsible for the resulting injury. — 77

4. *American Motorcycle Association v. Superior Court.* Under a comparative negligence formula of recovery, the equitable indemnity doctrine should be modified so as to permit partial indemnity among concurrent tortfeasors on a proportional basis. — 78

5. *Kingston v. Chicago & N.W. Ry.* A party causing a fire that unites with another man-made fire is liable for all damages caused by the united fires. — 79

6. *Summers v. Tice.* When two or more persons by their acts are possibly the sole cause of harm, and the plaintiff has introduced evidence that one of the two persons is culpable (responsible), then the defendant has the burden of proving that the other person was the sole cause of the harm. — 80

7. *Sindell v. Abbott Laboratories.* Where an innocent tort plaintiff brings an action against multiple manufacturers of a product that has allegedly injured the plaintiff, but the plaintiff cannot identify which manufacturer's product in fact caused the plaintiff's injuries, the plaintiff's action nevertheless may proceed where it is possible to measure each manufacturer's market share of the product; where the manufacturers of a substantial share of the product are joined in the action; and where, if the named-manufacturers cannot show they did not manufacture the injury-causing product, they may cross-complain against other manufacturers, not joined in the action, which they can allege might have supplied the injury-causing product. — 81

8. *Herskovits v. Group Health Cooperative.* A defendant's conduct that increases the risk of death by decreasing the chances of survival is sufficient to take the issue of proximate cause to the jury. — 84

9. *General Electric Co. v. Joiner.* Abuse of discretion is the proper standard to be applied by an appellate court in reviewing a trial court's decision to admit or exclude scientific evidence. — 85

10. *Ryan v. New York Central R.R.* Damages can be awarded only when the injury is immediate and not the remote result of defendant's negligence. — 86

11. *Berry v. Sugar Notch Borough.* A person's right to recover for injuries caused by the negligence of another is not automatically precluded because he was violating some ordinance at the time he was injured. — 87

12. *Brower v. New York Central & H.R.R.* A negligent party is liable for harm caused by the intervening acts of a third person if that person's acts should have been foreseen. — 88

13. *Wagner v. International Ry.* A party whose negligence has caused harm or the risk thereof is liable to all persons who are injured in the course of reasonable rescue attempts. — 89

CHAPTER 5

14. *In re Polemis & Furness, Withy & Co.* Once the negligence of a party has been established, he may be held liable for all the consequences, foreseeable or not, of his conduct.   90

15. *Overseas Tankship (U.K.) Ltd. v. Morts Dock & Engineering Co., Ltd. (Wagon Mound [No. 1]).* An injury must be reasonably foreseeable before liability for it can be imposed.   91

16. *Palsgraf v. Long Island R.R.* The risk reasonably to be perceived defines the duty to be obeyed.   92

17. *Marshall v. Nugent.* The defendant remains liable for the full consequences of his negligent act when the intervening force is one a reasonable man would have foreseen as likely to occur under the circumstances, and the issue of foreseeability remains a question of fact for the jury.   94

18. *Virden v. Betts and Beer Construction Company.* As a matter of law, proximate cause is not established where a defendant's negligence is not a substantial factor in bringing about the plaintiff's injury.   95

19. *Hebert v. Enos.* A claim of negligence may be dismissed as a matter of law where the plaintiff cannot show that his injuries were a reasonably foreseeable consequence of the defendant's negligent conduct.   96

20. *Mitchell v. Rochester Railway.* Proximate damages are ordinary and natural results of the negligence charged and those that are usual and may, therefore, be expected.   97

21. *Dillon v. Legg.* The zone of danger rule does not bar a recovery for negligent infliction of emotional distress where a close family member outside the zone views an accident causing an injury or death to another family member.   98

New York Central R.R v. Grimstad

Railroad (D) v. Barge captain (P)

264 F. 334 (2d Cir. 1920).

NATURE OF CASE: Suit to recover damages for wrongful death.

FACT SUMMARY: Grimstad's (P) husband, captain of a barge owned by New York Central R.R. (D), fell into the water and drowned. The boat was not equipped with life preservers, and the victim did not know how to swim.

RULE OF LAW
A negligent party is liable only for those damages that were actually caused by his negligence.

FACTS: Grimstad's (P) husband, who did not know how to swim, was captain of the *Grayton*, a barge owned by New York Central R.R. (the Railroad) (D). While docked in Brooklyn, the *Grayton* was struck by a tugboat. Mrs. Grimstad (P) came out of the *Grayton's* cabin and found her husband in the water, arms outstretched. She ran back into the cabin and returned with a small line, but by then her husband had disappeared. Mrs. Grimstad (P) later brought suit under the Federal Employers' Liability Act, seeking damages for the death of her husband. Mrs. Grimstad (P) alleged that his drowning had been the result of the Railroad's (D) negligence in failing to equip the *Grayton* with life-preservers and other safety appliances, including life buoys. From a jury verdict in favor of Mrs. Grimstad (P), the Railroad (D) appealed, arguing that any negligence on its part had been inconsequential because Grimstad would have drowned anyway.

ISSUE: If a party is shown to have been negligent, will he be held liable for all damages suffered by another person?

HOLDING AND DECISION: (Ward, C.J.) No. A negligent party is liable only for those damages that were actually caused by his negligence. The jury found that the Railroad (D) was negligent in not equipping the Grayton with life preservers, but a life preserver is intended to be put on before a person gets into the water. A life buoy, on the other hand, is to be thrown to a person who has already fallen into the water, but there has been no showing that the absence of life buoys contributed to Grimstad's death. It is likely that Mrs. Grimstad (P) would have found a buoy too late to save her husband. Or, she might not have thrown it accurately enough for him to seize it. In fact, even if Grimstad had been able to grasp a life buoy, he might not have been saved from drowning. Thus, there was no showing that the Railroad's (D) negligence, if any, caused Grimstad's death. Therefore, the Railroad's (D) motion to dismiss the complaint should have been granted. Reversed.

ANALYSIS

Causation is a necessary element of any cause of action that sounds in tort. Thus, a party is not liable unless his conduct can be shown to have been the cause in fact of the damages suffered by someone else. It is sometimes said that the defendant's conduct is actionable only if the plaintiff would have incurred no damages "but for" the defendant's acts. The "but for" test does not enjoy widespread acceptance, however, since it does not adequately dispose of the causation issue in every case. Courts generally prefer to ignore any prescribed causation test, most electing instead to resolve the causation issue according to the facts of each particular case.

━━■■■━━

Quicknotes

CAUSE IN FACT The event without which an injury would not have been incurred.

━━■■■━━

Zuchowicz v. United States

Decedent's estate (P) v. Federal government (D)

140 F.3d 381 (2d Cir. 1998).

NATURE OF CASE: Appeal from damage award for plaintiff in negligence action.

FACT SUMMARY: Mrs. Zuchowicz (P) brought suit against the Government (D), alleging the Government's (D) negligence in prescribing an overdose of Danocrine, thereby causing her to develop primary pulmonary hypertension.

RULE OF LAW
Where a negligent act increases the chances that a particular type of accident would occur, and such an accident does in fact occur, a court may conclude that the negligent conduct was the cause of the injury.

FACTS: Mrs. Zuchowicz (P) filed a prescription for Danocrine at the Naval Hospital. The prescription incorrectly instructed her to take 1600 milligrams of Danocrine per day. Defendants stipulated its doctors and/or pharmacists were negligent and violated the prevailing standard of care by prescribing this dosage. Mrs. Zuchowicz (P) took 1600 milligrams per day for one month, and 800 milligrams per day thereafter. She experienced abnormal weight gain, bloating, edema, hot flashes, night sweats, a racing heart, chest pains, dizziness, headaches, acne, and fatigue. She was examined by an obstetrician/gynecologist who told her to stop taking the drug. Shortly thereafter, she was diagnosed with primary pulmonary hypertension (PPH). She was on the waiting list for a lung transplant when she became pregnant. She gave birth to a son and died one month later. Mrs. Zuchowicz's (P) expert witness testified that he was confident that the prescribed overdose caused her illness. The district court awarded plaintiff's husband, as representative of Mrs. Zuchowicz's (P) estate, $1,034,236.02 in damages. The Government (D) appealed.

ISSUE: Where a negligent act increases the chances that a particular type of accident would occur, and such an accident does in fact occur, may a court conclude that the negligent conduct was the cause of the injury?

HOLDING AND DECISION: (Calabresi, J.) Yes. Where a negligent act increases the chances that a particular type of accident would occur, and such an accident does in fact occur, a court may conclude that the negligent conduct was the cause of the injury. On the basis of the expert testimony alone the court could have held that the prescribed overdose more likely than not caused Mrs. Zuchowicz's (P) illness. In order for the causation element to be satisfied, the trier of fact must be able to determine, by a preponderance of the evidence, that the defendant's

negligence was responsible for the injury. Here the trier of fact must be able to conclude that the overdose was, more likely than not, the cause of Mrs. Zuchowicz's (P) illness and ultimate death. Courts have held that where a negligent act was deemed wrongful because the act increased the chances that a particular type of accident would occur, and such an accident did in fact happen, this was sufficient to support a finding by the trier of fact that the negligent conduct caused the injury. Then the burden shifts to the negligent party to show evidence rebutting such but for cause and showing that the wrongful conduct was not a substantial factor. Here Mrs. Zuchowicz (P) met her burden of demonstrating that the excessive dosage was a substantial factor in causing her illness. Affirmed.

ANALYSIS

Cause-in-fact is also an issue in slip-and-fall cases. In such cases courts have noted that the mere fact that such injury could have occurred in the absence of negligence is insufficient to break the chain of causation, where the defendant's conduct greatly increases the chances of injury and is of the type that would normally lead to the happening of such an injury, *Reynolds v. Texas & Pacific Ry.*, 37 La. Ann. 694, 698 (1885).

▬▬

Quicknotes

CAUSATION The aggregate effect of preceding events that bring about a tortious result; the causal connection between the actions of a tortfeasor and the injury that follows.

CAUSE IN FACT The event without which an injury would not have been incurred.

▬▬

Union Stock Yards Co. of Omaha v. Chicago, Burlington, & Quincy R.R.

Terminal company (P) v. Railroad company (D)

196 U.S. 217 (1905).

NATURE OF CASE: Suit for recovery of damages.

FACT SUMMARY: Union Stock Yards Co. of Omaha (P) brought suit against the Chicago, Burlington, & Quincy Railroad (D) for recovery of damages it paid to one of its employees who was injured as the result of a defective nut in one of the switching cars, which was undetected since both parties failed to conduct a reasonable inspection.

🏛 RULE OF LAW
When two parties commit a joint offense neither can seek indemnity or contribution from the other, unless the action of one party was primarily responsible for the resulting injury.

FACTS: Union Stock Yards Co. of Omaha (Union) (P) was responsible for moving the switching cars for the Chicago, Burlington, & Quincy Railroad (the Railroad) (D) in its stockyard. One of the cars had a defective nut, which either party could have discovered through reasonable inspection; neither party carried out such an inspection and Union's (P) employee suffered injuries. Union (P) paid damages to the employee and sued the Railroad (D) for recovery.

ISSUE: When two parties commit a joint offense can either seek indemnity or contribution from the other?

HOLDING AND DECISION: (Day, J.) No. When two parties commit a joint offense neither can seek indemnity or contribution from the other, unless the action of one party was primarily responsible for the resulting injury. The general rule is that one of several tortfeasors may not recover against another, even if he was compelled to pay all the damages for any injuries sustained. An exception to the rule has been found so that the principal wrongdoer be made to bear the ultimate loss, and thus less culpable parties have been able to avoid liability. In *Gray v. Boston Gas Light Co.*, 114 Mass. 149 (1873), the court stated the rule that if two parties, acting together, commit an illegal or wrongful act, then the party who is held responsible cannot have indemnity or contribution from the other because each is equally culpable for the damage. The rule does not apply, however, when one party commits the action, and the other is exposed to liability and suffers damage therefrom. In that case, the party may recover against the party whose wrongful act exposed him to liability. Here both parties were negligent in failing to inspect the car before putting it into use by persons who may be injured. This case does not fall into the exception to the

general rule barring recovery of indemnity or contribution. Affirmed.

▌ ANALYSIS

At common law where joint tortfeasors have acted in concert, the release by the plaintiff of one affected a release as to all other defendants, in the absence of an agreement otherwise. The tortfeasors were considered a single person with an undividable duty of care to the plaintiff. Modern courts, however, have rejected this rationale.

Quicknotes

CONTRIBUTION The right of a person or party who has compensated a victim for his injury to seek reimbursement from others who are equally responsible for the injury in proportional amounts.

INDEMNITY The duty of a party to compensate another for damages sustained.

TORTFEASOR Party that commits a tort or wrongful act.

American Motorcycle Association v. Superior Court

Association (D) v. Motorcycle racer (P)

Cal. Sup. Ct., 578 P.2d 899 (1978).

NATURE OF CASE: Appeal from denial of claim for partial indemnity.

FACT SUMMARY: Glen Gregos was injured in a cycle meet negligently organized by American Motorcycle Association (AMA) (D). AMA (D) cross-complained for contribution from Gregos's parents for the negligence allocable to the improper supervision of Glen.

🏛 RULE OF LAW
Under a comparative negligence formula of recovery, the equitable indemnity doctrine should be modified so as to permit partial indemnity among concurrent tortfeasors on a proportional basis.

FACTS: Glen Gregos was injured during a cycle meet and brought an action against American Motorcycle Association (AMA) (D) for damages. Liability was found on AMA's (D) part and damages awarded. AMA (D) then cross-complained for partial indemnity for the negligence of Gregos's parents for their negligent supervision of Gregos. The cross-complaint was dismissed, and AMA (D) appealed.

ISSUE: Under a comparative negligence formula of recovery, should the equitable indemnity doctrine be modified so as to permit a partial indemnity among concurrent tortfeasors on a proportional basis?

HOLDING AND DECISION: (Tobriner, J.) Yes. While the comparative negligence theory requires the assessment of fault attributable to each defendant, joint and severable liability is not completely wiped away by the development. A plaintiff should still be able to obtain full recovery from any one defendant who was responsible; however, in most cases the percentage of liability will also operate as the percentage of the entire judgment that a particular defendant will pay. Furthermore, partial indemnity should be permitted as among concurrent tortfeasors on a proportional basis. Reversed.

DISSENT: (Clark, J.) The principle of joint and several liability is inconsistent with a comparative negligence formula. In this respect the majority opinion is undermining the formula. Furthermore, the incentive to settle a case for a proportional amount is lost where the possibility exists for recovery of all the judgment from one party.

▶ ANALYSIS

The majority opinion is somewhat vague on when joint and several liability is available after a determination of the percentages of fault. Clearly, the court did not want to deprive the plaintiffs the opportunity to collect a judgment from one tortfeasor if all others are insolvent.

◼▬◼

Quicknotes

COMPARATIVE NEGLIGENCE Doctrine whereby the court in assessing the appropriate measure of damages compares the relative fault of the parties and reduces the amount of damages to be collected by the plaintiff in proportion to his degree of fault.

INDEMNITY The duty of a party to compensate another for damages sustained.

JOINT AND SEVERAL LIABILITY Liability amongst tortfeasors allowing the injured party to bring suit against any of the defendants, individually or collectively, and to recover from each up to the total amount of damages awarded.

◼▬◼

Kingston v. Chicago & N.W. Ry.

Fire victim (P) v. Railroad company (D)

Wis. Sup. Ct., 211 N.W. 913 (1927).

NATURE OF CASE: Action for damages in negligence.

FACT SUMMARY: Sparks from a train united with a fire of unknown origin to destroy Kingston's (P) property.

RULE OF LAW
A party causing a fire that unites with another man-made fire is liable for all damages caused by the united fires.

FACTS: Sparks from a train owned by Chicago and N.W. Ry. (Chicago) (D) caused a fire. The fire spread and united with another fire of a relatively minor nature, which was apparently set by an unknown third party. The united fires destroyed Kingston's (P) property. Chicago (D) attempted to argue that the uniting of the two fires, either of which would have destroyed Kingston's (P) property, absolved it of liability since the other fire was an intervening cause and would have destroyed Kingston's (P) property anyway.

ISSUE: Where two unnatural fires unite to destroy property and one of the fires is of unknown origin, is the defendant liable?

HOLDING AND DECISION: (Owen, J.) Yes. If both parties starting the separate blazes were known they would be jointly liable for the destruction of Kingston's (P) property. The fact that one of the parties is unknown will not excuse Chicago (D) from its joint and several liability. Here, either fire would have destroyed the property. In such a case, the mere fact that one of the parties is unknown is immaterial. This is not a case where a lesser fire is swallowed up by a much greater fire, thereby losing its identity. The fires were approximately equal in size and magnitude. Kingston (P) need not prove the origin of the other fire. If it had a natural origin and would have burned Kingston's (P) property anyway, Chicago (D) might not be liable. Here, since both fires were caused by human negligence or design, Chicago (D) is jointly and severally liable. Affirmed.

ANALYSIS

Where two defendants are negligent and their conduct unites to cause a single injury, the courts may apportion the negligence between them awarding damages based on the proportion. In *Smith v. J.C. Penney Co.*, 525 P.2d 1299 (1974), the court found that the manufacturer of a coat containing flammable material was a joint tortfeasor with the party who negligently set the coat on fire. The same rationale applies where two parties collide with plaintiff's vehicle. *Madduk v. Donaldson*, 108 N.W. 2d 33 (1961).

Quicknotes

JOINT AND SEVERAL LIABILITY The liability of multiple tort-feasors whose causal connection to the injury cannot be separated and who are therefore found equally liable; all tortfeasors are responsible for the entire amount of the injury.

Summers v. Tice

Shooting victim (P) v. Gunman (D)

Cal. Sup. Ct., 199 P.2d 1 (1948).

NATURE OF CASE: Damages for personal injury.

FACT SUMMARY: Summers (P) sued two defendants for personal injury caused when both defendants shot in his direction.

🏛 RULE OF LAW
When two or more persons by their acts are possibly the sole cause of harm, and the plaintiff has introduced evidence that one of the two persons is culpable (responsible), then the defendant has the burden of proving that the other person was the sole cause of the harm.

FACTS: Summers (P) and the two defendants were members of the same hunting party. Both defendants fired at the same time at a quail in the direction of Summers (P). Summers (P) was struck in the eye by a shot from one of the two guns. There was no evidence from which to determine which gun had caused the injury. The trial court held both defendants liable. They appealed on grounds they were not joint tortfeasors, they were not acting in concert, and there was insufficient evidence to show which defendant was guilty of the negligence which caused the injuries.

ISSUE: When two persons by their acts are possibly the sole cause of harm, and the plaintiff has introduced evidence that one of the two persons is culpable, do the defendants have the burden of proving which of them was the sole cause of the harm?

HOLDING AND DECISION: (Carter, J.) Yes. When two or more persons by their acts are possibly the sole cause of harm, and the plaintiff has introduced evidence that one of the two persons is culpable, then each defendant has the burden of proving that the other person was the sole cause of the harm. The reason behind the rule that each joint tortfeasor is responsible for the whole damage is the practical unfairness of denying the injured person redress simply because he cannot prove how much damage each did, when it is certain that between the defendants they did all the damage. The rule applies whenever the harm has plural causes, and not merely when the causes acted in conscious concert. Here it is clear that the two defendants were the sole cause of plaintiff's injuries. Plaintiff has introduced evidence that one of the two defendants is culpable. The defendants now have the burden of proving which of them is the sole cause of the harm. Judgment for plaintiff is affirmed.

▶ *ANALYSIS*

At common law, two situations in which two or more defendants acted tortiously toward the plaintiff gave rise to what is now referred to as joint and several liability: where the defendants acted in concert to cause the harm, and where the defendants acted independently but caused indivisible harm. Liability in the case of concerted action is a form of vicarious liability, in which all the defendants will be responsible for the harm actually caused by only one of the defendants.

Quicknotes

JOINT AND SEVERAL LIABILITY Liability amongst tortfeasors allowing the injured party to bring suit against any of the defendants, individually or collectively, and to recover from each up to the total amount of damages awarded.

TORTFEASOR Party that commits a tort or wrongful act.

Sindell v. Abbott Laboratories

Daughter of drug recipient (P) v. Drug manufacturer (D)

Cal. Sup. Ct., 607 P.2d 924 (1980).

NATURE OF CASE: Appeal from dismissal of putative class actions for personal injuries allegedly resulting from prenatal exposure to diethylstilbestrol (DES).

FACT SUMMARY: Sindell (P) brought class actions alleging that she and other women similarly situated to her had suffered various personal injuries from prenatal exposure to diethylstilbestrol (DES), which numerous drug manufacturers (D) had produced, marketed and distributed over a 30-year period, but she could not identify which named drug manufacturer (D) had produced the DES given to her mother.

RULE OF LAW

Where an innocent tort plaintiff brings an action against multiple manufacturers of a product that has allegedly injured the plaintiff, but the plaintiff cannot identify which manufacturer's product in fact caused the plaintiff's injuries, the plaintiff's action nevertheless may proceed where it is possible to measure each manufacturer's market share of the product; where the manufacturers of a substantial share of the product are joined in the action; and where, if the named-manufacturers cannot show they did not manufacture the injury-causing product, they may cross-complain against other manufacturers, not joined in the action, which they can allege might have supplied the injury-causing product.

FACTS: Sindell (P) brought class actions alleging that she and other women similarly situated to her had suffered various personal injuries from prenatal exposure to diethylstilbestrol (DES), a synthetic compound of the female hormone estrogen that was administered to women during pregnancy for the purpose of preventing miscarriage. Daughters of women to whom DES was administered were at risk of suffering from cancerous vaginal and cervical growths and possibly requiring expensive and repeated testing, monitoring, surgeries and treatment. DES was manufactured, marketed, and distributed between 1941 and 1971 by over 200 producers from an identical drug formula. In 1947, the Food and Drug Administration (FDA) authorized the marketing of DES as a miscarriage preventative, but only on an experimental basis, with a requirement that the drug contain a warning label to that effect. In one action, Sindell (P) alleged that various drug manufacturers (D) were jointly and individually negligent in that they manufactured marketed and promoted DES as a safe and efficacious drug to prevent miscarriage, without adequate testing or warning, and without monitoring or

reporting its effect, and that they knew or should have known that, in fact, DES was a carcinogenic substance that was dangerous to the daughters of the mothers to whom it was administered. In a second action, Sindell (P) alleged that the drug manufacturers (D) were jointly liable regardless of which particular brand of DES was ingested by Sindell's (P) mother because the drug manufacturers (D) collaborated in marketing, promoting and testing the drug, relied upon each other's tests, and adhered to an industrywide safety standard. She also alleged that the drug was produced from a common and mutually agreed upon formula as a fungible drug interchangeable with other brands of the same product. Finally, she alleged that the drug manufacturers (D) were jointly liable since they acted in concert, on the basis of express and implied agreements, and in reliance upon and ratification and exploitation of each other's testing and marketing methods. The trial court dismissed Sindell's (P) actions on the grounds that she could not prove which of the named drug manufacturers (D) had produced the DES given to her mother. The state's highest court granted review.

ISSUE: Where an innocent tort plaintiff brings an action against multiple manufacturers of a product that has allegedly injured the plaintiff, but the plaintiff cannot identify which manufacturer's product in fact caused the plaintiff's injuries, may the plaintiff's action nevertheless proceed where it is possible to measure each manufacturer's market share of the product; where the manufacturers of a substantial share of the product are joined in the action; and where, if the named manufacturers cannot show they did not manufacture the injury-causing product, they may cross-complain against other manufacturers, not joined in the action, which they can allege might have supplied the injury-causing product?

HOLDING AND DECISION: (Mosk, J.) Yes. Where an innocent tort plaintiff brings an action against multiple manufacturers of a product that has allegedly injured the plaintiff, but the plaintiff cannot identify which manufacturer's product in fact caused the plaintiff's injuries, the plaintiff's action nevertheless may proceed where it is possible to measure each manufacturer's market share of the product; where the manufacturers of a substantial share of the product are joined in the action; and where, if the named manufacturers cannot show they did not manufacture the injury-causing product, they may cross-complain against other manufacturers, not joined in the action, which they can allege might have supplied the

Continued on next page.

injury-causing product. Although the general rule is that a plaintiff's injuries must be caused directly by the defendant, or by an instrumentality directly controlled by the defendant, there are three existing exceptions to this rule. The first exception, also known as the "alternative liability" theory, is that under certain circumstances, where a plaintiff cannot identify which of two or more defendants caused an injury, the burden of proof may shift to the defendants to show that they were not responsible for the harm. Here, the drug manufacturers (D) argue that the alternative liability theory is inapplicable because they are in no better position than Sindell (P) to identify which among them actually manufactured the DES given to Sindell's (P) mother. However, even if that were so, that would not per se prevent the application of the theory, since the manufacturers (D) might be able to show they did not manufacture the injury-causing substance—as where they did not start manufacturing DES until after Sindell (P) was born. Nevertheless, the alternative liability theory is inapplicable here because not all DES manufacturers have been joined in Sindell's (P) actions, so that it would be impossible to properly apportion liability among them under the alternative liability theory. Here, since any one of 200 companies that manufactured DES might have made the product that harmed Sindell (P), there is no rational basis upon which to infer that any defendant in this action caused her injuries, nor even a reasonable possibility that they were responsible. The second exception to the general rule arises when there has been "concert of action" among multiple potential tortfeasors. However, here, the record does not demonstrate the requisite common plan or tacit understanding among the defendants necessary to sustain the exception. The third exception to the general rule, known as the "enterprise theory" of liability, also is inapplicable here. Thus, none of the existing exceptions apply, and, seemingly, the dismissal of the actions should be upheld. However, the court decides to craft a fourth exception that will enable Sindell's (P) actions to go forward, as there are forceful arguments in favor of holding that she has a cause of action, the most persuasive of which is that as between an innocent plaintiff and negligent defendants, the latter should bear the cost of the injury. Sindell (P) is not at fault in failing to provide evidence of causation, and although the absence of such evidence is not attributable to the DES manufacturers (D) either, their conduct in marketing a drug the effects of which are delayed for many years played a significant role in creating the unavailability of proof. Also, from a broader policy standpoint, the DES manufacturers (D) are better able to bear the cost of injury resulting from the manufacture of a defective product. Accordingly, as here, where all defendants produced a drug from an identical formula and the manufacturer of the DES that caused the plaintiff's injuries cannot be identified, through no fault of the plaintiff, an expanded, modified alternative liability theory is applicable. Under this new theory, it is reasonable to measure the likelihood that any of the defendants supplied the product which

allegedly injured plaintiff by the percentage which the DES sold by each of them bears to the entire production of the product sold by all the manufacturers. To make this exception fair to the manufacturers (D), those manufacturers (D) representing a substantial share of the market for the product (here, DES) must be joined—so that the injustice of shifting the burden of proof to defendants to demonstrate that they could not have made the substance which injured the plaintiff is significantly diminished. The presence in the action of a substantial share of the appropriate market also provides a ready means to apportion damages among the defendants, and each defendant will be held liable for the proportion of the judgment represented by its share of that market unless it demonstrates that it could not have made the product which caused the plaintiff's injuries. Once a plaintiff has met her burden of joining the required defendants, they in turn may cross-complain against other manufacturers, not joined in the action, which they can allege might have supplied the injury-causing product. Under this approach, each manufacturer's (D) liability would approximate its responsibility for the injuries caused by its own products. It is acknowledged that it may be impossible to divide liability with mathematical exactitude, but, in such cases, the trier of fact will do the best it can. There also will be practical problems involved in defining the market and determining market share, but these are largely matters of proof. Reversed.

DISSENT: (Richardson, J.) A causal link between a plaintiff's injuries and a defendant's product is essential in products liability cases, and Sindell (P) fails to establish such a link. Thus, here, it remains wholly speculative and conjectural whether any of the named defendants actually caused Sindell's (P) injuries. The majority, while stating in its new rule that this element of actual causation can be satisfied by joining those manufacturers who produced a "substantial percentage" of the injurious product, does not define or provide guidance as to what constitutes a "substantial" share of the relevant market. Thus, not only does the majority ignore well-established precedent, it also lets plaintiffs pick and choose their defendants.

▶ **ANALYSIS**

The California Supreme Court, which established the market share rule in *Sindell* held that each defendant could be held liable for the shares of absent or insolvent defendants no matter how small its share of the market. The court gradually stepped back from that holding, first holding in *Murphy v. E.R. Squibb & Sons, Inc.,* 710 P.2d 247, 255 (Cal. 1985), that the "substantial share" requirement of *Sindell* was not met when the plaintiff sued only one manufacturer with a 10 percent market share, and then holding, in *Brown v. Superior Court (Abbott Laboratories, RPI),* 751 P.2d 470

Continued on next page.

(Cal. 1988), that a defendant was responsible only for its proportionate share of the loss, so that the entire loss could not be imposed on a defendant with an "insignificant" market share. These refinements to the initial rule were necessary because calculating market share in a case such as *Sindell* proved quite difficult, given that DES was marketed for multiple purposes and sold in different formats.

Quicknotes

ENTERPRISE LIABILITY Apportionment of liability between each participant in an industry equal to the participant's market share.

JOINT LIABILITY Liability owed to an injured party by two or more parties where each party has the right to insist that the other tortfeasors be joined to the matter.

MARKET SHARE LIABILITY The apportionment of liability between each participant in an industry equal to the participant's market share.

Herskovits v. Group Health Cooperative

Lung cancer victim (P) v. Medical group (D)

Wash. Sup. Ct., 664 P.2d 474 (1983).

NATURE OF CASE: Appeal from summary judgment denying damages for medical malpractice.

FACT SUMMARY: Herskovits (P) died of lung cancer after his chances of survival were reduced by Group Health Cooperative's (D) late diagnosis of his cancer.

🏛 RULE OF LAW
A defendant's conduct that increases the risk of death by decreasing the chances of survival is sufficient to take the issue of proximate cause to the jury.

FACTS: Herskovits (P) died of lung cancer. Herskovits's (P) chances of survival were reduced from 39 percent to 25 percent by Group Health Cooperative's (Cooperative's) (D) failure to diagnose his cancer on his first visit. After Herskovits (P) died, his estate sued Cooperative (D) for professional negligence on the basis that Cooperative's (D) late diagnosis reduced Herskovits's (P) chances for survival. Cooperative (D) moved for a judgment notwithstanding the verdict, contending that Herskovits (P) would have probably died of lung cancer even if his diagnosis had been made earlier. The motion was granted. Herskovits (P) appealed.

ISSUE: Is the fact that a defendant's conduct increases the risk of death by decreasing the chances of survival sufficient to take the issue of proximate cause to the jury?

HOLDING AND DECISION: (Dore, J.) Yes. A defendant's conduct that increases the risk of death by decreasing the chances of survival is sufficient to take the issue of proximate cause to the jury. The criterion is whether Cooperative (D) deprived Herskovits (P) of a significant chance to survive rather than absolute proof that Cooperative's (D) conduct caused Herskovits's (P) death. A 36 percent reduction in Herskovits's (P) chances of survival is sufficient evidence of causation for a jury to consider the possibility that Cooperative's (D) failure to timely diagnose Herskovits's (P) illness was the proximate cause of his death. To decide otherwise would be a blanket release from liability anytime there was less than a 50 percent chance of survival, regardless how flagrant defendant's negligence. Reversed.

CONCURRENCE: (Pearson, J.) While the majority's decision is correct, its reasoning is not. A more rational approach would be to allow recovery even where the plaintiff could not ultimately prove that he was denied a cure but could prove he was denied a chance of a cure.

DISSENT: (Dolliver, J.) A better rule would be one that comports with the standard of proof of proximate cause, i.e., the plaintiff in a malpractice case must prove that defendant's negligence, in probability, proximately caused the death.

▌ ANALYSIS

In an analogous case, *Jackson v. Johns-Manville Sales Corp.*, 781 F.2d 394 (5th Cir. 1986), the plaintiff had contracted asbestosis and sued the defendant for the over 50 percent probability that he would eventually contract cancer due to his earlier asbestos exposure. The defendant argued that the plaintiff could not recover for the loss since the development of cancer represented a future injury based on a present cause of action. The plaintiff countered that the cancer action had to be brought together with the asbestosis action because a suit for future cancer would be barred by the procedural rule that prevents splitting causes of action. The court held that it would allow recovery for "probable future consequences" of the plaintiff's exposure to asbestos.

∎▭∎

Quicknotes

CAUSE IN FACT The event without which an injury would not have been incurred.

JUDGMENT N.O.V. A judgment entered by the trial judge reversing a jury verdict if the jury's determination has no basis in law or fact.

PROXIMATE CAUSE The natural sequence of events without which an injury would not have been sustained.

SUMMARY JUDGMENT Judgment rendered by a court in response to a motion by one of the parties, claiming that the lack of a question of material fact in respect to an issue warrants disposition of the issue without consideration by the jury.

∎▭∎

General Electric Co. v. Joiner

Manufacturer (D) v. Electrician (P)

522 U.S. 136 (1997).

NATURE OF CASE: Writ of certiorari to determine appropriate standard of review.

FACT SUMMARY: General Electric Co. (D) sought to exclude scientific evidence introduced by Joiner (P) to support his expert testimony that his exposure to PCB's caused his development of small-cell lung cancer.

RULE OF LAW

Abuse of discretion is the proper standard to be applied by an appellate court in reviewing a trial court's decision to admit or exclude scientific evidence.

FACTS: Joiner (P), an electrician, worked with electrical transformers, requiring him to often stick his hands and arms into the coolant to make repairs. It was later discovered that the coolant fluid of many transformers were contaminated with PCB's. Joiner (P) was diagnosed with small-cell lung cancer. He sued General Electric Co. (D), manufacturers of the transformers and coolant. Joiner (P) linked his development of cancer to his exposure to the PCB's and their derivatives. Joiner (P) had been a smoker for eight years, both his parents were smokers, and there was a history of lung cancer in his family. General Electric (D) removed to federal court and moved for summary judgment. The district court granted summary judgment for General Electric (D) because (1) there was no genuine issue as to whether Joiner (P) had been exposed to furans and dioxins, and (2) Joiner's (P) expert testimony failed to show a link between exposure to PCB's and small-cell lung cancer. The court of appeals reversed, holding the district court erred in excluding Joiner's (P) expert testimony. General Electric (D) appealed.

ISSUE: Is abuse of discretion the proper standard to be applied by an appellate court in reviewing a trial court's decision to admit or exclude scientific evidence?

HOLDING AND DECISION: (Rehnquist, C.J.) Yes. Abuse of discretion is the proper standard to be applied by an appellate court in reviewing a trial court's decision to admit or exclude scientific evidence. Application of this standard to this case indicates the district court did not abuse its discretion. Joiner (P) claimed that his exposure to PCB's promoted his development of lung cancer. In support of this claim he introduced expert testimony. The district court agreed with General Electric (D) that the experts' reliance on animal studies did not support Joiner's (P) contention that his exposure to PCB's contributed to his development of cancer. The issue here was not whether animal studies can ever be a proper foundation for expert testimony, but rather whether in this case the expert testimony was sufficiently supported by the animal studies relied upon. Since the studies relied upon by Joiner's (P) experts were so dissimilar from the facts in the case, the district court did not err in rejecting the experts' reliance on the studies. The court also concluded that the four epidemiological studies relied upon were not a sufficient basis for the experts' opinions. These studies did not support the experts' testimony either. A court may decide to exclude scientific evidence where the analytical gap is too great between the data and the opinion offered. Thus the district court did not abuse its discretion in excluding the experts' testimony. Reversed and remanded.

CONCURRENCE: (Breyer, J.) Since modern life depends upon manufactured substances, judges must fulfill their *Daubert* gatekeeping functions to assure that litigation does not prohibit the production of certain chemicals.

CONCURRENCE AND DISSENT: (Stevens, J.) The court of appeals expressly decided that a "weight of the evidence" standard was acceptable. Under this standard an expert could have reasonably concluded that an inference was raised that PCB's promote lung cancer.

ANALYSIS

Here the court of appeals construed the decision in *Daubert v. Merrell Dow Pharmaceuticals, Inc.*, 509 U.S. 579 (1993), as altering the standard to be applied in deciding whether to admit or exclude scientific evidence. The Supreme Court, however, construed *Daubert* as maintaining the "gatekeeper" role of the trial court in screening scientific evidence under the Federal Rules of Evidence. This gatekeeper function has also been applied to the admission of technical evidence. *Kumho Tire Co. v. Carmichael*, 526 U.S. 137 (1999).

Quicknotes

SUMMARY JUDGMENT Judgment rendered by a court in response to a motion by one of the parties, claiming that the lack of a question of material fact in respect to an issue warrants disposition of the issue without consideration by the jury.

Ryan v. New York Central R.R.

Homeowner (P) v. Railroad (D)

N.Y. Ct. App., 35 N.Y. 210 (1866).

NATURE OF CASE: Action for damages for injury due to negligence.

FACT SUMMARY: Fire destroyed Ryan's (P) house. The fire started when a spark from New York Central Railroad's (D) train engine ignited a wood shed. The fire spread through several houses before reaching Ryan's (P).

RULE OF LAW

Damages can be awarded only when the injury is immediate and not the remote result of defendant's negligence.

FACTS: Ryan's (P) home in Syracuse was destroyed by a fire that spread from New York Central Railroad's (Central's) (D) woodshed, which had been ignited by a spark from Central's (D) train engine either through careless management or insufficient condition. Ryan's (P) house was 130 feet from the shed. Several other houses were also destroyed.

ISSUE: When a person's structure is set afire through his negligence or the negligence of his servant, is he liable for injury suffered to the structures of all others to which the fire spreads?

HOLDING AND DECISION: (Hunt, J.) No. Liability would extend only to the owner of the first structure, that is the structure upon which the spark lands. The result to be anticipated is that the structure upon which the spark lands will be damaged or destroyed. But the spread of the fire to other structures is not the necessary or usual result. The defendant has no control over that and cannot be responsible. The immediate result of the negligence was destruction of Central's (D) own woodshed. All other damage was remote. To hold defendant liable for all resulting damage would be to create a liability too great for any individual; all persons run some risk as to their neighbor's conduct. Affirmed.

ANALYSIS

Supposedly, a defendant is liable for damage that is the natural and probable consequence of his act. In New York, there has been created an arbitrary rule that the wrongdoer is liable for fire only to the first, adjoining property owner, as illustrated above. Here, as the first structure to be struck by sparks belonged to Central (D), it was not liable to anyone. Thus, it would not make any difference whether the adjoining structure was one large building or thirty small stores. Only the first, adjoining property owner could recover even if the fire covered the entire block,

whereas with a series of small stores, the ones after the first on the same size block would not be covered. The court touched but did not rest its decision upon whether one should be liable for all damage from an intentionally set fire as opposed to a negligent set fire where liability may be limited to the first, adjoining property.

Quicknotes

FORESEEABILITY A reasonable expectation that an act or omission would result in injury.

PROXIMATE CAUSE The natural sequence of events without which an injury would not have been sustained.

REMOTE DAMAGES Damages that are unexpected and unforeseeable, and over which the negligent party has no control.

Berry v. Sugar Notch Borough

Motorman (P) v. Railway company (D)

Pa. Sup. Ct., 43 A. 240 (1899).

NATURE OF CASE: Action for damages for negligence.

FACT SUMMARY: While driving the car in which he was a motorman in excess of the speed limit, Berry (P) was injured when a tree was blown down and fell on the roof of the car.

🏛 RULE OF LAW
A person's right to recover for injuries caused by the negligence of another is not automatically precluded because he was violating some ordinance at the time he was injured.

FACTS: An ordinance required that the cars run by the Wilkes-Barre and Wyoming Valley Traction Company not exceed a speed of eight miles per hour. Berry (P), a motorman for that line, was operating a car in excess of that speed during a windstorm when a tree was blown down and crashed into the roof of the car. Claiming that Sugar Notch (D), the borough where the accident occurred, had been negligent in permitting the tree to remain because it was diseased, Berry (P) brought suit to recover for his personal injuries. On appeal for a judgment in favor of Berry (P), Sugar Notch (D) continued to argue that his violation of the speed law precluded his recovery. It was asserted that Berry's (P) speed was the immediate cause of his injury because it was his particular speed that caused him to be at the place of the accident at the moment the tree blew down. Furthermore, urged Sugar Notch (D), even if the speed was not the sole efficient cause of the accident, it at least contributed to its severity and materially increased the damage.

ISSUE: Does the fact that a person injured by another's negligence was violating some ordinance at the time he was injured automatically preclude him from recovering for his injuries?

HOLDING AND DECISION: (Fell, J.) No. One's right to recover for injuries sustained as the result of another's negligence is not automatically precluded simply because he was himself violating some ordinance at the time he was so injured. In this case, the speed did not cause or contribute to the accident. If it had, the appropriate ground for denying recovery in such a case would be that Berry (P) was guilty of contributory negligence and not that he had violated some ordinance. Turning to the argument that Berry's (P) speed placed him in the position where the tree could fall on his car: that was a matter of chance and something no foresight could have predicted. It could just as well have been that the fast speed would have carried him beyond the tree to a place of safety. So, in the sense argued, Berry's (P) speed was not the immediate cause of his injury. It may well be that the speed did add to the severity of the accident and the amount of damage, however, the jury has no way to make such a determination and no guide for differentiating between the injury actually suffered and what would have been suffered had the car been running at eight miles per hour or less. There is, therefore, no way to take such a factor into account, and recovery was properly granted. Affirmed.

▶ ANALYSIS

Basically, Sugar Notch (D), in its defense, argued that the proximate cause of Berry's (P) injuries was his violation of the speed limit ordinance. The burden of proof is on the plaintiff to show the proximate cause of his injuries by presenting direct or circumstantial evidence that it is more probable than not that he was injured by the neglect of the defendant. In effect, Sugar Notch (D) attempted to show that Berry (P) was contributorily negligent, but there was no basis to show that his violation of the speed ordinance was a proximate cause.

Quicknotes

CONTRIBUTORY NEGLIGENCE Behavior on the part of an injured plaintiff falling below the standard of ordinary care that contributes to the defendant's negligence, resulting in the plaintiff's injury.

PROXIMATE CAUSE The natural sequence of events without which an injury would not have been sustained.

Brower v. New York Central & H.R.R.

Horsecart owner (P) v. Railroad (D)

N.J. Sup. Ct., 103 A. 166 (1918).

NATURE OF CASE: Suit to recover damages for loss of property.

FACT SUMMARY: The New York Central & H.R.R.'s (D) freight train collided with Brower's (P) cart at a grade-crossing. The stunned driver was unable to prevent bystanders from stealing items that the cart had been carrying.

> 🏛 **RULE OF LAW**
> A negligent party is liable for harm caused by the intervening acts of a third person if that person's acts should have been foreseen.

FACTS: A New York Central & H.R.R. (the Railroad) (D) freight train collided with Brower's (P) horse drawn cart at a grade-crossing. The horse was killed, and the cart and harness were destroyed. The driver of the cart was stunned by the accident and thus was unable to prevent onlookers from stealing the contents of the cart, including empty barrels and a keg of cider. The train carried two detectives hired by the Railroad (D) to prevent theft, but neither made any effort to stop the people from stealing those articles. Brower (P) sued to recover damages from the Railroad (D) and won a judgment which included an award for the value of the stolen items. On appeal, the Railroad (D) denied liability for the purloined articles, arguing that their loss had resulted from the intervening acts of third persons.

ISSUE: Is a negligent party always absolved of liability for damages occasioned by the acts of third-party intervenors?

HOLDING AND DECISION: (Swayze, J.) No. A negligent party is liable for harm caused by the intervening acts of a third person if that person's acts should have been foreseen. The Railroad's (D) negligence was responsible for the condition of the driver, and the loss of the items from the cart was a natural and probable consequence of the collision which stunned him. Obviously, the intervening acts of thieves were foreseeable, because the Railroad (D) placed two detectives on the train to guard against theft. Thus, the jury was entitled to find that the Railroad (D) should be held liable for the value of the stolen articles.

DISSENT: (Garrison, J.) The chain of causation between the original negligence and the loss of the contents of the cart was broken by the intervening criminal acts of the thieves. Their acts cannot be deemed foreseeable unless one accepts the proposition that crimes are a normal event and that lawful behavior is exceptional.

▶ **ANALYSIS**

Intervening causes, whether natural or human, may break the chain of causation and relieve the original negligent actor of liability for the harm suffered by a plaintiff. Of course, the intervening force must be one over which the negligent party has no control if he is to be absolved of liability. Moreover, as the *Brower* court recognized, the chain of causation is not broken if the conduct of the intervening force could reasonably have been foreseen by the negligent actor. The rule of the *Brower* case is representative of the weight of authority and has been reiterated by countless courts.

Quicknotes

FORESEEABILITY A reasonable expectation that an act or omission would result in injury.

INTERVENING ACT An event whose occurrence breaks the causal chain between the tortfeasor's acts and the resulting injury.

PROXIMATE CAUSE The natural sequence of events without which an injury would not have been sustained.

Wagner v. International Ry.

Train passenger (P) v. Railroad (D)

N.Y. Ct. App., 133 N.E. 437 (1921).

NATURE OF CASE: Suit seeking damages for personal injuries.

FACT SUMMARY: Wagner's (P) cousin was thrown from an International Railway (D) car. Wagner (P) went searching for his cousin's body and was himself injured when he fell from a trestle.

🏛 RULE OF LAW
A party whose negligence has caused harm or the risk thereof is liable to all persons who are injured in the course of reasonable rescue attempts.

FACTS: Wagner (P) and his cousin Herbert boarded a crowded International Railway (D) (the Railroad) car. The conductor failed to close the doors of the car. The train was traveling at six to eight miles per hour when, without reducing speed, it rounded a bend. Herbert was pitched out of the car near a point at which the Railroad's (D) trestle changed to a bridge. The car crossed the bridge before stopping and Wagner (P), after disembarking, had to walk 445 feet to reach the site where his cousin had been thrown from the train. While atop the bridge, Wagner (P) lost his footing in the darkness, fell from the structure, and sustained injuries for which he later sued the Railroad (D). At trial, the judge instructed the jury that the Railroad's (D) negligence toward Herbert did not render it liable to Wagner (P) unless, as Wagner (P) maintained, the Railroad's (D) conductor had invited him to go to the bridge and had followed with a lantern. The jury returned a verdict in favor of the Railroad (D) and Wagner (P) appealed, contending that the charge to the jury had been improper.

ISSUE: Is a negligent actor liable to others who attempt to rescue those injured or imperiled by his negligent conduct?

HOLDING AND DECISION: (Cardozo, J.) Yes. A party whose negligence has caused harm or the risk thereof is liable to all persons who are injured in the course of reasonable rescue attempts. To create a danger is to invite rescue efforts. It is natural and probable that rescue attempts will be undertaken. The negligent actor is liable to the rescuer, even to the one who has time to stop and reflect before acting. It is the negligence that creates the likelihood of the rescue, and since Wagner (P) acted reasonably and was not contributorily negligent, the Railroad (D) is liable for his injuries.

▶ ANALYSIS

Wagner v. International Railway is consistent with the weight of authority. A tortfeasor may be held liable for the consequences of various foreseeable responses to his actions. The rule which makes the negligent actor liable for injuries sustained by a person engaged in a reasonable rescue attempt has been recognized and applied in a number of cases. It is based on the assumption that it is reasonable to anticipate that, if a person is injured or imperiled by the conduct of another, some third party will likely endeavor to prevent or mitigate the potential harm. Of course, the tortfeasor will not be held liable for injuries suffered by a would-be rescuer whose efforts were patently foolhardy or unreasonable.

━━◼━━

Quicknotes

FORESEEABILITY A reasonable expectation that an act or omission would result in injury.

PERIL OF RESCUERS An extension of the definition of foreseeable plaintiffs to include those persons who undertake to rescue the party put in danger by the tortfeasor; the tortfeasor thus owes a duty of care to any rescuers whom he has put in peril by exposing the plaintiff to injury.

In re Polemis & Furness, Withy & Co.

[Parties not identified.]

K.B., 3 K.B. 560 (1921).

NATURE OF CASE: Suit to recover damages for negligence.

FACT SUMMARY: The owners (P) of a ship chartered it to a business firm (D). One of the firm's (D) servants dropped a plank into a hold where benzine was stored, causing the ship to burn.

RULE OF LAW
Once the negligence of a party has been established, he may be held liable for all the consequences, foreseeable or not, of his conduct.

FACTS: The owners (P) of a ship chartered it to a firm (D) for use in transporting goods. One of the firm's (D) servants, while unloading cargo, negligently dropped a wooden plank into one of the ship's holds. The friction caused by the plank evidently created a spark, which ignited vapors from a quantity of benzine stowed in the hold. As a result, the ship burned. The owners (P) brought suit against the firm (D) that had chartered the vessel, and the matter was submitted to arbitration. The arbitrators found that the fire had been caused by the dropped plank, that the incident had been the result of negligence on the part of the firm's (D) servants, and that the charter agreement did not absolve the firm (D) from liability for losses attributable to its negligence. The arbitrators also found that it could not reasonably have been anticipated that the falling plank would cause a fire, but that the likelihood of some damage to the ship could have been anticipated. The court affirmed the award in favor of the owners (P), but the firm (D) appealed, arguing that liability should not attach because the particular harm that resulted from the dropped plank could not have been anticipated.

ISSUE: Does the liability of a negligent party extend only to those damages that could have been expected to result from his conduct?

HOLDING AND DECISION: (Lord Bankes, J.) No. Once the negligence of a party has been established, he may be held liable for all the consequences, foreseeable or not, of his conduct. The rule urged by the firm (D) has some support, but it clearly represents a minority position. The dropping of the plank constituted negligence, and it could have been anticipated that this act would cause some damage to the ship. The firm (D) is therefore liable, notwithstanding the fact that the nature and extent of the harm which actually occurred could not have been expected to result from the dropping of the board.

CONCURRENCE: (Lord Warrington, J.) The fact that some damage could have been anticipated renders the firm (D) guilty of negligence. Once this proposition has been established, it is clear that the firm (D) is liable for all damages that were the direct consequence of its acts.

CONCURRENCE: (Lord Scrutton, J.) If an act could be expected to cause damage, the party performing that act is negligent and thus becomes liable for any and all consequences of his conduct. Since dropping the plank could have been expected to cause some damage, the firm (D) is liable for all the harm that actually occurred.

ANALYSIS

The rule of the *Polemis* case is a party is negligent only if his conduct could have been expected to cause some damage, but once his negligence has been established, a party is liable for all damage that actually occurred, whether or not the nature and extent of the harm were foreseeable. A majority of American jurisdictions still subscribe to the *Polemis* rule. Of course, under *Polemis* a negligent party is not liable for harm that resulted only because of a foreseeable efficient intervening cause, because such a force breaks the causal link between the original negligence and the harm ultimately suffered.

Quicknotes

FORESEEABILITY A reasonable expectation that an act or omission would result in injury.

REMOTE DAMAGES Damages that are unexpected and unforeseeable, and over which the negligent party has no control.

Overseas Tankship (U.K.) Ltd. v. Morts Dock & Engineering Co., Ltd. (Wagon Mound [No. 1])

Ship company (D) v. Dock owner (P)

P.C. Austl. (1961) A.C. 388.

NATURE OF CASE: Action for negligence.

FACT SUMMARY: A ship owned by Overseas Tankship Ltd. (D) spilled oil. The oil was later ignited and destroyed a dock owned by Morts Dock and Engineering Co., Ltd. (P).

🏛 RULE OF LAW
An injury must be reasonably foreseeable before liability for it can be imposed.

FACTS: When a ship owned by Overseas Tankship Ltd. (Overseas) (D) left Sydney harbor, it negligently discharged oil into the water. The oil floated around a dock owned by Morts Dock and Engineering Co., Ltd. (Morts) (P). Welding operations were suspended until it was determined that the oil was not flammable. Some molten metal dropped on a piece of material floating on some debris. This apparently ignited the oil and the dock burned. The court found that Overseas (D) was liable since its negligent oil spillage was the direct cause of Morts's (P) loss. Overseas (D) alleged that this was a freak accident that was totally unforeseeable.

ISSUE: Must injury directly caused by defendant's negligence be foreseeable before it is actionable?

HOLDING AND DECISION: (Viscount Simonds, J.) Yes. Not every direct cause of injury is actionable. The defendant must reasonably be able to foresee the risk of that particular injury. We reject the doctrine espoused in *Polemis*. An injury must be caused by defendant's direct actions and the injury must be reasonably foreseeable. It is not the act itself that is actionable, but the damage resulting from the incident. Where these damages cannot be foreseen they are not deemed actionable. The igniting of the oil was a freak incident and was totally unforeseeable. [Appeal allowed.]

⚑ *ANALYSIS*

See also *Doughly v. Turner Manufacturing Co., Ltd.*, 1 Q.B. 518 (1964), where it was not foreseeable that a cover which had fallen into a vat would explode and splash hot liquid on plaintiff. The foreseeability rule has not been extended to cover the "thin skull victim" rule. A plaintiff who is injured because of unforeseeable physical defects may still collect. A defendant takes his victim as he finds him. See *Smith v. Brain Leech and Co., Ltd.*, 2 Q.B. 405 (1962).

Quicknotes

CAUSATION The aggregate effect of preceding events that bring about a tortious result; the causal connection between the actions of a tortfeasor and the injury that follows.

THIN SKULL VICTIM RULE Defendant takes victim as he finds him.

Palsgraf v. Long Island R.R.

Train passenger (P) v. Railroad (D)

N.Y. Ct. App., 162 N.E. 99 (1928).

NATURE OF CASE: Action for damages for personal injury due to negligence.

FACT SUMMARY: Mrs. Palsgraf (P) was injured on Long Island R.R.'s (R.R.'s) (D) train platform when a guard helped a passenger aboard a moving train, jostling his package, causing it to fall to the tracks. The package, containing fireworks, exploded creating a shock, which tipped a scale on Mrs. Palsgraf (P).

RULE OF LAW
The risk reasonably to be perceived defines the duty to be obeyed.

FACTS: Mrs. Palsgraf (P) purchased a ticket to Rockaway Beach from Long Island R.R. (R.R.) (D) and was waiting on the train platform. While standing on the platform, two men ran to catch a train that was pulling out from the platform. The first man jumped aboard but the second man, who appeared as if he might fall, was helped aboard by a guard who had kept the door open so they could jump aboard; a guard on the platform also helped by pushing him onto the train. The man was carrying a package wrapped in newspaper. In the process, the man dropped his innocent-looking package, which fell to the tracks. The package contained fireworks and exploded. The shock of the explosion was apparently of great enough strength to tip over some scales at the other end of the platform. The scales fell on Mrs. Palsgraf (P) and injured her. Mrs. Palsgraf (P) was awarded damages and R.R. (D) appealed.

ISSUE: Did there exist a duty by R.R. (D) to Mrs. Palsgraf (P) by which R.R. (D) would be liable had it breached that duty by its negligence?

HOLDING AND DECISION: (Cardozo, C.J.) No. If there was no foreseeable hazard as the result of an outwardly seeming innocent act with reference to the injured party, the act did not become a tort because it happened to be a wrong, though not to the injured party. Negligence is not enough upon which to base liability—there must be a duty to the injured party that could have been averted or avoided by observance of the duty. There can be no duty owed to an injured party when the wrong was committed toward someone else. The range of the duty is limited by the range of danger. The risk reasonably to be perceived defines the duty to be obeyed. There was nothing to suggest that the parcel from its appearance contained fireworks. Had the guard purposefully thrown down the package, he would have had no warning of a threat of harm to Mrs. Palsgraf (P). Just because the act was inadvertent

does not impose liability. In the abstract, negligence itself is not a tort. To be a tort it must result in the commission of a wrong. A wrong imports the violation of a right. If the wrong was not willful, it must be shown by the plaintiff that the act as to him had such great possibilities of danger, so many and so apparent, as to entitle him to protection against it though the harm was unintended. Had there been liability for the negligence toward Mrs. Palsgraf (P), she would recover for all injury "however novel or extraordinary." Accordingly, the judgment is reversed in favor of R.R. (D).

DISSENT: (Andrews, J.) The concept that "there is no negligence unless there is in the particular case a legal duty to take care, and this duty must be one owed to the plaintiff himself and not to others" is too narrow. Negligence in itself is a wrong. The rule of *In re Polemis*, 3 K.B. 560 (1921), is the correct statement of the law. A person who does a negligent act should be liable for its proximate results. Mrs. Palsgraf's (P) claim is for a breach of duty to herself and there cannot only be a duty when the harm is expected. Her right is not lesser to the right of the man with the parcel.

▶ ANALYSIS

Cardozo states that negligence is a matter of relationship between the parties. That relationship must be based upon the foreseeability of harm to the person who is, in fact, injured. Just because defendant's act was negligent, it is not necessarily wrong to the injured party. The act must be negligent and wrong to the injured party to enable him to sue in his own right. If there is no duty to the injured party, there can be no violation of a right, so even if an act was negligent it could not have violated a wrong to the injured party. The dissent, on the other hand, states that each person owes a duty of due care to society at large. Each person must refrain from any act that unreasonably threatens the safety of others. Accordingly, any party injured by a negligent act would suffer a wrong as the duty owed to each member of society at large would have been violated. A right of action must then arise despite the unforeseeability of the injury. The Restatement has accepted the view of this case that without any duty there can be no negligence, hence, never any liability to the unforeseeable injured party. Note that the determination on any question of duty is a question of law and never one for the jury. Cardozo, on the question of duty, went even farther by suggesting that the defendant could owe a duty to one

Continued on next page.

particular interest of the injured party but not to a different interest of the same party. That is to say that there could be a duty to the injured party's property interest but not to his person. So, if defendant negligently sets afire plaintiff's unoccupied building and plaintiff is injured extinguishing the blaze, damages only to the building are recoverable, or vice versa, depending upon the original duty. This theory advanced in the dictum of Palsgraf was approved by the Restatement of Torts § 281, but it has been widely opposed by most other courts. In fact, there is much authority against it and even Prosser has called this aspect of Cardozo's view "artificial." There are of course interests that, as a matter of public policy, should not be protected against certain types of wrongful conduct, but it does not follow from this that protection should always be limited to the interest which is threatened in advance.

■■

Quicknotes

FORESEEABILITY A reasonable expectation that an act or omission would result in injury.

PROXIMATE CAUSE The natural sequence of events without which an injury would not have been sustained.

■■

Marshall v. Nugent

Injured pedestrian (P) v. Car driver (D)

222 F.2d 604 (1st Cir. 1955).

NATURE OF CASE: For damages based on negligence.

FACT SUMMARY: Marshall (P) was struck by a car as he was attempting to warn oncoming traffic that a Socony-Vacuum Oil Co. (D) truck, driven by Prince, was blocking traffic.

🏛 RULE OF LAW
The defendant remains liable for the full consequences of his negligent act when the intervening force is one that a reasonable man would have foreseen as likely to occur under the circumstances, and the issue of foreseeability remains a question of fact for the jury.

FACTS: Prince, a truck driver for Socony-Vacuum Oil Co. (Socony) (D), intruded his truck into the ice-covered opposing traffic lane. He caused an oncoming car driven by Harriman—in which Marshall (P) was a passenger—to skid to a stop off of the road. No injuries occurred. Prince stopped to assist, blocking his traffic lane with his truck. Upon Prince's suggestion, Marshall (P) began walking up the hill to warn oncoming traffic. Nugent's (D) car then came around the curve, swerved to avoid hitting the truck, skidded, and struck Marshall (P). Marshall (P) charged both Socony (D) and Nugent (D) as joint tortfeasors. Socony (D) argued that Prince's negligence, having caused no injury, was not the proximate cause of the subsequent injury when Nugent's (D) car hit Marshall (P) since the injury was not foreseeable. The jury found against Socony (D) for $25,000 and for Nugent (D). (This opinion concerns only the Socony appeal.)

ISSUE: Is the defendant liable when the injury results from an act of another, which act is deemed by the jury to be a foreseeable intervening act?

HOLDING AND DECISION: (Magruder, C.J.) Yes. In the development of the doctrine of proximate causation, the courts have attempted to confine the liability of the negligent actor to those harmful consequences that result from a risk, the foreseeability of which causes the defendant's conduct to be negligent. However, the term "proximate" does not mean that the defendant's act must be the immediate or next cause of the plaintiff's injury. Often the injury may be brought about by an intervening force of nature or act of a third person which seems quite remote in a chain of events (e.g., proximate cause has been found where the plaintiff fainted, fracturing his skull, following a near collision). Many cases have held that a defendant, whose negligence causes a traffic tie-up, is liable for injuries and/or damages caused by an oncoming motorist. In the instant case, it was foreseeable that Marshall (P), having been delayed on a business journey by Prince's negligence, would get out on the highway and assist so that the journey might continue. The issue of the foreseeability of the risk and contributory negligence was a proper question of fact for the jury whose decision will stand. Affirmed.

▶ ANALYSIS

The Restatement of Torts § 453(e) holds that the defendant is not liable for consequences which, looking backward after the incident, with complete knowledge of all that has occurred, would appear to be "highly extraordinary." The main requisite for liability—to be decided by the jury—is that the response to the defendant's negligent act be a normal one. An abnormal response breaks the chain of causality.

━━━

Quicknotes

CONTRIBUTORY NEGLIGENCE Behavior on the part of an injured plaintiff falling below the standard of ordinary care that contributes to the defendant's negligence, resulting in the plaintiff's injury.

FORESEEABILITY A reasonable expectation that an act or omission would result in injury.

PROXIMATE CAUSE The natural sequence of events without which an injury would not have been sustained.

━━━

Virden v. Betts and Beer Construction Company

Injured worker (P) v. Construction company (D)

Iowa Sup. Ct., 656 N.W. 2d 805 (2003).

NATURE OF CASE: Appeal from reversal of summary judgment granted to defendant in negligence action.

FACT SUMMARY: Virden (P) contended that construction companies' (D) faulty installation of a ceiling was the proximate cause of his fall from a tall ladder he was using to repair the ceiling.

RULE OF LAW

As a matter of law, proximate cause is not established where a defendant's negligence is not a substantial factor in bringing about the plaintiff's injury.

FACTS: Virden (P), a high school maintenance worker, had to reinstall an angle iron that had fallen from the ceiling of the school's new wrestling room, which was built by Betts & Beer Construction and Stroh Corporation (the "construction companies") (D). As he was bolting the iron into place, he fell from the top of the 10-foot ladder on which he was standing. Neither Virden (P) nor the school contacted the construction companies (D) before he commenced work, nor did Virden (P) seek any assistance in securing the ladder, the placement of which was hampered by weight lifting equipment. He sued the construction companies (D), claiming that their negligent construction proximately caused his fall. The trial court granted summary judgment to the construction companies (D), but the state's intermediate appellate court reversed. The state's highest court granted review.

ISSUE: As a matter of law, is proximate cause established where a defendant's negligence is not a substantial factor in bringing about the plaintiff's injury?

HOLDING AND DECISION: (Neuman, J.) No. As a matter of law, proximate cause is not established where a defendant's negligence is not a substantial factor in bringing about the plaintiff's injury. The construction companies' (D) duty was to ensure that users of the room were not injured by parts falling from the ceiling. A breach of that duty is only actionable negligence if it is also the proximate cause of an injury. To satisfy proximate causation, (1) the defendant's conduct must have in fact caused the damages; and (2) the policy of the law must require the defendant to be legally responsible for them. Regarding the first element, the plaintiff must, at a minimum, prove that the damages would not have occurred but for the defendant's negligence. Here, this but-for test is satisfied, because Virden (P) would not have had to get on the ladder but for the construction companies' (D) negligence.

However, Virden (P) must also show that the construction companies' (D) negligence was a substantial factor in bringing about his injury. Because the duty to construct a solid ceiling is not to protect repairmen from perching on tall ladders but to prevent collapsing parts of the ceiling from falling on persons below, it was not foreseeable that a negligently welded angle iron would cause a ladder to tip or collapse—and here it is clear that the instrumentality of Virden's (P) injury was such a ladder, not the defective angle iron. Therefore, the trial court correctly granted summary judgment to the construction companies (D). Reversed.

ANALYSIS

The court noted that summary judgment on the question of proximate cause is rarely granted, since issues of proximate cause, like negligence, are generally left to the jury to resolve as fact matters. However, in exceptional circumstances, the issue of proximate cause may be decided as a matter of law on summary judgment where the material facts fail to show any causal link between the negligence and injury. The exception case is one where, after construing the evidence in its most favorable light and resolving all doubts in favor of the party seeking to establish proximate cause, the relationship between cause and effect nonetheless is so apparent and so unrelated to defendant's conduct that no reasonable jury could conclude defendant's fault was a proximate cause of plaintiff's injuries.

Quicknotes

ACTIONABLE Unlawful activity from which a cause of action may arise.

NEGLIGENCE Conduct falling below the standard of care that a reasonable person would demonstrate under similar conditions.

SUMMARY JUDGMENT Judgment rendered by a court in response to a motion made by one of the parties, claiming that the lack of a question of material fact in respect to an issue warrants disposition of the issue without consideration by the jury.

Hebert v. Enos

Neighbor (P) v. Neighbor (D)

Mass App. Ct., 806 N.E.2d 452 (2004).

NATURE OF CASE: Appeal from summary judgment for defendant in negligence action.

FACT SUMMARY: Hebert (P) contended that Enos's (D) faulty repairs of a second-floor toilet was a legal cause of the electrical shock and injuries Hebert (P) suffered when he went to water Enos's (D) flowers.

🏛 RULE OF LAW
A claim of negligence may be dismissed as a matter of law where the plaintiff cannot show that his injuries were a reasonably foreseeable consequence of the defendant's negligent conduct.

FACTS: Hebert (P) received a severe electrical shock when he went to water Enos's (D) flowers. Hebert (P) claimed that Enos's (D) faulty repairs of a second-floor toilet caused the toilet to overflow, and that the flooding water reacted with the home's electrical system, creating an electrical current that shocked and injured Hebert (P) when he touched the outside water faucet. Hebert (P) brought suit against Enos (D) for negligence, and Enos (D) moved for summary judgment, which the trial court granted on the ground that Hebert's (P) injuries were not a reasonably foreseeable consequence of Enos's (D) negligence. The state's intermediate appellate court granted review.

ISSUE: May a claim of negligence be dismissed as a matter of law where the plaintiff cannot show that his injuries were a reasonably foreseeable consequence of the defendant's negligent conduct?

HOLDING AND DECISION: (Kafker, J.) Yes. A claim of negligence may be dismissed as a matter of law where the plaintiff cannot show that his injuries were a reasonably foreseeable consequence of the defendant's negligent conduct. Hebert (P) established that Enos's (D) faulty toilet repair resulted in flooding, deterioration of electrical wiring inside the house, and, ultimately, severe electrical shock to Hebert (P) when he touched the outside faucet. Nonetheless, summary judgment is appropriate, despite this uninterrupted causal chain, if Hebert (P) cannot show that his injuries were a reasonably foreseeable result of Enos's (D) negligent conduct. Here, in light of the likelihood, character, and location of the harm, the injuries to Hebert (P) were a "highly extraordinary" consequence of a defective second-floor toilet, such that the law does not require a defendant in Enos's (D) position to guard against them. Merely because water and electricity are involved does not require a higher standard of care than is traditionally applied in negligence theory; the appropriate

standard is whether the defendant exercised care that is reasonable in the circumstances. Because Enos (D) could not have reasonably foreseen the harm that befell Hebert (P), the unbroken causal chain that results from Enos's (D) negligence does not legally constitute proximate causation of Hebert's (P) injuries. Affirmed.

▶ ANALYSIS

The issue of foreseeability is ordinarily a question of fact for the jury, but as this case demonstrates, a court may decide the issue as a matter of law in the absence of evidence that the risk that resulted in the plaintiff's injury should reasonably have been anticipated by the defendant. As a practical matter, in deciding the foreseeability question, it is not critical whether the court defines a duty as limited to guarding against reasonably foreseeable risk of harm or whether it defines the necessary causal connection between a breach of duty and some harm as one in which the harm was a reasonably foreseeable consequence of the breach of a duty.

━━■■━━

Quicknotes

NEGLIGENCE Conduct falling below the standard of care that a reasonable person would demonstrate under similar conditions.

PROXIMATE CAUSE The natural sequence of events without which an injury would not have been sustained.

SUMMARY JUDGMENT Judgment rendered by a court in response to a motion made by one of the parties, claiming that the lack of a question of material fact in respect to an issue warrants disposition of the issue without consideration by the jury.

━━■■━━

Mitchell v. Rochester Ry.

Pregnant train passenger (P) v. Railroad (D)

N.Y. Ct. App., 45 N.E. 354 (1896).

NATURE OF CASE: Appeal from decision in a negligence action.

FACT SUMMARY: Mitchell (P) sued Rochester Railway Co. (D) for negligence when Mitchell (P) was frightened by the horses pulling Rochester Railway Co.'s (D) horse car, causing her to faint and ultimately to have a miscarriage.

🏛 RULE OF LAW
Proximate damages are ordinary and natural results of the negligence charged and those that are usual and may, therefore, be expected.

FACTS: Mitchell (P) was standing at a crosswalk waiting to board one of Rochester Railway Co.'s (Rochester's) (D) cars. While just about to step aboard the car, one of Rochester's (D) horse cars came down the street. As the car drew near to Mitchell (P), the team of horses drawing the car turned to the right and came close enough to Mitchell (P) that she was standing between the horses' heads when they were stopped. Mitchell (P) testified that from fright and excitement caused by the proximity of the horses, she became unconscious and that the result was ultimately a miscarriage and consequent illness. Medical testimony was given to the effect that the mental shock Mitchell (P) received was sufficient to produce that result. At trial, Rochester (D) was held negligent, and Mitchell (P) was held free from all contributory negligence. Rochester (D) appealed.

ISSUE: Are proximate damages the ordinary and natural results of the negligence charged and those that are usual and may, therefore, be expected?

HOLDING AND DECISION: (Martin, J.) Yes. Proximate damages are ordinary and natural results of the negligence charged and those that are usual and may, therefore, be expected. The single question presented here is whether Mitchell (P) is entitled to recover from Rochester's (D) negligence, which occasioned her fright and alarm and resulted in her injuries. Here, it cannot be properly said that Mitchell's (P) miscarriage was the proximate result of Rochester's (D) negligence. Mitchell's (P) injuries were plainly the result of an accident or unusual combination of circumstances, which could not have been reasonably anticipated and over which Rochester (D) had no control. Hence, her damages were too remote to justify a recovery in this action. No recovery can be had for injuries sustained by fright occasioned by the negligence of another, where there is no immediate personal injury. Reversed and dismissed.

▶ ANALYSIS

Early cases required actual contact or "impact" to a plaintiff before that plaintiff was permitted to recover for negligently inflicted emotional distress. Resistance by the courts to recovery for emotional distress was based on the premise that such damages were too remote and also, that many spurious suits would be brought if such recoveries were permitted. Many courts, however, did stretch the "impact" concept and allowed plaintiffs to recover for even the slightest impact, as long as some type of impact had occurred. For example, in *Kenney v. Wong Len*, 128 A. 343 (N.H. 1925), the plaintiff was allowed recovery when evidence revealed that a mouse hair in a spoonful of stew touched the inside of plaintiff's mouth.

◼▬◼

Quicknotes

CONTRIBUTORY NEGLIGENCE Behavior on the part of an injured plaintiff falling below the standard of ordinary care that contributes to the defendant's negligence, resulting in the plaintiff's injury.

PROXIMATE CAUSE The natural sequence of events without which an injury would not have been sustained.

◼▬◼

Dillon v. Legg

Mother of infant killed in car crash (P) v. Driver of car (D)

Cal. Sup. Ct., 441 P.2d 912 (1968) (en banc).

NATURE OF CASE: Action for emotional distress.

FACT SUMMARY: Dillon (P) saw her daughter get hit by Legg's (D) car.

RULE OF LAW

The zone of danger rule does not bar a recovery for negligent infliction of emotional distress where a close family member outside the zone views an accident causing an injury or death to another family member.

FACTS: Legg (D) negligently struck Dillon's (P) infant daughter with his vehicle, killing her. Both Dillon (P) and her other daughter (P) witnessed the accident. The daughter (P) saw it from a curb near the accident and Dillon (P) saw it from a distance. Both Dillon (P) and her daughter (P) brought an action for negligent infliction of emotional distress. The daughter's (P) claim was allowed, but Dillon's (P) was dismissed because she was not within the zone of danger created by Legg's (D) actions. Dillon (P) appealed.

ISSUE: May a close family member viewing the negligent injury or death of another family member recover for negligent infliction of emotional distress even if outside the zone of danger?

HOLDING AND DECISION: (Tobriner, J.) Yes. Whether or not a plaintiff who witnesses the negligent injury of a close family member is within the zone of danger should be irrelevant to the allowance of recovery for the shock and trauma suffered by viewing the accident. A defendant's duty should not be fixed by arbitrary rules such as the zone of danger. The harm complained of by Dillon (P) was foreseeable, and Legg (D) owed her a duty of care. As to the possibility of fraudulent and indefinable claims, the danger of such actions is no greater than in other cases involving emotional harm. The court would be avoiding its responsibility to separate fraudulent from legitimate claims by barring all plaintiffs alleging such an injury. As to indefinable claims, the tort concept of foreseeability may provide adequate limits to liability. Factors which may be considered are: (1) was plaintiff near the scene of the accident; (2) was the shock or emotional trauma due to seeing or merely hearing about the accident; and (3) the closeness of the relationship between the plaintiff and the victim. Here, Dillon (P) saw the accident; the injuries were caused by the sight of the accident; and she was the parent of the victim. All of these factors are clearly foreseeable, and she should be permitted to recover. Reversed.

DISSENT: (Traynor, C.J.) The zone of danger rule is correct.

DISSENT: (Burke, J.) Too many unanswered questions are left by the majority. Examples are emotional injury from a mistaken belief of injury; how near is "near;" how close a family member must the victim be for plaintiff to recover, etc.

ANALYSIS

Dillon is a minority holding. The zone of danger rule is applied in most jurisdictions and recovery is limited to fear for one's own safety or from physical manifestations of the trauma. What constitutes physical injury varies within the jurisdictions. In *Cosgrove v. Beymer*, 244 F. Supp. 824, (D. Del. 1965), dizziness, nervousness, and a mild headache were deemed insufficient. In *Daley v. LaCroix*, 384 Mich. 4, 179 N.W. 2d 390 (1970), emotional disturbances and traumatic neurosis were deemed to constitute physical injury.

Quicknotes

INTENTIONAL INFLICTION OF EMOTIONAL DISTRESS Intentional and extreme behavior on the part of the wrongdoer with the intent to cause the victim to suffer from severe emotional distress, or with reckless indifference, resulting in the victim's suffering from severe emotional distress.

NEGLIGENT INFLICTION OF EMOTIONAL DISTRESS Violation of the duty of care owed to another that occurs when an individual creates a foreseeable risk of injury to the other person, which causes emotional distress resulting in some physical harm to that person.

CHAPTER 6

Affirmative Duties

Quick Reference Rules of Law

PAGE

1. *Buch v. Amory Manufacturing Co.* A landowner has no duty to warn a trespasser of the
existence of a dangerous condition or object even if the trespasser is a mere child.   100

2. *Hurley v. Eddingfield.* A physician is not required to treat anyone who requests medical
attention.   101

3. *Montgomery v. National Convoy & Trucking Co.* A duty to warn of an existing danger must be
carried out in a manner reasonably calculated to prevent harm.   102

4. *Robert Addie & Sons (Collieries), Ltd. v. Dumbreck.* Although a landowner may not
deliberately harm a trespasser, a landowner has no duty to protect a trespasser from risks or
dangers.   103

5. *Rowland v. Christian.* Where a land occupier is aware of a concealed condition involving, in
the absence of precautions, an unreasonable risk of harm to those coming in contact
with it, and is aware that a person is about to come in contact with it, the failure to warn or
to repair the condition constitutes negligence.   104

6. *Coggs v. Bernard.* A party is liable for negligent acts committed in the course of performing a
contract even if the contract itself, because of a lack of consideration, could not have been
enforced.   105

7. *Erie Railroad Co. v. Stewart.* A party who voluntarily assumes a duty not imposed upon
him by law may be deemed negligent if, without proper notice, he discontinues his
performance of that duty.   106

8. *Moch Co. v. Rensselaer Water Co.* A party whose performance of a contract incidentally
confers a benefit upon third parties does not owe any duty to continue to perform in a manner
that is satisfactory to those parties.   107

9. *Kline v. 1500 Massachusetts Avenue Apartment Corp.* A landlord is responsible for
maintaining the common areas of his property so as to minimize the risk that tenants may be
exposed to an unreasonable risk of criminal attack.   108

10. *Tarasoff v. Regents of University of California.* Where a person bears a special relationship
to a party or others who may be the victim of the conduct, it is reasonably foreseeable a legally
cognizable duty arises to protect or control the third party.   109

Buch v. Amory Manufacturing Co.

Injured child (P) v. Mill owner (D)

N.H. Sup. Ct., 44 A. 809 (1897).

NATURE OF CASE: Suit seeking damages for personal injuries.

FACT SUMMARY: Eight-year-old Buch (P) wandered into an Amory Manufacturing Co. (Amory) (D) mill and injured his hand when it was crushed by machinery. One of Amory's (D) overseers had observed Buch (P), but had not forced Buch (P) to leave the premises.

🏛 RULE OF LAW
A landowner has no duty to warn a trespasser of the existence of a dangerous condition or object even if the trespasser is a mere child.

FACTS: Eight-year-old Buch (P) was a trespasser in an Amory Manufacturing Co. (Amory) (D) mill. One of Amory's (D) overseers saw Buch (P) and told him to leave the premises, but this warning went unheeded because Buch (P) understood no English. The overseer made no other efforts to have Buch (P) removed, despite the fact that potentially dangerous weaving machinery was being operated within the mill. Buch (P) crushed his hand in a machine his thirteen-year-old brother, an Amory (D) employee, was teaching him to run. Buch (P) later sued to recover damages and, after Amory's (D) motion for a directed verdict had been denied, the jury returned a verdict in Buch's (P) favor. Amory (D) then appealed.

ISSUE: Is a landowner obligated to warn a child trespasser of the presence of potential dangers?

HOLDING AND DECISION: (Carpenter, C.J.) No. A landowner has no duty to warn a trespasser of the existence of a dangerous condition or object, even if the trespasser is a mere child. Moral obligations notwithstanding, Amory (D) was not bound to warn young Buch (P) of the dangerous machines or to protect him against harm. An adult trespasser need not be warned even of latent dangers. Similarly, a landowner has no duty to warn the child trespasser of an open and visible peril. The law recognizes a clear distinction between the duty to do no wrongful act and the duty to protect others against danger. The latter duty is moral only, and its breach has no legal significance. The situation is unchanged by the fact that the party choosing not to fulfill this moral duty is the owner of the property upon which harm occurs. No legal duty to protect a trespasser from harm exists, and for that reason judgment must be rendered in favor of Amory (D).

▶ ANALYSIS

Buch v. Amory Manufacturing Co. illustrates the distinction, in terms of liability, between active and passive conduct. Active negligence subjects a party to liability for damages caused by his conduct. A failure to act, on the other hand, does not ordinarily make a party liable for any of the damages he could have prevented, no matter how easily he could have caused the harm to be averted. Thus, no one is required by law to act as a "Good Samaritan." Of course, where one party has created the danger with which another party is threatened, or the two enjoy some special relationship, a duty to warn of or protect against the peril may arise. Note that the facts of the *Buch* case would likely result in a different outcome today since the duties of landowners to trespassers, particularly to those whose presence has been discovered, has been expanded since *Buch* was decided.

Quicknotes

GOOD SAMARITAN LAW A statute relieving a bystander from tort liability for the attempted rescue of another.

TRESPASSERS Persons present on the land of another without the knowledge or express permission of the owner, and to whom only a minimum duty of care is owed for injuries incurred while on the premises.

Hurley v. Eddingfield

Decedent's estate (P) v. Family physician (D)

Ind. Sup. Ct., 59 N.E. 1058 (1901).

NATURE OF CASE: Appeal of judgment for the defendant in wrongful death action.

FACT SUMMARY: A decedent's estate (P) sued the decedent's family physician (D) when the physician (D) refused to come to the decedent's aid.

🏛 RULE OF LAW
A physician is not required to treat anyone who requests medical attention.

FACTS: Prior to dying, the decedent had sent a messenger to retrieve the decedent's licensed family physician (D). The physician (D) refused to render aid to the decedent and the decedent subsequently died. The decedent's estate (P) sued the physician (D) for wrongfully causing the death of his intestate. The lower court found in favor of the physician (D) and the estate (P) appealed.

ISSUE: Was the physician lawfully required to come to the decedent's aid?

HOLDING AND DECISION: (Baker, J.) No. The physician (D) was not required to come to the decedent's aid. The act regulating the practice of medicine requires only that those who are licensed must meet certain qualifications, and subjects those who practice without a license to certain penalties. The State does not require those who are licensed to practice at all or according to certain terms against their will. Affirmed.

▶ ANALYSIS

This case exemplifies the sense of individualism that pervaded the law at the time.

▬▬

Quicknotes

WRONGFUL DEATH An action brought by the beneficiaries of a deceased person, claiming that the deceased's death was the result of wrongful conduct by the defendant.

▬▬

Montgomery v. National Convoy & Trucking Co.

Injured car driver (P) v. Trucking company (D)

S.C. Sup. Ct., 195 S.E. 247 (1937).

NATURE OF CASE: Suit seeking damages for personal injuries.

FACT SUMMARY: Two National Convoy & Trucking Co. (D) trucks stalled on an icy highway, blocking it completely. Because no warning had been posted, Montgomery (P) saw the trucks too late to avoid a collision.

RULE OF LAW

A duty to warn of an existing danger must be carried out in a manner reasonably calculated to prevent harm.

FACTS: Two National Convoy & Trucking Co. (National) (D) trucks stalled on an icy highway, completely blocking the road. The trucks had stalled not far from a hill, and the drivers of the trucks knew, or should have known, that the icy conditions made it impossible for a car coming over the hill to avoid hitting the trucks if they were not seen until the car had actually started down the hill. Nevertheless, the drivers posted no warnings except for the truck lights and some highway flares which were placed at the site of the stalled vehicles. About 15 minutes after the trucks had stopped Montgomery's (P) car came over the hill and could not stop in time to prevent a collision. Montgomery (P) sustained injuries, and ultimately won a judgment against National (D). On appeal, National (D) argued that the scope of its drivers' duty had not obligated them to post a warning at or before the top of the hill.

ISSUE: Will a party be absolved of liability if he has given at least some warning of a condition of which he was obligated to make the public aware?

HOLDING AND DECISION: (Baker, J.) No. A duty to warn of an existing danger must be carried out in a manner reasonably calculated to prevent harm. The drivers were guilty of no active negligence, but their failure to post an adequate warning constituted negligence by omission. The flares and lights were not effective to warn of the danger that drivers faced. Through no fault of their own, the drivers had created a traffic hazard, and they had a duty to warn other motorists of that danger. They did not adequately discharge that duty, because other drivers were not apprised of the peril in time to avoid contact. Since National's (D) drivers negligently failed to provide a sufficient warning, the judgment in favor of Montgomery (P) must be affirmed.

ANALYSIS

The rule of *Montgomery v. National Convoy & Trucking Co.* is supported by reason and logic and is declarative of the weight of authority. The duty to warn of impending danger may derive from various circumstances. But, in all contexts, it can be discharged only by providing a warning which promises to put parties on reasonable notice of the dangerous condition. It is expected that the party owing the duty to warn will, in effect, place himself in the position of those in need of the warning, and will then provide a notice that will be effective in light of all pertinent factors and circumstances.

Quicknotes

DUTY TO WARN An obligation owed by an owner or occupier of land to persons who come onto the premises, to inform them of defects or active operations which may cause injury.

MISFEASANCE The commission of a lawful act in a wrongful manner.

NONFEASANCE The omission, or failure to perform, an obligation.

Robert Addie & Sons (Collieries), Ltd. v. Dumbreck

Ash removal company (D) v. Father of deceased (P)

Scot. Ct. Sess., A.C. 358 (1929).

NATURE OF CASE: Damages for wrongful death.

FACT SUMMARY: Despite warnings to keep off Robert Addie & Sons (Collieries), Ltd. (Addie) (D) property, Dumbreck's (P) four-year-old son went onto Addie's (D) land and was killed by a wheel which was part of a coal ash removal system.

RULE OF LAW
Although a landowner may not deliberately harm a trespasser, a landowner has no duty to protect a trespasser from risks or dangers.

FACTS: Robert Addie & Sons (Collieries), Ltd. (D) operated a coal ash removal system in an open field. The field was surrounded by a hedge, but gaps in the hedge enabled people to enter or traverse the field almost at will. Addie's (D) employees constantly warned both children and adults to keep off the premises, and a sign on one of the field's two gates warned that trespassers would be prosecuted. Nevertheless, people of all ages frequently crossed or played on the field. Part of Addie's (D) ash removal system consisted of a large wheel around which wound a heavy cable when the system's motor was in operation. The wheel was unprotected except for four boards that covered the top of the wheel but left a large space exposed at the bottom. Dumbreck's (P) four-year-old son was sitting on or near the boards covering the wheel when he was sucked into the mechanism by the pulley. Death resulted, and Dumbreck (P) sued Addie (D). Judgment was rendered in favor of Dumbreck (P), but on appeal Addie (D) argued that it had owed the child no duty of care since he had been a mere trespasser.

ISSUE: Does a landowner have a duty to protect trespassers from dangerous conditions on his property?

HOLDING AND DECISION: (Lord Hailsham, J.C.) No. Although a landowner may not deliberately harm a trespasser, a landowner has no duty to protect a trespasser from risks or dangers. The trespasser, unlike the invitee or the licensee, is owed no duty of care. Young Dumbreck was a mere trespasser, and the fact that Addie (D) knew that outsiders frequented its premises did not confer upon the child the status of a licensee. Addie (D) therefore owed young Dumbreck no duty of care and was entitled to judgment. Affirmed.

CONCURRENCE: (Viscount Dunedin, J.) The legal distinctions between invitee, a licensee, and a trespasser are clear and rigid, although disputes may arise when the facts of a case are analyzed in terms of these categories. A trespasser does not rise to the status of a licensee unless his presence has been permitted or willingly tolerated by the landowner. Addie (D) took every reasonable step to exclude outsiders. Thus, all intruders, including the unfortunate child, qualify as mere trespassers to whom no duty of care was or is owed.

ANALYSIS

Courts today are reluctant to apply the harsh common law rule that no duty of care is owed to a trespasser. In this country, the common law rule is often circumvented by elevating the apparent trespasser to the status of a licensee, or by holding that the trespasser had been "discovered" by the landowner, and thus was owed a duty of care.

Quicknotes

ATTRACTIVE NUISANCE DOCTRINE The assignment of liability to an owner or occupier of land who permits a dangerous instrumentality to remain on the property, knowing it is likely to attract children who have access to it, and who fails to take reasonable steps to prevent such injury.

INVITEE A person who enters upon another's property by an express or implied invitation and to whom the owner of the property owes a duty of care to guard against injury from those hazards that are discoverable through the exercise of reasonable care.

LICENSEES Persons known to an owner or occupier of land, who come onto the premises voluntarily and for a specific purpose although not necessarily with the consent of the owner.

TRESPASSERS Persons present on the land of another without the knowledge or express permission of the owner, and to whom only a minimum duty of care is owed for injuries incurred while on the premises.

Rowland v. Christian

Injured houseguest (P) v. Homeowner (D)

Cal. Sup. Ct., 443 P.2d 561 (1968).

NATURE OF CASE: Appeal from a motion for summary judgment.

FACT SUMMARY: Rowland (P), a licensee in the apartment of Christian (D), was injured by a broken water faucet handle. Christian (D) knew about the broken handle, but did not warn Rowland (P).

🏛 RULE OF LAW
Where a land occupier is aware of a concealed condition involving, in the absence of precautions, an unreasonable risk of harm to those coming in contact with it, and is aware that a person is about to come in contact with it, the failure to warn or to repair the condition constitutes negligence.

FACTS: Rowland (P), a social guest in Christian's (D) apartment, was injured by a cracked water faucet handle that broke in his hand. Rowland (P) asked permission to use the bathroom, and Christian (D) was aware of the cracked handle on the water faucet in the bathroom, having informed the landlord of the need to repair it. Christian (D) did not inform Rowland (P) of the danger, however. Rowland (P) brought an action for negligence against Christian (D), and Christian (D) moved for and was granted summary judgment. Rowland (P) appealed.

ISSUE: Where a land occupier is aware of a concealed condition on the land involving, in the absence of precautions, an unreasonable risk of harm to those coming in contact with it, and, is aware that a person is about to come in contact with it, is the failure to warn or to repair, negligence?

HOLDING AND DECISION: (Peters, J.) Yes. Where a land occupier is aware of a concealed condition involving, in the absence of precautions, an unreasonable risk of harm to those coming in contact with it, and is aware that a person is about to come in contact with it, the failure to warn or to repair the condition constitutes negligence. Common law has departed from the usual rules of negligence where persons have been injured after entering upon the land of another. In such cases, the courts, having developed out of a feudal society based upon land ownership, have looked to see first whether the injured was an invitee (business guest), licensee (social guest), or trespasser. These classifications have grown obsolete in a modern industrial society. "A man's life or limb does not become less worthy of protection by the law … because he has come upon the land of another without permission or with permission but without a business purpose." A guest should be reasonably legally entitled to rely upon a warning of the dangerous condition so that he, like the host, can be able to take special precautions against it. Reversed.

DISSENT: (Burke, J.) The court, by overturning centuries of tort law, has failed to provide guiding legal principles and has invaded the province of the legislature.

▌ ANALYSIS

California was the first state to do away with the status of an entrant upon land. Few states have followed. Colorado now considers status to be just one factor in determining negligence, but not determinative in itself. The more common approach is to no longer distinguish between invitees and licensees but to retain the distinction as to the status of trespassers.

■━■

Quicknotes

FORESEEABILITY OF HARM An inquiry into the relatedness of events that contributed to the plaintiff's injury; whether the harm was foreseeable determines whether the tortfeasor's conduct was the proximate cause of the injury.

INVITEE A person who enters upon another's property by an express or implied invitation and to whom the owner of the property owes a duty of care to guard against injury from those hazards that are discoverable through the exercise of reasonable care.

LICENSEES Persons known to an owner or occupier of land, who come onto the premises voluntarily and for a specific purpose although not necessarily with the consent of the owner.

■━■

Coggs v. Bernard

Owner of brandy casks (P) v. Cask mover (D)

K.B., 92 Eng. Rep. 107 (1703).

NATURE OF CASE: Suit to recover for damages to property.

FACT SUMMARY: Bernard (D) agreed to move casks of brandy for Coggs (P), who allegedly gave no consideration in exchange for that service. While Bernard (D) was moving the casks, they became damaged.

RULE OF LAW

A party is liable for negligent acts committed in the course of performing a contract even if the contract itself, because of a lack of consideration, could not have been enforced.

FACTS: Bernard (D) agreed to move some casks of brandy for Coggs (P). The casks were damaged during the move, and Coggs (P) sued and won judgment. Bernard (D) moved for arrest of judgment, contending that it had not been alleged that he was a common porter or that he had received any reward or consideration.

ISSUE: Is a party liable for his negligent performance of a contract that could not have been enforced?

HOLDING AND DECISION: (Gould, J.) Yes. A party is liable for negligent acts committed in the course of performing a contract even if the contract itself, because of a lack of consideration, could not have been enforced. Anyone who undertakes to carry another's goods is liable for harm caused by his negligence, and it makes no difference that he is not a common porter and received no consideration. Coggs (P) entrusted Bernard (D) with the casks, and it was because Bernard (D) began performance and ultimately acted negligently that damages were suffered. Therefore, the judgment in favor of Coggs (P) was appropriate.

CONCURRENCE: (Holt, C.J.) The fact that Coggs (P) entrusted his goods to Bernard (D) was sufficient consideration to obligate Bernard (D) to take adequate care of them. If the contract had been purely executory, no action would lie against Bernard (D), but since Bernard (D) had begun performance, he is liable for the harm to Coggs' (P) property.

▶ ANALYSIS

Coggs v. Bernard was illustrative of the confluence of tort law and contract law. More than a century later, in *Thorne v. Deas*, 4 Johns. Cas. 84 (N.Y. Sup. Ct. 1809), the court was confronted with a case by the co-owner of a ship who lost the vessel after the other co-owner had failed to fulfill his gratuitous promise to obtain insurance. The court denied recovery, noting that there had been no consideration and that the defendant's conduct had constituted mere nonfeasance. Had the defendant embarked upon performance, and thereafter been guilty of misfeasance, the plaintiff would have been entitled to recover, the *Thorne v. Deas* court reasoned. The plaintiffs in both *Coggs v. Bernard* and *Thorne v. Deas* might succeed today by invoking the doctrine of promissory estoppel.

Quicknotes

FAILURE TO WARN The failure of an owner or occupier of land to inform persons present on the property of defects or active operations that may cause injury.

MALFEASANCE The commission of an unlawful act.

MISFEASANCE The commission of a lawful act in a wrongful manner.

NEGLIGENCE PER SE Conduct amounting to negligence as a matter of law because it is either so contrary to ordinary prudence or it is in violation of statute.

PROMISSORY ESTOPPEL A promise that is enforceable if the promisor should reasonably expect that it will induce action or forbearance on the part of the promisee, and does in fact cause such action or forbearance, and it is the only means of avoiding injustice.

Erie Railroad Co. v. Stewart

Railroad (D) v. Injured truck passenger (P)

40 F.2d 855 (6th Cir. 1930).

NATURE OF CASE: Suit seeking damages for personal injuries.

FACT SUMMARY: Stewart (P) was a passenger in a vehicle that was struck by a train. The Railroad (D) customarily maintained a watchman at the site, but he had provided no warning until too late to prevent the accident.

🏛 RULE OF LAW
A party who voluntarily assumes a duty not imposed upon him by law may be deemed negligent if, without proper notice, he discontinues his performance of that duty.

FACTS: Stewart (P) was a passenger in an automobile truck that was struck by an Erie R. R. (the Railroad) (D) train. The Railroad (D) customarily maintained a watchman at the crossing where the accident occurred, although no statute or ordinance required it to do so, and Stewart (P) was aware of the fact that the watchman was ordinarily on duty. On the day of the accident, however, the watchman was in or near his shanty and provided no warning of the oncoming train until too late to prevent the collision. Stewart (P) sued the Railroad (D) to recover for injuries sustained in the accident, and at trial the jury was instructed that the watchman's absence, after a long period of having been stationed at the site to the knowledge of Stewart (P), would constitute negligence as a matter of law. The Railroad (D), appealing from a judgment in Stewart's (P) favor, argued that the jury instruction had been erroneous.

ISSUE: May a party be charged with negligence if he abruptly abandons performance of a duty which he had voluntarily assumed?

HOLDING AND DECISION: (Hickenlooper, C.J.) Yes. A party who voluntarily assumes a duty not imposed upon him by law may be deemed negligent if, without proper notice, he discontinues his performance of that duty. The Railroad (D) had no statutory duty to post a watchman, but by doing so it invited motorists to proceed in reliance upon the implied assurance that any dangers would be made known in time to avert catastrophe. The Railroad (D) was not necessarily required to retain a watchman around the clock, but any time that the watchman's duties were not being carried out, the Railroad (D) had a responsibility to apprise the public of that fact. Its failure to do so was prima facie evidence of negligence, and in the absence of anything to rebut the allegation of negligence, the judgment in favor of Stewart (P) was appropriate. Affirmed.

CONCURRENCE: (Tuttle, J.) It is enough that the Railroad (D) had created a duty to post a watchman by virtue of having done so in the past. It should have assumed that the public at large would rely upon the existence of the watchman, and it is thus superfluous to show that Stewart (P) himself actually relied upon the presence of an adequate lookout.

▶ ANALYSIS

Many other cases can be found in which negligence has been predicated upon the defendant's abandonment of a voluntary course of conduct that had been undertaken to promote the safety of the plaintiff. A large number of these cases seem to accept the proposition that liability will not attach unless actual reliance can be demonstrated. The reliance upon which liability depends need not always be that of the plaintiff, however. In some cases it has been deemed sufficient that a third party refrained from acting on behalf of the plaintiff because of that third party's reliance upon the defendant's continuation of a custom.

Quicknotes

FAILURE TO WARN The failure of an owner or occupier of land to inform persons present on the property of defects or active operations that may cause injury.

NEGLIGENCE PER SE Conduct amounting to negligence as a matter of law because it is either so contrary to ordinary prudence or it is in violation of statute.

PRIMA FACIE EVIDENCE Evidence presented by a party that is sufficient, in the absence of contradictory evidence, to support the fact or issue for which it is offered.

Moch Co. v. Rensselaer Water Co.

Warehouse destroyed by fire (P) v. Water company (D)

N.Y. Ct. App., 159 N.E. 896 (1928).

NATURE OF CASE: Suit to recover for damage to property.

FACT SUMMARY: Rensselaer Water Co. (D) contracted to supply water to the city of Rensselaer. A fire destroyed a warehouse owned by Moch Co. (P). Adequate water service could have prevented the fire from spreading to the warehouse.

🏛 RULE OF LAW
A party whose performance of a contract incidentally confers a benefit upon third parties does not owe any duty to continue to perform in a manner that is satisfactory to those parties.

FACTS: Rensselaer Water Co. (Water Co.) (D) contracted to supply water for the city of Rensselaer. Water was to be furnished for sewer flushing, street sprinkling, and schools and other public buildings. Homeowners and businesses were to receive water at a reasonable rate, and water was to be supplied for service at fire hydrants. A fire broke out in the city, and eventually spread to a warehouse owned by the Moch Co. (P). Both the warehouse and its contents were destroyed. Moch (P) brought suit against Water Co. (D), alleging that Water Co. (D) had been notified of the fire, but had failed to supply water in adequate amounts and at satisfactory pressure to prevent the fire from spreading. Moch (P) claimed that the loss of its property had resulted from Water Co.'s (D) failure to fulfill its contract with the city. The trial court denied Water Co.'s (D) motion to dismiss the complaint, but the appellate division reversed. Moch (P) then appealed.

ISSUE: May a third party recover in tort for a promisor's failure to perform his contractual obligations?

HOLDING AND DECISION: (Cardozo, C.J.) No. A party whose performance of a contract incidentally confers a benefit upon third parties does not owe any duty to continue to perform in a manner which is satisfactory to those parties. The fact that one has begun to act does not always obligate him to continue to do so. If conduct has proceeded to such a state that its discontinuation would be likely to cause injury, a duty arises to continue that conduct. But to hold an actor liable to one party for failure to pursue his conduct toward another party with whom he has contracted, would be to unduly extend the common law rules of tort liability. In fact, it would subject the parties to a contract to actions by a potentially infinite number of tort claimants. Moch (P) also cannot recover as a third-party beneficiary of the contract because Water Co. (D) obviously had no intention of being answerable to

individual consumers. Nor does any statute enlarge Water Co.'s (D) duty to the extent that a third party may recover in tort for Water Co.'s (D) ineffectual performance. Therefore, the judgment in Water Co.'s (D) favor must be affirmed.

▶ ANALYSIS

Moch Co. v. Rensselaer Water Co. stands for the proposition that the failure to perform a contract can result in tort liability only if the party claiming damages was in privity with the breaching party. The earliest cases almost always excused water suppliers when their failure to provide enough water or sufficient pressure caused unnecessary damages as the result of a fire. The *Moch* case, however, seems inconsistent with the landmark case of *MacPherson v. Buick Motor Co.,* 217 N.Y. 382, Ill. N.E. 1050 (1916), in which it was held that the breach of a contractual obligation will result in liability to a third party if the injuries suffered by that individual were foreseeable.

Quicknotes

MISFEASANCE The commission of a lawful act in a wrongful manner.

NONFEASANCE The omission, or failure to perform, an obligation.

PRIVITY OF CONTRACT A relationship between the parties to a contract that is required in order to bring an action for breach.

Kline v. 1500 Massachusetts Avenue Apartment Corp.

Renter (P) v. Landlord (D)

439 F.2d 477 (D.C. Cir. 1970).

NATURE OF CASE: Appeal from denial for damages for negligence.

FACT SUMMARY: Kline (P) sued 1500 Massachusetts Ave. Apartment Corporation (D) for damages after she was attacked in a common area of the apartment building, contending it breached its duty to provide adequate security measures.

🏛 **RULE OF LAW**
A landlord is responsible for maintaining the common areas of his property so as to minimize the risk that tenants may be exposed to an unreasonable risk of criminal attack.

FACTS: In 1959, Kline (P) rented an apartment from 1500 Massachusetts Ave. Apartment Corporation (the Corporation) (D). At the time, there was a doorman on duty 24 hours a day, an employee at the front desk observing all persons using the elevators, and two garage attendants regulating who entered the building from the garage. By 1966, no doorman was present, the front desk was unattended, the garage was left virtually unguarded, and there was an increased number of criminal assaults against the tenants occurring in the common hallways of the building. Kline (P) and others had repeatedly informed the Corporation (D) of these attacks, but nothing was done. In September 1966, a female tenant was attacked in the hallway near Kline's (P) apartment, and two months later, Kline (P) was attacked in the same hallway. She sued, contending the Corporation (D) was liable for not providing adequate security measures. The district court held landlords have no such duty to protect their tenants. Kline (P) appealed.

ISSUE: Is a landlord responsible for maintaining the common areas of his property so as to minimize tenant exposure to an unreasonable risk of criminal attacks?

HOLDING AND DECISION: (Wilkey, J.) Yes. A landlord is responsible for maintaining the common areas of his property so as to minimize tenant exposure to an unreasonable risk of criminal attack. The landlord is the only party with control over the common areas of the property. Therefore, he, and not the tenants is in a position to take necessary protective steps. The landlord is not an insurer of the tenant's safety, but he is obligated to minimize the risk of foreseeable harm. In this case, the standard of reasonable care is the amount of security protections maintained when Kline (P) rented the apartment. She was led to expect this level of care and relied on it in renting the apartment. Therefore, given the clear foreseeability of the

attack and the lack of reasonable protective measures, the Corporation (D) was negligent. Reversed and remanded.

DISSENT: (MacKinnon, J.) Kline (P) presented no evidence that the attacker was not another tenant rather than an intruder. Therefore, if it were another tenant rather than an intruder, the lack of security measures would not be the proximate cause of the attack, and the Corporation (D) could not be held liable.

▷ **ANALYSIS**

The recognition of a special duty owed by a landlord to a tenant has been adopted in other jurisdictions. In *Johnston v. Harris,* 387 Mich. 569, 198 N.W. 2d 409 (1972), a landlord was held liable for an attack on a tenant occurring in a dimly lit, unlocked vestibule of the apartment. In *Sampson v. Saginaw Professional Building Inc.*, 224 N.W. 2d 843 (1975), the Michigan Supreme Court extended the duty of the landlord to invitees of the tenant.

•━━■■■━━•

Quicknotes

DUTY OF A LANDLORD TO COMMON AREAS A landlord owes a duty to all persons injured as the result of defects present in shared areas of the leasehold accessible to the public.

DUTY TO PROTECT TENANTS Generally speaking, a landlord owes a duty to tenants for any defects or other injurious instrumentalities on the property, including those not located in common areas, which are known to the landlord and which he fails to repair, and which are otherwise not the result of the tenant's own negligence.

FORESEEABILITY A reasonable expectation that an act or omission would result in injury.

•━━■■■━━•

Tarasoff v. Regents of University of California

Parents of murder victim (P) v. Psychologist and university (D)

Cal Sup. Ct., 551 P.2d 334 (1976).

NATURE OF CASE: Action in damages for wrongful death.

FACT SUMMARY: Moore (D), a psychologist, failed to notify Tatiana (plaintiff's daughter) that one of his patients threatened to kill her.

🏛 RULE OF LAW
Where a person bears a special relationship to a party or others who may be the victim of the conduct, it is reasonably foreseeable a legally cognizable duty arises to protect or control the third party.

FACTS: Poddar was a patient of Dr. Moore (D), a psychologist employed by the University of California at Berkeley (the University) (D). During a therapy session, Poddar told Moore (D) that he was going to kill Tatiana. Moore (D) informed the campus police who finally released Poddar since he appeared rational. Poddar killed Tatiana several days later. Tarasoff (P), Tatiana's parents, brought a wrongful death action against Powelson (D), Moore's superior and the University (D) on the ground that they had negligently failed to either warn Tatiana or to restrain Poddar. The court sustained a general demurrer on the ground that the defendants did not owe a duty to Tatiana. Tarasoff (P) argued that the special relationship of doctor to patient created a duty to protect Tatiana.

ISSUE: Does the presence of a special relationship create a duty to protect others from the conduct of the actor?

HOLDING AND DECISION: (Tobriner, J.) Yes. As a general rule a person is not liable for the conduct of another. An exception is created where a special relationship exists between the person and the actor or the person and a third party. These types of special relationships impose duties to prevent injury that may be caused by the actor or to protect a third party from injury. A doctor/patient relationship gives rise to this duty. Moore (D) had a duty to protect Tatiana from Poddar. The law recognizes that certain conduct must be prevented or certain interests protected. In such cases a right of action is granted or a penalty assessed. The basic tenet is whether there is a reasonably foreseeable likelihood of an unwarranted risk. Here the relationship exists; the right to life is deemed a protectible interest; and the risk was readily foreseeable. In such cases the law imposes a duty on the party to protect third parties from the actor's conduct. While the doctor/patient relationship requires the keeping of confidences, this privilege is outweighed by the need to protect human life. Reversed and remanded.

CONCURRENCE AND DISSENT: (Mosk, J.) I concur solely on the ground that Moore (D) had predicted that Poddar would kill. We are not concerned with whether he should have recognized whether the killing was likely to occur.

DISSENT: (Clark, J.) I dissent solely on the basis that the relationship required the keeping of confidences.

▶ ANALYSIS

In *Bellah v. Greenson*, C.A. 1st, 1 Civ. 39770 (1977), the parents of a suicidal teenager who died from a self-inflicted overdose of sleeping pills, relied on the above case in a wrongful death action against the girl's psychiatrist. The parents claimed that the psychiatrist had failed to personally take measures to prevent the suicide; that he had failed to warn others of her proclivity; and that he had also failed to warn them that their daughter was consorting with heroin addicts. The appellate court declined to extend the holding of *Tarasoff* to the case and distinguished it in that here there was a danger of self-inflicted harm rather than harm to others.

Quicknotes

DUTY TO PROTECT/AID A moral duty and not one imposed by law; no liability attaches to those persons who fail to undertake a rescue or otherwise aid a person in need absent a special relationship between them.

NEGLIGENT FAILURE TO PROTECT The breach of duty by a person with a special relationship or other fiduciary duty owed to the plaintiff, to intercede and prevent a threatened injury.

PSYCHOTHERAPIST/PATIENT PRIVILEGE The right of a patient to refuse to reveal confidential information given during the course of a relationship with a physician entered into for the purpose of treatment.

SPECIAL RELATIONSHIP A relationship between two persons that imposes a fiduciary responsibility to act where one is threatened with injury, such as the relationship between a parent and child.

Strict Liability

Quick Reference Rules of Law

PAGE

1. *Intel Corp. v. Hamidi.* The tort of trespass to chattel does not encompass an electronic communication that neither damages the recipient computer system nor impairs its functioning. — 113

2. *Poggi v. Scott.* Conversion is exercising an unjustifiable and unwarranted dominion and control over another's property that causes injury to the property owner. — 114

3. *Moore v. Regents of the University of California.* Where plaintiff has neither title to the property alleged to have been converted nor possession thereof, he cannot maintain an action for conversion. — 115

4. *Gehrts v. Batteen.* An owner of a domesticated animal may be liable for harm caused by his pet if the owner knows, or has reason to know, that the animal has abnormally dangerous propensities, regardless of the amount of care exercised by the owner. If an owner does not have actual knowledge, an action can still survive if an ordinary prudent person should have foreseen the event that caused the injury and taken steps to prevent the injury. — 117

5. *Spano v. Perini Corp.* (1) One who engages in blasting is responsible for damage caused without any showing of fault. (2) Proof of trespass is not necessary for recovery in strict liability. — 118

6. *Indiana Harbor Belt R.R. v. American Cyanamid Co.* Strict liability will not be imposed against the manufacturer of a toxic chemical for accidents occurring during transportation. — 119

7. *Vogel v. Grant-Lafayette Electric Cooperative.* Excessive stray voltage is actionable as a private nuisance if the trier of fact determines that such voltage unreasonably interferes with a person's interest in the private use and enjoyment of land. — 120

8. *Michalson v. Nutting.* A property owner is not liable for damage to the adjoining property of another that is caused by the roots of a tree growing on his land. — 121

9. *Fontainebleau Hotel Corp. v. Forty-Five Twenty-Five, Inc.* A landowner may make reasonable and lawful use of his own property as long as he does not interfere with the legal rights of his neighbors or create a nuisance. — 122

10. *Rogers v. Elliott.* Whether or not a particular activity constitutes a nuisance depends upon the way in which it would affect a person of ordinary sensitivity and temperament. — 123

11. *Ensign v. Walls.* The fact that an alleged nuisance existed long before those objecting to it moved into the vicinity does not necessarily prevent a court from ordering it abated. — 124

12. *Boomer v. Atlantic Cement Co.* Although a nuisance will be enjoined even when a marked disparity is shown in economic consequence between the effect of the injunction and the effect of the nuisance, if the practical effect of the injunction will be to close a production plant, a court will condition on equitable grounds the continuance of the injunction on the payment of permanent damages. — 125

13. *Anonymous.* Complaints regarding an obstruction on the King's highway are to be brought to the King for resolution and not via a private action. — 126

14. *Ira S. Bushey & Sons, Inc. v. United States.* An employer is vicariously liable for the reasonably foreseeable conduct of its employees performed within the scope of employment, even when such conduct was not motivated by a purpose of serving the employer. — 127

15. *Petrovich v. Share Health Plan of Illinois, Inc.* A health maintenance organization (HMO) may be held vicariously liable for the negligence of its independent-contractor physicians under the doctrines of apparent and implied authority. — 128

Intel Corporation v. Hamidi

Employer (P) v. Employee (D)

Cal. Sup. Ct., 71 P.3d 296 (2003).

NATURE OF CASE: Appeal of summary judgment in trespass to chattel action.

FACT SUMMARY: Intel Corporation (Intel) (P) sued Hamidi (D) for trespass to chattel when Hamidi (D) sent e-mails to current Intel (P) employees.

📖 RULE OF LAW
The tort of trespass to chattel does not encompass an electronic communication that neither damages the recipient computer system nor impairs its functioning.

FACTS: Hamidi (D), a former Intel Corporation (P) employee, sent six e-mails on Intel's (P) e-mail system, to up to 35,000 current Intel (P) employees, criticizing Intel's (P) employment practices. Although the content of Hamidi's (D) e-mails caused discussion among employees and managers, the messages did not damage Intel's (P) computer system or impair its functioning. Intel (P) sued, claiming that by communicating with its employees over the company's e-mail system, Hamidi (D) committed the tort of trespass to chattels. The trial court granted Intel's (P) motion for summary judgment and the court of appeal affirmed.

ISSUE: Does the tort of trespass to chattel encompass an electronic communication that neither damages the recipient computer system nor impairs its functioning?

HOLDING AND DECISION: (Werdegar, J.) No. The tort of trespass to chattel does not encompass an electronic communication that neither damages the recipient computer system nor impairs its functioning because the e-mail does not interfere with the possessor's use or possession of the computer system itself. Intel's (P) claimed loss of productivity caused by employees reading and reacting to Hamidi's (D) messages and its (P) efforts to block the messages, is not an injury to Intel's (P) interest in its computers because the computers worked as intended and were unharmed by the communications. The tort of trespass to chattels allows recovery for interferences with the possession of personal property which causes some injury. Even though Intel (P) was requesting only injunctive relief, it still had to prove actual harm. Intel's (P) workers were distracted from their work not because of the frequency of Hamidi's (D) messages, but because of the content of the e-mails and, therefore, it was not the functioning of Intel's (P) computer system which was allegedly harmed. The law of trespass to chattel should not be extended to cover an otherwise harmless e-mail whose contents are objectionable. Moreover, intangible intrusions on land are not actionable as trespass. Since Intel (P) did not claim Hamidi's (D) e-mail physically damaged its servers, it could not prove trespass to land even if the computer were treated as a type of real property. Computers are personal, not real property. Hamidi (D) had no tangible presence on Intel (P) property. Reversed.

CONCURRENCE: (Kennard, J.) Like a person who makes unwanted calls to a cell phone, Hamidi's (D) e-mails to Intel's (P) employees did not damage Intel's (P) computer system or impair its functioning and therefore the tort of trespass to chattels was not established.

DISSENT: (Brown, J.) The time required to review and delete Hamidi's (D) e-mails undermined the utility of Intel's (P) expensive computer system. Intel (P) objects to Hamidi's (D) use of Intel (P) property to display his message. Even if, however, Intel (P) objected only to the content of the e-mails, it still deserved an injunction.

DISSENT: (Mosk, J.) Hamidi's (D) actions are synonymous with someone intruding into a private office mailroom, taking the mail cart and dropping off unwanted mail on 30,000 desks. Hamidi's (D) actions did not occur in a public forum.

▶ ANALYSIS

Trespass to chattels has successfully been used to hold spammers—senders of unsolicited commercial bulk e-mail—liable to Internet service providers because such e-mail overburdens the provider's computers and makes the system harder for recipients to use.

◼▬◼

Quicknotes

TRESPASS TO CHATTELS Action for damages sustained as a result of defendant's unlawful interference with plaintiff's personal property.

◼▬◼

Poggi v. Scott

Owner of wine barrels (P) v. Seller of wine barrels (D)

Cal. Sup. Ct., 139 P. 815 (1914).

NATURE OF CASE: Appeal from judgment of nonsuit in a conversion action.

FACT SUMMARY: Scott (D) inadvertently sold Poggi's (P) wine barrels and Poggi (P) sued for conversion.

RULE OF LAW
Conversion is exercising an unjustifiable and unwarranted dominion and control over another's property that causes injury to the property owner.

FACTS: Poggi (P) stored his wine in a basement space he rented initially from Mouser and then from Sanitary Laundry Company (Laundry Company). When Mouser sold the building to Scott (D), Mouser informed Scott (D) of Poggi's (P) lease with the Laundry Company. Scott (D) subsequently sold what he believed to be broken empty barrels stored in the basement. The barrels actually contained Poggi's (P) wine. The men Scott (D) sold the barrels to were subsequently arrested for theft of the wine. Poggi (P) sued Scott (D) to recover damages suffered as a result of Scott's (D) conversion of about two hundred barrels of Poggi's (P) wine. The jury found in favor of Scott (D) and Poggi (P) appealed.

ISSUE: Is Scott (D) liable for conversion?

HOLDING AND DECISION: (Henshaw, J.) Yes. Scott (D) is liable for conversion because he exercised an unjustifiable and unwarranted dominion and control over Poggi's (P) property resulting in injury to Poggi (P). Neither knowledge, nor intent, nor negligence is necessary to prove conversion. An action for conversion rests upon the interference with the property of another resulting in injury. Conversion occurs when there is a breach of an absolute duty, the existence of bad faith is irrelevant. Scott (D) sold barrels that did not belong to him, it does not matter that he did not know the barrels contained wine. Moreover, Scott (D) had no right to sell the barrels whether they contained wine or not, and the fact he did so means he exercised an unjustifiable and unwarranted dominion and control over the property of another. Reversed.

ANALYSIS

As this case demonstrates, conversion was initially considered a strict liability tort.

Quicknotes

ABATEMENT A decrease or lessening of something; in equity, a suspension or dismissal of a cause of action.

INJUNCTION A remedy imposed by the court ordering a party to cease the conduct of a specific activity.

INVERSE CONDEMNATION Taking of private property for public use so as to impair or decrease the value of property near or adjacent to, but not a part of, the property taken.

NUISANCE Use of property that interferes with the lawful use of another's property.

Moore v. Regents of the University of California

Cancer patient (P) v. University (D)

Cal. Sup. Ct., 793 P.2d 479 (1990).

NATURE OF CASE: Appeal from decision denying defendants' demurrer in a conversion action.

FACT SUMMARY: After the Medical Center of the University of California at Los Angeles (D) removed tissue from Moore's (P) body and, without Moore's (P) knowledge, developed a cell-line from the tissue capable of producing pharmaceutical products of great therapeutic value, financially benefiting from doing so, Moore (P) sued for conversion.

🏛 RULE OF LAW
Where plaintiff has neither title to the property alleged to have been converted nor possession thereof, he cannot maintain an action for conversion.

FACTS: Moore (P), a cancer patient with hairy-cell leukemia, sought medical treatment at the Medical Center of the University of California at Los Angeles (UCLA) (D). As part of the treatment, Moore's (P) spleen was removed. After removal of the spleen, and without Moore's (P) consent or knowledge, two UCLA (D) doctors discovered that Moore's (P) tissue was unique and, through genetic engineering, developed a cell-line capable of producing valuable pharmaceutical products. UCLA (D) then entered into contracts with pharmaceutical companies and was paid hundreds of thousands of dollars pursuant to the contracts. UCLA (D) never informed Moore (P) about these happenings and continued to take tissue from Moore (P) for seven years after the removal of his spleen. Moore (P), after discovering that UCLA (D) had taken his tissue and profited financially thereby, sued UCLA (D) for conversion. The trial court sustained all UCLA's (D) demurrers to Moore's (P) complaint, and Moore (P) appealed. The court of appeals reversed the trial court and decided in Moore's (P) favor on the conversion issue. UCLA (D) appealed.

ISSUE: Where plaintiff has neither title to the property alleged to have been converted nor possession thereof, can he maintain an action for conversion?

HOLDING AND DECISION: (Panelli, J.) No. Where plaintiff has neither title to the property alleged to have been converted nor possession thereof, he cannot maintain an action for conversion. Since Moore (P) clearly did not expect to retain possession of his cells following their removal, in order to sue for their conversion he must have retained an ownership interest in them. There are several reasons to doubt that he did retain such interest. First, no reported judicial decision supports Moore's (P) claim, either directly or by close analogy; second, California

statutory law drastically limits any continuing interest of a patient in excised cells; third, the subject matters of UCLA's (D) patent—the patented cell-line and the products derived from it—cannot be Moore's (P) property. Also, there are three reasons why it is inappropriate to impose liability for conversion upon the allegations of Moore's (P) complaint. First, a fair balancing of relevant policy considerations counsels against extending the tort; second, problems in this area are better suited to legislative resolution; and third, the tort of conversion is not necessary to protect Moore's (P) rights since Moore (P) can base liability on existing disclosure obligations rather than rely on an unprecedented extension of the conversion tort. Reversed.

CONCURRENCE AND DISSENT: (Broussard, J.) Because Moore (P) alleged that UCLA (D) wrongfully interfered with his right to determine, prior to the removal of body parts, how these parts would be used after removal, Moore's (P) complaint states a cause of action under traditional common law conversion principles.

DISSENT: (Mosk, J.) Acceptance of legislative dominance does not require judicial passivity in the application of traditional common law principles of conversion to recent explosive growth in the commercialization of biotechnology. Here, Moore (P) also has argued a nondisclosure cause of action, which the court feels is adequate to solve the problem of this case. But the nondisclosure cause of action does not protect Moore's (P) right to participate in the benefits UCLA (D) will reap as a result of selling a product produced from Moore's (P) tissues. Therefore, the nondisclosure cause of action is not an adequate substitute for the conversion remedy, which does protect the right.

▶ ANALYSIS

Justice Mosk's dissent in this case discussed at length the reasons that a nondisclosure cause of action could not adequately protect a person in Moore's (P) position. Mosk stated that the nondisclosure cause of action only gives a patient a right to refuse consent, *i.e.*, to prohibit commercialization of his tissue; it does not give him the right to consent to that commercialization on the condition that he share in its proceeds. Also, the nondisclosure cause of action fails to reach a major class of defendants: all those outside the strict physician-patient relationship with the plaintiff.

Continued on next page.

Quicknotes

BREACH OF FIDUCIARY DUTY The failure of a fiduciary to observe the standard of care exercised by professionals of similar education and experience.

CONVERSION The act of depriving an owner of his property without permission or justification.

DEMURRER The assertion that the opposing party's pleadings are insufficient and that the demurring party should not be made to answer.

INFORMED CONSENT An individual's consent to a particular occurrence following full disclosure of the consequences of that decision.

Gehrts v. Batteen

Dog bite victim (P) v. Dog owner (D)

S.D. Sup. Ct., 620 N.W. 2d 775 (2001).

NATURE OF CASE: Appeal of summary judgment in favor of Batteen (D) in dog bite action.

FACT SUMMARY: Nielsen's (D) dog bit Gehrts (P) and Gehrts (P) sued for damages.

🏛 RULE OF LAW
An owner of a domesticated animal may be liable for harm caused by his pet if the owner knows, or has reason to know, that the animal has abnormally dangerous propensities, regardless of the amount of care exercised by the owner. If an owner does not have actual knowledge, an action can still survive if an ordinary prudent person should have foreseen the event that caused the injury and taken steps to prevent the injury.

FACTS: Nielsen (D) left her St. Bernard, Wilbur, in the back of her (D) pickup truck when she went to visit Gehrts's (P) home. Wilbur was secured by a harness attached to a restraining device that allowed the dog to move freely between the sides of the pickup box, but limited his movement between the front and back. Gehrts (P) attempted to pet Wilbur, with Nielsen's (P) permission, and received injuries to her nose and forehead as a result of Wilbur biting her. Gehrts (P) subsequently sued Nielsen (D) in negligence and strict liability and the trial court granted summary judgment in favor of Nielsen (D). Gehrts (P) appealed.

ISSUE: Was Nielsen (D) liable for the harm Wilbur caused?

HOLDING AND DECISION: (Gilbertson, J.) No. Nielsen (D) was not liable for the harm Wilbur caused because Nielsen (D) did not know, or have reason to know, that Wilbur had abnormally dangerous propensities and an ordinary prudent person could not have foreseen the event that caused the injury and taken steps to prevent the injury. An owner of a domesticated animal may be liable for harm caused by his pet if the owner knows or has reason to know that the animal has abnormally dangerous propensities, regardless of the amount of care exercised by the owner. Absent an actual attack, barking, barring its teeth and straining at its leash is sufficient to establish such propensities. If an owner does not have actual knowledge, an action can still survive if an ordinary prudent person should have foreseen the event that caused the injury and taken steps to prevent the injury. In the present case, there is no evidence that Nielsen (D) had any knowledge that Wilbur had dangerous propensities. St. Bernards are by nature gentle dogs and Wilbur specifically had never

growled, bared his teeth or acted aggressively toward any person. Furthermore, it was not proven that Nielsen (D) failed to use reasonable care in the circumstances because a prudent person would not have foreseen the danger. There was no evidence that Nielsen (D) was aware that Gehrts (P) owned a dog or that the scent of a dog would be on Gehrts (P) and that the scent of a strange dog would cause Wilbur to attack Gehrts (P). In addition, it is mere speculation to suggest that if Nielsen (D) restrained Wilbur in a different way while Gehrts (P) was petting him, Gehrts (P) would not have been bitten. Lastly, it is up to the legislature to adopt a strict liability standard for injuries caused by dogs, not the courts. Affirmed.

DISSENT: (Sabers, J.) It is premature to say that the facts in this case warrant summary judgment. Precedent holds that summary judgment is not appropriate in negligence actions. There are numerous genuine issues of material fact in this case that should be resolved by a jury.

▌ ANALYSIS
Other state legislatures, such as California, have mandated strict liability in dog bite actions.

Quicknotes

NEGLIGENCE Conduct falling below the standard of care that a reasonable person would demonstrate under similar conditions.

STRICT LIABILITY Liability for all injuries proximately caused by a party's conducting of certain inherently dangerous activities without regard to negligence or fault.

SUMMARY JUDGMENT Judgment rendered by a court in response to a motion by one of the parties, claiming that the lack of a question of material fact in respect to an issue warrants disposition of the issue without consideration by the jury.

Spano v. Perini Corp.

Garage owner (P) v. Construction company (D)

N.Y. Ct. App., 250 N.E.2d 31 (1969).

NATURE OF CASE: Property damage based on strict liability.

FACT SUMMARY: Blasting by Perini Corp. (D) on its own land wrecked Spano's (P) garage on nearby property.

RULE OF LAW
(1) One who engages in blasting is responsible for damage caused without any showing of fault.
(2) Proof of trespass is not necessary for recovery in strict liability.

FACTS: Spano (P) owns a garage that was wrecked by shock waves from a dynamite blast set off by Perini Corp (D) on nearby property. There was no physical trespass caused by the blast nor was there any proof of negligence on the part of the defendant. In addition to the foregoing, suit was also brought for damages to an automobile that had been in the garage at the time of the blast. The two suits were consolidated and judgment was for Spano and Davis (P). Perini Corp. (D) appealed.

ISSUE:
(1) Is one who engages in blasting responsible for damage caused without any showing of fault?
(2) Is proof of trespass necessary for recovery in strict liability?

HOLDING AND DECISION: (Fuld, C.J.)
(1) Yes. One who engages in blasting is responsible for damage caused without any showing of fault. This case recognizes that under the doctrine of strict liability, an actor is liable for damage caused by abnormally dangerous activity without regard to fault. The rationale is that he who engages in an abnormally dangerous activity should bear the losses as opposed to the injured and innocent victim.
(2) No. Proof of trespass is not necessary for recovery in strict liability. The early common law would have distinguished between the physical invasion, which was a trespass, and the concussion, which would be in nuisance. For purposes of strict liability the distinction has been abandoned. Reversed and remanded.

ANALYSIS

This case indicates the traditional approach to strict liability. If an activity cannot be made safe even by the exercise of utmost care, then strict liability applies. This is the majority view. In many jurisdictions the protection of strict liability has been extended to food, drugs, and products. In those jurisdictions, if a defect exists in the product when it left the manufacturer, the manufacturer will be absolutely liable.

Quicknotes

STRICT LIABILITY Liability for all injuries proximately caused by a party's conducting of certain inherently dangerous activities without regard to negligence or fault.

ULTRAHAZARDOUS ACTIVITIES Dangerous activities that give rise to strict liability by presenting a risk of serious harm to the community that cannot be removed through any exercise of due care.

Indiana Harbor Belt R.R. v. American Cyanamid Co.

Railroad (P) v. Chemical manufacturing company (D)

916 F.2d 1174 (7th Cir. 1990).

NATURE OF CASE: Appeal of damages awarded for injury to property.

FACT SUMMARY: American Cyanamid Co. (D), manufacturer of a dangerous chemical, was held strictly liable when a quantity of it spilled during transportation.

🏛 RULE OF LAW
Strict liability will not be imposed against the manufacturer of a toxic chemical for accidents occurring during transportation.

FACTS: American Cyanamid Co. (D), a chemical manufacturer, engaged a railroad car to transport 20,000 gallons of liquid acrylonitrile, a toxic substance, to a processing plant in New Jersey. While the car was sitting in a Chicago railroad yard owned by Indiana Harbor Belt R.R. (P), about 5,000 gallons spilled, which necessitated an evacuation of nearby homes and nearly $1 million in cleanup. Indiana Harbor Belt R.R. (P) filed suit against American Cyanamid (D) to recover the cost of cleanup, contending that the transportation of toxic chemicals was an ultrahazardous activity for which the manufacturer should be strictly liable. A district court, sitting in diversity, agreed and so instructed the jury. A verdict for damages was rendered, and American Cyanamid (D) appealed.

ISSUE: Will strict liability be imposed against the manufacturer of a toxic chemical for accidents occurring during transportation?

HOLDING AND DECISION: (Posner, J.) No. Strict liability will not be imposed against the manufacturer of a toxic chemical for accidents occurring during transportation. The Restatement (Second) of Torts, at § 520, lists six factors to be considered in determining whether an activity is ultrahazardous: (1) great probability of harm; (2) potentially serious level of harm; (3) the activity is not a matter of common usage; (4) harm cannot be prevented by utmost care; (5) the activity is inappropriate for the location; and (6) the social value of the activity is not sufficient to offset the risks. The basic purpose behind the ultrahazardous activity doctrine is to encourage the use of alternative methods when possible. In this case, no alternative exists to transport chemicals other than truck transport, which is not inherently safer. It would not be feasible to reroute the shipment of all hazardous materials around Chicago. Moreover, the negligence regime is perfectly adequate for deterring railway spills. Finally, the ultrahazardous activity doctrine concentrates on the activity, not the subject of the activity. American Cyanamid (D) is not considered to be engaged in an abnormally dangerous activity just because a product it manufactures becomes dangerous when handled. It is the transportation, not the manufacture of the chemical, which is under scrutiny. For these reasons, strict liability is inappropriate in this context. Reversed and remanded.

▶ ANALYSIS

The classic case of ultrahazardous activity is dynamite blasting in an urban area. It entails a great risk of harm, and a less dangerous (albeit more expensive) method of building demolition exists—the wrecking ball. The ultrahazardous activity rule will make the demolisher strictly liable if he chooses the more dangerous method.

━■━

Quicknotes

STRICT LIABILITY Liability for all injuries proximately caused by a party's conducting of certain inherently dangerous activities without regard to negligence or fault.

ULTRAHAZARDOUS ACTIVITIES Dangerous activities that give rise to strict liability by presenting a risk of serious harm to the community that cannot be removed through any exercise of due care.

━■━

Vogel v. Grant-Lafayette Electric Cooperative

Farmers (P) v. Electric cooperative association (D)

Wis. Sup. Ct., 548 N.W.2d 829 (1996).

NATURE OF CASE: Suit for damages based on negligence on private nuisance.

FACT SUMMARY: On theories of negligence and private nuisance, the Vogels (P), dairy farmers, sought recovery for injuries sustained by their herd of cows as a result of stray voltage allegedly caused by Grant-Lafayette Electric Cooperative (GLEC) (D).

> ## 🏛 RULE OF LAW
> Excessive stray voltage is actionable as a private nuisance if the trier of fact determines that such voltage unreasonably interferes with a person's interest in the private use and enjoyment of land.

FACTS: The Vogels (P) are dairy farmers and members of Grant-Lafayette Electric Cooperative (GLEC) (D). Shortly after the Vogels (P) built a new milking facility, their herd began exhibiting violent or erratic behavior while in the facility. The herd also suffered from excessive and chronic mastitis, and as a result, the Vogels (P) suffered a decline in their herd's milk production and cows were repeatedly culled from the herd. The Vogels (P) contacted GLEC (D) because they suspected the cows were suffering from the effects of excessive stray voltage. GLEC (D) installed an isolator at its transformer on the Vogels' (P) farm in order to reduce the risk of excessive stray voltage. After installation of the isolator, the behavior and other problems of the herd improved immediately. The Vogels (P) brought suit against GLEC (D) for negligence and nuisance. GLEC (D) denied the allegations and contended the Vogels (P) were contributorily negligent in the design, maintenance, and operation of their equipment. A jury found that GLEC (D) was negligent and that it had created a nuisance, and the Vogels (P) were found one-third negligent. A verdict was entered for $200,000. GLEC (D) appealed on the basis that stray voltage is not a private nuisance. The Vogels (P) appealed claiming GLEC (D) committed an intentional nuisance and therefore the award could not be reduced for contributory negligence. The court of appeal held the trial court erred in submitting the nuisance claim to the jury and struck that portion of the award. The Vogels (P) appealed.

ISSUE: Is excessive stray voltage actionable as a private nuisance if the trier of fact determines that such voltage unreasonably interferes with a person's interest in the private use and enjoyment of land?

HOLDING AND DECISION: (Bradley, J.) Yes. Excessive stray voltage is actionable as a private nuisance if the trier of fact determines that such voltage unreason-ably interferes with a person's interest in the private use and enjoyment of land. Private nuisance is defined as: "a nontrespassory invasion of another's interest in the private use and enjoyment of land," Restatement of Torts (Second) § 821D. GLEC (D) argued that the term invasion constitutes a "unilateral encroachment." In other words, it constitutes an action by the defendant to which the plaintiff objects, not one which the plaintiff requested and facilitated. Thus, the Vogels' (P) act of requesting service and connecting its service to that of GLEC's (D) defeats their nuisance claim and the court of appeals agreed. However, a request for electric service does not negate the element of invasion of nuisance. The Vogels' (P) request for electric service did not include excessive stray voltage. Such stray voltage is actionable if it unreasonably interferes with a person's interest in the private use and enjoyment of land. The Vogels (P) also argued that GLEC's (D) invasion was intentional under § 825(b) since it knew the stray voltage was substantially certain to result from its conduct under the basic laws of electricity. However, it is only unreasonable levels of stray voltage that may give rise to liability for an intentional invasion. The Vogels (P) failed to demonstrate evidence that GLEC (D) had knowledge of any unreasonable levels of stray voltage being released on their farm. The Vogels (P) also argued the invasion was intentional because it was continuing. This argument failed for the same reason. Reversed.

▶ ANALYSIS

Many jurisdictions impose an "unreasonable" requirement in nuisance laws. Such jurisdictions only hold activity actionable if the interference with the plaintiff's use and enjoyment of his property is unreasonable. Whether an activity is unreasonable is determined by weighing the expected benefits of the conduct against their anticipated costs. Restatement (Second) of Torts § 826.

■=■

Quicknotes

CONTRIBUTORY NEGLIGENCE Behavior on the part of an injured plaintiff falling below the standard of ordinary care that contributes to the defendant's negligence, resulting in the plaintiff's injury.

NUISANCE Use of property that interferes with the lawful use of another's property.

■=■

Michalson v. Nutting

Property owner (P) v. Adjoining property owner (D)

Mass. Sup. Jud. Ct., 175 N.E. 490 (1931).

NATURE OF CASE: Appeal from dismissal of bill in equity seeking mandatory and permanent injunctions.

FACT SUMMARY: The plaintiffs (P) sought a court order requiring the defendants (D) to prevent the roots of their tree from encroaching on and causing injury to the plaintiffs' (P) property.

🏛 RULE OF LAW
A property owner is not liable for damage to the adjoining property of another that is caused by the roots of a tree growing on his land.

FACTS: The plaintiffs (P) brought a bill in equity alleging that roots from a poplar tree growing on the defendants' (D) property had penetrated the plaintiffs' (P) land and had filled up sewer and drain pipes there, causing damages, and also had grown under the cement cellar of the plaintiffs' (P) house, causing the cement to crack and crumble, and threatening the house's foundation. The plaintiffs (P) sought a mandatory injunction compelling the removal of the roots, a permanent injunction restraining the defendants (D) from allowing the roots to encroach on plaintiffs' (P) land, and damages. The trial court ruled that the defendants (D) were not liable for the asserted damages and dismissed the bill with costs. The state's highest court granted review.

ISSUE: Is a property owner liable for damage to the adjoining property of another that is caused by the roots of a tree growing on his land?

HOLDING AND DECISION: (Wait, J.) No. A property owner is not liable for damage to the adjoining property of another that is caused by the roots of a tree growing on his land. It is well established that a property owner has the right to grow trees on his land and is not liable to an adjoining property owner for the shade or overhanging branches that emanate from a tree(s) on his land. There is no distinction in principle between damage caused by shade and overhanging branches and the penetration of roots onto adjoining property. The neighbor's recourse is not through the courts, but in his own hands: he can cut the overhanging limbs, as well as the penetrating roots. By leaving the neighbors to work out such annoyances between themselves, the law prevents the bringing of "innumerable and, in many instances, purely vexatious" actions. Affirmed.

legal injury. While the tree roots caused real injury, this injury did not constitute actionable nuisance because the injured neighbor could resort to self-help and destroy the roots. Presumably, such destruction could kill the tree, in which case the owner of the tree would have no legal recourse for the tree's death.

Quicknotes

MANDATORY INJUNCTION An injunction that compels a defendant to either perform an act or to refrain from doing a particular act.

PERMANENT INJUNCTION A remedy imposed by the court ordering a party to cease the conduct of a specific activity until the final disposition of the cause of action.

▶ ANALYSIS

The court in this case found that the injury at issue was "damnum absque injuria," which is Latin for harm without

Fontainebleau Hotel Corp. v. Forty-Five Twenty-Five, Inc.

Expanding hotel (D) v. Neighboring hotel (P)

Fla. Dist. Ct. App., 114 So. 2d 357 (1959).

NATURE OF CASE: Suit seeking injunctive relief.

FACT SUMMARY: The Fontainebleau Hotel Corp. (D) began construction of a building addition which threatened to cast a shadow upon the sunbathing area of a hotel owned by Forty-Five Twenty-Five, Inc. (P).

RULE OF LAW

A landowner may make reasonable and lawful use of his own property as long as he does not interfere with the legal rights of his neighbors or create a nuisance.

FACTS: The Fontainebleau Hotel, owned and operated by the Fontainebleau Hotel Corp. (D), commenced construction of a fourteen-story addition. Forty-Five Twenty-Five, Inc. (P), owner of the Eden Roc Hotel (Eden Roc), sought to enjoin the erection of the addition, claiming that it would cast a shadow on an area which Eden Roc guests used for sunbathing. Forty-Five Twenty-Five (P) alleged that the addition had been maliciously inspired and that it violated a building ordinance and interfered with various easements owned by Forty-Five Twenty-Five (P). A chancellor, after taking evidence, granted a temporary injunction. His memorandum opinion clearly stated that the sole basis for his ruling had been "the proposition that no one has a right to use his property to the injury of another." Fontainebleau Hotel Corp. (D) appealed from the order granting the temporary injunction.

ISSUE: Is a landowner absolutely precluded from using his property in a manner that will be injurious to others?

HOLDING AND DECISION: (Per curiam) No. A landowner may make reasonable and lawful use of his own property as long as he does not interfere with the legal rights of his neighbors or create a nuisance. Even at common law, a landowner enjoyed no legal right to the free flow of light and air across his neighbor's property. Thus, the fact that the Fontainebleau's addition may block sunlight that would otherwise reach the Eden Roc does not mean that there has been, or will be, an interference with a legal right belonging to Forty-Five Twenty-Five (P). No reason is suggested for departing from the rule stated, and if its operation proves to be offensive to public policy objectives, the only recourse is through appropriate ordinances. The order granting a temporary injunction must be reversed.

ANALYSIS

As the *Fontainebleau* court noted, American jurisdictions have consistently refused to recognize an easement for the air and light that pass through neighboring properties. Theoretically, conduct that interferes with air or light could nonetheless be characterized as a nuisance. Most courts, though, seem to think of nuisances as consisting of invasions rather than mere interferences. Thus, an activity that caused excessive bright lights at inopportune times of the day would be more likely to be abated than would conduct which prevented the transmittal of rays of sunlight. A further complication is the fact that courts are reluctant to find that a condition constitutes a nuisance if its only undesirable effect is to create aesthetic displeasure.

Quicknotes

DOCTRINE OF "ANCIENT LIGHTS" A doctrine descended from English common law that granted an interest in land for the unobstructed passage of light and air after 20 years of uninterrupted use.

EASEMENT OF "LIGHTS" An interest in land granted for the unobstructed passage of light and air, from English common law.

INJUNCTIVE RELIEF A court order issued as a remedy, requiring a person to do, or prohibiting that person from doing, a specific act.

NUISANCE Use of property that interferes with the lawful use of another's property.

SIC UTERE TUO UT ALIENUM NON LADEAS One's use of property should be done so as not to injure another.

Rogers v. Elliott

Sunstroke victim (P) v. Church custodian (D)

Mass. Sup. Jud. Ct., 15 N.E. 768 (1888).

NATURE OF CASE: Suit to recover damages for harm caused by an alleged nuisance.

FACT SUMMARY: Elliott (D), the custodian of a church, insisted upon ringing the church bell despite notice from a physician that the noise from the bell caused Rogers (P) to suffer physical harm.

RULE OF LAW

Whether or not a particular activity constitutes a nuisance depends upon the way in which it would affect a person of ordinary sensitivity and temperament.

FACTS: Elliott (D) was custodian and manager of a Roman Catholic Church in a small Massachusetts town. One of his activities consisted of ringing a bell in the church each day. In a house not far from the church, Rogers (P) was recovering from a severe case of sunstroke. After Elliott (D) rang the bell on Saturday, Rogers (P) suffered convulsions that his physician attributed to the noise from the bell. The doctor visited Elliott (D) and informed him that the ringing of the bell the next day would again affect Rogers's (P) physical condition, but Elliott (D) replied that he had no love for Rogers (P) and would continue to ring the bell even if his own mother were sick. The following day, Elliott's (D) ringing of the bell caused further damage to Rogers (P), who sued Elliott (D) on the theory that the bell ringing constituted a nuisance.

ISSUE: May the hypersensitivity of one particular complainant be taken into account in determining whether or not an activity constitutes a nuisance?

HOLDING AND DECISION: (Knowlton, J.) No. Whether or not a particular activity constitutes a nuisance depends upon the way in which it would affect a person of ordinary sensitivity and temperament. Property may be put to legitimate and proper use, and what is a lawful use must be determined by reference to an objective standard. If the effects upon unusually sensitive individuals were taken into account, the permissibility of a particular land use might be subject to daily change, depending upon the identities and levels of tolerance of the people who were to be found in the vicinity at a given moment. Obviously, no semblance of certainty or continuity can be achieved unless it is the effect upon a normal person which is used as a standard for measuring the propriety of an activity. The presence of express malice may have a bearing on the issue, but this case presents insufficient facts from which to infer express malice. Thus, the case involves merely the protests of a single hypersensitive individual who is not entitled to relief in the absence of a showing that the conduct complained of was unreasonably objectionable even to the average person. Judgment on the verdict.

ANALYSIS

The rule ordinarily applied in tort cases is that the defendant "takes the plaintiff as he finds him." In other words, the defense that the plaintiff was hypersensitive or was particularly susceptible to injury usually is unavailing. In the context of nuisance cases, however, the rule of *Rogers v. Elliott* is almost always recognized and applied. The *Rogers v. Elliott* holding seems particularly appropriate in those cases where the individual of normal sensibilities need not be a merely imaginary creature because several such people actually exist in close proximity to the hypersensitive plaintiff and the defendant, and have offered no objection to the defendant's conduct.

Quicknotes

HYPERSENSITIVE PLAINTIFFS In tort law, a plaintiff who has the potential to suffer a greater degree of unforeseeable injury than an ordinary person due to their unique or individual nature (*i.e.*, the eggshell-skull plaintiff) thus increasing the damages owing to defendant, who will be held liable for the entire range of injury; put another way, the defendant "takes the plaintiff as he finds him."

MALICE The intention to commit an unlawful act without justification or excuse.

NUISANCE Use of property that interferes with the lawful use of another's property.

Ensign v. Walls

Homeowner (P) v. Dog breeder (D)

Mich. Sup. Ct., 34 N.W.2d 549 (1948).

NATURE OF CASE: Suit to enjoin an alleged nuisance.

FACT SUMMARY: Ensign (P) and others (P) claimed that Walls's (D) dog-breeding business constituted a nuisance. Walls (D) had operated the business for years before most of those protesting had moved into the neighborhood.

🏛 RULE OF LAW
The fact that an alleged nuisance existed long before those objecting to it moved into the vicinity does not necessarily prevent a court from ordering it abated.

FACTS: For some years, Walls (D) had bred St. Bernard dogs in the city of Detroit. Ensign (P) and other nearby property owners (P) sued for an injunction preventing Walls (D) from continuing to operate. It was alleged that her business created noise, offensive odors, and a vermin problem, and that dogs occasionally escaped and wandered around the neighborhood. Walls (D) denied that her activities constituted a nuisance, and also claimed that an injunction should not issue since she had operated her business since 1926 and had invested considerable money in it, while many of those who objected to her activities had only recently moved into the neighborhood. The lower court ruled that an injunction should issue, and Walls (D) appealed.

ISSUE: May a court order a nuisance abated despite the fact that it existed long before those objecting to it came on the scene?

HOLDING AND DECISION: (Carr, J.) Yes. The fact that an alleged nuisance existed long before those objecting to it moved into the vicinity does not necessarily prevent a court from ordering it abated. That the nuisance predated the appearance of the protestors is but one factor to be considered in determining whether or not the condition should be abated. It is appropriate to note that an activity that presents no problems in an isolated locale may become offensive when the surrounding neighborhood becomes more densely populated. In such circumstances, public policy mandates that operations injurious to health and comfort are to be excluded from populous areas. Ample evidence supports the conclusion that Walls's (D) business constituted a nuisance, and it was within the discretion of the trial judge to grant injunctive relief. Walls (D) argued that a complete shutdown of her operations was an unnecessarily drastic measure, but no evidence has been presented, which tends to show that Walls (D) could conduct her business without causing a nuisance. Therefore, the decree affording injunctive relief must be affirmed.

▶ ANALYSIS

The result of *Ensign v. Walls* is consistent with that reached by numerous other courts. That is, the defense that the plaintiff "came to the nuisance" rarely prevails. A minority of courts reason that if the nuisance predated the arrival of the plaintiff, relief should be denied on the theory that the plaintiff knowingly assumed whatever hardships result from the nuisance. The majority rule, however, is rooted in the notion that a landowner enjoys a right to the use and control of his property, and can never be deprived of that right even by a neighbor whose unreasonable land use began long ago.

■◼■

Quicknotes

DAMNUM ABSQUE INJURIA When an injury is sustained but the law affords no means of recovery.

INJUNCTIVE RELIEF A court order issued as a remedy, requiring a person to do, or prohibiting that person from doing, a specific act.

NUISANCE Use of property that interferes with the lawful use of another's property.

■◼■

Boomer v. Atlantic Cement Co.

Landowner (P) v. Cement plant (D)

N.Y. Ct. App., 257 N.E.2d 870 (1970).

NATURE OF CASE: Action for an injunction to enjoin maintenance of a nuisance and for damages.

FACT SUMMARY: Property owners (P) sued a cement plant (D) alleging that pollution emanating from the plant had injured their lands. The trial court refused an injunction, but did authorize successive actions for damages.

🏛 RULE OF LAW
Although a nuisance will be enjoined even when a marked disparity is shown in economic consequence between the effect of the injunction and the effect of the nuisance, if the practical effect of the injunction will be to close a production plant, a court will condition on equitable grounds the continuance of the injunction on the payment of permanent damages.

FACTS: The Atlantic Cement Co., Inc. (Atlantic) (D) operated a large cement plant near Albany, New York, in which it had invested $45,000,000 and employed over 300 workers. A group of neighboring landowners (P) brought actions for injunction and damages against Atlantic (D) alleging injury to their property from dirt, smoke, and vibration emanating from the plant. The trial court held that a nuisance existed, but denied the issuance of an injunction. Rather, it awarded the landowners (P) damages up to the time of trial, thus permitting them to maintain successive actions at law for damages thereafter as further injury was incurred. Atlantic (D) appealed.

ISSUE: Where the issuance of an injunction to enjoin the maintenance of a manufacturing operation as a nuisance would have the effect of closing the plant, may a court award permanent damages as an alternative?

HOLDING AND DECISION: (Bergan, J.) Yes. Courts should be wary of using a decision in private litigation as a purposeful mechanism to achieve direct public objectives greatly beyond the rights and interests before the court. The judicial establishment is neither equipped in the limited nature of any judgment it can pronounce nor prepared to lay down and implement an effective policy for the elimination of air pollution. This is a problem government alone is to resolve. Although an injunction should not be denied because the damage to a plaintiff is slight as compared to the defendant's expense of abating a nuisance, to follow this rule literally in this case would have the immediately drastic effect of closing the plant. One alternative would be to grant the injunction but postpone its effect to a specified future date to give opportunity for

technical advances to permit Atlantic (D) to eliminate the nuisance. However, it is unlikely that Atlantic (D) by itself will be able to eliminate its pollution in the near future. The rate of the research is simply beyond its control. A better alternative would be to grant the injunction unless Atlantic (D) pays the landowners (P) permanent damages as may be fixed by the court. An amount of $185,000 would fairly compensate the landowners (P) for all past and future injury they have and will suffer. Reversed and remitted.

DISSENT: (Jasen, J.) The majority has in effect licensed a continuing wrong. Furthermore, once permanent damages are assessed and paid, the incentive to alleviate the wrong would be eliminated. Moreover, Atlantic (D) should not be allowed, as a private party, inverse condemnation; the public is not being benefited. Finally, the landowners (P) are being forced to accept servitude on their land for the benefit of a private party.

▌ ANALYSIS

In determining whether or not to enjoin a nuisance, a court "may take into consideration the relative economic hardship which will result to the parties from the granting or denial of the injunction, the good faith or intentional misconduct of each, and the interest of the general public in the continuation of the defendant's enterprise." Prosser, *Law of Torts* (1971 4th ed.) ch. 15, § 90 p. 604. Another factor, as this case illustrates, is the financial investment each party has made in his land.

Quicknotes

ABATEMENT A decrease or lessening of something; in equity, a suspension or dismissal of a cause of action.

INJUNCTION A remedy imposed by the court ordering a party to cease the conduct of a specific activity.

INVERSE CONDEMNATION The taking of private property for public use so as to impair or decrease the value of property near or adjacent to, but not a part of, the property taken.

NUISANCE Use of property that interferes with the lawful use of another's property.

Anonymous

[Parties not identified.]

Y.B. Mich. 27 Hen. 8, f. 27, pl. 10 (1536).

NATURE OF CASE: Action for damages arising from an obstruction in the road preventing passage.

FACT SUMMARY: The plaintiff sued the defendant for obstructing the King's highway.

RULE OF LAW
Complaints regarding an obstruction on the King's highway are to be brought to the King for resolution and not via a private action.

FACTS: The plaintiff sued the defendant for causing an obstruction on the King's highway that prevented the plaintiff from passing through, whereas previous to the obstruction the plaintiff was able to pass.

ISSUE: Did the plaintiff bring his case to the proper venue?

HOLDING AND DECISION: (Baldwin, C.J.) No. The plaintiff did not bring his action to the proper venue. It is up to the King to resolve matters involving nuisances on his highways, not the courts. Many people could be harmed by the defendant's actions. Therefore, if we allow the plaintiff's action, the defendant could theoretically be punished 100 times over for the same malfeasance. The plaintiff needs to go tell the King about his concerns. Judgment for the defendant.

DISSENT: (Fitzherbert, J.) If an individual is harmed, above and beyond the normal harm that everyone experiences by such a nuisance on the King's highway, then that individual is entitled to bring a private action. The plaintiff in the present action was inconvenienced more than any other person and he, therefore, should be allowed to have this action for his special harm.

ANALYSIS

In present day, public nuisances are still usually resolved via administrative regulation, and private actions are maintainable only for special harms.

▬▬▬

Quicknotes

PUBLIC NUISANCE An activity that unreasonably interferes with a right common to the overall public.

▬▬▬

Ira S. Bushey & Sons, Inc. v. United States

Drydock owner (P) v. Coast Guard (D)

398 F.2d 167 (2d Cir. 1968).

NATURE OF CASE: Appeal in an action for damages based on employer's vicarious liability.

FACT SUMMARY: While returning to his docked United States Coast Guard ship, Lane, an intoxicated seaman, opened the drydock valves, causing both the ship and Ira S. Bushey & Sons, Inc.'s (P) drydock to partially sink.

RULE OF LAW

An employer is vicariously liable for the reasonably foreseeable conduct of its employees performed within the scope of employment, even when such conduct was not motivated by a purpose of serving the employer.

FACTS: Lane, an intoxicated seaman, was returning at night from shore leave to his ship, a United States Coast Guard vessel in drydock. However, before going aboard, Lane opened a valve that controlled the flooding of the drydock tanks. As a result, both the ship and the Ira S. Bushey & Sons, Inc. (Bushey) (P) drydock were damaged. Bushey (P) sought damages based on the Government's (D) vicarious liability for Lane's actions. The Government (D) denied liability, relying on § 228(1) of the Restatement (Second) of Agency, which stated that the conduct of a servant is within the scope of his employment only if it is actuated at least in part by a purpose to serve the master. However, the trial court rejected that argument and held that an expansion of the employer's liability would serve the public policy of a more intensive screening of employees and allocation of resources. The Government (D) appealed.

ISSUE: Is an employer vicariously liable for the reasonably foreseeable conduct of its employees within the scope of their employment, even when such conduct was not motivated by a purpose of serving the employer?

HOLDING AND DECISION: (Friendly, J.) Yes. An employer is vicariously liable for the reasonably foreseeable conduct of its employees performed within the scope of employment, even when such conduct was not motivated by a purpose of serving the employer. Although courts have traditionally gone to great lengths to find that the motive of the negligent employee was to serve the master, we believe that this "motive test" can be highly artificial. In the instant case, while surely Lane was not serving the Government (D) in his destructive action, nevertheless his conduct was not so "unforeseeable" as to make it unfair to charge the Government (D) with responsibility. It was surely foreseeable that sailors will return to their ships in an intoxicated state; and that intoxicated crew members, in crossing the drydock, might intentionally or negligently damage it. Such an allocation of a reasonably foreseeable risk is fair, and the Government (D) must bear the loss. Affirmed.

▌ ANALYSIS

Although the doctrine of respondeat superior enjoys a virtually unquestioned acceptance in all common-law jurisdictions, nevertheless, writers have usually been unable to identify and to defend its precise rationale. Much effort has been expended to place the stringent rules of respondeat superior within the traditional negligence framework. Young B. Smith, "Frolic and Detour," 23 *Colum. L. Rev.* 444, 445-456 (1923), listed nine rationales for vicarious liability: control, profit, revenge, carefulness and choice, identification, evidence, indulgence, danger, and satisfaction. However, he then concluded that none of them could account for the doctrine. The profit rationale would seem to be the most reasonable. Simply stated, it holds that just as the employer gains from his worker's activities, so too should he bear the losses from those activities.

Quicknotes

FORESEEABILITY A reasonable expectation that an act or omission would result in injury.

VICARIOUS LIABILITY The imputed liability of one party for the unlawful acts of another.

Petrovich v. Share Health Plan of Illinois, Inc.

Patient (P) v. HMO (D)

Ill. Sup. Ct., 719 N.E.2d 756 (1999).

NATURE OF CASE: Medical malpractice suit alleging negligence in failing to timely diagnose illness.

FACT SUMMARY: Petrovich (P), now deceased, brought suit against her physicians and Share Health Plan of Illinois, Inc. (D), her HMO, on the basis that both were responsible for the negligent and late diagnosis of her tongue cancer.

RULE OF LAW

A health maintenance organization (HMO) may be held vicariously liable for the negligence of its independent-contractor physicians under the doctrines of apparent and implied authority.

FACTS: Petrovich (P) alleged that her physician and HMO, Share (D), were responsible for the negligent and late diagnosis of her tongue cancer. Share Health Plan of Illinois, Inc. (Share) (D) was an independent practice association-model, which means that it was the financing entity that arranges for and pays for health care by contracting with independent medical groups and practitioners. Share paid its medical groups through a method of compensation called capitation. Share (D) also maintained a "quality assurance program" to all of its members. The handbook stated that Share (D) would meet all of the member's healthcare needs and provide "comprehensive high quality services." The handbook did not identify the physicians as independent contractors, but rather as "Share physicians." While Petrovich (P) did not read the entire handbook, she read portions of it as needed. Petrovich (P) believed her physicians to be employees of Share (D).

ISSUE: May a health maintenance organization (HMO) be held vicariously liable for the negligence of its independent-contractor physicians under the doctrines of apparent and implied authority?

HOLDING AND DECISION: (Bilandic, J.) Yes. A health maintenance organization (HMO) may be held vicariously liable for the negligence of its independent-contractor physicians under the doctrines of apparent and implied authority. Under the doctrine of apparent authority, a principal is bound by both the actual authority it gives to another as well the authority that it appears to give. Where such appearance of authority is created, a principal may not later deny agency to the detriment of an innocent third party, who has reasonably relied upon such agency and suffered injury. In *Gilbert v. Sycamore Municipal Hospital*, 622 N.E.2d 788 (1993), the court held a hospital vicariously liable for injuries sustained as a result of an independent-contractor physician's negligence. The court

stated that the requirements necessary to provide apparent agency against a hospital were a "holding out" by the hospital and "justifiable reliance" by the patient. The court applies the same factors to the HMO context. Here the holding out prong could be established since she was not given notice that her care was being provided by independent contractors. Justifiable reliance prong is met if the patient relies upon the HMO and not a specific physician to provide health care. Share (D) argued that justifiable reliance could not be established where the patient did not actually select the HMO since there was no nexus between the HMO's alleged wrongful conduct and the patient's injury. However, in a situation such as this where the patient has no choice as to his HMO, the person is likewise relying upon the HMO to provide health care. In determining whether implied authority exists, the issue is whether the alleged agent retains the right to control the means of performing the work. Where a person's independent contractor status is effectively negated, liability may attach under the doctrine of respondeat superior. Petrovich (P) argued that Share's (D) control over her attending physicians negated their independent contractor status. Share (D) argued that since it cannot control a physician's medical judgment, it cannot be vicariously liable under the implied authority doctrine. The Illinois State Medical Society supports imposing vicarious liability upon HMOs for the medical malpractice of their physician under the doctrine of implied authority. Here the facts and circumstances show that Share's (D) system of control over its physicians negated their independent contractor status to Petrovich's (P) detriment. Affirmed.

ANALYSIS

The distinction between independent contractor and employee was articulated in *Sanford v. Goodridge*, 13 N.W.2d 40, 43 (1944). There the court stated that an independent contractor "is one who . . . possesses independence in the manner and method of performing the work he has contracted to perform for the other party." The other party "must relinquish the right of control ordinarily enjoyed by an employer." Furthermore, if the employer has "the right to dictate and control the manner, means, and details of performing the service," then he is liable for any torts committed by the independent contractor under the doctrine of respondeat superior.

■=■=■

Continued on next page.

Quicknotes

APPARENT AUTHORITY The authority granted to an agent to act on behalf of the principal in order to effectuate the principal's objective, which is not expressly granted but which is inferred from the principal's conduct.

IMPLIED AUTHORITY Inferred power granted to an agent to act on behalf of the principal in order to effectuate the principal's objective.

RESPONDEAT SUPERIOR Rule that the principal is responsible for tortious acts committed by its agents in the scope of their agency or authority.

VICARIOUS LIABILITY The imputed liability of one party for the unlawful acts of another.

Products Liability

Quick Reference Rules of Law

PAGE

1. *Winterbottom v. Wright.* A contracting party, unless he has undertaken a public duty, has no   *132*
liability to third parties who are injured as a result of a breach of the contract.

2. *MacPherson v. Buick Motor Co.* A manufacturer will be strictly liable for injury caused by his   *133*
product where, if negligently made, it will be dangerous to the life of any potential user.

3. *Escola v. Coca Cola Bottling Co. of Fresno.* The manufacturer of a defective product should be   *134*
held strictly liable for any injuries that result from the use of the product.

4. *Casa Clara Condominium Association, Inc. v. Charley Toppino & Sons, Inc.* The economic   *136*
loss rule prohibits tort recovery when a product damages itself, causing economic loss, but
does not cause personal injury or damage to any property other than itself.

5. *Speller v. Sears, Roebuck and Co.* The circumstantial approach to proving a product liability   *138*
action requires proof that the product did not perform as intended and all other causes
for the product's failure, that are not attributable to the defendants, have been excluded.

6. *Campo v. Scofield.* A manufacturer will not be liable if it does everything necessary to   *139*
make a machine function properly for the purpose for which it was designed, if the machine is
without any latent defect, and if the machine's functioning creates no danger that is not
known to the user.

7. *Volkswagen of America, Inc. v. Young.* An automobile manufacturer may be held liable for   *140*
injuries sustained in a so-called "second collision" if those injuries were the result of the
manufacturer's negligent design of the vehicle.

8. *Barker v. Lull Engineering Co.* A product is defectively designed (1) if it does not perform as   *141*
safely as the ordinary consumer would expect, when used in an intended or reasonably
foreseeable manner, or (2) if the benefits of the product's design are outweighed by the risk of
danger inherent in such design.

9. *MacDonald v. Ortho Pharmaceutical Corp.* The manufacturer of birth control pills owes a   *142*
direct duty to the consumer to warn her of the dangers inherent in the use of the pill.

10. *Vassallo v. Baxter Healthcare Corp.* A defendant is not liable under the implied warranty of   *143*
merchantability for failure to warn or to provide instructions about risks that were not
reasonably foreseeable at the time of sale, or could not have been reasonably discovered
through reasonable testing, prior to the marketing of the product.

11. *Hood v. Ryobi America Corp.* A manufacturer may be liable for placing a product on the   *145*
market that bears inadequate instructions and warnings or that is defective in design.

12. *Daly v. General Motors Corp.* A plaintiff's negligent conduct will reduce his recovery in strict   *146*
products liability by an amount proportionate to his fault.

13. *Geier v. American Honda Motor Co.* A "no airbag" lawsuit conflicts with the objectives of a   *147*
Federal Motor Vehicle Safety Standard, and is therefore preempted.

14. *Wyeth v. Levine.* Federal regulatory law does not preempt state tort law where the state law   *148*
does not frustrate the achievement of congressional objectives.

Winterbottom v. Wright

Injured coachman (P) v. Coach supplier (D)

Ex., 152 Eng. Rep. 402 (1842).

NATURE OF CASE: Action for damages based on negligence.

FACT SUMMARY: Winterbottom (P) was injured while driving a defective mail coach which the government had bought from Wright (D) pursuant to a supply-maintenance contract.

🏛 RULE OF LAW
A contracting party, unless he has undertaken a public duty, has no liability to third parties who are injured as a result of a breach of the contract.

FACTS: Wright (D) agreed to supply and maintain mail coaches for the use of the Postmaster General. Atkinson also had a contract with the Postmaster General to supply horses and coachmen to operate the mail coaches. Winterbottom (P), one of Atkinson's coachmen, was injured when one of the coaches supplied by Wright (D) broke down. Winterbottom (P) brought suit against Wright (D), contending that his injuries were the result of Wright's (D) negligent performance of the contract with the Postmaster General.

ISSUE: Is a contracting party who has not undertaken a public duty, liable to third persons who are injured as a result of a breach of the contract?

HOLDING AND DECISION: (Abinger, C.B.) No. Parties to a contract are liable only to each other for breaches of the contract, unless privity with respect to the contract and therefore may not sue either party to the contract. If such an action were permitted, contracting parties would be exposed to a potentially unlimited number of suits by strangers to the contract, even in the situation where the breach has been excused or waived. Winterbottom (P) was not privy to the contract between the Postmaster General and Wright (D), and therefore may not maintain an action against him.

▶ ANALYSIS

The harsh *Winterbottom* decision was followed by the majority of courts in the United States during the second half of the 19th century, but a number of exceptions developed. The New York court in *Thomas v. Winchester*, 6 N.Y. 397 (1852), allowed a negligence action by a woman who was poisoned against a chemist who had sold the falsely labeled poison to her druggist. The court's rationale was that the poison was an "imminently dangerous" article, while the defective mail coach in *Winterbottom* was not. Other applications of the "imminently dangerous" exception proved difficult, however, and the New York court in

MacPherson v. Buick Motor Co., 217 N.Y. 382 (1916), finally formulated a general rule of liability of remote manufacturers which eliminated privity as a requirement.

■■■

Quicknotes

LATENT DEFECTS A defect that cannot be discovered upon ordinary examination.

NUISANCE Use of property that interferes with the lawful use of another's property.

PRIVITY OF CONTRACT A relationship between the parties to a contract that is required in order to bring an action for breach.

■■■

MacPherson v. Buick Motor Co.

Injured car owner (P) v. Car manufacturer (D)

N.Y. Ct. App., 111 N.E. 1050 (1916).

NATURE OF CASE: Action for damages for negligence.

FACT SUMMARY: MacPherson (P) purchased a car for his wife (P) who was injured when a defective wheel collapsed.

RULE OF LAW

A manufacturer will be strictly liable for injury caused by his product where, if negligently made, it will be dangerous to the life of any potential user.

FACTS: MacPherson (P) purchased a Buick (D) for his wife (P) telling the salesman of this fact. A wheel on the car collapsed because it was negligently manufactured. Buick (D) obtained the wheels from another manufacturer, but the defect could have easily been discovered by a reasonable inspection. MacPherson (P) and his wife (P) brought suit for property damage and personal injury resulting from the accident. Buick (D) defended on the grounds that an automobile was not a dangerous instrument, therefore strict liability was inappropriate; and that no privity existed between it and the wife (P) since the car was purchased by Mr. MacPherson (P). Judgment was rendered for MacPherson (P) on the ground that negligence in the manufacture of an automobile rendered it dangerous to life and property, and it was foreseeable that Mrs. MacPherson (P) might use the car.

ISSUE: Will strict liability be applied whenever a product which, if negligently made, will be dangerous to the life of any potential user?

HOLDING AND DECISION: (Cardozo, J.) Yes. Strict liability in tort will be applied to any manufacturer who voluntarily places his product in the stream of commerce, knowing that if it is negligently manufactured it is likely to cause severe injury. Buick (D) knew or should have known that if its car tires were made negligently, severe injury would be likely to result. Buick (D) had a duty to inspect the tires before selling the car to the public. Since it was foreseeable that others might use the product and be injured thereby, privity is not required. Affirmed.

DISSENT: (Bartlett, C.J.) The defective wheel was not imminently dangerous to human life. The manufacturer should not be liable except where there is an imminent danger that the negligence will cause serious injury.

▌ ANALYSIS

After *MacPherson*, every jurisdiction abandoned the privity requirement where the product was likely to cause death or serious injury. In *Hanna v. Fletcher*, 231 F.2d 469 (D.C. Cir. 1956), the court held a contractor liable where a third party was later injured when part of a building collapsed due to faulty construction. No privity was required.

■■■

Quicknotes

DUTY TO INSPECT Regarding products liability, the examination of a product for defects prior to releasing the product to a consumer precludes product liability claims from being imposed under a negligence theory, unless those defects arose as the result of manufacturing or design defects.

NEGLIGENCE Conduct falling below the standard of care that a reasonable person would demonstrate under similar conditions.

STRICT LIABILITY Liability for all injuries proximately caused by a party's conducting of certain inherently dangerous activities without regard to negligence or fault.

■■■

Escola v. Coca Cola Bottling Co. of Fresno

Injured waitress (P) v. Cola manufacturer (D)

Cal. Sup. Ct., 150 P.2d 436 (1944).

NATURE OF CASE: Suit to recover damages for personal injuries.

FACT SUMMARY: Escola (P), a waitress in a restaurant, was injured when a Coca-Cola Bottling Co. of Fresno (D) bottle exploded while being placed in a refrigerator.

🏛 RULE OF LAW
The manufacturer of a defective product should be held strictly liable for any injuries that result from the use of the product.

FACTS: Escola (P) was a waitress in a restaurant that served a soft drink manufactured by the Coca-Cola Bottling Co. of Fresno (Coca-Cola) (D). Escola (P) was in the process of refrigerating bottles of Coca-Cola (D) that had been delivered to the restaurant at least 36 hours before. As the fourth bottle was being placed in the refrigerator, it exploded, causing severe injuries to Escola (P). In her suit for damages, Escola (P) alleged negligence on the part of Coca-Cola (D) and successfully relied on the doctrine of res ipsa loquitur. Coca-Cola (D) appealed, arguing that its negligence had not been established.

ISSUE: Does the liability of a manufacturer of a defective product depend upon a showing of negligence?

HOLDING AND DECISION: (Gibson, J.) [In an opinion not fully reprinted in the casebook, the majority of the court affirmed Escola's (P) judgment, basing its affirmance on the doctrine of res ipsa loquitur.]

CONCURRENCE: (Traynor, J.) No. The manufacturer of a defective product should be held strictly liable for any injuries that result from the use of the product. In the modern commercial setting, a consumer rarely has the opportunity to inspect the items which he purchases, yet it is imperative that defective merchandise be prevented from reaching potential users. Public policy mandates that liability be imposed upon the manufacturer, who is best able to prevent defects and is at the same time singularly able to spread the costs of bearing the risk of harm. And, the liability of the manufacturer should not depend upon proof of his negligence, because it will be a rare case in which an injured party, unfamiliar with the manufacturer's production process, will be able to ascertain the precise nature of that negligence. Where foodstuffs are involved, strict criminal liability is imposed by statute upon producers of defective goods, and the potential injuries which may result from the use of products other than food, justifies application of the strict liability doctrine to civil actions against manufacturers of all products. A retailer always owes his customer an implied warranty of safety, but since the retailer usually can recover from the manufacturer for judgments obtained by injured consumers, it makes sense to impose liability upon the manufacturer directly. Consumers are constantly bombarded with representations concerning a product's utility and worth, and justifiably rely upon the manufacturer's assertions in that regard. It is, therefore, fair that when defective products do reach the market, the manufacturer should be held strictly liable for injuries to any party who uses such products properly. Clearly, the facts of this case compel the conclusion that the judgment in favor of Escola (P) should be affirmed.

▌ ANALYSIS

Justice Traynor's concurring opinion in *Escola v. Coca-Cola Bottling Co. of Fresno* was one of the earliest and most thorough arguments in favor of strict liability in products liability cases. Today, of course, strict liability is widely accepted as the appropriate standard in such cases. Note that the plaintiff must establish that the defect in the product manufactured by the defendant was the legal cause of his injuries. And, liability will not attach if it is proved that the defect that caused the plaintiff's injuries was not present when the product left the control of the defendant. Recovery will also be denied upon a showing that the plaintiff was injured only because he chose to use the product in a manner other than the producer intended or could have anticipated.

▬▭

Quicknotes

DUTY TO INSPECT Regarding products liability, the examination of a product for defects prior to releasing the product to a consumer precludes product liability claims from being imposed under a negligence theory, unless those defects arose as the result of manufacturing or design defects.

NEGLIGENCE Conduct falling below the standard of care that a reasonable person would demonstrate under similar conditions.

RES IPSA LOQUITUR A rule of law giving rise to an inference of negligence where the instrument inflicting the injury is in the exclusive control of the defendant and where such harm could not ordinarily result in the absence of negligence.

Continued on next page.

STRICT LIABILITY Liability for all injuries proximately caused by a party's conducting of certain inherently dangerous activities without regard to negligence or fault.

Casa Clara Condominium Association, Inc. v. Charley Toppino & Sons, Inc.

Homeowner association (P) v. Concrete supplier (D)

Fla. Sup. Ct., 620 So. 2d 1244 (1993).

NATURE OF CASE: Appeal from dismissal of a negligence action to recover economic losses.

FACT SUMMARY: Casa Clara Condominium Association, Inc. (P) sued Charley Toppino & Sons, Inc. (Toppino) (D) in negligence to recover economic losses suffered after building its homes with defective concrete supplied by Toppino (D).

RULE OF LAW
The economic loss rule prohibits tort recovery when a product damages itself, causing economic loss, but does not cause personal injury or damage to any property other than itself.

FACTS: Casa Clara Condominium Association, Inc. (Casa Clara) (P) sued Charley Toppino & Sons, Inc. (Toppino) (D) in an action for negligence after Toppino (D) supplied concrete to Casa Clara (P) for the construction of condominiums. The concrete (which contained a high salt content) caused the reinforcing steel in the condos to rust, which, in turn, caused the concrete to break off. Casa Clara's (P) claims against Toppino (D) included breach of common law implied warranty, products liability, negligence, and violation of the building code. The circuit court dismissed all counts against Toppino (D) in each case. The district court, on appeal, applied the economic loss rule and held that, because no person was injured and no other property damaged, Casa Clara (P) had no cause of action against Toppino (D) in tort.

ISSUE: Does the economic loss rule prohibit tort recovery when a product damages itself, causing economic loss, but does not cause personal injury or damage to any property other than itself?

HOLDING AND DECISION: (McDonald, J.) Yes. The economic loss rule prohibits tort recovery when a product damages itself, causing economic loss, but does not cause personal injury or damage to any property other than itself. This rule is the fundamental boundary between contract law, which is designed to enforce the expectancy interests of the parties, and tort law, which imposes a duty of reasonable care and thereby encourages citizens to avoid causing physical harm to others. Economic loss has been defined as damages for inadequate value, costs of repair, and replacement of the defective product or consequent loss of profits—without any claim of personal injury or damage to other property. In other words, economic losses are disappointed economic expectations, which are protected by contract law, rather than tort law. Here, Casa

Clara (P) finds a tort remedy attractive because it permits the recovery of greater damages than an action in contract and may avoid the conditions of the contract. However, Casa Clara (P) homeowners are seeking purely economic damages—no one has sustained any physical injury, and no property other than the structures built with Toppino's (D) concrete has sustained any damage. Casa Clara (P) argues that holding it to contract remedies is unfair and homeowners in general should be exempted from the operation of the economic loss rule. But there are protections for home buyers, such as statutory warranties, the general warranty of habitability, and the duty of sellers to disclose defects, as well as the ability of the house buyer to inspect a house for defects. Coupled with the home buyers' power to bargain over price, these protections are sufficient when compared to the mischief that could be caused by allowing tort recovery for purely economic losses. Affirmed.

CONCURRENCE AND DISSENT: (Barkett, C.J.) Here, although Casa Clara (P) homeowners assert that their homes are literally crumbling around them because Toppino's (D) concrete was negligently manufactured, the courts have said "too bad!" That answer is unacceptable in light of the principle underlying Florida's Access to Courts provision: absent compelling countervailing public policies, wrongs must have remedies.

CONCURRENCE AND DISSENT: (Shaw, J.) Under negligence theory, purely economic loss cannot be recovered by parties to a contract when the loss is to property that is the subject of the contract. However, the logic of this restriction is inapplicable in this instance. The rationale of the economic loss rule is that parties who have bargained for the distribution of risk of loss should not be permitted to circumvent their bargain after loss occurs. But the economic loss theory was never intended to defeat tort causes of action that would otherwise lie for damages to a third party by a defective product.

ANALYSIS

The *Casa Clara* rule has been adopted as the law by most courts. A strong minority of courts, however, takes the position the strict liability rule of Restatement § 402A should prevail over warranty disclaimers even in circumstances where there has been only economic loss. Some courts take the middle ground and apply § 402A only when

Continued on next page.

there has been "sudden" damage to the product, resulting in personal injury.

▬▬

Quicknotes

ECONOMIC LOSS RULE For products liability losses, economic losses can include repair and replacement costs as well as lost profits and the commercial value lost due to inadequate use.

WARRANTY OF HABITABILITY An implied warranty owed by a landlord to a tenant to provide leased premises in properly maintained in a habitable condition prior to leasing the premises and during the duration of the lease.

▬▬

Speller v. Sears, Roebuck and Co.

Fire victim (P) v. Manufacturer and retailer (D)

N.Y. Ct. App. 790 N.E.2d 252 (2003).

NATURE OF CASE: Appeal of summary judgment in favor of Sears, Roebuck and Co. (D) in a products liability action.

FACT SUMMARY: Speller (P) sued Sears, Roebuck and Co. (Sears) (D) after her (P) decedent, Sandra, died and Sandra's (P) son was injured in a fire allegedly caused by a defective refrigerator, which Sears (P) sold.

RULE OF LAW
The circumstantial approach to proving a product liability action requires proof that the product did not perform as intended and all other causes for the product's failure, that are not attributable to the defendants, have been excluded.

FACTS: Speller's (P) decedent, Sandra, died in a house fire that also injured Sandra's (P) seven-year-old son. The fire originated in the kitchen. Speller (P) sued Sears, Roebuck and Co. (Sears) (D), Whirlpool Corporation, and the property owner alleging negligence, strict products liability, and breach of warranty. Speller (P) asserted that the fire was caused by defective wiring in the refrigerator, which was manufactured by Whirlpool (D) and sold by Sears (D). Sears (D) and Whirlpool (D) moved for summary judgment on the basis of a report by the New York City Fire Marshal concluding that a stovetop grease fire was the cause of the fire. In opposition, Speller (P) presented three expert opinions that contradicted the Fire Marshal's findings and placed blame for the fire on the defective refrigerator. Sears (D) was granted summary judgment, and Speller (P) appealed.

ISSUE: Did Speller (P) raise a triable issue of fact concerning whether the defective refrigerator caused the fire?

HOLDING AND DECISION: (Graffeo, J.) Yes. Speller (P) raised a triable issue of fact concerning whether the defective refrigerator caused the fire because she proved that all other causes for the product's failure, that were not attributable to the defendant, had been excluded. A product manufacturer or others in the distribution chain will be liable if someone is injured as a result of a defective product if the defect was a substantial factor in causing the injury. In the present case, the wiring of the refrigerator was not tested because it was consumed in the fire. Speller (P) had to prove her claim circumstantially by establishing that the refrigerator caused the house fire and therefore it did not perform as intended. The circumstantial approach is a viable route to prove a products liability case. However, in addition to proving that the product did not perform as intended, all other causes for the product's failure that are not attributable to the defendants must be excluded. Sears's (D) motion argued that the injuries were not caused by their product, but by a grease fire that began on the stove. Speller (P), however, came forward with competent evidence, in the form of three expert witnesses, excluding the stove as the origin of the fire, and concluding that the fire originated in the refrigerator. The three expert witnesses were an electrical engineer, a fire investigator, and a former Deputy Chief of the New York City Fire Department. Their testimony regarding the source of the fire raised a triable question of fact, which, if credited by the jury, was sufficient to rebut Sears's (D) alternative cause evidence. Based on Speller's (P) proof, a reasonable jury could conclude that Speller (P) excluded all other causes of the fire. Reversed.

ANALYSIS

The holding into this case is consistent with the Restatement (Third) of Torts: Product Liability § 3 (1998).

Quicknotes

PRODUCT LIABILITY The legal liability of manufacturers and sellers for damages and injuries suffered by buyers, users, and even bystanders because of defects in goods purchased.

SUMMARY JUDGMENT Judgment rendered by a court in response to a motion by one of the parties, claiming that the lack of a question of material fact in respect to an issue warrants disposition of the issue without consideration by the jury.

Campo v. Scofield

[Parties not identified.]

N.Y. Ct. App. 95 N.E.2d 802, 804 (1950).

NATURE OF CASE: [Nature of case not stated in casebook excerpt.]

FACT SUMMARY: [Facts not stated in casebook excerpt.]

🏛 RULE OF LAW
A manufacturer will not be liable if it does everything necessary to make a machine function properly for the purpose for which it was designed, if the machine is without any latent defect, and if the machine's functioning creates no danger that is not known to the user.

FACTS: [Facts not stated in casebook excerpt.]

ISSUE: Is a manufacturer liable for injuries incurred by a machine that functioned properly when used normally and had no latent defects or hidden dangers?

HOLDING AND DECISION: (Fuld, J.) No. A manufacturer will not be liable if it does everything necessary to make a machine function properly for the purpose for which it was designed, if the machine is without any latent defect, and if the machine's functioning creates no danger that is not known to the user. A manufacturer does not have to furnish a machine that does not wear out in order to guard against injury resulting from deterioration. A manufacturer, therefore, has no duty to guard against an injury from a patent peril or from a source manifestly dangerous because the very nature of the product puts the user on notice of the possible dangers surrounding it.

▌ANALYSIS

The court is inferring here that a manufacturer is not required to make a machine accident-proof or foolproof.

▬▬▬

Quicknotes

LATENT DEFECTS A defect that cannot be discovered upon ordinary examination.

▬▬▬

Volkswagen of America, Inc. v. Young

Car manufacturer (D) v. Car crash victim (P)

Md. Ct. App., 321 A.2d 737 (1974).

NATURE OF CASE: Suit seeking damages for wrongful death.

FACT SUMMARY: Young's (P) decedent was killed when the back seat of his Volkswagen (D) tore loose following a collision with another vehicle.

RULE OF LAW
An automobile manufacturer may be held liable for injuries sustained in a so-called "second collision" if those injuries were the result of the manufacturer's negligent design of the vehicle.

FACTS: Young's (P) decedent stopped his 1968 Volkswagen of America, Inc. (Volkswagen) (D) car at a traffic light and was struck from behind by a negligently driven Ford. He suffered fatal injuries when he was tossed into the rear of his car after colliding with the back seat. This so-called "second collision" resulted when the bracketing pieces and seat adjustment mechanisms of the back seat tore loose from the body of the car. Young (P) brought suit in federal district court, alleging that the Volkswagen (D) Beetle had been so designed and manufactured as to be hazardous, not merchantable, and not fit for its intended purpose. Upon motion of Volkswagen (D), the federal court certified to the Maryland Court of Appeals the question of whether a vehicle's intended use included its involvement in an accident, and whether a manufacturer could be held liable for injuries caused by improper design and manufacture of a vehicle even though the defect did not contribute to the occurrence of the accident from which the injuries resulted.

ISSUE: Is a vehicle manufacturer liable for the additional injuries that an accident victim sustains as a result of the defective design of the vehicle?

HOLDING AND DECISION: (Eldridge, J.) Yes. An automobile manufacturer may be held liable for injuries sustained in a so-called "second collision" if those injuries were the result of the manufacturer's negligent design of the vehicle. In *Evans v. General Motors Corporation*, 359 F.2d 822 (7th Cir. 1966), it was held that a manufacturer is not liable in such a case since an automobile's intended use does not include its involvement in accidents. But the modern trend is clearly to follow the rule of *Larsen v. General Motors Corporation*, 391 F.2d 495 (8th Cir. 1968), wherein it was held that injuries resulting from a "second collision" are the responsibility of the manufacturer if those injuries occurred because of the faulty design of the vehicle. The *Larsen* court emphasized that automobile manufacturers should anticipate that their products will be involved in accidents and are therefore obligated to make vehicles that will be reasonably safe even if collisions occur. Economy of manufacture, attractiveness, and utility of the vehicle are factors to be considered in determining whether a reasonably safe product has been created, and the manufacturer cannot be held liable for dangerous design features that are obvious and apparent. But traditional principles of negligence dictate that liability should attach when latent design defects cause a "second collision" or otherwise exacerbate injuries. Imposition of liability in such cases does not make the manufacturer an insurer, nor does it obligate the manufacturer to produce cars that are injury proof. And, it cannot seriously be contended that the result reached in this case should be imposed only pursuant to legislative mandate. While this type case is not one in which strict liability should be imposed, to hold automobile manufacturers liable under the circumstances of this case is wholly consistent with the evolution of negligence law.

ANALYSIS

The thoughts articulated by the Maryland Court of Appeals in *Volkswagen of America, Inc. v. Young* are consistent with the results reached in most recent "second collision" cases. For instance, there appears to be little opposition to the important proposition that accidents are within the scope of an automobile's intended use. It is worthwhile to note that, although the *Young* decision expressly rejects the strict liability standard, strict liability was imposed in a California case that involved facts strikingly similar to those of the *Young* case. See *Cronin v. J.B.E. Olson Corp.*, 8 Cal. 3d 121, 501 P.2d 1153, 104 Cal. Rptr. 433 (1972).

Quicknotes

DESIGN DEFECT A defect that exists in a product regardless of the method of manufacture or amount of due care exercised by those in the commercial chain of distribution, but instead as the result of flaws in the product's design.

NEGLIGENCE Conduct falling below the standard of care that a reasonable person would demonstrate under similar conditions.

STRICT LIABILITY Liability for all injuries proximately caused by a party's conducting of certain inherently dangerous activities without regard to negligence or fault.

Barker v. Lull Engineering Co.

Injured construction worker (P) v. Manufacturer of construction loader (D)

Cal. Sup. Ct., 573 P.2d 443 (1978).

NATURE OF CASE: Appeal from denial of damages in products liability action.

FACT SUMMARY: Barker (P) sought to recover under a strict liability theory for injuries sustained while operating a machine manufactured by Lull Engineering Co. (D), claiming that the defective design of the machine proximately caused these injuries.

🏛 RULE OF LAW

A product is defectively designed (1) if it does not perform as safely as the ordinary consumer would expect, when used in an intended or reasonably foreseeable manner, or (2) if the benefits of the product's design are outweighed by the risk of danger inherent in such design.

FACTS: Lull Engineering Co. (Lull) (D) manufactured a "high-lift loader," designed for use on level terrain. In August 1970, while operating the machine on uneven terrain in order to lift some lumber, Barker (P) felt the loader vibrate. Jumping off the loader to escape harm, he was struck by a heavy piece of lumber and seriously injured. When Barker (P) brought suit, the trial court instructed the jury "that strict liability for a defect in design of a product is based on a finding that the product was unreasonably dangerous for its intended use." Following a verdict for Lull (D), Barker (P) appealed, claiming that the trial court erred in giving this instruction.

ISSUE: Is it prejudicial error for a trial court to instruct the jury that strict liability for defective design requires a finding that the product was unreasonably dangerous for its intended use?

HOLDING AND DECISION: (Tobriner, C.J.) Yes. In *Cronin v. J.B.E. Olson Corp.*, 8 Cal.3d 121, 501 P.2d 1153, 104 Cal. Rptr. 433 (1972), the California Supreme Court rejected the use of the "unreasonably dangerous" standard for defining "defect" in product liability actions. The "unreasonably dangerous" terminology suggested that recovery should be permitted only if a product is more dangerous than contemplated by the average consumer. Often, however, the consumer cannot know what to expect, as he has no idea how safe the product could be made. Thus, a manufacturer's liability should not be so circumscribed. While *Cronin* involved a "manufacturing defect," the rationale of the case is equally applicable to "design defects." Hence, a trial court may properly instruct that a product is defective in design (1) if it has failed to perform as safely as the ordinary consumer would expect, when used in an intended or reasonably foreseeable manner, or (2) if the

benefits of the product's design are outweighed by the risk of danger inherent in such design. Furthermore, with respect to the risk-benefit standard, once the plaintiff makes a prima facie showing that the injury was proximately caused by the product's design, the manufacturer has the burden of proving the design is not defective. Here, the trial court did not instruct the jury properly but, rather, used the "unreasonably dangerous" standard. In light of the *Cronin* decision, this is prejudicial error. Reversed.

▶ ANALYSIS

Barker v. Lull Engineering Co. is a major expansion of the concept of product defect. Other states have likewise rejected the Restatement's "unreasonably dangerous" terminology, *e.g.*, *Azzarello v. Black Bros. Co., Inc.*, 480 Pa. 547, 391 A. 2d 1020 (1978). Furthermore, at least one case has squarely adopted the standard developed by the California Supreme Court in *Barker v. Lull: Caterpillar Tractor Co. v. Beck*, 593 P.2d 871 (Alaska 1979).

Quicknotes

DESIGN DEFECT A defect that exists in a product regardless of the method of manufacture or amount of due care exercised by those in the commercial chain of distribution, but instead as the result of flaws in the product's design.

PROXIMATE CAUSE The natural sequence of events without which an injury would not have been sustained.

STRICT LIABILITY Liability for all injuries proximately caused by a party's conducting of certain inherently dangerous activities without regard to negligence or fault.

MacDonald v. Ortho Pharmaceutical Corp.

Birth control pill users (P) v. Pharmaceutical manufacturer (D)

Mass. Sup. Jud. Ct., 475 N.E.2d 65 (1985).

NATURE OF CASE: Appeal from decision granting judgment notwithstanding the verdict.

FACT SUMMARY: MacDonald (P) appealed from the court's decision granting Ortho Pharmaceutical Corp.'s (Ortho) (D) motion for judgment notwithstanding the verdict in favor of MacDonald (P), contending that as a manufacturer of an oral contraceptive, Ortho (D) had a direct duty to MacDonald (P), the consumer, to warn her of inherent dangers.

🏛 RULE OF LAW
The manufacturer of birth control pills owes a direct duty to the consumer to warn her of the dangers inherent in the use of the pill.

FACTS: Ortho Pharmaceutical Corp. (Ortho) (D) manufactured birth control pills eventually prescribed to MacDonald (P). Ortho (D) provided a booklet outlining the dangers inherent in the use of the pill to MacDonald's (P) gynecologist. The individual pill dispenser also contained warnings in compliance with United States Food and Drug Administration (FDA) requirements. Neither warning mentioned a "stroke," though each mentioned blood clotting and possible fatal consequences. MacDonald (P), who suffered a stroke and permanent brain damage, sued Ortho (D), alleging essentially the failure to warn properly. The jury found Ortho (D) negligent for failure to give sufficient warnings of the dangers inherent in the pill's use. Upon motion by Ortho (D), the court entered a judgment in favor of Ortho (D) notwithstanding the jury's verdict, finding that Ortho's (D) duty to warn was satisfied by giving adequate warnings to the physician. MacDonald (P) appealed.

ISSUE: Does the manufacturer of birth control pills owe a direct duty to the consumer to warn her of the dangers inherent in the use of the pill?

HOLDING AND DECISION: (Abrams, J.) Yes. The manufacturer of birth control pills owes a direct duty to the consumer to warn her of the dangers inherent in the use of the pill. While noting that this is a departure from the ordinary "prescription drug" rule, the prescription of oral contraceptives differs from the ordinary prescription drug situation in the following ways. The consumer is much more involved in the decision to use the pill. There are substantial risks associated with the pill, and direct warnings from the manufacturer are feasible. There is limited participation (annually) by the physician, and there may be inadequate communication between physician and patient regarding the dangers inherent in the use of the pill.

Given these distinctions, Ortho (D) cannot rely on warnings issued to physicians to satisfy its common law duty to warn. (The court went on to determine that the dispenser warning, although in compliance with FDA regulations, was not sufficient as a matter of law, and upheld the jury's decision that the warning was not unreasonable as a matter of law.) Reversed and remanded.

DISSENT: (O'Connor, J.) Adequate warning to the physician in compliance with FDA regulations is sufficient as a matter of law to comply with Ortho's (D) duty to warn.

▶ ANALYSIS

The expanded liability recognized in the present case has been expanded to other areas. In *Lauperi v. Sears, Roebuck & Co.*, 787 F.2d 726 (1st Cir. 1986), the *MacDonald* reasoning was used to expand the scope of liability to the manufacturer of smoke alarms for the failure to adequately warn the consumer.

Quicknotes

JUDGMENT NOTWITHSTANDING THE VERDICT A judgment entered by the trial judge reversing a jury verdict if the jury's determination has no basis in law or fact.

NEGLIGENCE Conduct falling below the standard of care that a reasonable person would demonstrate under similar conditions.

Vassallo v. Baxter Healthcare Corp.

Breast implant recipient (P) v. Manufacturer (D)

Mass. Sup. Jud. Ct., 696 N.E.2d 909 (1998).

NATURE OF CASE: Products liability action.

FACT SUMMARY: Vassallo (P) brought suit, seeking recovery of damages for injuries sustained as a result of the rupturing of her silicone breast implants on the basis that the implants were negligently designed and that the manufacturer negligently failed to provide adequate warnings in breach of the implied warranty of merchantability.

🏛 RULE OF LAW
A defendant is not liable under the implied warranty of merchantability for failure to warn or to provide instructions about risks that were not reasonably foreseeable at the time of sale, or could not have been reasonably discovered through reasonable testing, prior to the marketing of the product.

FACTS: Vassallo (P) underwent breast implant surgery. About 15 years later, she underwent a mammogram after suffering from chest pains under her left armpit. The mammogram showed that the breast implants had possibly ruptured. The silicone gel implants were removed and replaced with saline implants. During the surgery the surgeon noted severe, permanent scarring of Vassallo's (P) pectoral muscles that was attributed to the silicone gel. The left implant had ruptured and the right had several pinholes through which the silicon could escape. Testimony revealed that there was knowledge regarding the possible adverse long-term consequences of leaking silicone into the body; however, Heyer-Schulte Corp. (D), the manufacturer, conducted few animal and no clinical, studies regarding the safety of its silicone gel implants. While Heyer-Schulte (D) did furnish warnings to doctors, they did not address the possibility of gel bleed, ruptures or the consequences of silicone gel escaping into the body. Vassallo (P) brought suit for damages on the basis that the implants were negligently designed, accompanied by negligent product warnings and in breach of the implied warranty of merchantability, resulting in her injuries. The jury found in favor of Vassallo (P). The judge entered a separate memorandum of decision in favor of Vassallo (P). Baxter Healthcare Corp. (Baxter) (D) appealed.

ISSUE: Is a defendant liable under the implied warranty of merchantability for failure to warn or to provide instructions about risks that were not reasonably foreseeable at the time of sale, or could not have been reasonably discovered through reasonable testing, prior to the marketing of the product?

HOLDING AND DECISION: (Greaney, J.) No. A defendant is not liable under the implied warranty of merchantability for failure to warn or to provide instructions about risks that were not reasonably foreseeable at the time of sale, or could not have been reasonably discovered through reasonable testing, prior to the marketing of the product. The manufacturer will be held accountable to the standard of knowledge of an expert in the relevant field, and is subject to a continuing duty to warn consumers of risks discovered following the sale of the particular product. Baxter (D) argued that products liability law regarding the implied warranty of merchantability should be reformulated to adopt a "state of the art" standard conditioning the manufacturer's liability on the actual or constructive knowledge of the risks. The duty to warn under the implied warranty of merchantability presumes that a manufacturer is fully informed of all the risks associated with a product, regardless of the state of the art at the time of sale. Thus, the manufacturer is strictly liable for failure to warn of associated risks. The majority of states follow the Restatement (Second) of Torts § 402A comment j principle that the seller must warn against a danger "if he has knowledge, or by the application of reasonable, developed human skill and foresight should have knowledge of, the danger." This state follows the minority rule, which applies a hindsight analysis to the duty to warn. The rationale for the hindsight rule in strict liability jurisdictions is that the goal of providing an incentive to manufacturers to take reasonable measures for consumer protection would not be advanced if liability were imposed with respect to risks that were incapable of being discovered. In light of the modern trend regarding the duty to warn in products liability cases and the Restatement (Third) of Torts, the law in Massachusetts is revised to state that a defendant will not be held liable under an implied warranty of merchantability for failure to warn or provide instructions about risks that were not reasonably foreseeable at the time of sale or could not have been reasonably discovered through reasonable testing prior to the marketing of the product. The manufacturer will be held accountable to the standard of knowledge of an expert in the relevant field, and is subject to a continuing duty to warn consumers of risks discovered following the sale of the particular product. This standard applies to all claims on which a final judgment has not yet been entered or to which an appeal is pending or the appeal period has not yet expired and to all claims commenced after this ruling. Affirmed.

Continued on next page.

⟩ ANALYSIS

The majority of jurisdictions follow the Restatement of Torts (Second) § 402A comment j rule requiring a warning if the seller has knowledge, or if "by the application of reasonable, developed human skill and foresight should have knowledge of the danger." Restatement of Torts (Third): Products Liability § 2(c) comment m ratifies this rule and clarifies that the manufacturer has a duty to perform testing prior to marketing a product to discover risks. Furthermore, a seller of the product is also charged with knowledge of the risks as discovered by the reasonable testing.

━■━

Quicknotes

FAILURE TO WARN The failure of an owner or occupier of land to inform persons present on the property of defects or active operations that may cause injury.

IMPLIED WARRANTY OF MERCHANTABILITY An implied promise made by a merchant in a contract for the sale of goods that such goods are suitable for the purpose for which they are purchased.

REASONABLE FORESEEABILITY A reasonable expectation that an act or omission would result in injury.

━■━

Hood v. Ryobi America Corp.

Injured consumer (P) v. Manufacturer (D)

181 F.3d 608 (4th Cir. 1999).

NATURE OF CASE: Appeal from summary judgment for defendant.

FACT SUMMARY: Hood (P) alleged that Ryobi America Corp. (D) failed to adequately warn of dangers of using an allegedly defectively designed saw.

🏛 RULE OF LAW
A manufacturer may be liable for placing a product on the market that bears inadequate instructions and warnings or that is defective in design.

FACTS: Hood (P) purchased a saw manufactured by Ryobi America Corp. (Ryobi) (D) to use for home repairs. The saw itself warned that the saw blade guards that were attached to the saw should never be removed. The owner's manual also contained similar warnings. Disregarding the warnings, Hood (P) removed the saw blade guards and was later seriously injured when the spinning saw blade flew off the saw. Hood claimed that Ryobi's (D) warnings were not adequate because they were not specific enough, and that the saw had been defectively designed. Hood (P) sued under negligence, strict liability, and breach of warranty. The district court granted Ryobi's (D) motion for summary judgment and Hood (P) appealed.

ISSUE: May a manufacturer be liable for placing a product on the market that bears inadequate instructions and warnings or that is defective in design?

HOLDING AND DECISION: (Wilkinson, C.J.) Yes. A manufacturer may be liable for placing a product on the market that bears inadequate instructions and warnings or that is defective in design. A warning need only be one that is reasonable under the circumstances. Ryobi's (D) warnings were clear and unequivocal. Ryobi (D) placed three labels on the saw itself and at least four warnings in the owner's manual. The warnings were adequate as a matter of law. Affirmed.

▌*ANALYSIS*

The court declined to hold the manufacturer liable because of the affirmative misuse by Hood (P). The additional warnings Hood (P) had claimed were necessary were found by the court to be more confusing and unnecessary. Some courts rule on the issue of the adequacy of the warnings as a matter of law. Other courts leave this issue for the jury to decide.

Quicknotes

DUTY TO WARN An obligation owed by an owner or occupier of land to persons who come onto the premises, to inform them of defects or active operations which may cause injury.

NEGLIGENCE Conduct falling below the standard of care that a reasonable person would demonstrate under similar conditions.

PRODUCT LIABILITY The legal liability of manufacturers and sellers for damages and injuries suffered by buyers, users, and even bystanders because of defects in goods purchased.

STRICT LIABILITY Liability for all injuries proximately caused by a party's conducting of certain inherently dangerous activities without regard to negligence or fault.

Daly v. General Motors Corp.

Fatal car accident victim (P) v. Car manufacturer (D)

Cal. Sup. Ct., 575 P.2d 1162 (1978).

NATURE OF CASE: Appeal from denial of damages in products liability action.

FACT SUMMARY: After decedent sustained fatal injuries when thrown from his car, which was manufactured by General Motors Corp. (D), Daly (P) claimed the defective design of the door lock caused decedent to be thrown. But General Motors (D) contended that decedent was ejected through his failure to use the car's safety devices.

> 🏛 **RULE OF LAW**
> A plaintiff's negligent conduct will reduce his recovery in strict products liability by an amount proportionate to his fault.

FACTS: In October 1970, decedent was driving his Opel on the freeway when it hit the metal divider. Thrown from the car, he sustained fatal head injuries. Daly (P), on behalf of the widow and children, alleged defective product design, claiming that the exposed pushbutton of the door lock was forced open in the collision, causing decedent to be ejected. General Motors Corp. (D) introduced evidence that the car contained a seat belt harness and a door lock, either of which would have prevented decedent's ejection and, further, that decedent was intoxicated and failed to use these protections. Daly (P) appealed from a verdict for General Motors (D).

ISSUE: Do comparative fault principles apply in strict product liability cases, so that plaintiff's negligent conduct proportionately reduces his recovery in strict liability?

HOLDING AND DECISION: (Richardson, J.) Yes. Strict liability is imposed on manufacturers in order to avoid placing the burden of loss on injured persons who are unable to protect themselves from manufacturing defects. But that part of a plaintiff's damages which results from his own fault should not be apportioned to others. Thus, comparative principles should apply to proportionately reduce his recovery in strict liability. This principle is not retroactive, however. In this case, since the issue of comparative fault was first raised on appeal, there was no basis for having the jury evaluate the evidence under comparative fault principles. The principles will apply in the event of retrial, however. Reversed.

CONCURRENCE AND DISSENT: (Jefferson, J.) The jury cannot accurately measure or compare a defendant's strict liability with a plaintiff's negligence; thus, it will be unable to fairly apportion liability.

DISSENT: (Mosk, J.) Negligence is a concept foreign to products liability. The issues are whether a product is defective and whether the defect caused the injury; the victim's conduct is irrelevant to these issues.

▶ ANALYSIS

As a general rule, contributory negligence (failure to guard against or discover defects) is not a defense to a strict products liability action, while assumption of the risk is a defense. Some states, California now among them, have extended the concept of comparative fault to strict products liability actions, e.g., *Butand v. Suburban Marine & Sporting Goods, Inc.*, 555 P. 2d 42 (Alaska 1976). In these states, assumption of the risk has merged with comparative principles and is no longer a separate defense.

Quicknotes

DESIGN DEFECT A defect that exists in a product regardless of the method of manufacture or amount of due care exercised by those in the commercial chain of distribution, but instead as the result of flaws in the product's design.

STRICT LIABILITY Liability for all injuries proximately caused by a party's conducting of certain inherently dangerous activities without regard to negligence or fault.

Geier v. American Honda Motor Co.

Injured driver (P) v. Manufacturer (D)

529 U.S. 861 (2000).

NATURE OF CASE: Review of dismissal of tort claims.

FACT SUMMARY: Geier (P) was seriously injured when her car struck a tree and sued American Honda Motor Co. (D) for allegedly negligently and defectively designing a car without a driver's side airbag.

🏛 RULE OF LAW
A "no airbag" lawsuit conflicts with the objectives of a Federal Motor Vehicle Safety Standard, and is therefore preempted.

FACTS: Geier (P), who was injured when her car hit a tree, alleged that American Honda Motor Co. (Honda) (D) was negligent in not equipping the car with air bags or other passive restraint devices. The district court dismissed the suit, claiming it was preempted by federal standards that gave manufacturers a choice as to whether to install airbags. The court of appeals affirmed. Geier (P) appealed. The United States Supreme Court granted certiorari.

ISSUE: Does a "no airbag" lawsuit conflict with the objectives of a Federal Motor Vehicle Safety Standard, and is it therefore preempted?

HOLDING AND DECISION: (Breyer, J.) Yes. A "no airbag" lawsuit conflicts with the objectives of a Federal Motor Vehicle Safety Standard, and is therefore preempted. Ordinary preemption principles apply to this case. The National Traffic and Motor Vehicle Safety Act authorized the promulgation of federal standards and preempted state law safety standards. Affirmed.

DISSENT: (Stevens, J.) An interim regulation, motivated by the Secretary of Transportation's desire to foster gradual development of a variety of passive restraint devices, should not deprive state courts of jurisdiction over claims of negligence or defective design. Honda (D) has not overcome the presumption against preemption in this case.

▶ ANALYSIS

The dissent would have permitted preemption of tort claims only if they created a special burden on the federal regulatory scheme. The preemption was based on inferences from regulatory history and commentary alone. The majority deferred to the Department of Transportation's own interpretation of the federal standards.

Quicknotes

DEFECTIVE DESIGN A product that is manufactured in accordance with a particular design; however, such design is inherently flawed so that it presents an unreasonable risk of injury.

FEDERALISM A scheme of government whereby the power to govern is divided between a central government and localized governments.

NEGLIGENCE Conduct falling below the standard of care that a reasonable person would demonstrate under similar conditions.

PREEMPTION Judicial preference recognizing the presumption in favor of federal legislation over state legislation of the same subject matter.

Wyeth v. Levine

Drug manufacturer (D) v. Drug recipient (P)

555 U.S. 555 (2009).

NATURE OF CASE: Appeal, on grounds that certain federal regulations preempt state tort law, from state's highest court's affirmance of a jury verdict for a plaintiff in a product liability action.

FACT SUMMARY: Levine (P) contended that notwithstanding the federal Food and Drug Administration's (FDA's) approval of Wyeth's (D) warning label for Wyeth's (D) drug Phenergan, the warning label was inadequate by state tort law standards. Wyeth (D) asserted that state tort law was preempted by federal regulatory law in this area.

🏛 RULE OF LAW

Federal regulatory law does not preempt state tort law where the state law does not frustrate the achievement of congressional objectives.

FACTS: Wyeth (D) manufactured the antinausea drug Phenergan. The warnings on Phenergan's label had been deemed sufficient by the federal Food and Drug Administration (FDA) when it approved Wyeth's (D) new drug application in 1955 and when it later approved changes in the drug's labeling. After a clinician injected Levine (P) with Phenergan by the "IV-push" method, whereby a drug is injected directly into a patient's vein, the drug entered Levine's (P) artery, she developed gangrene, and doctors amputated her forearm. Levine (P) brought a state-law damages action on theories of common-law negligence and strict liability, alleging, inter alia, that Wyeth (D) had failed to provide an adequate warning about the significant risks of administering Phenergan by the IV-push method. Although Phenergan's labeling warned of the danger of gangrene and amputation following inadvertent intra-arterial injection, Levine (P) alleged that the labeling was defective because it failed to instruct clinicians to use the IV-drip method of intravenous administration instead of the higher risk IV-push method. More broadly, she alleged that Phenergan is not reasonably safe for intravenous administration because the foreseeable risks of gangrene and loss of limb are great in relation to the drug's therapeutic benefits. A state jury ruled for Levine (P), and the state's highest court affirmed. Wyeth (D), claiming that federal regulatory law preempted the state's tort law in this area appealed, and the United States Supreme Court granted certiorari.

ISSUE: Does federal regulatory law preempt state tort law where the state law does not frustrate the achievement of congressional objectives?

HOLDING AND DECISION: (Stevens, J.) No. Federal regulatory law does not preempt state tort law where the state law does not frustrate the achievement of congressional objectives. The argument that Levine's (P) state-law claims are preempted because it is impossible for Wyeth (D) to comply with both the state law duties underlying those claims and its federal labeling duties is rejected. Although a manufacturer generally may change a drug label only after the FDA approves a supplemental application, the agency's "changes being effected" (CBE) regulation permits certain pre-approval labeling changes that add or strengthen a warning to improve drug safety. Pursuant to the CBE regulation, Wyeth (D) could have unilaterally added a stronger warning about IV-push administration, and there is no evidence that the FDA would ultimately have rejected such a labeling change. Wyeth (D) is incorrect in its understanding that the FDA, rather than the manufacturer, bears primary responsibility for drug labeling. Instead, federal law and regulations provide that the manufacturer bears responsibility for the content of its label at all times. In addition, Wyeth's (D) argument that requiring it to comply with a state-law duty to provide a stronger warning would interfere with Congress's purpose of entrusting an expert agency with drug labeling decisions is meritless because it relies on an untenable interpretation of congressional intent and an overbroad view of an agency's power to pre-empt state law. The history of the Food, Drug, and Cosmetic Act (FDCA) shows that Congress did not intend to preempt state-law failure-to-warn actions. In advancing the argument that the FDA must be presumed to have established a specific labeling standard that leaves no room for different state-law judgments, Wyeth (D) relies not on any statement by Congress but on the preamble to a 2006 FDA regulation declaring that state-law failure-to-warn claims threaten the FDA's statutorily prescribed role. Although an agency regulation with the force of law can preempt conflicting state requirements, this case involves no such regulation but merely an agency's assertion that state law is an obstacle to achieving its statutory objectives. Here, however, the FDA's statement is not entitled to deference, as it is at odds with congressional purposes, and it reverses the FDA's own longstanding position that state law is a complementary form of drug regulation without providing a reasoned explanation for such a change of course. Affirmed.

DISSENT: (Alito, J.) Contrary to the majority's assertion that the issue presented is a narrow one, the real issue is whether a state tort jury can countermand the FDA's considered judgment that Phenergan's FDA-mandated

Continued on next page.

warning label renders its intravenous (IV) use "safe." Federal law relies on the FDA to make safety determinations like the one it made here. The FDA has long known about the risks associated with IV push in general and its use to administer Phenergan in particular, but nevertheless concluded that the drug is safe and effective when used in accord with the authorized warning label. Levine's (P) injuries did not come about because the label was too weak—it was because the providers who administered the drug ignored the warning label altogether. Thus, while the case is appropriately one for medical malpractice, permitting it to be a frontal assault on the FDA's regulatory regime for drug labeling upsets the well-settled meaning of the Supremacy Clause and settled conflict preemption jurisprudence. Congress made its "purpose" plain in authorizing the FDA—not state tort juries—to determine when and under what circumstances a drug is "safe." Because the FDA did weigh the costs and benefits associated with IV push, and, given the "balance" that the FDA struck between those costs and benefits, preemption of tort suits that would upset that balance is required by precedent. And, unlike the FDA, juries are ill-equipped to perform the FDA's cost-benefit-balancing function. Juries address actualities, whereas the FDA addresses probabilities and takes a much longer view. Thus, the FDA conveys its warnings with one voice, rather than whipsawing the medical community with 50 (or more) potentially conflicting ones. Under the majority's ruling, however, parochialism may prevail. Because the state's law in this instance cannot coexist peacefully with federal law, it must be preempted.

▶ ANALYSIS

The decision in this case was limited to brand-name drugs, but not generics, which are regulated by a different statutory scheme. In *Pliva, Inc. v. Mensing*, 131 S. Ct. 2567 (2011), the Court held that federal drug regulations applicable to generic drug manufacturers directly conflict with, and thus preempt, state-law tort claims alleging a failure to provide adequate warning labels. Thus, while failure to warn claims against generics manufacturers may no longer be brought under state law, it is not clear that other types of state-law claims, such as design defect claims, against such manufacturers are equally preempted. The distinction between *Pliva* and *Wyeth* turned on the fact that a brand-name manufacturer seeking new drug approval is responsible for the accuracy and adequacy of its label, whereas a manufacturer seeking generic drug approval is responsible for ensuring that its warning label is the same as the label of the brand name drug. In distinguishing the cases, the Court acknowledged that from the plaintiff's perspective it made little difference whether the drug taken was a brand-name drug or a generic, since the drug chemically was the same. The dissent in *Pliva* went further, claiming that the distinction was "absurd" and predicting the decision will make generic drugs a riskier proposition for consumers, and reduce demand for gener-

ics, at least among consumers who can afford brand-name drugs.

Quicknotes

GENERIC MEANING A term that encompasses a class of related products and lacks the requisite distinctiveness for federal trademark protection.

PREEMPTION Doctrine holding that matters of national interest take precedence over matters of local interest; the federal law takes precedence over state law.

REGULATORY POWER Power granting authority pursuant to statute to a government agency or body to govern a particular area.

TORT A legal wrong resulting in a breach of duty by the wrongdoer, causing damages as a result of the breach.

Quick Reference Rules of Law

PAGE

1. *Sullivan v. Old Colony Street Ry.* Damages are awarded to afford monetary equivalent for the actual loss caused by the wrong of another. — 152

2. *Zibbell v. Southern Pacific Co.* The amount of damages recoverable is calculated to be commensurate with the injury sustained. — 153

3. *McDougald v. Garber.* Some degree of cognitive awareness is a prerequisite to a plaintiff's recovery of damages for the loss of the enjoyment of life, and such damages should be treated as part of the plaintiff's recovery of damages for pain and suffering. — 154

4. *O'Shea v. Riverway Towing Co.* Where an adequate means of determining the impact of inflation on the present value of lost wages exists, inflation may be considered in calculating the amount recoverable. — 156

5. *Duncan v. Kansas City Southern Railway.* A general damage award will be found to be excessive and reversed if the trier of fact has abused its discretion in assessing the amount of damages and a review of prior awards will be undertaken in order to determine the highest or lowest point that is reasonably within that discretion. A future medical care award will be reversed if the trier of fact relied on an erroneous life expectancy figure. — 157

6. *Kemezy v. Peters.* The plaintiff does not have the burden of introducing evidence regarding the defendant's net worth for purposes of providing the jury with information necessary to make a proper award of punitive damages. — 158

7. *State Farm Mutual Automobile Insurance Co. v. Campbell.* In determining the validity of a punitive damage award, consideration is given to the degree of reprehensibility of the defendant's misconduct, the disparity between the actual or potential harm suffered by the plaintiff and the punitive damages award, and the difference between the punitive damages award by the jury and the civil penalties authorized or imposed in comparable cases. — 159

8. *Harding v. Town of Townshend.* The presence of liability insurance has no bearing on the liability of the defendant for his wrongful acts. — 161

Sullivan v. Old Colony Street Ry.

[Parties not identified.]

Mass. Sup. Jud. Ct., 83 N.E. 1091, 1092 (1908).

NATURE OF CASE: Action for damages.

FACT SUMMARY: [Facts not included in casebook excerpt.]

🏛 **RULE OF LAW**
Damages are awarded to afford monetary equivalent for the actual loss caused by the wrong of another.

FACTS: [Facts not included in casebook excerpt.]

ISSUE: Are damages awarded as monetary compensation for injury?

HOLDING AND DECISION: (Rugg, C.J.) Yes. Damages are awarded to afford a monetary equivalent for the actual loss caused by the wrongful conduct of another. The rule of damages is a practical instrumentality for doing justice through economic compensation.

▶ **ANALYSIS**

The fundamental remedial goal in the law of torts is to restore the victim to the state of being he or she enjoyed before the tort was committed. Because it is not physically possible to erase the pain and ramifications of physical or mental injuries, the restoration must come in the form of economic compensation. This is the fundamental theory supporting damage awards.

▬▬

Quicknotes

DAMAGES Monetary compensation that may be awarded by the court to a party, who has sustained injury or loss to his person, property or rights due to another party's unlawful act, omission or negligence.

▬▬

Zibbell v. Southern Pacific Co.

[Parties not identified.]

Cal. Sup. Ct., 116 P. 513, 520 (1911).

NATURE OF CASE: [Nature of case not stated in casebook excerpt.]

FACT SUMMARY: [Facts not stated in casebook excerpt.]

🏛 RULE OF LAW
The amount of damages recoverable is calculated to be commensurate with the injury sustained.

FACTS: [Facts not stated in casebook excerpt.]

ISSUE: Must the amount of recoverable damages equal the extent of the injury sustained?

HOLDING AND DECISION: (Henshaw, J.) Yes. The amount of recoverable damages must be commensurate with the injury sustained. Although money is an inherently poor substitute for the ability to relieve pain and suffering, it is the only standard of measure available to a court to calculate compensation for tortuously induced injury. As such, the amount of money awarded must be made as closely commensurate with the amount of pain and suffering imposed. It cannot be beyond all proportion to the actual injury.

▶ ANALYSIS

The most unguided area in tort law is the field of estimating the amount of damage due a particular victim. It is relatively clear what types of injuries are recoverable in damages, yet the amount actually due is often very difficult to ascertain. Usually damage awards must be made by contrasting degrees of injury. Generally, a broken arm will recover less than a severed arm. However, how much less is open for debate.

Quicknotes

ACTUAL DAMAGES Measure of damages necessary to compensate victim for actual injuries suffered.

▬▬■■▬▬

McDougald v. Garber

Patient injured during surgery (P) v. Doctor (D)

N.Y. Ct. App. 536 N.E.2d 372 (1989).

NATURE OF CASE: Appeal from award of non-pecuniary damages.

FACT SUMMARY: During surgery performed by Garber (D), McDougald (P) suffered oxygen deprivation, resulting in irreversible brain damage and a permanent comatose condition.

🏛 RULE OF LAW
Some degree of cognitive awareness is a prerequisite to a plaintiff's recovery of damages for the loss of the enjoyment of life, and such damages should be treated as part of the plaintiff's recovery of damages for pain and suffering.

FACTS: Emma McDougald (P) underwent a Caesarean section and tubal ligation. Garber (D) performed the surgery. During surgery, McDougald (P) suffered oxygen deprivation that resulted in irreversible brain damage and left her in a permanent comatose condition. McDougald (P) sued Garber (D) and the anesthesiologists in a malpractice action. McDougald (P) was awarded approximately $1,000,000 for conscious pain and suffering and approximately $3,500,000 for the loss of the pleasure and pursuits of life. The trial judge reduced McDougald's (P) total award to a single award of $2,000,000 against Garber (D). On cross-appeal, the appellate division affirmed and granted leave for Garber's (D) appeal to the New York Supreme Court. Garber (D) on appeal contended that the trial court erred, both (1) in instructing the jury that McDougald's (P) awareness was irrelevant to its consideration of damages for loss of enjoyment of life; and (2) in directing the jury to consider that aspect of damages separately from pain and suffering.

ISSUE: Must some degree of cognitive awareness be a prerequisite for a plaintiff's recovery of damages for the loss of the enjoyment of life, and should such damages be treated as part of the plaintiff's recovery of damages for pain and suffering?

HOLDING AND DECISION: (Wachtler, C.J.) Yes. Some degree of cognitive awareness is a prerequisite of a plaintiff's recovery of damages for the loss of enjoyment of life, and such damages should be treated as part of the plaintiff's recovery of damages for pain and suffering. Damages for nonpecuniary loss for loss of enjoyment of life are among those that can be awarded to compensate a plaintiff. However, an award of money damages to a person who has no awareness of the loss of such enjoyment serves no compensatory purpose. An award of damages in such circumstances has no meaning or utility to the injured

person. The advocates of separate awards contend that because pain and suffering and loss of enjoyment of life can be distinguished conceptually, they must be treated separately if the plaintiff is to be compensated fully for each distinct injury suffered. Such an analytical approach may be warranted when the subject is pecuniary damages that are easily subject to calculation. However, translating human suffering into dollars and cents may not be accomplished by applying a mathematical formula, but rests on a legal fiction. The figure that emerges is unavoidably distorted. If anything, the distortion will be amplified by repetition. Affirmed; new trial granted on issue of nonpecuniary damages.

DISSENT: (Titone, J.) The majority's holding neither comports with the fundamental principles of tort compensation nor furnishes a satisfactory, logically consistent framework for compensating nonpecuniary loss. The loss of enjoyment of life is an objective damage item, conceptually distinct from conscious pain and suffering. An award for loss of enjoyment of life should therefore have been given even in the absence of any awareness of that loss on the part of McDougald (P). Such an award is not altered or rendered punitive by the fact that the unaware injured McDougald (P) cannot experience the pleasure of having it.

▶ ANALYSIS

Pain and suffering, called "general" damages, have been the source of much debate in the legal community. Some commentators have called for their abolition, stating that, at the societal level, they are nothing more than a device for wealth distribution and have nothing to do with compensation. Most accept the need for such damages, however, for reasons cited in the present case. The difficulty with the majority view is that a wrongdoer pays less compensation when his actions turn the victim into a "vegetable" than had the victim retained consciousness.

Quicknotes

COMPENSATORY DAMAGES Measure of damages necessary to compensate victim for actual injuries suffered.

NONPECUNIARY LOSS Damages that cannot be calculated or accurately estimated in monetary terms.

PAIN AND SUFFERING DAMAGES In tort law, damages for pain and suffering are compensable only to the extent

Continued on next page.

that some form of physical injury, or at least nominal damages, can be shown.

PUNITIVE DAMAGES Damages exceeding the actual injury suffered for the purposes of punishment, deterrence and comfort to plaintiff.

=■=

O'Shea v. Riverway Towing Co.

Injured ship's cook (P) v. Riverboat company (D)

677 F.2d 1194 (7th Cir. 1982).

NATURE OF CASE: Appeal from an award for damages for lost earnings.

FACT SUMMARY: Riverway Towing Co. (D) contended it was improper for the trial court to take inflation into account in calculating O'Shea's (P) loss of future wages.

RULE OF LAW
Where an adequate means of determining the impact of inflation on the present value of lost wages exists, inflation may be considered in calculating the amount recoverable.

FACTS: Mrs. O'Shea (P) was injured while getting off a harbor boat operated by Riverway Towing Co. (Riverway) (D). She sued for damages, including the loss of future earnings due to her inability to continue working as a ship's cook. The trial court accepted the testimony of O'Shea's (P) economist who estimated that inflation would continue to rise approximately 5-8 percent between the time of the award and the end of O'Shea's (P) working career. Based on this calculation, he arrived at an overall damage figure for lost wages and then discounted it to reflect the present value of the award. In discounting for present value, he included a large allowance for projected inflationary impact. Riverway (D) appealed the trial court's award based on this testimony, contending it was improper as a matter of law to take inflation into account in projecting future wages.

ISSUE: May inflation be considered in calculating damages for lost wages?

HOLDING AND DECISION: (Posner, J.) Yes. Where an adequate means of determining the potential impact of inflation on the present value of lost wages exists, inflation may be considered in calculating the amount recoverable. In this case, the current long term interest rate provided an adequate gauge of future inflationary impact on the value of money. Therefore, the testimony presented a fair representation of the inflationary impact on the award as it is based on this interest rate. Consequently, the testimony and award was proper. Affirmed.

ANALYSIS

This case illustrates that all awards which are meant to compensate for future losses must be discounted to represent their present value. This involves determining what amount in today's dollars when invested safely will yield the amount of the total award on a future date. Because of the state of the economy over the last 25 years, the impact of inflation must be considered to arrive at an accurate compensation amount.

■■■

Quicknotes

COMPENSATORY DAMAGES Measure of damages necessary to compensate victim for actual injuries suffered.

■■■

Duncan v. Kansas City Southern Railway

Train collision victims (P) v. Railway company (D)

La. Sup. Ct., 773 So. 2d 670 (2000).

NATURE OF CASE: Certiorari review of damage award in personal injury action.

FACT SUMMARY: One girl was killed, her sister, Rachel, was severely injured, and another sister was less seriously injured when the van in which they were riding collided with a train.

RULE OF LAW
A general damage award will be found to be excessive and reversed if the trier of fact has abused its discretion in assessing the amount of damages and a review of prior awards will be undertaken in order to determine the highest or lowest point that is reasonably within that discretion. A future medical care award will be reversed if the trier of fact relied on an erroneous life expectancy figure.

FACTS: One sister was killed, one sister, Rachel, was rendered a quadriplegic, and a third sister suffered less serious injuries when the church van in which they were riding collided with a locomotive at a railroad crossing. The Duncans (P), the parents of the girls, filed suit against Kansas City Southern Railway (KCS) (D) to recover damages. A jury found the driver of the van and the railroad liable for the accident and awarded damages totaling $27,876,813.31. Of the total amount, $8 million was for general damages for Rachel for physical pain and suffering, mental anguish, and loss of enjoyment of life and $17 million was for Rachel's future medical expenses. The court of appeals affirmed and the Louisiana Supreme Court granted certiorari.

ISSUE: Was the jury's award of damages excessive?

HOLDING AND DECISION: (Johnson, J.) Yes. The jury's award of general damages was so excessive as to be set aside because the trier of fact abused its discretion in assessing the amount of damages. The jury's award for future medical expenses was also excessive based on an erroneous life expectancy figure. General damages cannot be fixed with pecuniary exactitude. Since the trier of fact is given such vast discretion in calculating such damages, their judgment should rarely be set aside if the trier of fact exercised appropriate discretion. In the present case, however, the trier of fact did abuse its discretion in assessing the amount of damages. The $8 million in general damages awarded to Rachel for her physical pain and suffering, mental anguish, and loss of enjoyment of life is beyond that which a reasonable trier of fact could assess for the effects of Rachel's particular injury under the circumstances surrounding her injury. While the sight of Rachel in her wheelchair may have elicited some sympathetic feelings from the jury, it is abundantly clear that the effects of this accident on Rachel were devastating. Prior to the accident, Rachel was an eleven-year-old-girl who was enjoying a full life. As a result of the accident, Rachel is unable to function physically in the same manner as before, is severely injured, and has suffered immense mental distress. Although Rachel suffers greatly, the general damage award of $8 million is excessive and the trial court abused its discretion. Cases having plaintiffs with similar injuries reveals the highest amount that could reasonably be awarded under the facts of this case is $6 million and, therefore, the award is adjusted as such. Furthermore, future medical expenses will be reduced from $17 million to $10,528,722 based on a life expectancy for Rachel of 57 years, based on her treating physician's assessment, and not 81 years, as the Duncans' (P) expert predicted. Future medical expenses must be established with some degree of certainty based on medical testimony that they are indicated and that sets out their cost.

ANALYSIS

Cases involving serious personal injury usually involve the same issues as were raised in this case.

Quicknotes

DAMAGES Monetary compensation that may be awarded by the court to a party who has sustained injury or loss to his or her person, property or rights due to another party's unlawful act, omission or negligence.

Kemezy v. Peters

Individual (P) v. Policeman (D)

79 F.3d 33 (7th Cir. 1996).

NATURE OF CASE: 42 U.S.C. § 1983 action.

FACT SUMMARY: Kemezy (P) sued Peters (D), an off-duty policeman moonlighting as a security guard, for injuries sustained during an altercation at a bowling alley.

RULE OF LAW
The plaintiff does not have the burden of introducing evidence regarding the defendant's net worth for purposes of providing the jury with information necessary to make a proper award of punitive damages.

FACTS: Kemezy (P) brought suit against Peters (D), a policeman, under 42 U.S.C. § 1983, alleging Peters (D) wantonly beat him with a nightstick during an altercation in a bowling alley in which Peters (D) was moonlighting as a security guard. The jury awarded Kemezy (P) $10,000 in compensatory damages and $20,000 in punitive damages. Peters (D) appealed, challenging the punitive damages award on the basis that it was Kemezy's (P) burden to show evidence of Peters's (D) net worth.

ISSUE: Does the plaintiff have the burden of introducing evidence regarding the defendant's net worth for purposes of providing the jury with information necessary to make a proper award of punitive damages?

HOLDING AND DECISION: (Posner, C.J.) No. The plaintiff does not have the burden of introducing evidence regarding the defendant's net worth for purposes of providing the jury with information necessary to make a proper award of punitive damages. This is the law in the majority of jurisdictions. The purpose of punitive damages is to punish the defendant and to deter him and others from engaging in similar, wrongful conduct. This is due to several reasons. First, compensatory damages do not always compensate a victim fully. Where this is the case, punitive damages are necessary in order to ensure that tortious conduct is not underdeterred. This is necessary when the cost of mere compensation for the action is low; thus, the defendant would not be deterred from the action if he derived greater benefit from the conduct than the loss incurred. Similarly, where the defendant's tortious conduct may be undetected, he may evaluate the risk in term of the likelihood of being caught. Punitive damages also demonstrate society's abhorrence of deliberate or reckless wrongdoing and relieve the criminal justice system of some of the pressure of enforcement. None of these purposes depend upon proof of the defendant's income or wealth. Affirmed.

ANALYSIS

Punitive damages have been a vehicle of the common law for centuries. This presents a difficult issue in the context of products liability. In *Owens-Corning Fiberglass Corp. v. Garrett*, 682 A.2d 1143, 1166-1167 (1996), the court set forth a two-part test for punitive damages in products liability cases, requiring the plaintiff to demonstrate by clear and convincing evidence the defendant's "actual knowledge of the defect and deliberate disregard of the consequences" to its users.

Quicknotes

COMPENSATORY DAMAGES Measure of damages necessary to compensate victim for actual injuries suffered.

PUNITIVE DAMAGES Damages exceeding the actual injury suffered for the purposes of punishment, deterrence and comfort to plaintiff.

State Farm Mutual Automobile Insurance Co. v. Campbell

Insurer (D) v. Insured (P)

538 U.S. 408 (2003).

NATURE OF CASE: Certiorari review of damages awarded in a bad faith, fraud, and intentional infliction of emotional distress action.

FACT SUMMARY: Campbell (P) sued State Farm Mutual Automobile Insurance Co. (State Farm) (D), his automobile insurer, for bad faith, fraud, and intentional infliction of emotional distress action when State Farm (D) refused to settle a claim brought against Campbell (P) by Ospital's estate and by Slusher.

> 🏛 **RULE OF LAW**
> In determining the validity of a punitive damage award, consideration is given to the degree of reprehensibility of the defendant's misconduct, the disparity between the actual or potential harm suffered by the plaintiff and the punitive damages award, and the difference between the punitive damages award by the jury and the civil penalties authorized or imposed in comparable cases.

FACTS: Campbell (P) caused a collision that killed Ospital and left Slusher permanently disabled. Ospital's estate and Slusher sued Campbell (P) for wrongful death and in tort. Campbell's (P) insurance company, State Farm Mutual Automobile Insuracne Co. (State Farm) (D) refused to settle with Ospital and Slusher even though Ospital and Slusher agreed to settle for the policy limit of $25,000 each. State Farm (D) assured Campbell (P) State Farm (D) would represent Campbell's (P) interests, Campbell's (P) assets were safe and Campbell (P) did not need to procure separate counsel. A jury found Campbell (P) to be at fault and awarded $185,849 to Ospital and Slusher. Initially, State Farm (D) refused to cover the $135,849 in excess liability and refused to post a bond so Campbell (P) could appeal. State Farm (D) told Campbell (P) that he may as well put a for sale sign on his house. Campbell (P) obtained his own attorney, filed his appeal and, in the meantime, agreed to let Slusher and Ospital's attorney represent him (P) in a case against State Farm (D) for bad faith, fraud, and intentional infliction of emotional distress. In exchange, Slusher and Ospital agreed not to seek satisfaction from Campbell (P), but would play a central role in the bad faith action, including receiving 90 percent of any verdict against State Farm (D). The appeals court denied Campbell's (P) appeal in the wrongful death and tort actions and State Farm (D) paid the entire judgment, including the amounts in excess of the policy limits. Despite State Farm's (D) payment, Campbell (P) filed suit against State Farm (D) alleging bad faith, fraud, and intentional infliction of emotional distress. The trial court found

in favor of Campbell (P) and awarded him $2.6 million in compensatory damages and $145 million in punitive damages. The award was subsequently reduced to $1 million and $25 million, respectively. The appeals court affirmed the $1 million and reinstated the $145 million in punitive damages. The United States Supreme Court granted certiorari.

ISSUE: Is an award of $145 million in punitive damages, where full compensatory damages are $1 million, excessive and in violation of the Due Process Clause?

HOLDING AND DECISION: (Kennedy, J.) Yes. An award of $145 million in punitive damages, where full compensatory damages are $1 million, is excessive and in violation of the Due Process Clause because the reprehensibility of State Farm's (D) misconduct could have been punished in a more modest way and still have satisfied State objectives. The disparity between the actual or potential harm suffered by Campbell (P) and the punitive damages awarded was significant, and the difference between the punitive damages award by the jury and the civil penalties authorized or imposed in comparable cases was great. Although States have discretion over the amount of punitive damages allowed, there are constitutional limitations on these awards. The imposition of grossly excessive or arbitrary punishments on a tortfeasor, are prohibited because of fundamental notions of fairness. Moreover, because defendants subjected to punitive damages in civil cases do not have the same protections applicable in criminal proceedings, such awards pose an acute danger of arbitrary deprivation of property. In the present case, it was erroneous for the $145 million to be reinstated. Although State Farm's (D) handling of the claims against Campbell (P) was reprehensible, in that they would probably get a judgment over the policy limits, but still went to trial and then told Campbell (D) to sell his house, a more modest punishment for these actions could have satisfied the State's legitimate objectives. Instead, this case was used to expose State Farm's (D) perceived nationwide deficiencies, and a State does not have a legitimate concern in imposing punitive damages to punish a defendant for unlawful acts committed outside the State's jurisdiction. A State cannot punish a defendant for conduct that may have been lawful where it occurred. Lawful out-of-state conduct may be probative when it demonstrates the deliberateness and culpability of the defendant's action in the State where it is tortuous, but that conduct must have a nexus to the specific harm suffered by the plaintiff. Moreover, the courts

Continued on next page.

erred in awarding punitive damages to punish and deter conduct that bore no relation to Campbell's (P) harm. Due process does not permit courts to adjudicate the merits of other parties' hypothetical claims against a defendant. Furthermore, the disparity between the actual or potential harm suffered by Campbell (P) and the punitive damages award is much too large to be valid. Few awards exceeding a single-digit ratio between punitive and compensatory damages will satisfy due process. Usually an award of no more than four times the amount of compensatory damages is the maximum. The ratio in the present case is 145 to 1. The measure of punishment in this case was neither reasonable nor proportionate to the amount of harm to Campbell (P) and to the general damages recovered. The harm Campbell (P) suffered was minor economic damage and not physical, and the excess verdict was paid before the complaint was filed. Lastly, the disparity between the punitive damages award and the civil penalties authorized or imposed in comparable cases is great. The civil sanction is a $10,000 fine for an act of fraud. Reversed and remanded.

DISSENT: (Scalia, J.) The Due Process Clause provides no substantive protections against excessive or unreasonable awards of punitive damages.

DISSENT: (Thomas, J.) The Constitution does not constrain the size of punitive damage awards.

DISSENT: (Ginsburg, J.) Punitive damage issues are traditionally within the States' domain until legislators initiate system-wide change.

▶ ANALYSIS

There is much analysis in legal literature concerning the theoretical basis and practical operation of punitive damages in tort cases.

Quicknotes

BAD FAITH Conduct that is intentionally misleading or deceptive.

DUE PROCESS CLAUSE Clauses, found in the Fifth and Fourteenth Amendments to the United States Constitution, providing that no person shall be deprived of "life, liberty, or property, without due process of law."

FRAUD A false representation of facts with the intent that another will rely on the misrepresentation to his detriment.

INTENTIONAL INFLICTION OF EMOTIONAL DISTRESS Intentional and extreme behavior on the part of the wrongdoer with the intent to cause the victim to suffer from severe emotional distress, or behavior performed with reckless indifference, resulting in the victim's suffering from severe emotional distress.

PUNITIVE DAMAGES Damages exceeding the actual injury suffered for the purposes of punishment, deterrence and comfort to plaintiff.

Harding v. Town of Townshend

Accident victim (P) v. City (D)

Vt. Sup. Ct., 43 Vt. 536 (1871).

NATURE OF CASE: Action on the case for damages sustained by the plaintiff.

FACT SUMMARY: Harding (P) was injured when Townshend (D) failed to maintain a safe highway. Townshend (D) claimed its liability should be diminished by the amount Harding (P) recovered from his insurance.

🏛 RULE OF LAW
The presence of liability insurance has no bearing on the liability of the defendant for his wrongful acts.

FACTS: Townshend (D) had a duty to maintain its highways so as not to cause Harding (P) and others similarly situated to be injured thereon. Harding (P) was injured, but received some compensation from his insurance. The only issue at trial was damages. Townshend (D) claimed the amount of Harding's (P) recovery from them should be diminished by what he received from his insurer, because Harding (P) is entitled to only one recovery.

ISSUE: Is a defendant entitled to deduct from the amount of damages a sum paid to plaintiff by insurers in respect to such damage?

HOLDING AND DECISION: (Peck, J.) No. The one who causes the injury should bear the loss. The insurer has no relationship, such as privity or being a joint tortfeasor, with Townshend (D) that should allow it to be subrogated to the rights of the injured party, even though an insurer may be so subrogated. Here, the superior equity is in the insurers who pay the second recovery, not in the wrongdoers. Reversed.

▌ANALYSIS

The Collateral Benefits Rule has its supporters and detractors in academic circles, although it remains entrenched in American courts. In some jurisdictions, a setoff may be allowed by statute, especially in attempts to keep medical malpractice insurance costs down. In some cases, a governmental agency that provides insurance may be allowed a setoff. The recovery it paid under the insurance may be deducted from what the U.S., as tortfeasor, was held liable for under a judgment. But the principal case states the majority view.

■▬■

Quicknotes

JOINT TORTFEASORS Two or more parties that either act in concert, or whose individual acts combine to cause a single injury, rendering them jointly and severally liable for damages incurred.

PRIVITY Commonality of rights or interests between parties.

■▬■

Harding v. Town of Townshend

Accident action 27 v. Civ (U)

(Vt. Sup. Ct. 43 Vt. 536, 1871)

NATURE OF CASE: Action on the case for dam- ages sustained by the plaintiff.

FACT SUMMARY: Harding (P) was injured when Townshend (D) failed to maintain a safe highway. Townshend (D) claimed its liability should be diminished by the amount Harding (P) recovered from his insurance.

RULE OF LAW
The presence of liability insurance has no bear- ing on the liability of the defendant for his wrongful acts.

FACTS: Townshend (D) had a duty to maintain its highways so as not to cause Harding (P) and others injury who should to be harmed thereon. Harding (P) was injured, but received some compensation from his insur- er. The only issue at trial was damages. Townshend (D) claimed the amount of Harding's (P) recovery from them should be diminished by what he recovered from his insurer because Harding (P) is entitled to only one recovery.

ISSUE: Is defendant entitled to deduct from the amount of damages a sum paid to plaintiff by insurer in respect to such damage?

HOLDING AND DECISION: (Ross, J.) No. The one who causes an injury should bear the loss. The insurer has no relationship, such as privity or being a joint tortfea- sor, with Townshend (D), that should allow it to be subrogated to the right of the injured party; even though the insurer may be so subrogated after, the superior equity is in the insured who may the injured (to every injury from the wrongdoer). Reversed.

ANALYSIS

The Collateral Benefits Rule finds acceptance and deroga- tion in aggregate circles, although it remains embodied in American courts. In some jurisdictions it actually may be abrogated by statute, especially in attempts to keep medi- cal malpractice insurance costs down. In some cases, a gov- ernmental agency that provides insurance may be allowed a setoff. The recovery if paid under the insurance may be deducted from what the tortfeasor should. In such matters, it is under a judgment, but the tortfeasor gets the same opportunity view.

Quicknotes

JOINT TORTFEASORS Two or more parties that either act in concert or whose individual acts combine to cause a single injury, rendering them jointly and severally liable for damages incurred.

PRIVITY Commonality of rights or interests between par- ties.

Tort Extensions: Insurance and No-Fault Systems

Quick Reference Rules of Law

PAGE

1. *Crisci v. Security Insurance Co.* In determining whether an insurer has given consideration to the interests of the insured in reference to an offer to settle a claim against the insured, the test is whether a prudent insurer, without policy limits, would have accepted the settlement offer. — 164

2. *Dimmitt Chevrolet, Inc. v. Southeastern Fidelity Insurance Corp.* In the context of a comprehensive liability insurance policy intended to cover hazardous waste pollution, "sudden" damages means those that are abrupt and unexpected. — 165

3. *Clodgo v. Rentavision, Inc.* In order to receive workers' compensation benefits a claimant must show that "but for" the claimant's employment and conditions of work, the injury would not have occurred. — 167

4. *Wilson v. Workers' Compensation Appeals Board.* Workers' compensation does not compensate injuries sustained while an employee travels to or from work. — 168

5. *Rainer v. Union Carbide Corporation.* The phrase "deliberate intention to produce injury or death" in a state workers' compensation statute, to act as an exception to the statute, requires an employer is determined to injure an employee and employ some means toward that end. — 169

Crisci v. Security Insurance Co.

Apartment owner (P) v. Insurance company (D)

Cal. Sup. Ct., 426 P.2d 173 (1967).

NATURE OF CASE: Appeal in action by insured against insurer.

FACT SUMMARY: Security Insurance Co. (D), having unreasonably refused to settle a claim against their insured, Crisci (P), for a lesser amount, is now held liable to Crisci (P) for her having lost a judgment far in excess of the original settlement offer.

🏛 RULE OF LAW
In determining whether an insurer has given consideration to the interests of the insured in reference to an offer to settle a claim against the insured, the test is whether a prudent insurer, without policy limits, would have accepted the settlement offer.

FACTS: Mrs. Crisci (P) carried a $10,000 general liability policy with Security Insurance Co. (Security) (D) who was obliged also to defend her and authorized to settle—in any suit. Mrs. DiMare, Mrs. Crisci's (P) tenant, sued her for $400,000 in injuries sustained in falling through the stairs of Mrs. Crisci's (P) apartment building. Security's (D) own attorney and claims manager predicted a minimum jury verdict of $100,000 for Mrs. DiMare if the jury believed the fall caused her psychosis. Security (D) knew that both sides' psychiatrists agreed that the psychosis could have been so caused, yet Security (D) still rejected settlement offers of $10,000 and $9,000 (of which Mrs. Crisci (P) offered to pay $2,500) for physical injuries. Security (D) offered only $3,000 to Mrs. DiMare for physical injuries and nothing for mental. They felt the jury would not believe her psychiatric evidence. However, the jury gave Mrs. DiMare a judgment of $101,000 of which Security (D) paid $10,000. Mrs. DiMare secured the balance from Mrs. Crisci (P) leaving her indigent and physically and emotionally ill. Mrs. Crisci (P) sued Security (D). The trial court awarded her $91,000 for Security's (D) refusal to settle and $25,000 for mental suffering. Security (D) argues that no recovery can be had against an insurer unless it can be shown that its failure to settle was based on actual dishonesty, fraud, or concealment.

ISSUE: In determining whether or not to settle a claim, must an insurer give the interests of the insured the same consideration it would give its own interests?

HOLDING AND DECISION: (Peters, J.) Yes. Following *Comunale v. Traders and General Insurance Co.*, 328 P.2d 198 (1958), this court held that, in every contract—including insurance policies—there is an implied covenant of good faith and fair dealing in that neither party will deprive the other of the benefits of a reasonable settlement which avoids litigation—such as is the common policy in insurance claims. When an insurer realizes that the insured is facing a possible recovery beyond the limits of the policy coverage, the insurer must give the interests of the insured the same consideration it would give its own interests and seek to settle within the limits of the policy. In determining whether an insurer is acting in good faith, the test is whether a prudent insurer without policy limits would have accepted the settlement offer. *Comunale* holds that only bad faith—much less than actual dishonesty or fraud—may impose liability. Further, it is not unreasonable for an insured who purchases a policy with limits to believe the policy is available with which to settle when the likelihood of a greater recovery is apparent. The insurer should not further his interests by rejecting a settlement unless he is also willing to absorb the possibly greater loss. Regarding the loss for mental suffering, the plaintiff may elect a tort or contract action where the injury stems from financial damage. The general rule in tort is that the injured party may recover from all damages—even those unanticipated—such as mental distress resulting from property loss. Affirmed.

▶ ANALYSIS

The traditional test, followed by most jurisdictions, holds the insurer who refuses to settle liable only for actual bad faith or when it has insisted on litigating with less than an even chance of winning. However, recent years have seen an increased application of the "no limit" test requiring an insurer to treat a claim as if it were against an insured whose policy was unlimited. The *Crisci* court, though applying the "no limit" test, suggested in its dicta that in the future it may adopt a rule of strict liability, holding the insurer liable for excess judgments whenever any offer within the policy limits has been rejected.

■■■■

Quicknotes

IMPLIED COVENANT A promise inferred by law from a document as a whole and the circumstances surrounding its implementation.

■■■■

Dimmitt Chevrolet, Inc. v. Southeastern Fidelity Insurance Corp.

Chevrolet dealership (P) v. Liability insurance company (D)

Fla. Sup. Ct., 636 So. 2d 700 (1993).

NATURE OF CASE: Certified question in appeal from summary judgment in a declaratory judgment action on an insurance policy.

FACT SUMMARY: Southeastern Fidelity Insurance Corp. (D) contended that it owed no duty to defend or indemnify Dimmit Chevrolet, Inc. (P) for environmental contamination resulting from oil leaking at a site since its policy covered only "sudden," i.e., abrupt, discharges.

RULE OF LAW
In the context of a comprehensive liability insurance policy intended to cover hazardous waste pollution, "sudden" damages means those that are abrupt and unexpected.

FACTS: Southeastern Fidelity Insurance Corp. (Southeastern) (P) provided comprehensive general liability insurance (CGL) to Dimmit Chevrolet, Inc. (Dimmitt) (D). The policy explicitly excluded coverage for all pollution except when a discharge was "sudden and accidental." Dimmitt (D) sold used crankcase oil generated by its business to Peak Oil Co. Peak was found by the Environmental Protection Agency (EPA) to have substantial pollution at its worksite from storage of waste sludge in unlined bins. The EPA also found Dimmitt (D) to be a potentially responsible party under CERCLA because it had generated and transported hazardous material to Peak. Thereafter, Southeastern (P) filed a declaratory judgment action against Dimmitt (D), seeking a declaration by the federal district court that Southeastern (P) owed no duty to defend and indemnify Dimmitt (D) under the CGL policy. The court granted summary judgment in favor of Southeastern (P) on the grounds that the CGL policy's pollution exclusion language was not ambiguous and the word "sudden" in the policy should be read to mean abrupt rather than intended. The pollution at Peak had occurred over a period of years and therefore could not be considered "sudden." Dimmitt (D) appealed.

ISSUE: In the context of a comprehensive liability insurance policy intended to cover hazardous waste pollution, does "sudden" damages mean those which are abrupt and unexpected?

HOLDING AND DECISION: (Per curiam) Yes. In the context of a comprehensive liability insurance policy intended to cover hazardous waste pollution, "sudden" damages means those which are abrupt and unexpected. Here, Dimmitt (D) asserts that the term "sudden" in the pollution exclusion clause of the policy at issue is ambiguous and therefore should be construed in Dimmitt's (D) favor. Dimmitt (D) also argues that the word "sudden" does not have a temporal meaning and that the term was intentionally written so as to provide coverage for unexpected and unintended discharge. Conversely, Southeastern (P) contends that the clause excludes coverage for all pollution except when the discharge or dispersal of the pollutant occurs abruptly and accidentally. The ordinary and common usage of the term "sudden" includes a temporal aspect with a sense of immediacy or abruptness. Applying the policy language to the facts of this case, the pollution damage was not within the scope of Southeastern's (P) policy. The pollution by Peak took place over a period of many years, and most of it occurred gradually. Affirmed.

CONCURRENCE: (Grimes, J.) Because I would rather have insurance companies cover these losses instead of parties such as Dimmitt (D), who did not actually cause the pollution damage, initially and erroneously, I departed from the basic rule of interpretation that language should be given its plain and ordinary meaning. But the words "sudden and accidental" cannot be contorted to mean "gradual and accidental," which must be done in order to provide coverage in this case.

DISSENT: (Overton, J.) The term "sudden and accidental" must be found to be ambiguous given that the term is, in fact, subject to more than one interpretation. It is clear that the term can mean "unexpected and unintended," a definition not limited to the time of occurrence, in addition to Southeastern's (P) asserted definition of "instantaneous and abrupt." The drafting history of the pollution exclusion clause leads to the conclusion that the insurance industry was attempting to exclude from coverage those polluters who committed their acts intentionally. The addition of the pollution exclusion clause, specifically the term "sudden and accidental," was presented by the insurance industries to the regulators to mean that coverage would continue for those events that were "unexpected and unintended."

ANALYSIS

As explained in the majority opinion in *Dimmitt*, comprehensive general liability (CGL) policies are standard insurance policies developed by the insurance industry. Such policies are the primary form of commercial insurance coverage obtained by businesses throughout the

Continued on next page.

United States. Before 1966, the standard CGL policy covered only property and personal injury damage that was caused by "accident." Beginning in 1970, the pollution exclusion clause at issue in *Dimmitt* was added to the standard policy. Finally, in 1984, an "absolute exclusion clause" was added to totally exclude coverage for pollution clean-up costs that arise from governmental directives.

■■■

Quicknotes

INDEMNIFICATION Reimbursement for losses sustained or security against anticipated loss or damages.

■■■

Clodgo v. Rentavision, Inc.

Employee (P) v. Employer (D)

Vt. Sup. Ct., 701 A.2d 1044 (1997).

NATURE OF CASE: Appeal from decision of state agency awarding workers' compensation benefits to claimant.

FACT SUMMARY: Clodgo (P) sought workers' compensation benefits for an injury sustained while engaged in horseplay during a lull between customers.

🏛 **RULE OF LAW**
In order to receive workers' compensation benefits a claimant must show that "but for" the claimant's employment and conditions of work, the injury would not have occurred.

FACTS: Clodgo (P), manager of one of Rentavision's stores, began firing staples with a staple-gun at a coworker during a lull between customers. The coworker fired staples back at Clodgo (P), hitting him in the eye. Clodgo (P) reported the injury and filed a claim for workers' compensation. The Commissioner of Labor awarded Clodgo (P) permanent partial disability and vocational rehabilitation benefits, medical expenses, attorney's fees and costs. Rentavision (D) appealed, claiming the Commissioner erred in granting such benefits for an injury sustained in the employee's horseplay.

ISSUE: In order to receive workers' compensation benefits, must a claimant show that "but for" the claimant's employment and conditions of work, the injury would not have occurred?

HOLDING AND DECISION: (Gibson, J.) Yes. In order to receive workers' compensation benefits a claimant must show that "but for" the claimant's employment and conditions of work, the injury would not have occurred. While it is true that the injury occurred during work hours and with a staple-gun provided by the employer, the claimant must also show that the injury occurred in the course of his employment. This is accomplished by showing the injury occurred during the period of time in which the claimant was on duty and at a location in which the employee was reasonably expected to be while fulfilling the duties of his employment. While some horseplay may be expected and does not automatically bar compensation, the issue is whether the employee's injury is too far removed from his duties. Factors to be considered are the extent and seriousness of the employee's deviation from his duties; whether the deviation was commingled with the performance of his duties; the extent to which such conduct was an accepted part of the employment; and the extent to which the nature of the employment anticipated there would be horseplay. Here the shooting of staple-guns was not intermingled with the accomplishment of some legitimate work duty, nor was there any evidence presented to conclude that it was an accepted part of the employment. Moreover, the dangerousness of the activity also supports the conclusion that such activity constituted a substantial deviation from the claimant's (P) work duties. Reversed.

DISSENT: (Morse, J.) The court has exceeded its limits in reviewing the agency's decision. There was evidence to support the Commissioner's conclusion that the horseplay engaged in by the claimant was not a substantial deviation from his duties.

▶ **ANALYSIS**

Workers' compensation statutes have evolved in many states to reduce liability of the employer based on specified conduct by the employees. Several states provide defenses to an employer where an employee has engaged in willful misconduct, drunkenness or aggression. Furthermore, many states bar or reduce the amount of a worker's recovery if the employee engaged in willful misconduct or disregard of safety regulations.

Quicknotes

WILLFUL MISCONDUCT Behavior that is committed with an intentional disregard for others' safety or care for others' property.

WORKERS COMPENSATION Fixed awards provided to employees for job-related injuries.

Wilson v. Workers' Compensation Appeals Board

Teacher injured on her way to school (P) v. Appeals board (D)

Cal. Sup. Ct., 545 P.2d 225 (1976).

NATURE OF CASE: Appeal from the denial of workers' compensation by the appeals board.

FACT SUMMARY: Wilson (P) was injured in an auto accident while on route to work.

🏛 RULE OF LAW
Workers' compensation does not compensate injuries sustained while an employee travels to or from work.

FACTS: Wilson (P), a teacher, was injured in an auto accident while on route to work. Her car contained some art supplies, graded assignments, and books to be used at school that day. The school did not require teachers to use their personal cars to commute to work, nor did they require that teachers work at home. The Workers' Compensation Appeals Board denied compensation because the home was not a second job site, the automobile trip was a matter of convenience, and the transportation of work related items was not the major purpose of the trip. Wilson (P) appealed.

ISSUE: Is workers' compensation available to compensate injuries sustained while an employee travels to or from work?

HOLDING AND DECISION: (Clark, J.) No. Workers' compensation does not compensate injuries sustained while an employee travels to or from work. The only exception to this rule is the presence of special or extraordinary circumstances. These circumstances do not exist here; there was no business reason for work at home. The work was done at home for the employee's own convenience. The job requirements demanded only that she report to the school grounds. The implicit requirement that she work after class hours did not require her to work at home. Nor is there an allegation that facilities at school were not sufficient to permit completion of preparatory chores. Nor does the transportation of materials constitute special circumstances. The transport did not require a special route or mode of transport, nor did it increase the risk of injury. The decision of the appeals board is affirmed.

DISSENT: (Tobriner, J.) The employee was required or expected to furnish her own means of transportation to the job. Thus, one of the special exceptions to the "going and coming" rules applies.

► ANALYSIS

This case illustrates the "going and coming rule." This rule has generated a great amount of litigation, due to the fact that the courts have never been very precise in deciding when a person is in transit or has arrived at the job site. This is not a failure of our judicial system though, but rather is caused by the nature of our society. Only a small number of people live and work in the same place. To meet this problem the courts look at each case as it comes before them and base their decisions on the finding of special and extraordinary circumstances such as the closeness of the employee to the job site or the fact that an employee is in a company owned parking lot, or the fact that travel was essential rather than incidental to the work being done.

Quicknotes

WORKERS COMPENSATION Fixed awards provided to employees for job-related injuries.

Rainer v. Union Carbide Corporation

Workers (P) v. Employers (D)

402 F.3d 608 (6th Cir. 2005).

NATURE OF CASE: Appeal from dismissal of action brought by employees against employer for subcellular damage allegedly sustained from exposure to carcinogenic substances at the workplace.

FACT SUMMARY: Workers (P) at a uranium-enrichment plant contended that the successive operator-employers (D) of the plant were liable to them for subcellular damage to their DNA and chromosomes resulting from the exposure to various radioactive substances, the presence of which was not disclosed to the workers (P). They also contended that their claims fell under an exception to the state's workers' compensation act.

> ## RULE OF LAW
> The phrase "deliberate intention to produce injury or death" in a state workers' compensation statute, to act as an exception to the statute, requires an employer is determined to injure an employee and employ some means toward that end.

FACTS: Workers (P) at a uranium-enrichment plant were exposed over many years to dangerous radioactive substances without their knowledge. Although not yet suffering from any symptoms of a clinical disease, they brought suit against successive operator-employers (D) of the plant, alleging that they had suffered subcellular damage to their DNA and chromosomes as a result of the prolonged exposure. Company documents revealed a disregard for worker safety, and that workers were not informed of the presence of the radioactive substances, which are dangerous carcinogens. The district court dismissed the action, finding that the state's workers' compensation act provided the exclusive remedy for such claims, brought by employees against their employers. Although the workers (P) acknowledged the normal exclusivity of this act, they asserted that their claims fell under one of the act's exceptions relating to an employer's deliberated intention to produce injury or death. In so arguing, the worker's (P) asserted that the phrase "deliberate intention" must "include conduct undertaken with the knowledge that it will produce a certain result, or is substantially certain to do so." The court of appeals granted review.

ISSUE: Does the phrase "deliberate intention to produce injury or death" in a state workers' compensation statute, to act as an exception to the statute, require that an employer is determined to injure an employee and employ some means toward that end?

HOLDING AND DECISION: (Gilman, J.) Yes. The phrase "deliberate intention to produce injury or death" in a state workers' compensation statute, to act as an exception to the statute, requires that an employer is determined to injure an employee and employ some means toward that end. Contrary to the workers' (P) contention, the phrase "deliberate intention" does not necessarily cover conduct that is undertaken with the knowledge that it will produce a certain result or is substantially certain to do so. Instead, the state's supreme court has interpreted this language to require that the employer has determined to injure the employee. That court has also indicated that "deliberate intention" does not equate to wanton and gross negligence and is much narrower than "intent" in tort law, where the "substantial certainty" analysis is proper. Although other jurisdictions have interpreted this phrase in accordance with the workers' (P) position, that is not the law of the state, which the federal courts sitting in that state must follow. Affirmed.

ANALYSIS

Some courts that have taken a broader view of the phrase "deliberate intention" than the court in this case have adopted the substantial certainty test from the Second Restatement of Torts. An element of that test provides that a specific intent to injure is not an essential element of an intentional tort where the actor proceeds despite a perceived threat of harm to others that is substantially certain, not merely likely, to occur.

Quicknotes

INTENTIONAL TORT A legal wrong resulting in a breach of duty, which is intentionally or purposefully committed by the wrongdoer.

Defamation

Quick Reference Rules of Law

PAGE

1. *Mims v. Metropolitan Life Insurance Co.* (1) Where a corporation is a defendant in a libel action, a writing is not published where it is dictated by a corporate employee to another corporate employee, who then writes the writing. (2) For purposes of a libel action, a writing is not published where the plaintiff's agent is the only third party to read the writing. — 173

2. *Firth v. State of New York.* (1) For statute of limitation purposes, the single publication rule is applicable to allegedly defamatory statements that are posted on an Internet website. (2) An unrelated modification to a different portion of a website does not constitute a republication. — 175

3. *Blumenthal v. Drudge.* Section 230 of the Communications Decency Act of 1996 immunizes an Internet service provider from a defamation claim for allegedly defamatory material created by an independent third party that is disseminated by the Internet service provider. — 176

4. *Parmiter v. Coupland.* A publication, without justification or lawful excuse, which is calculated to injure the reputation of another by exposing him to hatred, contempt, or ridicule, is a libel. — 177

5. *Muzikowski v. Paramount Pictures Corp.* To be liable for defamation *per se*, a defendant's statements (1) must not be capable of innocent interpretation, (2) must not be capable of being reasonably interpreted to refer to someone other than the plaintiff, and (3) must either be statements that the plaintiff committed a criminal offense, is inflicted with a venereal disease, is unable to perform in public office, or committed adultery, or be statements that prejudice the plaintiff in his profession. — 178

6. *Wilkow v. Forbes, Inc.* A statement is not actionable for libel if the speaker is expressing a subjective view, an interpretation, a theory, conjecture, or surmise, rather than claiming to be in possession of objectively verifiable facts. — 180

7. *Varian Medical Systems, Inc. v. Delfino.* Written defamatory communications published by means of the Internet are properly characterized as libel. — 181

8. *E. Hulton & Co. v. Jones.* Libel is a tortious act and consists of using language that others, knowing the circumstances, would reasonably think to be defamatory of the person complaining of it or injured by it. — 183

9. *Terwilliger v. Wands.* Words that claim a man is having extra-marital intercourse are not actionable without a demonstration of special damages, since they do not disparage the man's character or reputation. — 184

10. *Ellsworth v. Martindale-Hubbell Law Directory, Inc.* Special damages may be established by showing a diminishment of business and that the defamatory statements were likely to have caused the loss. — 185

11. *Faulk v. Aware, Inc.* The jury may award whatever compensatory and punitive damages it deems appropriate so long as it is reasonable. — 186

12. *Faulk v. Aware, Inc.* In a libel action, a plaintiff's damages need not be limited to the level of his actual earnings at the time of the libel. — 187

13. *Auvil v. CBS 60 Minutes.* To establish a claim of product disparagement, or trade libel, a   188
plaintiff must show that the defendant published a knowingly false statement that was harmful
to the interests of another with the intent to harm the plaintiff's pecuniary interests.

14. *Watt v. Longsdon.* Unless the defamation is a privileged communication, a person making   189
defamatory statements that are untrue will incur liability for his statements.

15. *Kennedy v. Cannon.* Attorneys are privileged and protected to a certain extent, at least, for   190
defamatory words spoken in a judicial proceeding if they have some relation thereto.

16. *Brown & Williamson Tobacco Corp. v. Jacobson.* An otherwise libelous statement is privileged if   191
it is a fair and accurate summary of government proceedings or investigations.

17. *New York Times Co. v. Sullivan.* A public official may not recover damages for a defamatory   192
falsehood concerning his official conduct unless he can prove that the statement was made
with actual malice.

18. *Curtis Publishing Co. v. Butts.* Where the standard of reporting on the activities of public   194
personalities is outside the limits associated with good, prudent journalism, the privilege is lost.

19. *Gertz v. Robert Welch, Inc.* Defamation of a party who is neither a public figure nor an official is   195
entitled to constitutional protections.

20. *Obsidian Finance Group, LLC v. Cox.* (1) Liability for a defamatory blog post involving a matter   196
of public concern cannot be imposed without proof of fault and actual damages. (2) For
purposes of defamation liability, a court-appointed bankruptcy trustee is not a public official.

Mims v. Metropolitan Life Insurance Co.

Alleged libel victim (P) v. Alleged libeler (D)

200 F.2d 800 (5th Cir. 1952).

NATURE OF CASE: Appeal from summary judgment for defendant-corporation in action for libel.

FACT SUMMARY: Mims (P), who alleged libel against Metropolitan Life Insurance Co. (the corporation) (D) arising from a letter sent by the corporation's (D) president to Senator Sparkman, a friend of Mims (P), contended for purposes of establishing libel there was sufficient publication of the letter arising from the dictation of the letter by the corporation's (D) president to a stenographer employed by the corporation (D), as well as from the receipt by Senator Sparkman of the letter, notwithstanding Senator Sparkman had solicited the letter at Mims's (P) request.

RULE OF LAW
(1) Where a corporation is a defendant in a libel action, a writing is not published where it is dictated by a corporate employee to another corporate employee, who then writes the writing.
(2) For purposes of a libel action, a writing is not published where the plaintiff's agent is the only third party to read the writing.

FACTS: Mims (P) had worked for the Alabama office of Metropolitan Life Insurance Co. (the corporation) (D) for 32 years. His employment was terminated after he failed to contribute to a political campaign fund. He believed the termination was occasioned by this failure, and he asked his friend, Senator Sparkman of Alabama, to ask the corporation's (D) president to explain why Mims (P) had been fired. The corporation's (D) president, located in New York, replied at length by letter, denying the discharge was in any way due to Mims's (P) refusal to contribute to the campaign fund, and stating in effect it was due to inefficiency and to unsatisfactory production in the branch agencies of which Mims (P) had been the manager. The letter, which had been dictated by the president to a company-employed stenographer, who wrote it, concluded the only mistake made by the corporation (D) was in giving Mims (P) so long an opportunity to make good, in the hope he might improve. The letter was then mailed to Senator Sparkman in reply to his inquiry, and was received and read by him in Washington, D.C. Mims (P) brought suit for libel in Alabama federal district court, asserting the statements in the letter were false, made with malice, and were therefore libelous and unprivileged. The district court granted summary judgment to the corporation, and the court of appeals granted review.

ISSUE:
(1) Where a corporation is a defendant in a libel action, is a writing published where it is dictated by a corporate employee to another corporate employee, who then writes the writing?
(2) For purposes of a libel action, is a writing published where the plaintiff's agent is the only third party to read the writing?

HOLDING AND DECISION: (Strum, J.)
(1) No. Where a corporation is a defendant in a libel action, a writing is not published where it is dictated by a corporate employee to another corporate employee, who then writes the writing. A corporate defendant can act only through its agents. Here, the president who dictated the letter, and the stenographer who transcribed it, were employed by and acting for the corporation (D) in the performance of a single corporate function, each supplying a component part thereof. When the letter was thus dictated and transcribed, it was not the act of two individuals acting separately. It was one corporate entity acting through two instrumentalities, neither of whom was a third party in relation to the corporation (D), because each was acting as a part of the corporate entity in the performance of a single corporate act, the production of the letter, in the regular course of their duties. For these reasons, there was insufficient publication to support a libel action. Affirmed as to this issue.
(2) No. For purposes of a libel action, a writing is not published where the plaintiff's agent is the only third party to read the writing. Here, Senator Sparkman was acting as Mims's (P) agent, because he was acting at Mims's (P) express request and with his approval—virtually as Mims's (P) alter ego. The corporation's (D) president replied to the person through whom the inquiry was made. The letter complained of having been solicited by Mims (P), through his representative Senator Sparkman, Mims (P) thereby impliedly consented that the corporation (D) reply through the same representative. As a matter of law, the corporation's (D) president effectively replied to Mims (P) himself. Without Mims's (P) solicitation, the letter would not have been written. For these reasons, there was insufficient publication in the District of Columbia to support a libel action. Because Mims (P) cannot establish publication, the issue of whether the letter was written with

Continued on next page.

malice and therefore not privileged, is not reached. Affirmed as to this issue. Affirmed.

DISSENT: (Rives, J.) Contrary to the majority's conclusion, there was publication both where the letter was written, as well as where it was received. Merely because a corporation can act only through its human agents should not immunize it from tort liability, since its corporate agents are just as much individual human beings as are the agents of natural persons. The same rules should apply to both. Under New York law, it has been held that publication results from dictation, where the stenographic notes have been transcribed. Although the case that announced that rule involved a stenographer employed by an individual, there was nothing in the opinion to indicate the rule would be different if the stenographer were employed by a corporation. Further, Senator Sparkman here was not acting as Mims's (P) agent. The matter was one of public interest and Senator Sparkman was properly acting in his capacity as a Senator of the United States. He was giving the corporation (D) an opportunity to offer an explanation before referring the matter to the Senate Elections Subcommittee, so the jury could have found Senator Sparkman was not the Mims's (P) alter ego.

▶ *ANALYSIS*

It has been held there has been sufficient publication to support a libel action where a corporate defendant has communicated libelous matter to employees who had no part in producing the writing, thus exceeding the normal necessities of preparing the writing. See, e.g., *Kennedy v. James Butler*, 245 N.Y. 204, 156 N.E. 666 (1927); *Pirre v. Printing Developments, Inc.*, 468 F. Supp. 1028, 1044 (S.D.N.Y.), *aff'd*, 614 F.2d 1290 (2d Cir. 1979). This approach is consistent with the Restatement (Second) of Torts (1977) § 577, comment (i), p. 204, and has been approved by leading commentators. Thus, if the language of the president's letter in this case had been communicated to an employee of the corporation whose duties were unconnected with the process by which the letter was produced, such communication might be regarded as an actionable publication.

▰▬▰

Quicknotes

LIBEL A false or malicious publication subjecting a person to scorn, hatred or ridicule, or injuring him or her in relation to his or her occupation or business.

PUBLICATION The communicating of a defamatory statement to a third party.

▰▬▰

Firth v. State of New York

Former employee (P) v. Former employer (D)

N.Y. Ct. App., 775 N.E.2d 463 (2002).

NATURE OF CASE: Appeal of dismissed defamation action.

FACT SUMMARY: Firth (P) sued the State of New York (State) (D) when it published a report online which criticized his job performance.

RULE OF LAW
(1) For statute of limitation purposes, the single publication rule is applicable to allegedly defamatory statements that are posted on an Internet website.
(2) An unrelated modification to a different portion of a website does not constitute a republication.

FACTS: The State Department of Education posted an executive summary with links to the full text of a report issued by the Office of the State Inspector General. The summary was critical of Firth's (P) managerial style and procurement of weapons. Firth (P) was formerly employed by the Department of Environmental Conservation as Director of the Division of Law Enforcement. More than one year after the report was on the website, Firth (P) filed a claim against the State of New York (State) (D) alleging that the report defamed him. The court of claims granted the State's (D) motion to dismiss on the basis that Firth (P) filed his action after the one-year statute of limitation and rejected Firth's (P) argument that the ongoing availability of the report via the Internet constituted a continuing wrong or new publication. The appellate division affirmed and Firth (P) appealed.

ISSUE:
(1) For statute of limitation purposes, is the single publication rule applicable to allegedly defamatory statements that are posted on an Internet website?
(2) If it is applicable, does an unrelated modification to a different portion of the website constitute a republication?

HOLDING AND DECISION: (Levine, J.)
(1) Yes. For statute of limitation purposes, the single publication rule is applicable to allegedly defamatory statements that are posted on an Internet website. Traditionally, the single publication rule held that although there might be thousands of copies of a newspaper containing a defamatory statement, there can be only one cause of action which runs from the date of that publication. Although a website might be altered at any time and publications are available only to those who see them, each hit or viewing of the report should

not be considered a separate publication that retriggers the statute of limitations. If a multiple publication rule was allowed, the statute of limitation would theoretically never expire or would take a long time to expire because communications posted on websites may be viewed by millions over an expansive geographic area for an indefinite period of time. The legislative intent to bar completely and forever all actions that as to the time of their commencement overpass the limitation there prescribed upon litigation would be thwarted. In addition, a multiplicity of actions, leading to potential harassment and excessive liability would occur, draining judicial resources. All of this would inhibit the dissemination of information over the Internet, which is one of its best attributes.

(2) No. An unrelated modification to a different portion of the website does not constitute a republication. When the State (D) added an unrelated report of the Inspector General on the DMV to the Education Department's website, it did not republish the report within one year of the filing of the claim. Republication retriggering the period of limitations occurs upon a separate aggregate publication from the original, on a different occasion, which is not merely a delayed circulation of the original edition, but actually reaches a new audience. The mere addition of unrelated information to a website cannot be equated with the repetition of defamatory matter in a separately published edition of a book or newspaper, for it is not reasonably inferable that the addition was made either with the intent or the result of communicating the earlier and separate defamatory information to a new audience. Moreover, the Internet would be harmed if we decided otherwise. Affirmed.

ANALYSIS

This case follows the Restatement (Second) of Torts § 577A.

Quicknotes

DEFAMATION An intentional false publication, communicated publicly in either oral or written form, subjecting a person to scorn, hatred or ridicule, or injuring him or her in relation to his or her occupation or business.

Blumenthal v. Drudge

Alleged defamation victim (P) v. Alleged defamer (D)

992 F. Supp. 44 (D.D.C. 1998).

NATURE OF CASE: Motion for summary judgment in defamation action.

FACT SUMMARY: America Online (AOL) (D), an Internet service provider, contended that it was immune from suit under § 230 of the Communications Decency Act of 1996 (CDA) for defamation allegedly caused by Drudge (D) through his online gossip column, which was hosted by AOL (D).

🏛 RULE OF LAW
Section 230 of the Communications Decency Act of 1996 immunizes an Internet service provider from a defamation claim for allegedly defamatory material created by an independent third party that is disseminated by the Internet service provider.

FACTS: Drudge (D) published an online gossip column, the Drudge Report. At some point, Drudge (D) and America Online (AOL) (D), an Internet service provider, entered into an agreement whereby in exchange for a flat monthly "royalty" of $3000, Drudge (D) would provide AOL (D) with the column, which AOL (D) would post on its website. The Drudge Report posted a story that claimed Blumenthal (P), who was about to begin employment as the President's assistant, had physically abused his wife, who also worked in the White House. The Blumenthals (P) brought a defamation action in federal district court against Drudge (D) and AOL (D). Drudge (D) retracted the story and apologized publicly. AOL (D) moved for summary judgment, claiming that it was immune from the defamation suit under § 230 of the Communications Decency Act of 1996 (CDA).

ISSUE: Does § 230 of the Communications Decency Act of 1996 immunize an Internet service provider from a defamation claim for allegedly defamatory material created by an independent third party that is disseminated by the Internet service provider?

HOLDING AND DECISION: (Friedman, J.) Yes. Section 230 of the Communications Decency Act of 1996 immunizes an Internet service provider from a defamation claim for allegedly defamatory material created by an independent third party that is disseminated by the Internet service provider. In the CDA, in recognition of the speed with which information may be disseminated and the near impossibility of regulating information content, Congress decided not to treat providers of interactive computer services such as AOL (D) like other information providers such as newspapers, magazines or television and radio stations, all of which may be held liable for publishing or

distributing obscene or defamatory material written or prepared by others. Here, AOL (D) had not participated in creating the Drudge Report story about the Blumenthals (P). Therefore, under the CDA, AOL (D) may not be treated as a publisher or speaker of the story, and, hence, it is immunized from tort liability in this situation. Notwithstanding that AOL (D) had an aggressive role in licensing the Drudge Report and promoting it on its site, Congress has made the policy choice, in some sort of tacit quid pro quo arrangement with the service provider community, whereby Congress has conferred immunity from tort liability as an incentive to Internet service providers to self-police the Internet for obscenity and other offensive material, even where the self-policing is unsuccessful or not even attempted. Moreover, it is clear from the statute that Congress made no distinction between publishers and distributors in providing immunity from liability. Even though it is equally clear that AOL (D) has taken advantage of this arrangement without accepting any of the burdens that Congress intended, the statutory language is clear, so that AOL (D) is immune from suit. The motion for summary judgment is granted.

▶ ANALYSIS

The CDA would not immunize AOL (D), or any other Internet service provider, with respect to any information AOL (D) or the provider developed or created entirely by itself. Also, there are situations in which there may be two or more information content providers responsible for material disseminated on the Internet—joint authors, a lyricist and a composer, for example. Here, however, the record showed that AOL (D) had not in any way participated in developing or creating the Blumenthal (P) story; if it had, the outcome of the case would have been different.

▬▬

Quicknotes

DEFAMATION An intentional false publication, communicated publicly in either oral or written form, subjecting a person to scorn, hatred or ridicule, or injuring him or her in relation to his or her occupation or business.

QUID PRO QUO What for what; in the contract context used synonymously with consideration to refer to the mutual promises between two parties rendering a contract enforceable.

▬▬

Parmiter v. Coupland

[Parties not identified.]

Ex., 151 Eng. Rep. 340, 342 (1840).

NATURE OF CASE: Action for libel.

FACT SUMMARY: [Parmiter (P) sued Coupland (D) for libel, arguing that Coupland (D) calculated injury to Parmiter's (P) reputation.]

RULE OF LAW

A publication, without justification or lawful excuse, which is calculated to injure the reputation of another by exposing him to hatred, contempt, or ridicule, is a libel.

FACTS: [Parmiter (P) sued Coupland (D) for libel, arguing that Coupland (D) calculated injury to Parmiter's (P) reputation after Coupland (D) published information about Parmiter (P) that Parmiter (P) felt was defamatory.]

ISSUE: Is a publication, without justification or lawful excuse, which is calculated to injure the reputation of another by exposing him to hatred, contempt, or ridicule a libel?

HOLDING AND DECISION: (Parke, B.) Yes. A publication, without justification or lawful excuse, which is calculated to injure the reputation of another by exposing him to hatred, contempt, or ridicule, is a libel. Here, Coupland (D) calculated to injure Parmiter's (P) reputation and did, with Coupland's (D) publication, expose Parmiter (P) to hatred, contempt, and ridicule. Coupland (D) thus committed libel. Judgment for Parmiter (P).

ANALYSIS

In fairly recent English cases, the courts have taken the position that in defamation actions, a plaintiff's suit may proceed if a large enough portion of the community feels that the statements made could constitute defamation and plaintiff is identifiable in the community as the defamed party. The current view in the United States in defamation actions is that a plaintiff can recover if any portion of the community can be identified which would find statements made about plaintiff to be defamatory. See, e.g., *Peck v. Tribune Co.*, 214 U.S. 185 (1909).

Quicknotes

LIBEL A false or malicious publication subjecting a person to scorn, hatred or ridicule, or injuring him or her in relation to his or her occupation or business.

Muzikowski v. Paramount Pictures Corp.

Little league coach (P) v. Motion picture company (D)

322 F.3d. 918 (7th Cir. 2003).

NATURE OF CASE: Appeal of allowed motion to dismiss defamation action.

FACT SUMMARY: Muzikowski (P) sued Paramount Pictures Corp. (D) for making a movie that allegedly defamed him (P).

RULE OF LAW
To be liable for defamation *per se*, a defendant's statements (1) must not be capable of innocent interpretation, (2) must not be capable of being reasonably interpreted to refer to someone other than the plaintiff, and (3) must either be statements that the plaintiff committed a criminal offense, is inflicted with a venereal disease, is unable to perform in public office, or committed adultery, or be statements that prejudice the plaintiff in his profession.

FACTS: Muzikowski (P) coached Little League Baseball teams in economically depressed areas. A book was written about a particular season of the League Muzikowski (P) co-founded, and a movie, based on the book, was subsequently made by Paramount Pictures Corp. (Paramount) (D). The book was written by Coyle, a volunteer assistant coach with one of the leagues, and billed as a work of non-fiction. The book focused primarily on the children Coyle coached, with some attention being given to the other coaches. Muzikowski (P) was the coach discussed most often in the book, and the discussion included personal details about his (P) life. In contrast, no character in the film is named Muzikowski (P), there is no reference to Little League Baseball and the credits disclaim any connection, other than inspiration, from non-fiction. Muzikowski (P) sued Paramount (D) claiming the movie defamed him because a character in the movie was easily identifiable as he (P) and was portrayed in negative way. Muzikowski (P) argued that this amounted to falsehoods about him and about his league. Muzikowski (P) contended that the main character in the movie is a portrayal of him because many facts about Muzikowski's (P) own life were in the book. The character in the movie experiences the same things as Muzikowski (P), except that Muzikowski (P) has never done some of the unflattering things that the character does—the character never overcomes his drinking habit and commits crimes. Press releases surrounding the release of the movie prompted comments by people that Paramount (D) was going to make a movie about Muzikowski (P). The district court granted Paramount's (D) motion to dismiss and Muzikowski (P) appealed.

ISSUE: Is Muzikowski (P) entitled to prove his claim under defamation *per se* theory?

HOLDING AND DECISION: (Wood, J.) Yes. Muzikowski (P) is entitled to prove his claim under defamation *per se* theory because there is evidence that Paramount's (D) statements could not be innocently interpreted or reasonably interpreted to refer to someone other than Muzikowski (P), and the statements prejudice Muzikowski (P) in his profession and have imputed that Muzikowski (P) has committed a criminal offense. Although there are differences between the character in the movie and Muzikowski (P), Muzikowski (P) might be able to produce evidence showing that there is in fact no reasonable interpretation of the movie that would support an innocent construction. Muzikowski (P) might be able to show that no one could think that anyone but Muzikowski (P) was meant by the character in the movie, and the changes in his character as portrayed in the movie only serve to defame him. Furthermore, Muzikowski's (P) complaint was sufficient to put Paramount (D) on notice of his claims. In his complaint, Muzikowski (P) describes such a close resemblance between himself (P) and the character in the movie that reasonable persons would understand that the character was actually intended to portray Muzikowski (P), and that Paramount (D) intended the movie mischaracterizations to refer to Muzikowski (P). In addition, Muzikowski (P) has pleaded a category of speech that is defamation *per se*. Muzikowski (P) asserts that the movie has injured him in his profession because in the movie the character is lying when he claims that he a securities broker, but in real life Muzikowski (P) is indeed a licensed securities broker. Moreover, Paramount (D) has imputed to Muzikowski (P) the commission of a crime of moral turpitude by having its character, steal. Reversed and remanded.

ANALYSIS

The court specifically found Paramount's (D) argument that it is reasonable to construe that the statements in question refer to the character in the movie and not Muzikowski (P) because the movie is a work of fiction and therefore it cannot reasonably be interpreted to refer to Muzikowski (P) is invalid. Just because a story is labeled fiction and does not purport to describe any real person, does not mean that it may not be defamatory per se.

Continued on next page.

Quicknotes

DEFAMATION An intentional false publication, communicated publicly in either oral or written form, subjecting a person to scorn, hatred or ridicule, or injuring him or her in relation to his or her occupation or business.

DEFAMATION PER SE An intentional false publication of words which, standing alone without proof, communicated publicly in either oral or written form, subject a person to scorn, hatred or ridicule.

MORAL TURPITUDE Intentional conduct demonstrating depravity or vileness and which is contrary to acceptable and traditional societal behavior.

Wilkow v. Forbes, Inc.

Businessman (P) v. Magazine (D)

241 F.3d 552 (7th Cir. 2001).

NATURE OF CASE: Appeal of judgment in favor of *Forbes, Inc.* (D) in libel action.

FACT SUMMARY: Wilkow (P) sued *Forbes, Inc.* (D) after *Forbes* (D) published an article about Wilkow (P) criticizing his filing for bankruptcy.

🏛 RULE OF LAW
A statement is not actionable for libel if the speaker is expressing a subjective view, an interpretation, a theory, conjecture, or surmise, rather than claiming to be in possession of objectively verifiable facts.

FACTS: *Forbes* Magazine (D) published an article about the grant of certiorari in a case in which Wilkow (P) was a party. The issue in that case was whether the absolute-priority rule in bankruptcy has a new-value exception. Under the absolute-priority rule, creditors may insist on priority of payment where secured creditors are paid in full before unsecured creditors retain any interest, and unsecured creditors are paid off before equity holders retain an interest. The court had held in the case that the equity investors could retain ownership of a commercial office building in exchange for about $6 million in new capital over a five-year period, even though the principal lender would fall about $38 million short of full repayment. The *Forbes* (D) article described this holding in its article, which was published seven months before the Supreme Court ultimately held the plan "doomed . . . by its provision for vesting equity in the reorganized business in the Debtor's partners without extending an opportunity for anyone else either to compete for that equity or to propose a competing reorganization plan." The *Forbes* (D) article took the lenders' side of the issue and stated that ". . . unscrupulous business owners [are allowed] to rob creditors." The article specifically accused a partnership led by Wilkow (P) of pleading poverty and filing for bankruptcy when the principle became due and of stiffing the bank by paying only $55 million on a $93 million loan while retaining ownership of the building. Wilkow (P) sued *Forbes* (D) for libel contending that *Forbes* (D) defamed him by asserting that he pleaded poverty when he was solvent and had filched the bank's money. Wilkow (P) argued that *Forbes* (D) should have at least told its readers that a downturn in the real estate market and the fact that it was a loan without recourse against the partners was the principal source of the bank's loss. The trial court found no libel and Wilkow (P) appealed.

ISSUE: Was the article libelous?

HOLDING AND DECISION: (Easterbrook, J.) No. The article was not libelous. A statement is not actionable for libel if the speaker is expressing a subjective view, an interpretation, a theory, conjecture, or surmise, rather than claiming to be in possession of objectively verifiable facts. In the present case characterizing the situation as "stiffing" and "rob" convey the article writer's objection to the new-value exception. The writer was expostulating against judicial willingness to allow debtors to retain interests in exchange for new value, not against debtors' seizing whatever opportunities the law allows. The article did not imply that Wilkow (P) did anything illegal. Most of the details in the article came from public documents. The colloquialisms used did not imply that Wilkow (P) was destitute and failing to pay his personal creditors. Although the article clearly disapproves of Wilkow's (P) conduct, an author's opinion about business ethics is not defamatory. It is likely that many readers of the article who are investors would have thought favorably of Wilkow (P) because he used every opening the courts allowed in order to drive the hardest bargain with lenders. Affirmed.

▶ ANALYSIS

Although investors may have looked at Wilkow (P) in a favorable light, lenders clearly would not appreciate Wilkow's (P) actions.

▬■

Quicknotes

LIBEL A false or malicious publication subjecting a person to scorn, hatred or ridicule, or injuring him or her in relation to his or her occupation or business.

▬■

Varian Medical Systems, Inc. v. Delfino

Allegedly defamed former employer (P) v. Allegedly libelous former employee (D)

Cal. App. Ct., 113 Cal. App. 4th 273 (2003).

NATURE OF CASE: Appeal from judgment for plaintiffs in an action for, inter alia, defamation, and from an injunction.

FACT SUMMARY: After Delfino (D) and Day (D), former employees of Varian Associates, Inc. (Varian) (P), were found by a jury to have defamed Varian (P) and two Varian executives (P) through a slew of thousands of derogatory postings on Internet bulletin boards, Delfino (D) and Day (D) contended, inter alia, that hyperbole on the Internet cannot be defamatory and that to the extent that speech on the Internet is defamatory, it can only constitute slander, not libel.

RULE OF LAW
Written defamatory communications published by means of the Internet are properly characterized as libel.

FACTS: Varian Associates, Inc. (Varian) (P) and two Varian executives (P) filed suit against Delfino (D) and Day (D), former Varian (P) employees for defamation, invasion of privacy, breach of contract, and conspiracy after Delfino (D) and Day (D) used Internet bulletin boards to post over 13,000 derogatory messages about Varian (P) and the executives (P). Rejecting Delfino's (D) and Day's (D) argument that their speech was constitutionally protected, a jury found them liable on all counts, and, given that Delfino (D) and Day (D) had vowed to continue to post derogatory messages until they died, the court issued a broad injunction to prevent further injury. On appeal, Delfino (D) and Day (D) contended, inter alia, that hyperbole on the Internet cannot be defamatory and that to the extent that speech on the Internet is defamatory, it can only be designated as slander, which requires proof of special damages, rather than libel, for which damages are presumed. The state's intermediate appellate court granted review.

ISSUE: Are written defamatory communications published by means of the Internet properly characterized as libel?

HOLDING AND DECISION: (Premo, J.) Yes. Written defamatory communications published by means of the Internet are properly characterized as libel. First, not all communication on the Internet must be considered non-defamatory. Although Internet message boards are freewheeling and irreverent, they are still subject to established legal and social norms. Here, there was sufficient evidence that Delfino's (D) and Day's (D) postings were defamatory, rather than mere hyperbole, opinion, or truth.

Delfino's (D) and Day's (D) argument that to the extent their Internet messages could be considered defamatory, they must be characterized as slander must also be rejected. They point out that the distinction is crucial because slander requires proof of special damages and libel does not and since Varian (P) and the executives (P) did not prove any special damages they cannot recover for defamation. The traditional distinction between libel and slander is that libel is written and slander is spoken, but Delfino (D) and Day (D) ignore this distinction and focus instead upon the practical difference, which involves the necessity to prove damages. Libel today is defined as a defamatory publication communicated "by writing, printing, picture, effigy, or other fixed representation to the eye," whereas slander is "orally uttered, and also communications by radio or any mechanical or other means." A review of the legislative history reveals that the state's legislature did not intend that "communications by radio or any mechanical or other means" include written communications made by a computer or other electronic device. Accordingly, the plain language of the defamation statutes is dispositive, so that the messages at issue were publications by writing. The messages were composed and transmitted in the form of written words just like newspapers, handbills, or notes tacked to a conventional bulletin board. They are representations "to the eye." Although it is true that when sent out over the Internet the messages may be deleted or modified and to that extent they are not "fixed," in contrast with the spoken word, they are certainly "fixed." Furthermore, the messages are just as easily preserved (as by printing them) as they are deleted or modified. In short, the only difference between the publications made in this case and traditionally libelous publications is that Delfino (D) and Day (D) chose to disseminate the writings electronically. Affirmed as to damages. [The trial court's injunction must be overruled to the extent it prohibits future postings on the Internet, as that prohibition constitutes an unconstitutional prior restraint.]

ANALYSIS

The advent of various social media has enabled almost everyone to be a broadcaster, and the consequences of and damages related to a defamatory broadcast via social media can be far more devastating than via traditional print media, since social media are instantaneous and can become "viral." While the court in this case acknowledged that many forms of publication available to us today

Continued on next page.

"cannot realistically be analyzed by reference to the traditional libel-slander dichotomy, which modern technology has rendered increasingly obsolete," the court's decision stands as a warning that new technologies will be subjected to defamation laws, regardless of how defamatory communications are characterized. Given the ease of sending communications via social media, as well as the Internet, users must be advised to be extremely cautious to avoid making defamatory statements, lest they be subject to defamation actions with potentially high damages.

━━━━

Quicknotes

DEFAMATION An intentional false publication, communicated publicly in either oral or written form, subjecting a person to scorn, hatred or ridicule, or injuring him or her in relation to his or her occupation or business.

LIBEL A false or malicious publication subjecting a person to scorn, hatred or ridicule, or injuring him or her in relation to his or her occupation or business.

━━━━

E. Hulton & Co. v. Jones

Newspaper (D) v. Writer (P)

A.C. 20 (1910).

NATURE OF CASE: Appeal from award of damages in a defamation action.

FACT SUMMARY: Jones (P) sued E. Hulton & Co. (D) for running an article implying that Jones (P) was seen in Paris with a woman who was not his wife, but Hulton (D) argued that they had used the name "Artemus Jones" as a fictitious name and did not intend to defame Jones (P).

RULE OF LAW

Libel is a tortious act and consists of using language that others, knowing the circumstances, would reasonably think to be defamatory of the person complaining of it or injured by it.

FACTS: Jones (P) had been a writer for a newspaper owned by E. Hulton & Co. (D). The paper ran an article written by its Paris correspondent stating that an "Artemus Jones" had been seen in Paris with a woman who was not his wife and therefore "you know—must be the other thing!" Jones (P) sued Hulton (D) for defamation, claiming that Hulton (D) had libeled him. Hulton (D) argued that the writer of the article had never heard of Jones (P) and was using a fictitious name for the object of the article. Jones (P) produced witnesses who said they had read the story and believed that it referred to Jones (P). At trial, the judge charged the jury that the issue was not what the writer had intended but how the statement would be understood. Jones (P) recovered upon a jury verdict, and on appeal by Hulton (D), the court of appeals affirmed. Hulton (D) appealed.

ISSUE: Does libel consist of using language that others, knowing the circumstances, would reasonably think to be defamatory of the person complaining of it or injured by it?

HOLDING AND DECISION: (Lord Loreburn, C.) Yes. Libel consists of using language that others, knowing the circumstances, would reasonably think to be defamatory of the person complaining of it or injured by it. It is no defense that the defendant does not intend to defame the plaintiff. Such a defendant has nonetheless imputed something disgraceful and injured the plaintiff. Hulton (D) may not excuse itself from malice, even by proving the article was written in the most benevolent spirit, or if can it show that the libel was not of or concerning Jones (P) by proving it had never heard of him. In any event, Jones (P) had been employed by Hulton (D), and his name was well known in the paper and in the district in which the paper was distributed. Therefore, the jury was entitled to infer recklessness, at least. Affirmed.

▶ ANALYSIS

Under the common law, as in this case, defamation was regarded as a strict liability tort. In other words, the defendant published at his peril. Actual malice, in the sense of spite or ill will, was presumed and did not need to be proven if the statement was defamatory on its face.

Quicknotes

DEFAMATION An intentional false publication, communicated publicly in either oral or written form, subjecting a person to scorn, hatred or ridicule, or injuring him or her in relation to his or her occupation or business.

LIBEL A false or malicious publication subjecting a person to scorn, hatred or ridicule, or injuring him or her in relation to his or her occupation or business.

MALICE The intention to commit an unlawful act without justification or excuse.

RECKLESSNESS The conscious disregard of substantial and justifiable risk.

Terwilliger v. Wands

Slandered party (P) v. Slanderer (D)

N.Y. Ct. App., 17 N.Y. 54 (1858).

NATURE OF CASE: Action to recover damages for slander.

FACT SUMMARY: Wands (D) said that Terwilliger (P) was having sexual intercourse with Mrs. Fuller, a married woman.

🏛 RULE OF LAW
Words that claim a man is having extra-marital intercourse are not actionable without a demonstration of special damages, since they do not disparage the man's character or reputation.

FACTS: Wands (D) told a third person that Terwilliger (P) was visiting Mrs. Fuller regularly for the purpose of having sexual intercourse with her, and that Terwilliger (P) would do all he could to keep Mrs. Fuller's husband in the penitentiary so that he could have access to her. The damages alleged were that Terwilliger (P) became ill and was unable to work after hearing of the reports circulated by Wands (D). Wands's (D) motion for a nonsuit was sustained.

ISSUE: Are words that claim a man is having extra-marital intercourse actionable as slanderous without a showing of special damages?

HOLDING AND DECISION: (Strong, J.) No. Words that have a natural and immediate tendency to produce injury are actionable per se, and are adjudged to be injurious, though no special loss or damage can be proved. However, words that do not apparently and upon their face impart such defamation as will of course be injurious, are not actionable per se, and special damages must be shown. The kind of special damages that must be shown to have resulted from the words are damages produced by, or through, impairing the reputation. The words must be defamatory in nature, and must, in fact, disparage the character, and this disparagement must be evidenced by some positive loss arising therefrom. Hence, words that do not degrade the character do not injure and cannot occasion loss. In this case, Wands's (D) words were defamatory, and it may be assumed that Terwilliger's (P) illness was a result of the words. However, this result does not prove that Terwilliger's (P) character was injured, and so Terwilliger (P) cannot recover for slander. Affirmed.

▶ ANALYSIS

This case demonstrates the difficulty of recovering if the slanderous words do not fall into one of the four categories that do not require the showing of special damages (pecuniary loss). Tort law scholar William Prosser states that since a plaintiff is seldom able to prove any specific pecuniary loss as a result of slander, the effect of the rule requiring a demonstration of such loss has to deny recovery unless slander fits into one of the four categories. The fourth category added was words that accuse a woman of unchastity. Such words are actionable per se, without a showing of special damages, because of their harmfulness to a woman's reputation. As this case demonstrates, the law reflects society's double standard, and this rule is not applied to men, since such accusations are not as damaging to their reputation.

━━■■■━━

Quicknotes

ACTIONABLE PER SE Language of such an extreme nature that the law will presume that the person who is the subject of the communication has suffered injury and for which proof of damages is not required.

DEFAMATION An intentional false publication, communicated publicly in either oral or written form, subjecting a person to scorn, hatred or ridicule, or injuring him or her in relation to his or her occupation or business.

SLANDER Defamatory statement communicated orally.

SPECIAL DAMAGES Damages caused by a specific act that are not the usual consequence of that act and which must be specifically pled and proven.

━━■■■━━

Ellsworth v. Martindale-Hubbell Law Directory, Inc.

Attorney (P) v. Law directory publisher (D)

N.D. Sup. Ct., 280 N.W. 879 (1938).

NATURE OF CASE: Action in damages for libel.

FACT SUMMARY: Ellsworth (P) alleged special damages resulting from Martindale-Hubbell Law Directory Inc.'s (D) failure to rate him in its Law Directory.

RULE OF LAW
Special damages may be established by showing a diminishment of business and that the defamatory statements were likely to have caused the loss.

FACTS: Martindale-Hubbell Law Directory, Inc. (Martindale-Hubbell) (D) failed to rate Ellsworth (P) in its Law Directory. Ellsworth (P) sued for libel, alleging that his referral business had declined because the failure to rate an attorney in the Law Directory speaks adversely of his professional character. No specific loss was alleged. Martindale-Hubbell (D) demurred, alleging that Ellsworth (P) had failed to establish special damages and without them a libel per quod action cannot be maintained.

ISSUE: Must the loss of specific clients be alleged to establish special damages?

HOLDING AND DECISION: (Nuessle, J.) No. Forwarders of legal matters rely on Martindale-Hubbell (D). The local attorney, more likely than not, doesn't even know the forwarder of the case. In such circumstances, it would be unfair and unfeasible to require that specific individuals be named in an allegation for special damages. Rather, a general decline in business plus defamation that is reasonably calculated to have resulted in the decline is sufficient to establish such damages. To hold otherwise would be to deny a remedy where a wrong has been committed. The defendant may allege other factors that might have resulted in the decline to destroy the presumption of special damages. Affirmed.

ANALYSIS

Some courts have held that specific losses must be alleged. *Shaw Cleaners and Dyers, Inc. v. Des Moines Dress Club*, 215 Iowa 1130 (1932). If plaintiff can introduce the testimony of a single person who was dissuaded from using or patronizing plaintiff as a result of the defamation there is prima facie evidence of special damages. *Storey v. Challends*, 8 C. & P. 234 (1837).

Quicknotes

DEFAMATION An intentional false publication, communicated publicly in either oral or written form, subjecting a person to scorn, hatred or ridicule, or injuring him or her in relation to his or her occupation or business.

LIBEL A false or malicious publication subjecting a person to scorn, hatred or ridicule, or injuring him or her in relation to his or her occupation or business.

SPECIAL DAMAGES Damages caused by a specific act that are not the usual consequence of that act and which must be specifically pled and proven.

Faulk v. Aware, Inc.

Television/Radio performer (P) v. Anti-Communist organization (D)

N.Y. Sup. Ct., 231 N.Y.S.2d 270 (1962).

NATURE OF CASE: Action for damages from slander and libel.

FACT SUMMARY: Faulk (P) was blacklisted as a Communist by Aware, Inc. (D).

RULE OF LAW
The jury may award whatever compensatory and punitive damages it deems appropriate so long as it is reasonable.

FACTS: Faulk (P), a performer, was blacklisted by Aware, Inc. (D) as being a Communist. The jury awarded Faulk (P) $1,000,000 in compensatory damages for loss of past and future earnings and mental anguish. It also awarded punitive damages of $1,250,000 against each of the three defendants. Aware, Inc. (D) and the others alleged that the award was excessive. Faulk (P) maintained that an award was solely in the province of the jury and could be overturned only if clearly excessive and unreasonable.

ISSUE: Will a jury award be overturned only when clearly excessive and unreasonable?

HOLDING AND DECISION: (Geller, J.) Yes. The exact effect of libel on a person's business reputation is impossible to adequately calculate. Therefore, it is deemed to be solely within the province of the jury. Their award will be set aside only if it is clearly excessive and unreasonable. Here, Faulk (P) established by expert testimony that he had lost substantial past and future income. Income trends for performers were testified to by experts. The testimony showed that Faulk's (P) income could have grown to as much as $500,000 a year. Mental anguish is also compensable. The compensatory award was clearly justified herein. The jury found that Aware, Inc. (D) had purposefully set out to ruin Faulk's (P) career and that of others. Punitive damages are discretionary with the jury. Here, it awarded more than was prayed for by Faulk (P). The jury, representing the community, assesses the penalty necessary to prevent further occurrences. Here it was reasonable. Affirmed.

ANALYSIS

Compensatory damages may be minimal and a jury may still award huge punitive awards. They are in the nature of penalties to prevent future activities. The more egregious the conduct and the more likely it is to reoccur, the greater the award of punitive damages which will be sustained. Compensatory damages must be proved. Punitive damages only need be included as part of the prayer in the pleadings.

Quicknotes

COMPENSATORY DAMAGES Measure of damages necessary to compensate victim for actual injuries suffered.

LIBEL A false or malicious publication subjecting a person to scorn, hatred or ridicule, or injuring him or her in relation to his or her occupation or business.

PUNITIVE DAMAGES Damages exceeding the actual injury suffered for the purposes of punishment, deterrence and comfort to plaintiff.

SLANDER Defamatory statement communicated orally.

Faulk v. Aware, Inc.

T.V./Radio performer (P) v. Anti-Communist organization (D)

N.Y. App. Div., 244 N.Y.S.2d 259 (1963).

NATURE OF CASE: Appeal from damages award in a defamation action.

FACT SUMMARY: Aware, Inc. (D) appealed from an award of damages for defamation of more than $3 million to Faulk (P), a radio and television performer, arguing that the compensatory damages were disproportionate to Faulk's (P) actual income and the punitive damages were not properly allocated between the defendants.

RULE OF LAW
In a libel action, a plaintiff's damages need not be limited to the level of his actual earnings at the time of the libel.

FACTS: Faulk (P), a radio and television performer, brought a libel action against Aware (D) and its owner, Hartnett (D), for statements made by them and widely distributed, charging Faulk (D) with Communist sympathies and affiliations. At trial, the jury awarded Faulk (P) compensatory damages of $1 million and punitive damages of $1.25 million against each defendant. Aware (D) and Hartnett (D) appealed.

ISSUE: In a libel action, must a plaintiff's damages be limited to the level of his actual earnings at the time of the libel?

HOLDING AND DECISION: (Rabin, J.) No. In a libel action, a plaintiff's earnings are an important factor in assessing damages suffered when his earnings are cut off, and his damages need not be limited to the level of his actual earnings at the time of the libel. However, in this case, the size of the verdict is greatly excessive and most unrealistic—even in the field of entertainment. In this case, Faulk's (P) potential earnings were fixed by his witnesses in amounts ranging from $100,000 to $1 million a year. The larger figure was arrived at by reference to the earnings of those who had reached the very top of the profession yet no explanation was given as to why Faulk's (P) earnings were so comparatively low, never more than $35,000 a year. The testimony of the experts left too much room for speculation. Thus, there is hardly justification for finding compensatory damages in the amount of $1 million, even making allowance for Faulk's (P) mental pain and suffering. The compensatory damages should be fixed at a figure no higher than $400,000. Regarding punitive damages, the jury awarded $1.25 million against both Aware (D) and Hartnett (D), even though Hartnett (D) was the author of the objectionable pamphlet, and he put it in places that would most hurt Faulk (P). The assessment of punitive

damages against Hartnett (D) should be in a much greater amount than against Aware (D); the maximum sum that should have been awarded against Aware (D) as punitive damages was $50,000 and against Hartnett (D), $100,000. Reversed.

ANALYSIS

In defamation actions, the plaintiff is entitled to recover for both general and special damages. For example, in a case where a defendant's words could be understood to cast aspersions not only on a product produced by plaintiff but on the plaintiff herself, then special damages could be recovered. Also, it is widely understood that, in slander cases, once special damages are proven (and there is no slander per se), a jury may award plaintiff general damages in addition to the special damages.

Quicknotes

COMPENSATORY DAMAGES Measure of damages necessary to compensate victim for actual injuries suffered.

LIBEL A false or malicious publication subjecting a person to scorn, hatred or ridicule, or injuring him or her in relation to his or her occupation or business.

PAIN AND SUFFERING DAMAGES In tort law, damages for pain and suffering are compensable only to the extent that some form of physical injury, or at least nominal damages, can be shown.

PUNITIVE DAMAGES Damages exceeding the actual injury suffered for the purposes of punishment, deterrence and comfort to plaintiff.

Auvil v. CBS 60 Minutes

Apple growers (P) v. Television news show (D)

67 F.3d 816 (9th Cir. 1996).

NATURE OF CASE: Appeal from summary judgment for defendants in a product defamation suit.

FACT SUMMARY: Washington state apple growers (P) brought suit against CBS "60 Minutes" (CBS) (D) alleging product disparagement as a result of a broadcast in which CBS (D) claimed that the growers (P) utilized a known carcinogen in the production of their apples.

🏛 RULE OF LAW
To establish a claim of product disparagement, or trade libel, a plaintiff must show that the defendant published a knowingly false statement that was harmful to the interests of another with the intent to harm the plaintiff's pecuniary interests.

FACTS: CBS's weekly news show "60 Minutes" aired a segment on daminozide, a chemical growth regulator sprayed on apples. The show was based on a Natural Resources Defense Council (NRDC) report on the risks associated with certain pesticides used on fruit. Scientific research had revealed that the chemical breaks down into a carcinogen. Following the broadcast, the sale of apples and apple products dropped markedly. Washington state apple growers (P) brought suit against CBS (D) and its local affiliates (D), the NRDC (D) and Fenton Communications (D) alleging product disparagement. The district court granted summary judgment in favor of CBS (D) on the basis that the growers (P) failed to prove the falsity of the message conveyed by the broadcast. The growers (P) appealed.

ISSUE: To establish a claim of product disparagement, or trade libel, must a plaintiff show that the defendant published a knowingly false statement that was harmful to the interests of another with the intent to harm the plaintiff's pecuniary interests?

HOLDING AND DECISION: (Per curiam) Yes. To establish a claim of product disparagement, or trade libel, a plaintiff must show that the defendant published a knowingly false statement that was harmful to the interests of another with the intent to harm the plaintiff's pecuniary interests. Thus, in order to sustain an action for product disparagement, the plaintiff must prove that the disparaging statements were false. Since the tort is substantially similar to defamation, the case law on defamation is applicable here. The growers (P) introduced evidence that no studies have been conducted showing the relation between the ingestion of daminozide and the development of cancer in humans. This evidence is insufficient to show a genuine issue of material fact regarding the claims that the pesticide in a potential carcinogen. Animal laboratory tests are a sufficient means for determining potential cancer risks to humans. All of the statements referenced were factual assertions. The growers (P) also claimed that summary judgment was inappropriate since a jury could find that the broadcast contained a false message. The argument fails as well. The Restatement (Second) of Torts § 651(1)(c) requires a plaintiff claiming product disparagement to provide the "falsity of the statement," not any overall message. Such a requirement would result in uncertainty and a chilling effect on speech. Since the growers (P) failed to raise a genuine issue of material fact the district court's grant of summary judgment is affirmed.

▮ ANALYSIS

Truth is an absolute defense to a suit for defamation. While products disparagement cases were addressed in the Restatement (Second) of Torts, there had been no case law regarding the plaintiff's burden of proving the falsity of the statements prior to this decision.

■=■

Quicknotes

DEFAMATION An intentional false publication, communicated publicly in either oral or written form, subjecting a person to scorn, hatred or ridicule, or injuring him or her in relation to his or her occupation or business.

■=■

Watt v. Longsdon

Oil company director (P) v. Co-worker (D)

K.B., 1 K.B. 130 (1930).

NATURE OF CASE: Appeal from an action for libel.

FACT SUMMARY: Watt (P) sued Longsdon (D) for three separate defamatory publications issued between Longsdon (D) and Browne, a coworker of Watt's (P), in which it was alleged that Watt (P) drank excessively and carried on extramarital relations.

RULE OF LAW
Unless the defamation is a privileged communication, a person making defamatory statements that are untrue will incur liability for his statements.

FACTS: Watt (P) sued Longsdon for three separate defamatory publications. In one communication Browne, a coworker of Watt's (P), sent a letter to Longsdon (D) in which he alleged that Watt (P) drank excessively, cavorted with women other than Watt's wife, and had been shown to be a thief and a liar. Longsdon (D) sent Browne's letter to the chairman of their company's board of directors. This was the first act of defamation. Longsdon (D) then wrote Browne a letter in which Longsdon (D) stated that he shared Browne's view of Watt (P) and requested Browne obtain corroborating statements from other informants. This letter was the second act of defamation. A few days later Longsdon (D) showed Browne's letter to Watt's wife resulting in their separation and a suit for divorce. The trial court found for Longsdon (D) on the ground that all three publications were privileged communication. Watt (P) appealed.

ISSUE: Is a person who makes defamatory statements, which are untrue, libel for those statements, unless the defamation is privileged?

HOLDING AND DECISION: (Lord Scrutton, J.) Yes. By the law of England there are occasions on which a person may make defamatory statements about another that are untrue without incurring any legal liability for his statements. These occasions involve privileged communications requiring a public or private duty or interest in the publication. However, even these communications may lose their privilege if they go beyond the limits of the duty or interest or if they are published with express malice. The occasions giving rise to a privileged communication are as follows: either (1) a duty to communicate information believed to be true to a person who has a material interest in receiving the information, or (2) an interest in the speaker to be protected by communicating information, or (3) a common interest in and reciprocal duty in respect of the subject matter of the communication. This court,

therefore, holds that the first two communications between Browne and Longsdon were privileged communications on the ground of a common interest in the affairs of the company they worked for. However, the communication to Mrs. Watt stands on a different footing. As a general rule, it is not desirable for anyone to interfere in the affairs of man and wife and in this case there was no moral or social duty in Longsdon to make the communication to Mrs. Watt. The decision of the trial court is reversed.

CONCURRENCE AND DISSENT: (Lord Greer, J.) The publication to Watt's (P) wife was not privileged. Although the publications to the chairmen of the company and to Mr. Browne may have been privileged, there is intrinsic evidence in the letter to Browne, and evidence in the hasty and unjustifiable communication to Watt's (P) wife, which would be sufficient to entitle Watt (P) to ask for a verdict on these publications on the ground of express malice. It is up to the jury to decide whether they are satisfied that in publishing the libels, Longsdon (D) was in fact giving effect to his malicious feelings toward Watt (P).

ANALYSIS

In the area of privileged communications, the courts are constantly weighing and balancing the interests in reputation with freedom to communicate in areas considered of social utility. In general, an action lies for the malicious publication of statements which are false in fact, and injurious to the character of another; and the law considers such publication as malicious, unless it is made by a person in the discharge of some duty.

Quicknotes

DEFAMATION An intentional false publication, communicated publicly in either oral or written form, subjecting a person to scorn, hatred or ridicule, or injuring him or her in relation to his or her occupation or business.

LIBEL A false or malicious publication subjecting a person to scorn, hatred or ridicule, or injuring him or her in relation to his or her occupation or business.

PRIVILEGED COMMUNICATION Statements made by people in a protected relationship which the law shields from forced disclosure, such as attorney-client, husband-wife, doctor-patient, etc.

Kennedy v. Cannon

Rape victim (P) v. Rapist's attorney (D)

Md. Ct. App., 182 A.2d 54 (1962).

NATURE OF CASE: Appeal from an action for slander.

FACT SUMMARY: Kennedy (P), a rape victim, brought this suit for slander against Cannon (D), the attorney of the alleged rapist, after Cannon (D) issued a statement to the local newspaper that Kennedy (P) had consented to the relation.

RULE OF LAW
Attorneys are privileged and protected to a certain extent, at least, for defamatory words spoken in a judicial proceeding if they have some relation thereto.

FACTS: After Cannon (D) consulted with his client Humphreys, who had been arrested and charged with the rape of Kennedy (P), Cannon (D) called the local newspaper inquiring about any information received in regard to the rape case. Cannon (D) was informed that the authorities had issued a story saying that Humphreys had signed a statement to the effect that he had intercourse with the Kennedy (P) woman. Thereupon, Cannon (D) proceeded to tell the newspaper everything Humphreys had related, including the assertion that Mrs. Kennedy (P) had consented to the intercourse. The newspaper published the information. As a result, Kennedy (P) alleges she suffered humiliation and harassment by annoying phone calls and eventually was forced to move out of the state. Kennedy (P) brought this action against Cannon (D), alleging that the words spoken by him to the newspaper were slanderous per se. The trial court granted Cannon's (D) motion for a directed verdict on the ground that when the state authorities undertook to publish a statement about the case damaging to Cannon's (D) client, Cannon (D) was justified and privileged in replying.

ISSUE: Are attorneys privileged and protected for defamatory words spoken in a judicial proceeding if they have some relation thereto?

HOLDING AND DECISION: (Sybert, J.) Yes. An attorney is absolutely privileged to publish false and defamatory statements of another in communications preliminary to, or during the course and as part of a judicial proceeding in which he participates as counsel, if it has some relation thereto. However, the scope of the privilege is restricted to communications such as those made between attorney and client, or in the examination of a witness, or in statements made to the court or jury. On the other hand, such absolute privilege will not attach to counsel's extrajudicial publications, related to the litigation,

which are made outside the purview of the judicial proceeding. It may be conceded that Cannon (D) indeed had a duty to act upon information he had gained as to the statement given by the state's attorney to the newspaper. However, the means he chose to fulfill the duty were not proper nor were they within the scope of his professional acts as an attorney in a pending case. Therefore, the granting of a directed verdict for Cannon (D) was erroneous, and the case should have been submitted to the jury. Reversed.

ANALYSIS

There are various other privileges in the area of defamation. Defamatory communications about another between husband and wife are absolutely privileged. Yet it is unclear on what basis this privilege depends. Some argue a husband and wife are more one person than two and consequently their communications are not a publication. Whether remarks to a stenographer are privileged publications in the interests of proper business practices has met with divided opinions, as has the issue of a defamatory publication in a will.

Quicknotes

DEFAMATION An intentional false publication, communicated publicly in either oral or written form, subjecting a person to scorn, hatred or ridicule, or injuring him or her in relation to his or her occupation or business.

DIRECTED VERDICT A verdict ordered by the court in a jury trial.

MITIGATION OF DAMAGES A plaintiff's implied obligation to reduce the damages incurred by taking reasonable steps to prevent additional injury.

PRIVILEGE A benefit or right conferred upon a person or entity beyond those conferred upon the general public.

SLANDER Defamatory statement communicated orally.

Brown & Williamson Tobacco Corp. v. Jacobson

Tobacco company (P) v. News commentator (D)

713 F.2d 262 (7th Cir. 1983).

NATURE OF CASE: Appeal from dismissal of action of damages for libel.

FACT SUMMARY: Jacobson (D), a television news commentator, broadcasted a critical expose, revealing Brown & Williamson Tobacco Corp.'s (P) confidential advertising strategy to attract young viewers.

RULE OF LAW
An otherwise libelous statement is privileged if it is a fair and accurate summary of government proceedings or investigations.

FACTS: In 1975, Brown & Williamson Tobacco Corp. (Brown & Williamson) (P), the manufacturer of the Viceroy cigarettes, hired an advertiser to develop an advertising strategy to attract younger viewers. Kennan, a market research firm hired by the advertiser submitted a report stating that "a cigarette, and the whole smoking process, is part of the illicit pleasure category. . . . In the young smoker's mind, a cigarette falls into the same category with wine, beer, shaving, wearing a bra." Brown & Williamson (P) rejected the advertiser's "illicit pleasure strategy" and fired the advertiser. Years later, the Federal Trade Commission (FTC) conducted an investigation of cigarette advertising and published a 1981 report of its findings. The report quoted the Kennan report and stated that Brown & Williamson (P) adopted many of its ideas in the Viceroy advertising campaign. Jacobson (D) soon after, broadcasted a "Perspective" of the tobacco industry advertising that quoted verbatim the rejected Kennan report, and stated incorrectly that it was used without modification by Brown & Williamson (P) in its Viceroy advertising strategy. Brown & Williamson (P) sued Jacobson (D) for defamation. Jacobson (D) contended that even if his broadcast were libelous it was privileged as a fair and accurate summary of the FTC's staff report on cigarette advertising. The district court granted Jacobson's (D) motion to dismiss based on free speech concerns. Brown & Williamson (P) appealed.

ISSUE: Is an otherwise libelous statement privileged if it is a fair and accurate summary of government proceedings or investigations?

HOLDING AND DECISION: (Posner, J.) Yes. An otherwise libelous statement is privileged if it is a fair and accurate summary of government proceedings or investigations. An unfair summary is one that amplifies the libelous effect that publication of the government report verbatim would have on a reader who reads it carefully. The FTC report conveys the message that a mar-

ket research firm submitted a report to Brown & Williamson (P) for enticing young people to smoke cigarettes, and Brown & Williamson (P) adopted many of the ideas in an advertising campaign it conducted five years ago. Jacobson's (D) broadcast conveys the message that Brown & Williamson (P) is currently conducting an advertising campaign in a manner designed to entice children by associating smoking with drinking, sex, and other illicit youthful pleasures. A rational jury might interpret that Jacobson's (D) broadcast carried a greater sting than the FTC report and was therefore unfair. Reversed and remanded.

ANALYSIS

On remand, Brown & Williamson (P) recovered $3,000,000 in actual damages, and $2,000,000 in punitive damages. The trial judge reduced the compensatory damages to $1. Brown & Williamson (P) appealed, and the compensatory damages were increased to $1,000,000. The $2,000,000 punitive damage award remained unchanged. See *Brown & Williamson Tobacco Corp. v. Jacobson*, 827 F.2d 1119 (7th Cir. 1987).

Quicknotes

LIBEL A false or malicious publication subjecting a person to scorn, hatred or ridicule, or injuring him or her in relation to his or her occupation or business.

PRIVILEGED COMMUNICATION Statements made by people in a protected relationship which the law shields from forced disclosure, such as attorney-client, husband-wife, doctor-patient, etc.

New York Times Co. v. Sullivan

Newspaper publisher (D) v. Police chief (P)

376 U.S. 254 (1964).

NATURE OF CASE: Civil action for damages for libel.

FACT SUMMARY: The *New York Times* (D) published a full-page advertisement critical of the manner in which the Montgomery, Alabama police, under Commissioner Sullivan (P), responded to civil rights demonstrations.

RULE OF LAW
A public official may not recover damages for a defamatory falsehood concerning his official conduct unless he can prove that the statement was made with actual malice.

FACTS: On March 29, 1960, the *New York Times* (D) carried a full page advertisement entitled "Heed Their Rising Voices," placed by several Negro clergymen of Alabama. The advertisement charged that southern Negro students engaged in nonviolent demonstrations were "being met by an unprecedented wave of terror by those who would deny and negate" the U.S. Constitution and Bill of Rights. The advertisement went on to describe certain alleged events in support of this charge, including various actions taken by the police of Montgomery, Alabama. L.B. Sullivan (P), the Police Commissioner of Montgomery, brought a civil libel action against the *New York Times* (D), claiming although the advertisement did not mention him by name, it attributed policy misconduct to him by inference. The trial judge instructed the jury that the advertisement was "libelous per se," leaving the *New York Times* (D) with no defense other than proving the statement true in all respects. Some of the statements were found to be inaccurate descriptions of events that had occurred in Montgomery, and Sullivan (P) was awarded $500,000. The Supreme Court of Alabama affirmed, and the *New York Times* (D) appealed on grounds of constitutional protection of speech and press.

ISSUE: Does the First Amendment limit the power of a state to award damages in a civil libel action brought by a public official against critics of his official conduct?

HOLDING AND DECISION: (Brennan, J.) Yes. If criticism of a public official's conduct is published without actual malice—that is, without knowledge that it was false and without reckless disregard of whether or not it was false—it is protected by the constitutional guarantees of freedom of speech and press. This qualified privilege to publish defamation of a public office is not limited to comment or opinion, but extends as well to false statements of fact, providing there was no actual malice. Behind this decision is a "profound national commitment to the principle that debate on public issues should be uninhibited, robust and wide-open," and that "right conclusions are more likely to be gathered out of a multitude of tongues, than through any kind of authoritative selection." There would be a pall of fear and timidity imposed upon those who would give voice to pure criticism by any rule that would compel such a critic of official conduct to guarantee the truth of all his factual assertions. In addition, any attempt to transmute criticism of government to personal criticism, and hence potential libel of the officials of whom the government is composed would be unconstitutional. Reversed and remanded.

CONCURRENCE: (Black, J.) The First and Fourteenth Amendments do not merely delimit a State's power to award damages to public officials against critics of their official conduct, but completely prohibit a State from exercising such a power. Furthermore, the requirement that malice be proved provides at best an evanescent protection for the right critically to discuss public affairs and certainly does not measure up to the safeguard embodied in the First Amendment. I therefore vote to reverse exclusively on the ground that the *[New York] Times* (D), and the individual defendants, had an absolute, unconditional right to publish in the *[New York] Times* (D) advertisement of their criticisms of the Montgomery agencies and officials (P).

ANALYSIS

Prior to the *Sullivan* case, there was a general recognition, at common law, of a qualified privilege known as "fair comment." Criticism of public officials' conduct and qualifications was allowed to be published as a matter of public concern—this much was undisputed. But sharp disagreement existed between state courts: the majority holding that the privilege of public discussion was limited to opinion and comment, and a vigorous minority insisting even false statements of fact were privileged, if made for the public benefit with an honest belief in their truth. The Supreme Court of Alabama was thus following the majority position in the instant case, and the holding of the Supreme Court came as something of a bombshell, termed by Prosser as "unquestionably the greatest victory won by the defendants in the modern history of the law of torts." Since *Sullivan*, the rule has been applied to criminal, as well as

Continued on next page.

civil, libel and has been extended to all public officers and employees, no matter how inferior their position.

■=■

Quicknotes

FIRST AMENDMENT Prohibits Congress from enacting any law respecting an establishment of religion, prohibiting the free exercise of religion, abridging freedom of speech or the press, the right of peaceful assembly and the right to petition for a redress of grievances.

LIBEL A false or malicious publication subjecting a person to scorn, hatred or ridicule, or injuring him or her in relation to his or her occupation or business.

MALICE The intention to commit an unlawful act without justification or excuse.

PUBLIC FIGURE/OFFICER Any person who is generally known in the community.

■=■

Curtis Publishing Co. v. Butts

Publishing company (D) v. Football coach (P)

388 U.S. 130 (1967).

NATURE OF CASE: Two appeals from verdicts in libel cases.

FACT SUMMARY: Butts (P), a coach, was accused of fixing a football game. Walker (P) had allegedly led a charge against national guardsmen.

🏛 RULE OF LAW
Where the standard of reporting on the activities of public personalities is outside the limits associated with good, prudent journalism, the privilege is lost.

FACTS: Two cases are consolidated herein. In *Curtis Publishing v. Butts*, Curtis (D) published an article concerning Butts (P), the coach of the University of Georgia's football team, alleging activities in connection with a football game with Alabama. A telephone conversation was held between Butts (P) and the Alabama coach in which someone allegedly overheard Butts (P) disclosing Georgia's game plan. The article alleged that Butts (P) had "fixed" the game. Witnesses established that the conversation involved only a general discussion of football, and a judgment for libel was awarded Butts (P) over Curtis's (D) claim of privilege. In *Walker*, [*Associated Press v. Walker*, 393 S.W.2d 671 (Tex. Civ. Ct. App. 1965)], Associated Press (D) published a newspaper article which inaccurately reported that Walker (P) had led a charge against national guardsmen who were escorting a black to classes in a white school. In both cases the juries found libel. Both Curtis (D) and Associated (D) argued that the holding in *New York Times v. Sullivan*, 376 U.S. 254 (1964), supra, should be extended to cover public figures. Both Walker (P) and Butts (P) were newsworthy because of their activities and/or positions.

ISSUE: Should liability be founded on the standard of journalistic care in libel cases involving parties who may fairly be deemed public figures?

HOLDING AND DECISION: (Harlan, J.) Yes. A balancing of the public's right to be informed of newsworthy events and an individual's right to be free from libel are at issue. Mistakes are inevitable in the reporting of public interest events. Public officials may rebut propaganda with counter-propaganda. Further, there is no issue of vindictiveness of a government wishing to protect itself from attack, *i.e.*, seditious libel. Finally, neither plaintiff is in a position of privilege occupied by many government officials. Therefore, the considerations present in *New York Times v. Sullivan* are not present herein. Rather, we opt for a test considering whether the publisher of the libel employed reasonable methods in obtaining its information. If it maintained a reasonable journalistic standard, no liability will be found. State law cannot alone control this area. It must be tested against First Amendment protections. In *Butts*, we find that the journalistic standard was not met. A careful consideration of the evidence would have convinced Curtis (D) that further investigation was required. The judgment of the Fifth Circuit is therefore affirmed. In *Walker*, no real evidence was adduced as to Associated Press's (D) standard of care. It must be reversed and remanded for such consideration.

CONCURRENCE: (Warren, C.J.) I would adopt the same standard for public figures as that applied to public officials.

CONCURRENCE AND DISSENT: (Black, J.) A purpose of the first Amendment was to keep the press free from the pursuit of libel judgments.

CONCURRENCE AND DISSENT: (Brennan, J.) We concur in *Walker*, but dissent as to *Butts*. More evidence is required to establish whether the journalistic standard of care has been met.

▶ ANALYSIS

The actual malice test is extended herein to public figures. Either malice or a reckless disregard of the truth is sufficient to impose liability. In *Meeropol v. Nizer*, 381 F. Supp. 29 (S.D.N.Y. 1974), the children of the Rosenbergs were deemed public figures based on the considerable publicity given to them as a result of their parents' trial and execution for treason. It was immaterial that they had renounced the public spotlight and changed their names.

■■■

Quicknotes

LIBEL A false or malicious publication subjecting a person to scorn, hatred or ridicule, or injuring him or her in relation to his or her occupation or business.

MALICE The intention to commit an unlawful act without justification or excuse.

NEGLIGENCE Conduct falling below the standard of care that a reasonable person would demonstrate under similar conditions.

PUBLIC FIGURE/OFFICER Any person who is generally known in the community.

■■■

Gertz v. Robert Welch, Inc.

Attorney (P) v. Publishing company (D)

418 U.S. 323 (1974).

NATURE OF CASE: Action for damages for libel.

FACT SUMMARY: Gertz (P), an attorney, was labeled Communist for his actions in connection with a civil action filed against a policeman.

🏛 RULE OF LAW
Defamation of a party who is neither a public figure nor an official is entitled to constitutional protections.

FACTS: Gertz (P) instituted a wrongful death action against a police officer. Gertz (P) did not take any further part in the trial. A Birch newspaper published an article from a contributor solely relying on his "extensive research." The article accused Gertz (P) of framing the policeman and of being a Communist. A judgment for a libel verdict in favor of Gertz (P) was reversed judgment n.o.v. on the basis of *New York Times v. Sullivan*, 376 U.S. 254 (1964). It was held that since malice had not been established, the article was constitutionally protected. Gertz (P) argued that he was neither a public figure nor an official and that defamation of a private party was not protected.

ISSUE: Is defamation of a party who is neither a public figure nor a public official entitled to a constitutional privilege?

HOLDING AND DECISION: (Powell, J.) Yes. The rights of the individual to be safe from defamation must be balanced against the rights of free speech and an unfettered press which are an essential concomitant of democracy. Errors are inevitable. However, not all errors are deemed constitutionally protected. If the defamed party has voluntarily or by circumstance been placed in the public eye or he is a public official, he is deemed newsworthy and the public has a right to know about him or to comment on his activities. No such corresponding right is granted with respect to private individuals. Private rights have, for the most part, been granted to the states through the Ninth and Tenth amendments. We do not lightly trammel on those rights. The right to be free from defamation is one such right. It is only abridged where mandated by the Constitution. So long as the state statute does not impose liability without fault, such actions for defamation may be maintained. Punitive damages may not be awarded under these statutes since they are unnecessary to accomplish the state interest and may serve to unnecessarily inhibit the press. Reversed.

CONCURRENCE: (Blackmun, J.) I concur solely on the ground that we need a definite rule in this area of law,

and the removal of punitive damages should allow the press to remain vigorous and unfettered.

DISSENT: (Burger, C.J.) The jury's verdict in favor of Gertz (P) should have been reinstated.

DISSENT: (Douglas, J.) I dissent based on the reasons stated by Justice Black in *New York Times*.

DISSENT: (Brennan, J.) I dissent based on the reasons I stated in *Rosenbloom*, [*Rosenbloom v. Metromedia, Inc.*, 403 U.S. 29 (1971)].

DISSENT: (White, J.) I do not see why the publishing industry should not be liable without fault for published falsehoods in this area or why it would be exempted from punitive damages. The rights of the private individual herein should be protected under state law.

▌ ANALYSIS

An assistant dean and professor of law was deemed a public official within the purview of *New York Times v. Sullivan* in *Gallman v. Carnes*, 254 Ark. 987 (1973). The principles in *Gertz* are only applicable to the media. They are not applied to other conditional privileges such as the right to give information to a prospective employer about a former employee, *Jacron Sales Co. v. Sindorf*, 350 A.2d 688 (Md. 1976).

Quicknotes

DEFAMATION An intentional false publication, communicated publicly in either oral or written form, subjecting a person to scorn, hatred or ridicule, or injuring him or her in relation to his or her occupation or business.

JUDGMENT N.O.V. A judgment entered by the trial judge reversing a jury verdict if the jury's determination has no basis in law or fact.

LIBEL A false or malicious publication subjecting a person to scorn, hatred or ridicule, or injuring him or her in relation to his or her occupation or business.

MALICE The intention to commit an unlawful act without justification or excuse.

PUBLIC FIGURE Any person who is generally known in the community.

PUNITIVE DAMAGES Damages exceeding the actual injury suffered for the purposes of punishment, deterrence and comfort to plaintiff.

Obsidian Finance Group, LLC v. Cox

Turnaround firm (P) v. Blogger (D)

740 F.3d 1284 (9th Cir. 2014).

NATURE OF CASE: Appeal from jury verdicts imposing defamation liability on a blogger.

FACT SUMMARY: Cox (D), a blogger, contended defamation liability could not be imposed on her for a blog comment she made about Obsidian Finance Group, LLC (Obsidian) (P) and its principal, Padrick (P), without proof of fault and actual damages because the comment, which asserted Padrick (P), who served as a bankruptcy trustee for Summit Accommodators, Inc. (Summit), had failed to pay Summit's taxes, concerned a matter of public concern. Cox (D) also contended Obsidian (P) and Padrick (P) should be considered public officials for defamation purposes.

RULE OF LAW

(1) Liability for a defamatory blog post involving a matter of public concern cannot be imposed without proof of fault and actual damages.

(2) For purposes of defamation liability, a court-appointed bankruptcy trustee is not a public official.

FACTS: Padrick (P), a principal of Obsidian Finance Group, LLC (Obsidian) (P), became the bankruptcy trustee for Summit Accommodators, Inc. (Summit), which had misappropriated funds from clients. Cox (D), a blogger with a history of making fraudulent allegations and seeking payoffs in exchange for retraction, accused Padrick (P) and Obsidian (P) of fraud, corruption, money-laundering, and other illegal activities in connection with the Summit bankruptcy. One factual allegation Cox (D) made was Padrick (P), in his capacity as bankruptcy trustee, failed to pay $174,000 in taxes owed by Summit. Padrick (P) and Obsidian (P) brought a defamation action against Cox (D) in federal district court, and the court permitted the action to proceed as to the factual allegation Cox (D) had made. The jury was instructed Cox's (D) knowledge of whether the statements at issue were true or false and her intent or purpose in publishing those statements were not elements of the claim and were not relevant to the determination of liability. The jury was also instructed damages were presumed and did not have to be proved. The jury awarded Padrick (P) $1.5 million and Obsidian (P) $1 million in compensatory damages. On appeal, Cox (D) contended liability could not be imposed without a showing of fault or actual damages, and Padrick (P) and Obsidian (P) were public officials for purposes of imposing defamation liability. The Ninth Circuit Court of Appeals granted review.

ISSUE: (1) Can liability for a defamatory blog post involving a matter of public concern be imposed without proof of fault and actual damages?

(2) For purposes of defamation liability, is a court-appointed bankruptcy trustee a public official?

HOLDING AND DECISION: (Hurwitz, J.)

(1) No. Liability for a defamatory blog post involving a matter of public concern cannot be imposed without proof of fault and actual damages. This case involves the intersection between *New York Times Co. v. Sullivan*, 376 U.S. 254 (1964) (which held when a public official seeks damages for defamation, the official must show "actual malice"—the defendant published the defamatory statement "with knowledge it was false or with reckless disregard of whether it was false or not") and *Gertz v. Robert Welch, Inc.*, 418 U.S. 323 (1974) (which held the First Amendment required only a "negligence standard for private defamation actions"). Padrick (P) and Obsidian (P) argue the *Gertz* negligence requirement applies only to suits against the institutional press, but that would restrict *Gertz* too narrowly. The *Gertz* court did not expressly limit its holding to the defamation of institutional media defendants, and the Supreme Court repeatedly refused in non-defamation contexts to accord greater First Amendment protection to the institutional media than to other speakers. As other circuits that have considered the issue have concluded, the protections of the First Amendment do not turn on whether the defendant was a trained journalist, formally affiliated with traditional news entities, engaged in conflict-of-interest disclosure, went beyond just assembling others' writings, or tried to get both sides of a story. Moreover, as the Supreme Court has observed, with the advent of the Internet and the decline of print and broadcast media, the line between the media and others who wish to comment on political and social issues becomes far more blurred. Thus, in defamation cases, the public-figure status of a plaintiff and the public importance of the statement at issue—to the identity of the speaker—provide the First Amendment touchstones. For these reasons, the *Gertz* negligence requirement for private defamation actions is not limited to cases with institutional media defendants. Nevertheless, Padrick (P) and Obsidian (P) argue they were not required to

Continued on next page.

prove Cox's (D) negligence because her accusations did not touch on a matter of public concern. Even assuming, arguendo, *Gertz* is limited to statements involving matters of public concern, Cox's (D) blog post qualifies. The post alleged Padrick (P) had committed tax fraud. Public allegations someone is involved in crime generally are speech on a matter of public concern. Cox's (D) post was not solely in her interest and that of a specific audience, but rather was published to the public at large, and the post was not "like advertising" and thus "hardy and unlikely to be deterred by incidental state regulation." Because Cox's (D) blog post addressed a matter of public concern, even assuming *Gertz* is limited to such speech, the district court should have instructed the jury it could not find Cox (D) liable for defamation unless it found she acted negligently. The court also should have instructed the jury it could not award presumed damages unless it found Cox (D) acted with actual malice. Reversed as to this issue.

(2) No. For purposes of defamation liability, a court-appointed bankruptcy trustee is not a public official. Although bankruptcy trustees are an integral part of the judicial process, neither Padrick (P) nor Obsidian (P) became public officials simply by virtue of Padrick's (P) appointment. Padrick (P) was neither elected nor appointed to a government position, and he did not exercise substantial control over the conduct of governmental affairs. No one would contend a debtor-in-possession has become a public official simply by virtue of seeking Chapter 11 protection, and there is no reason to reach a different conclusion as to the trustee who substitutes for the debtor in administering a Chapter 11 estate. Accordingly, because Padrick (P) and Obsidian (P) were not public officials, the jury did not have to be instructed under the *Sullivan* standard, it could impose liability for defamation only if she acted with actual malice. Affirmed as to this issue.
Reversed and remanded.

▶ ANALYSIS

Dun & Bradstreet, Inc. v. Greenmoss Builders, Inc., 472 U.S. 749 (1985), held presumed and punitive damages are constitutionally permitted in defamation cases without a showing of actual malice when the defamatory statements at issue do not involve matters of public concern. Thus, by holding Cox's (D) post concerned a matter of public concern, the court effectively required on remand Padrick (P) and Obsidian (P) prove Cox (D) acted with actual malice before such damages could be awarded, or, alternatively, prove they suffered actual damages.

Quicknotes

DEFAMATION An intentional false publication, communicated publicly in either oral or written form, subjecting a person to scorn, hatred or ridicule, or injuring him in relation to his occupation or business.

Quick Reference Rules of Law

PAGE

1. *Nader v. General Motors Corp.* In order to sustain a cause of action for invasion of privacy, the plaintiff must show that defendant's conduct was truly intrusive and that it was designed to elicit information that would not be available through normal inquiry or observation.
200

2. *Boring v. Google Inc.* (1) A plaintiff does not state a claim for invasion of privacy based on intrusion upon seclusion where, as a matter of law, the intrusion would not be highly offensive to a person of ordinary sensibilities. (2) A plaintiff does not have to plead damages to state a claim for trespass.
201

3. *Desnick v. American Broadcasting Co., Inc.* No invasion of privacy or trespass occurs when an individual posing as a patient, for investigative purposes, visits a doctor and secretly videotapes the consultation.
203

4. *Sidis v. F-R Publishing Corp.* Intimate, embarrassing facts concerning the private life of a one-time public figure are not actionable unless they go beyond the bounds of decency.
204

5. *Cox Broadcasting Corp. v. Cohn.* Accurate reporting of information contained in public records is not actionable.
205

6. *Haynes v. Alfred A. Knopf, Inc.* People who do not desire the limelight nevertheless have no legal right to extinguish it if the experiences that have befallen them are newsworthy.
206

7. *Time, Inc. v. Hill.* If a matter is of public interest, it is only actionable if the falsity was made with malice or in reckless disregard of the truth.
207

8. *In re NCAA Student-Athlete Name and Likeness Licensing Litig.* A defendant in a right-of-publicity action does not have a First Amendment right to use the plaintiff's likeness without the plaintiff's permission and without compensating the plaintiff where the defendant's use of the plaintiff's likeness is not transformative.
208

9. *Factors Etc., Inc. v. Pro Arts, Inc.* The owner of publicity may enjoin the sale or distribution of a likeness of the subject of the right even after the subject's death if the right was validly transferred to the owner during the lifetime of the subject.
211

Nader v. General Motors Corp.

Author (P) v. Corporation (D)

N.Y. Ct. App., 255 N.E.2d 765 (1970).

NATURE OF CASE: Suit for invasion of privacy.

FACT SUMMARY: Nader (P), an author and lecturer on automotive safety, claimed that General Motors Corp. (D) was engaging in a campaign of intimidation as a result of disclosures in his latest book.

🏛 RULE OF LAW
In order to sustain a cause of action for invasion of privacy, the plaintiff must show that defendant's conduct was truly intrusive and that it was designed to elicit information that would not be available through normal inquiry or observation.

FACTS: Nader (P) claimed that General Motors Corp. (GM) (D) began a campaign of intimidation against him when it learned of the pending publication of his book, "Unsafe at Any Speed," in order to suppress his criticism of and disclosure regarding its products. Nader (P) claimed such actions violated his right to privacy, and constituted an intentional infliction of emotional distress and interference with his economic advantage.

ISSUE: In order to sustain a cause of action for invasion of privacy, must the plaintiff show that defendant's conduct was truly intrusive and that it was designed to elicit information which would not be available through normal inquiry or observation?

HOLDING AND DECISION: (Fuld, C.J.) Yes. In order to sustain a cause of action for invasion of privacy, the plaintiff must show that defendant's conduct was truly intrusive and that it was designed to elicit information that would not be available through normal inquiry or observation. The mere gathering of information about a particular individual is not sufficient; the information sought must be of a private nature and the defendant's conduct must be unreasonably intrusive. Here the claims of invasion of privacy are not actionable. Nader (P) charged that GM (D) interviewed many persons who knew Nader (P), asking questions about him and disparaging his character. The allegations that GM (D) was responsible for threatening or harassing phone calls to Nader's (P) home are also not actionable, since they did not involve intrusion for the purpose of gathering confidential information. Affirmed.

CONCURRENCE: (Breitel, J.) It is inappropriate to decide that several of the allegations are referable only to the more restricted tort of intentional infliction of emotional distress rather than to the common-law right of privacy.

▶ ANALYSIS

The above allegations more properly fell into the categories of libel and intentional infliction of emotional distress. Nader (P) also alleged that GM (D) engaged in unauthorized wiretapping and eavesdropping. Such conduct has been recognized as a tortuous intrusion of privacy in many circuits. Nader (P) also alleged that GM (D) hired persons to keep him under surveillance. While mere observation in a public place is not actionable, if the surveillance is "overzealous" in the particular case it may be actionable.

Quicknotes

INTENTIONAL INFLICTION OF EMOTIONAL DISTRESS Intentional and extreme behavior on the part of the wrongdoer with the intent to cause the victim to suffer from severe emotional distress, or with reckless indifference, resulting in the victim's suffering from severe emotional distress.

INVASION OF PRIVACY The violation of an individual's right to be protected against unwarranted interference in his personal affairs, falling into one of four categories: (1) appropriating the individual's likeness or name for commercial benefit; (2) intrusion into the individual's seclusion; (3) public disclosure of private facts regarding the individual; and (4) disclosure of facts placing the individual in a false light.

Boring v. Google Inc.

Property owner (P) v. Internet data company (D)

362 Fed. Appx. 273 (3d Cir. 2010).

NATURE OF CASE: Appeal from dismissal of claims for, inter alia, invasion of privacy and trespass.

FACT SUMMARY: The Borings (P) contended they stated claims for, inter alia, invasion of privacy and trespass based on Google, Inc.'s (D) driving up their private road and taking images of their residence and swimming pool without their consent.

🏛 RULE OF LAW
(1) A plaintiff does not state a claim for invasion of privacy based on intrusion upon seclusion where, as a matter of law, the intrusion would not be highly offensive to a person of ordinary sensibilities.
(2) A plaintiff does not have to plead damages to state a claim for trespass.

FACTS: Google, Inc. (D), an Internet search engine company, has a "Street View" program, a feature on Google Maps that offers free access on the Internet to panoramic, navigable views of streets in and around major cities across the United States. To create the Street View program, Google (D) representatives attach panoramic digital cameras to passenger cars and drive around cities photographing the areas along the street. The Borings (P), who live on a private road clearly marked with a "Private Road, No Trespassing" sign, discovered Google (D) had taken colored imagery of their residence, including the swimming pool, from a vehicle in their residence driveway without obtaining any privacy waiver or authorization. They brought suit against Google (D), contending that, in driving up their road to take photographs for Street View and in making those photographs available to the public, Google (D) was liable to them for, inter alia, invasion of privacy and trespass. The federal district court dismissed all their claims. As to their invasion of privacy claim, the district court concluded they were unable to show Google's (D) conduct was highly offensive to a person of ordinary sensibilities. As to their trespass claim, the court concluded they failed to allege facts sufficient to establish they suffered any damages caused by the alleged trespass. The Third Circuit Court of Appeals granted review.

ISSUE:
(1) Does a plaintiff state a claim for invasion of privacy based on intrusion upon seclusion where, as a matter of law, the intrusion would not be highly offensive to a person of ordinary sensibilities?

(2) Does a plaintiff have to plead damages to state a claim for trespass?

HOLDING AND DECISION: (Jordan, J.)
(1) No. A plaintiff does not state a claim for invasion of privacy based on intrusion upon seclusion where, as a matter of law, the intrusion would not be highly offensive to a person of ordinary sensibilities. One of the grounds for invasion of privacy is intrusion upon seclusion. To make out this claim, a plaintiff must aver there was an intentional intrusion upon the seclusion of the plaintiff's private concerns that was substantial and highly offensive to a reasonable person, and must aver sufficient facts to establish the information disclosed would have caused mental suffering, shame, or humiliation to a person of ordinary sensibilities. No person of ordinary sensibilities would be shamed, humiliated, or have suffered mentally as a result of a vehicle entering into his or her ungated driveway and photographing the view from there. Any visitor or delivery person would have seen this view, and, significantly, the Borings (P) do not claim the image taken by Google (D) included any images of them. The Borings (P) are also incorrect that the determination, as a matter of law, of whether an intrusion is highly offensive may not be made at the pleading stage. For these reasons, their intrusion upon seclusion claim fails as a matter of law, and the district court did not err in dismissing it. Affirmed as to this issue.

(2) No. A plaintiff does not have to plead damages to state a claim for trespass. Trespass is a strict liability tort, involving the unprivileged, intentional intrusion upon land in possession of another. One does not need to suffer damages to suffer a trespass. Here, the Borings (P) have alleged Google (D) entered upon their property without permission. If proven, that is a trespass, pure and simple, and under the applicable state law, there is no requirement damages be plead, either nominal or consequential. Although the Borings (P) would have to prove actual damages on remand if they want to be awarded anything more than nominal damages, it was error for the district court to dismiss this claim. Reversed as to this issue.

Affirmed in part, reversed in part, and remanded.

Continued on next page.

▌ *ANALYSIS*

In addition to unreasonable intrusion upon the seclusion of another, other torts recognized under the umbrella of invasion of privacy include: appropriation of another's name or likeness; unreasonable publicity given to another's private life; and publicity that unreasonably places the other in a false light before the public. Here the court also rejected the Borings' (P) claim of invasion of privacy based upon publicity given to private life, because one element of that claim is the publicity "would be highly offensive to a reasonable person," and the court had already concluded Google's (D) conduct, as a matter of law, was not highly offensive.

Quicknotes

INTRUSION The unlawful entering on to or the taking of possession of another's property.

INVASION OF PRIVACY The violation of an individual's right to be protected against unwarranted interference in his personal affairs, falling into one of four categories: (1) appropriating the individual's likeness or name for commercial benefit; (2) intrusion into the individual's seclusion; (3) public disclosure of private facts regarding the individual; and (4) disclosure of facts placing the individual in a false light.

STRICT LIABILITY Liability for all injuries proximately caused by a party's conducting of certain inherently dangerous activities without regard to negligence or fault.

■=■

Desnick v. American Broadcasting Co., Inc.

Ophthalmic surgeons (P) v. Television network (D)

44 F.3d 1345 (7th Cir. 1995).

NATURE OF CASE: Appeal from dismissal of claims for trespass and invasion of privacy.

FACT SUMMARY: Doctors from the Desnick Eye Center (P) filed suit against American Broadcasting Co., Inc. (D) for sending reporters equipped with hidden video cameras pretending to be patients to the eye clinics.

🏛 RULE OF LAW
No invasion of privacy or trespass occurs when an individual posing as a patient, for investigative purposes, visits a doctor and secretly videotapes the consultation.

FACTS: Producers and reporters of the American Broadcasting Co., Inc. (ABC) (D) program *PrimeTime Live* prepared to run a story on the Desnick Eye Center (P) in which they would allege that Dr. Desnick was performing unnecessary cataract surgeries. ABC (D) had contacted Desnick, asking if they could tape a surgery at his office and stating that they would not conduct an ambush-type interview. Desnick consented. In addition to this taping, however, ABC (D) sent individuals posing as patients to other Desnick Eye Clinic (P) locations and equipped them with hidden cameras. Two doctors (P) at those clinics filed a suit against ABC (D), alleging that the methods used in sending undercover patients to the clinics constituted a trespass, invasion of privacy, fraud, and a violation of electronic surveillance statutes. The lower court dismissed these claims and the doctors (P) appealed.

ISSUE: Is an individual who poses as a patient for investigative purposes, visits a doctor, and secretly videotapes the consultation liable for invasion of privacy or trespass?

HOLDING AND DECISION: (Posner, C.J.) No. No invasion of privacy or trespass occurs when an individual posing as a patient, for investigative purposes, visits a doctor and secretly videotapes the consultation. There was no invasion of privacy because the test patients visited the Desnick Eye Clinics (P) during regular business hours, just like others there for eye examinations did, and did not disrupt the daily office activities. ABC's (D) test patients were similar to individuals who pose as prospective homebuyers to gather evidence of discrimination. No intimate or personal facts were revealed, and no other conversations were recorded other than the ones between the doctors and the test patients. There has been no trespass or trespass by fraud because the entry onto the property was not an interference with ownership or possession. The fact is that ABC's (D) test patients were there to get eye exams, even if

only for the purpose of uncovering any tampering with medical records or malpractice. State and federal wiretapping statutes permit a party to record a conversation as long as their purposes are not to commit a crime or tort, and it has been determined that the activities of the test patients do not fall into those categories. Although tabloid reporting of the type used by ABC (D) can be very aggressive, the First Amendment still protects it. If the broadcast itself does not contain actionable defamation, and no other crimes are committed in the process of creating the program, then the target of the story does not have a claim in tort even if the investigative tactics used by reporters and producers were surreptitious, confrontational, or even unscrupulous. Affirmed in part, reversed in part, and remanded.

▶ ANALYSIS

The tort of intrusion upon privacy can be very similar to trespass. While often a claim will be brought on both grounds, courts will not grant damages on both claims. The court here, in dismissing both claims, makes note of the fact that ABC (D) went to Desnick's place of business, which was open to the general public, rather than his personal residence. However, another court held trespass occurred when a camera crew went into a crowded restaurant during lunch time with the lights on and the camera rolling, causing some patrons to duck under tables and others to leave without paying. See *Le Mistral, Inc. v. Columbia Broadcasting System*, 61 A.D.2d 491, 402 N.Y. S.2d 815 (1978).

Quicknotes

INVASION OF PRIVACY The violation of an individual's right to be protected against unwarranted interference in his personal affairs, falling into one of four categories: (1) appropriating the individual's likeness or name for commercial benefit; (2) intrusion into the individual's seclusion; (3) public disclosure of private facts regarding the individual; and (4) disclosure of facts placing the individual in a false light.

TRESPASS Unlawful interference with, or damage to, the real or personal property of another.

Sidis v. F-R Publishing Corp.

Unwilling article subject (P) v. Publishing company (D)

113 F.2d 806 (2d Cir. 1940).

NATURE OF CASE: Action for invasion of privacy, malicious libel, and wrongful use of one's name and likeness.

FACT SUMMARY: The early life of a child genius was recounted in several articles appearing in *The New Yorker* (D).

RULE OF LAW
Intimate, embarrassing facts concerning the private life of a one-time public figure are not actionable unless they go beyond the bounds of decency.

FACTS: A writer for *The New Yorker* (D) wrote an article about what had happened to a one-time child genius, Sidis (P). The article was newsworthy and revealed many intimate and possibly embarrassing facts. It detailed a breakdown, Sidis's (P) shoddy surroundings, peculiar manner, and penchant for privacy. Sidis (P) had been the subject of many articles some 15-25 years earlier. A cartoon was included in the article. A subsequent article on another child prodigy briefly referred to the first article. An advertisement for *The New Yorker* (D) appeared in a newspaper mentioning that the current issue featured an article on Sidis (P). Sidis (P) brought suit for invasion of privacy, malicious libel, and the wrongful use of one's name and likeness for advertising purposes. *The New Yorker* (D) and its publisher, F-R Publishing Corp. (D), alleged that the article had been tastefully done, was newsworthy, and concerned a one-time public figure. The constitutional freedom of the press was raised as a defense.

ISSUE: Are intimate, embarrassing facts about a one-time public personality actionable?

HOLDING AND DECISION: (Clark, J.) No. There is a qualified privilege with respect to the printing of newsworthy stories about public figures. Intimate, even embarrassing facts concerning their private life may be published unless the article goes beyond the bounds of human decency. Sidis (P) was, at one time, a public figure. The interest of the public in what became of him outweighs his right to privacy. That right is not absolute. The article was tastefully done and is not outside of the privilege. Since it was true, it cannot be deemed libel. Therefore, the malice issue is immaterial. A malicious truth is not turned into libel. If the first article is not actionable, then the second article, which merely referred to the first one, is also not actionable. The advertisement mentioning that *The New Yorker* (D) had an article on Sidis's (D) life was not using his name or likeness to promote trade. Therefore, it is not actionable. Affirmed.

ANALYSIS

The nature of the publication is not controlling. In *Jenkins v. Dell Publishing Co.*, 251 F.2d 447 (3rd Cir. 1958), a detective magazine was held to have the same rights as *The New Yorker* or the *New York Times*. As long as the item is newsworthy it is protected. The picture of a football fan with his pants unzipped was deemed nonactionable even when titled, "a strange kind of love." *Neff v. Time, Inc.*, 405 F. Supp. 858 (1976).

Quicknotes

INVASION OF PRIVACY The violation of an individual's right to be protected against unwarranted interference in his personal affairs, falling into one of four categories: (1) appropriating the individual's likeness or name for commercial benefit; (2) intrusion into the individual's seclusion; (3) public disclosure of private facts regarding the individual; and (4) disclosure of facts placing the individual in a false light.

LIBEL A false or malicious publication subjecting a person to scorn, hatred or ridicule, or injuring him or her in relation to his or her occupation or business.

MALICE The intention to commit an unlawful act without justification or excuse.

PUBLIC FIGURE Any person who is generally known in the community.

Cox Broadcasting Corp. v. Cohn

Television station (D) v. Family of deceased rape victim (P)

420 U.S. 469 (1975).

NATURE OF CASE: Action in damages for invasion of privacy.

FACT SUMMARY: A television station owned by Cox Broadcasting Corp. (D) informed the public as to the name of a deceased rape victim.

RULE OF LAW
Accurate reporting of information contained in public records is not actionable.

FACTS: Cohn's (P) daughter was raped and died. A trial of the accused was held. Under state law, the publishing of the name of a rape victim was a misdemeanor. A television reporter learned the name of the decedent from public records made available at trial. The name was reported on a news program broadcast by a television station owned by Cox Broadcasting Corp. (D). The father of the decedent, Cohn (P), brought an action for invasion of privacy. The state courts held that the misdemeanor statute did not grant a private right of action, but suit could be maintained on a common-law tort of public disclosure. Cox (D) appealed on the grounds that publishing information contained in public records was not actionable and was protected under the First and Fourteenth Amendments.

ISSUE: Is a member of the news media privileged under the First and Fourteenth Amendments to accurately disclose anything contained in public records?

HOLDING AND DECISION: (White, J.) Yes. Public records are, by their nature, open to the public and matters of public information. A common law tort cannot make their disclosure actionable. The media could never tell with certainty what disclosures were actionable. On a more fundamental ground we hold that the freedom of the press outweighs Cohn's (P) right to privacy. Here the reporting was newsworthy, accurate, and a matter of public record. The accurate reporting of matters of public record is not privately actionable. Reversed.

CONCURRENCE: (Powell, J.) *Gertz v. Robert Welch, Inc.,* 418 U.S. 323 (1974), constitutionally requires that truth be an absolute defense in defamation actions brought by either public or private persons.

DISSENT: (Rehnquist, J.) There has been no final judgment in the case from which an appeal could be taken to the Supreme Court.

ANALYSIS

A party's zone of privacy does not extend to matters that are on the record. The state has no overriding or corresponding interest to protect. Having been thrust into the public eye because of the rape and subsequent trial, Cohn (P) became a limited public figure. The zone of privacy does not extend to the reporting of judicial events, which are deemed to be of general public interest. Land records, administrative hearings, etc., are all deemed to be matters of public record.

Quicknotes

INVASION OF PRIVACY The violation of an individual's right to be protected against unwarranted interference in his personal affairs, falling into one of four categories: (1) appropriating the individual's likeness or name for commercial benefit; (2) intrusion into the individual's seclusion; (3) public disclosure of private facts regarding the individual; and (4) disclosure of facts placing the individual in a false light.

PRIVATE FIGURES/CITIZENS An individual that does not hold a public office or that is not a member of the armed forces.

PUBLIC DISCLOSURE OF PRIVATE FACTS A form of invasion of privacy involving the disclosure of private facts regarding a person with which the public has no concern.

PUBLIC FIGURE Any person who is generally known in the community.

Haynes v. Alfred A. Knopf, Inc.

Subjects of social history (P) v. Book publishers (D)

8 F.3d 1222 (7th Cir. 1993).

NATURE OF CASE: Appeal from dismissal of an invasion of privacy action.

FACT SUMMARY: Haynes (P) sued Alfred A. Knopf, Inc. (D) for invasion of privacy after it published a book that included an account of Haynes's (P) young adulthood as a drunk, an adulterer, and a batterer.

🏛 RULE OF LAW
People who do not desire the limelight nevertheless have no legal right to extinguish it if the experiences that have befallen them are newsworthy.

FACTS: Haynes (P) and his wife Dorothy (P) sued Alfred A. Knopf, Inc. (Knopf) (D) and one of Knopf's (D) writers, Lemann (D), after Lemann (D) wrote a social history that included revelations about Haynes's (P) misconduct. The Hayneses (P) claimed that the book libeled them and invaded their right to privacy. The book, a history of migration of blacks from impoverished rural areas to urban areas, described Mr. Haynes's (P) descent from a well-paid worker and attributed this descent to his drunkenness, adultery, temper, and irresponsibility to his first wife. The book further described Mr. Haynes's (P) divorce from his first wife and marriage to his second wife, Dorothy (P). The Hayneses' (P) case was dismissed on a motion for summary judgment by Knopf (D) and Lemann (D). The Hayneses (P) appealed.

ISSUE: Do people who do not desire the limelight have a legal right to extinguish it if the experiences that have befallen them are newsworthy?

HOLDING AND DECISION: (Posner, C.J.) No. People who do not desire the limelight and do not deliberately choose a way of life calculated to thrust them into it nevertheless have no legal right to extinguish it if the experiences that have befallen them are newsworthy. This is so even if they would prefer those experiences to be kept private. The possibility of an involuntary loss of privacy is recognized in the modern formulations of the privacy tort. The tort requires not only that the private facts published be such as would make a reasonable party deeply offended but also that they be facts in which the publisher has no legitimate interest. The breach of privacy that the Hayneses (P) invoked in their appeal was not a proper surrogate for legal doctrines that are concerned with the accuracy of the private facts revealed. It is concerned with the propriety of stripping away the veil of privacy with which we cover the embarrassing, shameful truths about us. The revelations in this book are not about the intimate details of the Hayneses' (P) life; they are about Mr. Haynes's (P) mis-

conduct in the past. Every detail is germane to the story that the author wanted to tell, a story not only of legitimate but of transcendent public interest. The public needs the information conveyed by this book, including the information about the Hayneses (P), in order to evaluate the profound social and political questions that the book raises. On the basis of the evidence obtained in pretrial discovery, no reasonable judge could render a verdict for the Hayneses (P). Affirmed.

▶ ANALYSIS

As the *Haynes* case makes abundantly clear, when facts about a person who is not a public figure and who does not seek the public life are disclosed in the name of newsworthiness, there will always be a clash between that person's privacy interests and First Amendment freedoms. These First Amendment freedoms usually prevail over a person's privacy interests. There are situations, however, even the most newsworthy ones, where an individual's privacy concerns will overcome the First Amendment. These situations most often involve victims of rape or sexual assault and juvenile matters.

▬▬▬

Quicknotes

INVASION OF PRIVACY The violation of an individual's right to be protected against unwarranted interference in his personal affairs, falling into one of four categories: (1) appropriating the individual's likeness or name for commercial benefit; (2) intrusion into the individual's seclusion; (3) public disclosure of private facts regarding the individual; and (4) disclosure of facts placing the individual in a false light.

LIBEL A false or malicious publication subjecting a person to scorn, hatred or ridicule, or injuring him or her in relation to his or her occupation or business.

▬▬▬

Time, Inc. v. Hill

Magazine publisher (D) v. Crime victims (P)

385 U.S. 374 (1967).

NATURE OF CASE: Action in damage for being placed in a false light/invasion of privacy.

FACT SUMMARY: *Life Magazine* (D) published an article stating that a new play was a recreation of a real incident which was suffered by Hill (P) and his family.

🏛 RULE OF LAW
If a matter is of public interest, it is only actionable if the falsity was made with malice or in reckless disregard of the truth.

FACTS: A new play called "The Desperate Hours" opened on Broadway. *Life Magazine* (D), owned by Time (D), printed an article alleging that this was a dramatic recreation of a true event that had been suffered by the Hill (P) family. The Hill (P) family had been held by several convicts for 19 hours years earlier. Hill (P) brought an action under New York law on the grounds that he and his family were cast in a false light and that Time (D) maliciously printed the article knowing it was false and untrue. The court found the article was substantially false and the Hills (P) were no longer public figures. Judgment was rendered for Hill (P) over Time's (D) claim of public interest and constitutional privilege. Time (D) alleged that the opening of a new play was newsworthy and brought the Hills (P) back into the public eye. Time (D) also alleged that there was no malice present.

ISSUE: Is invasion of privacy only actionable if the report is of public interest, if it is false, malicious or is published in reckless disregard of the truth?

HOLDING AND DECISION: (Brennan, J.) Yes. One's right to privacy is not absolute. As members of society we must expect certain intrusions. The Hills (P) were once thrust into the public eye by events not of their own choosing. They do not remain public figures indefinitely. However, the opening of a new play on Broadway is of public interest and thrust them back in the public eye, albeit unwanted. Therefore, the article is protected under the rights accorded to a free press. It is immaterial that the article is for entertainment purposes and was published solely with the design of increasing circulation. This mode of news is of public interest and errors may occur. They are entitled to constitutional protections. Only if the errors involve malice or reckless disregard of the truth are they deemed actionable. Reversed and remanded for further consideration of the malice issue.

CONCURRENCE: (Douglas, J.) It was the fictionalized play which thrust Hill (P) back into the public light. Hill's (P) right to privacy ceased at this point.

CONCURRENCE AND DISSENT: (Harlan, J.) I feel a finding of negligence alone would expose Time (D) to liability. Where the plaintiff is a private person, negligence should be deemed sufficient.

DISSENT: (Fortas, J.) I dissent on the basis that the charge to the jury on the malice issue was sufficiently close to the constitutional standard to allow the verdict to stand.

▶ ANALYSIS

In *Spahn v. Julian Messner, Inc.,* 18 N.Y. 2d 324 (1966), Spahn (P) sued the publishers of an unauthorized biography of his life which contained many factual errors, distortions, and fanciful accounts. The court, while stating that no cause of action would exist if the biography were substantially true, found that due to the many errors Messner (D) was not entitled to the newsworthy defense. The failure to adequately research the facts was found to be a major factor in finding that Messner (D) had proceeded in reckless disregard of the truth.

Quicknotes

FALSE LIGHT In an action for invasion of an individual's right to privacy, the publication of facts that either attributes to the person beliefs that he does not hold or actions that he has not performed.

INVASION OF PRIVACY The violation of an individual's right to be protected against unwarranted interference in his personal affairs, falling into one of four categories: (1) appropriating the individual's likeness or name for commercial benefit; (2) intrusion into the individual's seclusion; (3) public disclosure of private facts regarding the individual; and (4) disclosure of facts placing the individual in a false light.

MALICE The intention to commit an unlawful act without justification or excuse.

PUBLIC FIGURE Any person who is generally known in the community.

RECKLESSNESS The conscious disregard of substantial and justifiable risk.

In re NCAA Student-Athlete Name and Likeness Licensing Litig.

Student athlete (P) v. Video game developer (D)

724 F.3d 1268 (9th Cir. 2013).

NATURE OF CASE: Appeal from judgment for plaintiff in a putative class action for violations of the right of publicity.

FACT SUMMARY: Electronic Arts (EA) (D), a video game developer, contended its college football and basketball video games contained sufficient transformative elements that gave it a First Amendment right to include likenesses of college athletes in the games without violating the athletes' right of publicity.

🏛 RULE OF LAW
A defendant in a right-of-publicity action does not have a First Amendment right to use the plaintiff's likeness without the plaintiff's permission and without compensating the plaintiff where the defendant's use of the plaintiff's likeness is not transformative.

FACTS: Electronic Arts (EA) (D), a video game developer, created college football and basketball video games that allowed users to control avatars representing college football and basketball players as those avatars participated in simulated games. One of these games was *NCAA Football*, in which EA (D) sought to replicate each school's entire team as accurately as possible. Every real football player on each team included in the game had a corresponding avatar in the game with the player's actual jersey number and virtually identical height, weight, build, skin tone, hair color, and home state. EA (D) attempted to match any unique, highly identifiable playing behaviors by sending detailed questionnaires to team equipment managers. Additionally, EA (D) created realistic virtual versions of actual stadiums; populated them with the virtual athletes, coaches, cheerleaders, and fans realistically rendered by EA's (D) graphic artists; and incorporated realistic sounds such as the crunch of the players' pads and the roar of the crowd. EA's (D) game differed from reality in that it omitted the players' names on their jerseys and assigned each player a home town that was different from the actual player's home town. However, users of the video game could upload rosters of names obtained from third parties so the names did appear on the jerseys. In such cases, EA (D) allowed images from the game containing athletes' real names to be posted on its website by users. Keller (P) was the starting quarterback for Arizona State University in 2005 before he transferred to the University of Nebraska, where he played during the 2007 season. In the 2005 edition of the game, the virtual starting quarterback for Arizona State wore number 9, as did Keller (P), and had the same height, weight, skin tone, hair color, hair

style, handedness, home state, play style (pocket passer), visor preference, facial features, and school year as Keller (P). In the 2008 edition, the virtual quarterback for Nebraska had these same characteristics, though the jersey number did not match, presumably because Keller (P) changed his number right before the season started. EA (D) did not obtain Keller's (P) permission to use his likeness, nor did it compensate him for such use. Objecting to this use of his likeness, Keller (P) filed a putative class action in federal district court asserting EA (D) violated his right of publicity under California law. The district court concluded EA (D) had no First Amendment defense against Keller's (P) right-of-publicity claims. The Ninth Circuit Court of Appeals granted review.

ISSUE: Does a defendant in a right-of-publicity action have a First Amendment right to use the plaintiff's likeness without the plaintiff's permission and without compensating the plaintiff where the defendant's use of the plaintiff's likeness is not transformative?

HOLDING AND DECISION: (Bybee, J.) No. A defendant in a right-of-publicity action does not have a First Amendment right to use the plaintiff's likeness without the plaintiff's permission and without compensating the plaintiff where the defendant's use of the plaintiff's likeness is not transformative. California's transformative use defense is a balancing test between the First Amendment and the right of publicity based on whether the work in question adds significant creative elements so as to be transformed into something more than a mere celebrity likeness or imitation. There are at least five factors to consider in determining whether a work is sufficiently transformative to obtain First Amendment protection. First, if "the celebrity likeness is one of the 'raw materials' from which an original work is synthesized," it is more likely to be transformative than if "the depiction or imitation of the celebrity is the very sum and substance of the work in question." Second, the work is protected if it is primarily the defendant's own expression, provided the expression is something other than the likeness of the celebrity. This factor requires an examination of whether a likely purchaser's primary motivation is to buy a reproduction of the celebrity, or to buy the expressive work of that artist. Third, a court should conduct an inquiry more quantitative than qualitative and ask whether the literal and imitative or the creative elements predominate in the work. Fourth, in close cases a court should inquire whether the marketability and economic value of the challenged work

Continued on next page.

derive primarily from the fame of the celebrity depicted. Fifth, and lastly, when an artist's skill and talent is manifestly subordinated to the overall goal of creating a conventional portrait of a celebrity so as to commercially exploit the celebrity's fame, the work is not transformative. An application of these tests leads to the conclusion EA's (D) use of Keller's (P) likeness does not contain significant transformative elements. EA (D) replicated Keller's (P) physical characteristics; users manipulate the characters in the performance of the same activity for which they are known in real life—playing football in this case; the context in which the activity occurs is also similarly realistic— realistic depictions of actual football stadiums and football game environments; and Keller was represented as what he was: the starting quarterback for Arizona State and Nebraska, in a setting that was identical to where the public found Keller (P) during his collegiate career: on the football field. For these reasons, EA (D) cannot prevail as a matter of law on the transformative use defense. Nonetheless, EA (D) urges the court to apply a broader First Amendment defense that previously has been adopted in the context of false endorsement claims under the Lanham Act. This defense was announced in *Rogers v. Grimaldi*, 875 F.2d 994 (2d Cir.1989). In *Rogers*, a key issue was whether the artistic work misled viewers into believing the celebrity being depicted in the work endorsed the work. The *Rogers* court determined titles of artistic or literary works were less likely to be misleading than the names of ordinary commercial products, and thus Lanham Act protections applied with less rigor when considering titles of artistic or literary works than when considering ordinary products. The court therefore held in the context of allegedly misleading titles using a celebrity's name, the balance between First Amendment rights and consumer confusion will normally not support application of the Lanham Act unless the title has no artistic relevance to the underlying work whatsoever, or, if it has some artistic relevance, unless the title explicitly misleads as to the source or the content of the work. While there is some applicability of *Rogers* to right-of-publicity situations, the *Rogers* test should not be imported wholesale for right-of-publicity claims. As the history and development of the *Rogers* test makes clear, it was designed to protect consumers from the risk of consumer confusion—the hallmark element of a Lanham Act claim. The right of publicity, on the other hand, does not primarily seek to prevent consumer confusion, but instead seeks to protect a celebrity's right to his or her likeness, in which the celebrity has made a significant investment. Here, Keller's (P) publicity claim is not founded on an allegation consumers are being illegally misled into believing he is endorsing EA (D) or its products. Thus, the reasoning of *Rogers*—that artistic and literary works should be protected unless they explicitly mislead consumers—is simply not responsive to Keller's (P) asserted interests here. For these, and other reasons, the invitation to extend *Rogers* to the case at bar is declined. Affirmed.

DISSENT: (Thomas, J.) The majority incorrectly focuses on the likeness of one athlete, rather than examining the transformative and creative elements in the video game as a whole. The majority approach therefore contradicts the holistic analysis required by the transformative use test. A broad view of the game at issue is that it is a work of interactive historical fiction, and, although the game changes from year to year, its most popular features predominately involve role-playing by the gamer. The gamer has the ability to make numerous decisions to create a virtual image of himself or herself. The gamer, for example, can decide whether to be a player or a coach, and, if a player, what kind of student to be. While it is true the college teams supplied in the game do replicate the actual college teams for that season, including virtual athletes who bear the statistical and physical dimensions of the actual college athletes, the NCAA football players in these games are not identified, and the gamer can morph them completely into virtual players with characteristics entirely different from those possessed by the actual players. Gamers can have players change teams, and can change the weather, crowd noise, mascots, and other environmental factors. In sum, the gamer controls the teams, players, and games, and it is possible for a gamer to never encounter Keller's (P) avatar, or that of any other actual player. These considerations favor First Amendment protection, since the athletic likenesses is but one of the raw materials from which the broader game is constructed. The work, considered as a whole, is primarily one of EA's (D) own expression. The creative and transformative elements predominate over the commercial use of likenesses. The marketability and economic value of the game comes from the creative elements within, not from the pure commercial exploitation of a celebrity image. The game is not a conventional portrait of a celebrity, but a work consisting of many creative and transformative elements. Further, the balancing in favor of First Amendment protection is called for when considering the right of publicity interests involved. As a quantitative matter, *NCAA Football* is different from other right of publicity cases in the sheer number of virtual actors involved. Most right of publicity cases involves either one celebrity, or a finite and defined group of celebrities. In contrast, *NCAA Football* includes not just Keller (P), but thousands of virtual actors. This consideration is of particular significance when examining whether the source of the product marketability comes from creative elements or from pure exploitation of a celebrity image. There is not, at this stage of the litigation, any evidence as to the personal marketing power of Keller (P), as distinguished from the appeal of the creative aspects of the product. Regardless, the sheer number of athletes involved inevitably diminishes the significance of the publicity right at issue. One could play *NCAA Football* thousands of times without ever encountering a particular

Continued on next page.

avatar. In context of the collective, an individual's publicity right is thus relatively insignificant, or potentially nonexistent. The logical consequence of the majority view is that all realistic depictions of actual persons, no matter how incidental, are protected by a state law right of publicity regardless of the creative context. This logic jeopardizes the creative use of historic figures in motion pictures, books, and sound recordings.

▶ ANALYSIS

The majority's response to Judge Thomas's dissenting argument that the sheer number of virtual actors, the absence of any evidence as to Keller's (P) personal marketing power, and the relative anonymity of each individual player in *NCAA Football*, was while these facts were not irrelevant to the analysis, the fact was EA (D) elected to use avatars that mimicked real college football players for a reason. The majority reasoned if EA (D) did not think there was value in having an avatar designed to mimic each individual player, it would not have gone to the lengths it did to achieve realism in this regard. The majority concluded, having chosen to use the players' likenesses, EA (D) could not now hide behind the numerosity of its potential offenses or the alleged unimportance of any one individual player.

■—■—■

Quicknotes

RIGHT OF PUBLICITY The right of a person to control the commercial exploitation of his name or likeness.

TRANSFORMATIVE TEST In right to publicity action, defense that the work is protected by the First Amendment if it contains significant transformative elements or that the value of the work does not derive primarily from a celebrity's fame.

■—■—■

Factors Etc., Inc. v. Pro Arts, Inc.

Exclusive license holder (P) v. Poster publisher (D)

579 F.2d 215 (2d Cir. 1978).

NATURE OF CASE: Appeal from injunction against distribution of a likeness.

FACT SUMMARY: After Factors Etc., Inc. (Factors) (P) purchased from Elvis Presley the exclusive license to exploit the name, image, and likeness of Presley, Pro Arts, Inc. (D) published and sold a poster bearing the photograph of Presley in memory of the entertainer's death, and Factors (P) obtained an injunction barring the poster's sale.

🏛 RULE OF LAW

The owner of publicity may enjoin the sale or distribution of a likeness of the subject of the right even after the subject's death if the right was validly transferred to the owner during the lifetime of the subject.

FACTS: Elvis Presley and his business associate, Colonel Tom Parker, assigned to Factors Etc., Inc. (Factors) (P) the exclusive license to exploit Presley's name, image, and likeness. Thereafter, Presley died. Pro Arts, Inc. (D) purchased the copyright to a photograph of Presley after his death and printed and sold posters bearing the legend, "In Memory" under the photograph. Factor (P) obtained an injunction against the further distribution of the poster on the ground that this was an infringement upon the right of publicity which Factor (P) owned as to Presley. Pro Arts (D) appealed.

ISSUE: May the owner of a right of publicity enjoin the sale or distribution of a likeness of the subject of the right even after the subject's death if the right was validly transferred to the owner during the lifetime of the subject?

HOLDING AND DECISION: (Ingraham, J.) Yes. The right of publicity belongs to the subject of the right and does not survive after his death unless the subject has exploited the right by transferring it before death. Without such a transfer, the right of publicity dies with the subject of it. Here, Elvis Presley transferred right of publicity reserving for himself a percentage of the royalties to be gained from the exploitation he licensed. The right was thus preserved for Factors (P) as purchaser and remains exclusive. Pro Arts (D) also contended that since Presley's death was a newsworthy event, its use of the likeness on the poster was privileged. However, the distribution of a poster is not within the privilege under these circumstances. Affirmed.

▶ ANALYSIS

In a similar case, *Lugosi v. Universal Pictures*, 603 P.2d 425 (Cal. 1979), Universal Studios was permitted to continue to distribute and publish the likeness of actor Bela Lugosi. Lugosi had not transferred his right of publicity nor had he exploited it during his lifetime by such publication or distribution of his own. Thus, the right was held to have died with Lugosi and not to have passed to his heirs or beneficiaries. The key element is exploitation during the lifetime of the subject of the right.

Quicknotes

ENJOIN The ordering of a party to cease the conduct of a specific activity.

RIGHT OF PUBLICITY The right of a person to control the commercial exploitation of his name or likeness.

CHAPTER 13

Misrepresentation

Quick Reference Rules of Law

PAGE

1. *Pasley v. Freeman.* Even if a party is under no obligation to give information, if he knowingly gives false information designed to injure, cheat, or deceive another person to that person's injury, he is liable for his misrepresentation. 214

2. *Vulcan Metals Co. v. Simmons Manufacturing Co.* An opinion is a fact, and when parties are so situated that a buyer may reasonably rely upon the expression of a seller's opinion, the fact that it is an opinion is not a defense to an action in deceit; but, there are some statements that no sensible man takes seriously. 216

3. *Swinton v. Whitinsville Savings Bank.* There is no liability for bare nondisclosure. 217

4. *Laidlaw v. Organ.* A buyer in sole possession of knowledge that would affect the price of products he is dealing in is not obliged by law to divulge the information. 218

5. *Edgington v. Fitzmaurice.* In order to show actionable fraud, the plaintiff must show the defendant knowingly made a false statement with the intent to induce the plaintiff to act in reliance on it, and that the plaintiff did in fact so act to his damage. 219

6. *Laborers Local 17 Health and Benefit Fund v. Philip Morris, Inc.* Proof of a direct injury sustained by the plaintiff is required in order to maintain a cause of action under the Racketeer Influenced and Corrupt Organizations Act (RICO) statute. 220

7. *Ultramares Corporation v. Touche.* There is no liability for negligent misrepresentations without privity between the plaintiff and defendant. 221

Pasley v. Freeman

Merchant (P) v. Individual who misrepresented credit standing (D)

K.B., 100 Eng. Rep. 450, 3 D. & E. (3 Term Rep.) 51 (1789).

NATURE OF CASE: Appeal from verdict for the plaintiffs in an action to recover damages for misrepresentation.

FACT SUMMARY: Freeman (D) falsely stated that Falch was a good credit risk and thereby induced Pasley (P) to deliver certain goods to Falch that were never paid for.

🏛 RULE OF LAW
Even if a party is under no obligation to give information, if he knowingly gives false information designed to injure, cheat, or deceive another person to that person's injury, he is liable for his misrepresentation.

FACTS: Although he knew that John Falch was not a good credit risk, Freeman (D) answered an inquiry by Pasley (P) by asserting that Falch's credit standing was good. Thereupon, Pasley (P) delivered certain goods to Falch on credit, but they were never paid for. Claiming that Freeman (D) had made misrepresentations to induce the giving of credit to Falch and thereby caused injury, Pasley (P) brought a successful action to recover the cost of the goods from Freeman (D). On motion for arrest of judgment, Freeman (D) argued that he had no obligation to give any information to Pasley (P), so no action could lie.

ISSUE: If a party who is under no obligation to do so nonetheless gives information to another knowing it to be false and to injure, cheat, or deceive him, does such misrepresentation provide a basis upon which the deceived party can recover for the injury suffered?

HOLDING AND DECISION: [Judge not listed in casebook excerpt.] Yes. If a party who is under no obligation to do so nonetheless gives information to another knowing it to be false and to injure, cheat, or deceive him, such misrepresentation provides a basis upon which the deceived party can recover for the injury suffered. Affirmed.

OPINION [DISSENTING]: (Grose, J.) The action by Pasley (P) is novel and is not maintainable. When Freeman (D) made statements as to the credit worthiness of Falch, he was making statements of opinion. Credit to which another is entitled is a matter of judgment and opinion. Any assertion relative thereto, therefore, is no basis for an action; especially where the party making it has no interest nor is in any collusion with the person respecting whose credit the assertion is made.

OPINION [CONCURRING]: (Buller, J.) Although a party may not be required or obligated to give any information, if he nonetheless knowingly gives false information designed to injure, cheat, or deceive another person, he is liable for the injury such misrepresentation occasions. This is not a case of a simple naked lie that is told without intent to injure or cheat, so it does not come under the rule that an action for such a lie is not maintainable. Clearly, Freeman (D) was not merely expressing his opinion, but he deliberately misstated the credit standing of Falch to deceive Pasley (P). It would be as repugnant to the law as it is to morality to allow such action without holding the party responsible for the injury it generates to be answerable for it. If one who has the option of keeping silent chooses to speak, he must not answer falsely so as to deceive and injure the inquiring party. If he does so, he, like Freeman (D), will be held accountable. It matters not if the party making the misrepresentation himself benefits therefrom, for the gist of the action is the injury done to the inquiring party. So, judgment for Pasley (P) was properly given.

CONCURRENCE: (Ashhurst, J.) The case turns on the injury done to the plaintiff and not whether the defendant meant to gain by his actions.

CONCURRENCE: (Lord Kenyon, C.J.) The plaintiff sought credit information about Falch from the defendant. The defendant fraudulently and knowingly deceived the plaintiffs, thus causing the plaintiffs considerable damage. The action is maintainable on the grounds of deceit in the defendant and injury and loss to the plaintiffs.

▶ ANALYSIS

The law on misrepresentation has its origins in the action on the case of deceit, which covers only the type of misrepresentation that misleads another into making a business judgment that results in financial loss. Although negligence is a more liberal and comprehensive theory of liability and therefore is usually a better cause of action to bring than deceit, it requires the presence of a duty to the injured party that cannot always be found.

■◀■

Quicknotes

DECEIT A false statement made either knowingly or with reckless disregard as to its truth and which is intended to

Continued on next page.

induce the plaintiff to act in reliance thereon to his detriment.

FRAUD A false representation of facts with the intent that another will rely on the misrepresentation to his detriment.

MISREPRESENTATION A statement or conduct by one party to another that constitutes a false representation of fact.

Vulcan Metals Co. v. Simmons Manufacturing Co.

Purchaser of vacuum parts and information (P) v. Seller of vacuums (D)

248 F. 853 (2d Cir. 1918).

NATURE OF CASE: Action for deceit, on appeal.

FACT SUMMARY: Simmons Manufacturing Co. (D) sold vacuum cleaner manufacturing machines to Vulcan Metals Co. (P), claiming that they were (inter alia) "perfect" and that the vacuum cleaners had never been marketed before.

🏛 RULE OF LAW
An opinion is a fact, and when parties are so situated that a buyer may reasonably rely upon the expression of a seller's opinion, the fact that it is an opinion is not a defense to an action in deceit; but, there are some statements that no sensible man takes seriously.

FACTS: Simmons Manufacturing Co. (Simmons) (D) sold Vulcan Metals Co. (Vulcan) (P) machinery for the manufacture of vacuum cleaners. Representations, challenged by Vulcan (P), were made to the effect that (1) the vacuum cleaners were: "perfect in even the smallest detail," "most economical," "everyone could afford one," "guaranteed perfect satisfaction," etc., and (2) that the vacuum cleaner had never before been put on the market. Vulcan (P) sued for deceit, charging the representations above were false. The trial court directed a verdict for Simmons (D) on each count. Vulcan (P) appealed, contending that both statements were false. Simmons (D) contended that the statements were mere opinion and therefore not actionable and they were substantively true since only 60 machines had ever been sold.

ISSUE: May an action for deceit (misrepresentation) lie where the representations challenged involve mere opinions as well as misrepresentations about a product sold?

HOLDING AND DECISION: (Hand, J.) Yes. An opinion is a fact, and when parties are so situated that a buyer may reasonably rely upon the expression of a seller's opinion, the fact that it is an opinion is not a defense to an action in deceit; but there are some statements that no sensible man takes seriously. Much depends on the relative equality of the parties involved in terms of their ability to know whether a statement is mere "dealer's talk" opinion or fact statement (the ability to examine the merchandise is but one factor in considering this question). Some statements are so patently "dealer's talk" that no sensible man would take them seriously. Here, the statements about the quality of the machines is clearly such "dealer's talk." No sensible man expects anything to be perfect. This is not true of the statement about previous sales, however. There, only the seller has reason to know the relative truth of such statements. Here, the misrepresentation is sufficiently material (to the salability of the vacuum cleaners) to be actionable. Reversed in part and affirmed in part.

▶ ANALYSIS

This case points up the general relationship between opinion and misrepresentation or deceit. Note the comparison made by Learned Hand in the decision. A political campaign manager or a politician will often make claims which no one really believes (*e.g.*, I will balance the budget. I will eradicate poverty). Such "puffing up" talk is done to show the candidate's intentions; it is not meant to be taken literally. No sensible man would ever rely upon it.

Quicknotes

DECEIT A false statement made either knowingly or with reckless disregard as to its truth and which is intended to induce the plaintiff to act in reliance thereon to his detriment.

MISREPRESENTATION A statement or conduct by one party to another that constitutes a false representation of fact.

Swinton v. Whitinsville Savings Bank

Buyer of termite-infested home (P) v. Home seller (D)

Mass. Sup. Jud. Ct., 42 N.E.2d 808 (1942).

NATURE OF CASE: Action to recover damages for fraudulent concealment.

FACT SUMMARY: Swinton (P) purchased a dwelling house, which was infested with termites, from Whitinsville Savings Bank (the Bank) (D). The Bank (D), through its salesman, knew of the termites and did not disclose this information to Swinton (P), nor was any such information asked for by Swinton (P).

RULE OF LAW
There is no liability for bare nondisclosure.

FACTS: Swinton (P) purchased a dwelling house from Whitinsville Savings Bank (the Bank) (D). Swinton (P) alleged that the Bank (D) knew that the home was infested with termites at the time of sale to Swinton (P) and that he had no idea nor any reasonable way at the time to tell whether termites were present or not. Swinton (P) made no allegation of any false statement or representation or of the uttering of a half-truth that may be tantamount to a falsehood. There was no intimation that the Bank (D) by any means prevented Swinton (P) from acquiring information as to the condition of the house. There was nothing to show any fiduciary relation between the parties. Based upon these facts, the trial court sustained a demurrer in favor of the Bank (D). Swinton (P) appealed.

ISSUE: Is there any duty to disclose facts when not requested to do so?

HOLDING AND DECISION: (Qua, J.) No. There is no liability for bare nondisclosure. The court states, "If the defendant was to be found liable on these facts, every seller would be liable who fails to disclose any nonapparent defect known to him in the subject of the sale which materially reduces its value and which the buyer fails to discover. Similarly it would seem that every buyer would be liable who fails to disclose any nonapparent virtue known to him in the subject of the purchase which materially enhances its value and of which the seller is ignorant. The law has not yet, we believe, reached the point of imposing upon the frailties of human nature a standard so idealistic as this." The demurrer was sustained on appeal.

ANALYSIS

This case may be considered a modern one that is based upon very old case law. The rule set down in this case, although still very much operable and in use today, has been eroded from the severity seen here to much more acceptable applications by numerous exceptions which have been created. This case does not represent the modern-day trend, which is toward more of a duty to disclose known material facts. Many states have specific statutes dealing with the subject of concealment in many fields, including that of real estate.

Quicknotes

LATENT DEFECTS A defect that cannot be discovered upon ordinary examination.

Laidlaw v. Organ

Tobacco seller (P) v. Tobacco buyer (D)

15 U.S. 178 (1817).

NATURE OF CASE: Appeal from an award for damages.

FACT SUMMARY: Organ (D) contracted to purchase tobacco from Laidlaw (P) without revealing information that would drastically raise the price of tobacco.

RULE OF LAW
A buyer in sole possession of knowledge that would affect the price of products he is dealing in is not obliged by law to divulge the information.

FACTS: Organ (D), a merchant in tobacco, learned of impending peace between the British and American forces before the news was made public. He then contracted to purchase tobacco from Laidlaw (P), who asked him if he knew anything that would affect the price of tobacco. Organ (D) did not reply. Subsequently, peace was announced, and the price of tobacco went up 30 percent to 50 percent. Laidlaw (P) sued, contending he had been defrauded. The trial court instructed the jury that Organ (D) was required to divulge the information, and the jury returned a verdict for Laidlaw (P). Organ (D) appealed.

ISSUE: Must a buyer divulge information he holds which may affect the price of products he is dealing in?

HOLDING AND DECISION: (Marshall, C.J.) No. A buyer in sole possession of information that would affect the price of products he is dealing in is not legally obliged to divulge the information. As long as nothing is said to mislead the ignorant party and the information is equally accessible to both, no duty to communicate exists. Therefore, the instruction was erroneous. Reversed and remanded for a new trial.

▶ ANALYSIS

This case illustrates the general rule that a buyer has no duty to disclose his superior knowledge to the seller. This is true for most transactions; however, in security transactions, special knowledge of buyers when they occupy positions which make them privy to inside information must be divulged or the sale violates securities laws.

■━■

Quicknotes

FRAUD A false representation of facts with the intent that another will rely on the misrepresentation to his detriment.

NONDISCLOSURE The failure to communicate certain facts to another person.

Edgington v. Fitzmaurice

Debenture purchaser (P) v. Society officers (D)

Ch., 29 Ch. 459 (1885).

NATURE OF CASE: Appeal from award of damages for fraud.

FACT SUMMARY: Edgington (P) contended he was fraudulently induced to buy debentures, resulting in his injury.

RULE OF LAW
In order to show actionable fraud, the plaintiff must show the defendant knowingly made a false statement with the intent to induce the plaintiff to act in reliance on it, and that the plaintiff did in fact so act to his damage.

FACTS: Edgington (P) bought debentures of a society of which Fitzmaurice (D) was a director. The prospectus prepared to solicit buyers stated that the money would be used to complete alterations and additions to buildings, to purchase horses and vans, and to develop the supply of fish used in the business. Edgington (P) sued when he discovered the money was used to pay off existing debts, contending he had been defrauded. At trial, he testified he would not have bought the debentures if he had known the money would not be used to acquire property stated in the prospectus. The trial court held Edgington (P) was influenced by the misstatement and entered a verdict in his favor. Fitzmaurice (D) appealed.

ISSUE: In order to show actionable fraud, must a plaintiff show he was induced by the defendant's knowingly or recklessly false statements to act to his damage?

HOLDING AND DECISION: (Lord Bowen, J.) Yes. In order to show an actionable fraud, a plaintiff must show the defendant knowingly made a false statement with the intent to induce the plaintiff to act in reliance on it and that the plaintiff did in fact act to his damage. It is clear that the statements in the prospectus were knowingly false. It is natural that when one advances money he asks what the money is to be used for. Unless there is evidence showing Edgington (P) did not act as a normal person, it cannot be said that he was not induced to purchase the debenture by the proposed use of the money. Affirmed.

▶ ANALYSIS

This case states the classic formulation of the tort of actionable fraud. The basis of the tort is the element of scienter. The defendant must make the statement or representation knowing it is to be false and with a reckless disregard for the truth or falsity of the representation. The doctrine of transferred intent operates to place liability on the defrauder whose misrepresentations induce another person other than the one to whom they are made to act to his damage.

■━■

Quicknotes

FRAUD A false representation of facts with the intent that another will rely on the misrepresentation to his detriment.

RECKLESSNESS The conscious disregard of substantial and justifiable risk.

SCIENTER Knowledge of certain facts; often refers to "guilty knowledge," which implicates liability.

■━■

Laborers Local 17 Health and Benefit Fund v. Philip Morris, Inc.

Labor union fund (P) v. Tobacco industry company representative (D)

191 F.3d 229 (2d Cir. 1999).

NATURE OF CASE: Suit to recover past and future damages alleging RICO violations and common law fraud.

FACT SUMMARY: The Laborers Local 17 Health and Benefit Fund (P) brought suit against tobacco companies (D) seeking recovery of past and future damages to recover money it expended in providing medical services to its members for smoking-related diseases.

RULE OF LAW

Proof of a direct injury sustained by the plaintiff is required in order to maintain a cause of action under the Racketeer Influenced and Corrupt Organizations Act (RICO) statute.

FACTS: The Laborers Local 17 Health and Benefit Fund (the Fund) (P) was established under the Employee Retirement Security Act of 1994 (ERISA) to provide health care to its union members. The Fund (P) brought suit against tobacco companies (D) alleging that they engaged in an advertising campaign that was intended to mislead the public as to the actual extent of the dangers of smoking to health. As a result, the Fund (P) paid millions of dollars in providing medical services to its participants who suffered from smoking-related diseases. The Fund (P) sought past and future damages to recover money expended as a result of smoking-related illness, alleging RICO violations and common law fraud.

ISSUE: Is proof of a direct injury sustained by the plaintiff required in order to maintain a cause of action under the RICO statute?

HOLDING AND DECISION: (Cardamone, J.) Yes. Proof of a direct injury sustained by the plaintiff is required in order to maintain a cause of action under the RICO statute. The first issue is whether the tobacco companies' (D) alleged wrongdoing was the proximate cause of the Fund's (P) injuries, or whether such causal connection is too remote to allow recovery as a matter of law. In order to sue under the RICO statute, a plaintiff must show that the violation was both the "but for" and proximate cause of the injury. In order to determine whether proximate cause exists, common law principles must be applied. This requires there to be some direct relation between the alleged harmful conduct and the injury sustained. If a plaintiff's claim consists merely of harm inflicted upon a third person by the defendant's conduct, then the plaintiff is too remote to recover. Here the Fund's (P) damages were entirely based upon the harm inflicted on its union mem-

bers. Since these injuries were indirect, the Fund (P) lacked standing to assert RICO claims against the tobacco companies (D). The Fund (P) further claimed that even if it lacked standing under the direct injury test, an exception to the rule applies where the defendants specifically intend to harm the plaintiffs. The court stated that an allegation of specific intent to injure does not overcome the fact that a direct injury must be sustained in order to maintain a RICO action. Reversed and remanded.

ANALYSIS

The court refers to three factors addressed in the case of *Holmes v. Securities Investor Protection Corp.,* 503 U.S. 258 (1992), that support its conclusion that a plaintiff lacks standing to sue for indirect injuries under the federal RICO statute. These include the following: (1) the less direct the injury, the more difficult it is to determine which of the plaintiff's injuries are attributable to the violation and which are the result of independent factors; (2) the recognition of claims for indirect injuries would require courts to adopt complicated rules for apportioning damages among the plaintiffs for the varying degrees of injuries in order to prevent multiple recoveries; and (3) the need to deal with the problems of calculating damages are unnecessary when those persons suffering direct injury may be relied upon to "vindicate the law as private attorneys general." Thus the Fund (P) could still bring a suit for subrogation of the funds expended and the individual members could bring suit to recover for their injuries.

Quicknotes

FRAUD A false representation of facts with the intent that another will rely on the misrepresentation to his detriment.

RICO Racketeer Influenced and Corrupt Organization laws; federal and state statutes enacted for the purpose of prosecuting organized crime.

Ultramares Corporation v. Touche

Money lender (P) v. Accounting corporation (D)

N.Y. Ct. App. 174 N.E. 441 (1931).

NATURE OF CASE: Appeal from denial of damages for negligent misrepresentation.

FACT SUMMARY: Ultramares Corporation (P) made monetary advances to Stern & Co. on the basis of an audit report, which was negligently prepared by Touche, Niven & Co. (D), a firm of public accountants.

RULE OF LAW
There is no liability for negligent misrepresentations without privity between the plaintiff and defendant.

FACTS: Stern & Co. employed Touche, Niven & Co. (Touche) (D), a firm of public accountants, to prepare and certify their balance sheets. This certification was necessary for Stern to obtain credit. Touche (D) conducted an independent audit and concluded Stern's net worth to be over $1 million. Touche (D) attached a certificate to the prepared balance sheets stating the sheets were true and correct. Actually, the sheets were wrong in all material respects due to the auditor's negligent reliance on false statements by Stern's officers. Ultramares Corporation (P) made monetary advances to Stern on the basis of the certified sheets and subsequently sued Touche (D) for negligent misrepresentation. The trial court overturned the jury verdict for Ultramares (P), holding that a lack of privity precluded a cause of action for negligent misrepresentation. The appellate court reversed, and Touche (D) appealed.

ISSUE: Is there any liability for misrepresentation without privity between plaintiff and defendant?

HOLDING AND DECISION: (Cardozo, C.J.) No. There is no liability for negligent misrepresentation absent privity between the plaintiff and defendant. In this case, the balance sheets were prepared primarily for the benefit of Stern & Co. for its use in developing its business. It was only incidentally or collaterally prepared for those to whom it might later be exhibited. As a result, the connection between Touche (D) and Ultramares (P) was too slight to support liability. An opposite holding would expand liability for negligent speech beyond proper limits. Reversed and remanded.

▶ ANALYSIS

This case is the leading common law decision on the extent of liability for negligent misrepresentation. It makes a distinction between the importance of privity in the products liability area and the importance of it in this context. Recent decisions have threatened to overturn the sanctity of privity in this context, especially under state law. In *Rosenblum v. Adler,* 461 A. 2d 138 (1983), the New Jersey Supreme Court noted Justice Cardozo's opinion in *McPherson v. Buick Motor Co.,* 111 N.E. 1050 (1916), wherein it was held that privity of contract was not essential to a products liability action, and held privity was not required in the context of an action for negligent misrepresentation.

Quicknotes

NEGLIGENT MISREPRESENTATION A misrepresentation that is made pursuant to a business relationship, in violation of an obligation owed, upon which the plaintiff relies to his detriment.

PRIVITY Commonality of rights or interests between parties.

CHAPTER 14

Economic Harms

Quick Reference Rules of Law

PAGE

1. *Lumley v. Gye.* A person who wrongfully and maliciously interferes with a contract between an employer and employee is liable for resulting damages. — 224

2. *Asahi Kasei Pharma Corp. v. Actelion Ltd.* A corporate entity that acquires a controlling interest in a contracting party is not shielded from liability for wrongful interference with the contracting party's contract where the acquiring entity's interference is not justified because it has used unlawful means to interfere with the contract. — 225

3. *Tarleton v. M'Gawley.* A person is liable for damage caused by his malicious interference with the prospective economic advantage of another. — 227

4. *People Express Airlines, Inc. v. Consolidated Rail Corp.* A defendant, who has breached its duty of care to avoid the risk of economic injury to particularly foreseeable plaintiffs, may be held liable for actual economic losses that are proximately caused by its breach of duty. — 228

5. *532 Madison Avenue Gourmet Foods, Inc. v. Finlandia Center, Inc.* (1) A landowner has no duty in negligence to protect an entire urban neighborhood against purely economic loss. (2) When businesses are forced to close their establishments because of the collapse of nearby structures, and incur damages as a result, if the businesses do not incur special damages beyond those suffered by the public, they do not have a valid cause of action for public nuisance. — 229

6. *Mogul Steamship Co. v. McGregor, Gow & Co.* Competition, regardless of severity, does not give rise to a cause of action unless attended by elements of dishonesty, intimidation, or illegality. — 231

7. *International News Service v. Associated Press.* News, once reduced to a concrete form, is property, and it is unfair competition to appropriate it for one's own commercial use prior to its fair exploitation by the gatherer. — 232

8. *The National Basketball Association v. Motorola, Inc.* Although a narrow "hot-news" misappropriation claim does survive preemption, the transmission of real-time NBA (P) games' scores and information tabulated from television and radio broadcasts of games in progress does not constitute a misappropriation of "hot-news" that is the property of the NBA (P). — 233

9. *Ely-Norris Safe Co. v. Mosler Safe Co.* A competitor cannot take away customers from another through the use of deceit. — 235

10. *Mosler Safe Co. v. Ely-Norris Safe Co.* In order to recover for palming off, a plaintiff must show he actually lost customers as a result of the defendant's action. — 236

Lumley v. Gye

Theater lessee (P) v. Man accused of interfering with theatrical contract (D)

K.B., 118 Eng. Rep. 749 (1853).

NATURE OF CASE: Action for damages for inducement of breach of contract.

FACT SUMMARY: Lumley (P) contended Gye (D) was liable in damages for inducing Wagner to breach her contract to sing exclusively for Lumley (P) in his theater.

🏛 RULE OF LAW
A person who wrongfully and maliciously interferes with a contract between an employer and employee is liable for resulting damages.

FACTS: Lumley (P) leased the Queen's Theater for the purpose of presenting operas for profit. He contracted with Wagner for her to perform at his theater for a set period of time with the condition that she was not to perform for anyone else during the term of the contract. After the contract was entered into, but prior to any performance under it, Gye (D) induced Wagner to breach the contract and perform in his employ. Lumley (P) sued for damages, and Gye (D) demurred, contending that no relation of master and servant was created because Wagner had not yet performed, and, therefore, no action for inducement to breach the contract was stated.

ISSUE: Is a person who wrongfully and maliciously interferes with an employment contract liable for resulting damages?

HOLDING AND DECISION: (Crompton, J.) Yes. A person who wrongfully and maliciously interferes with a contract between an employer and his employee is liable for resulting damages. In this case, Gye (D) was aware of the contract between Lumley (P) and Wagner and of its exclusive nature. He therefore acted maliciously in inducing Wagner to breach it. The relationship of master and servant exists from the time the binding contract is entered into, and it is irrelevant that actual performance had not yet occurred. Therefore, judgment must be entered for Lumley (P).

DISSENT: (Coleridge, J.) Remedies for breach of contract may be asserted only against the parties to the contract. Therefore, no recovery may be against a third party who maliciously causes the breach.

▶ ANALYSIS

Although this case involved the services of a performer with unique skills, subsequent cases expanded the holding to include all contractual arrangements. In *Bowen v. Hall*, 6 Q.B.D. 333 (1881), the holding in this case was applied to

grant recovery against a defendant who had induced a brick maker to breach a five-year exclusive contract.

▰▰◼

Quicknotes

INDUCEMENT OF BREACH OF CONTRACT An intentional tort whereby a defendant intentionally elicits the breach of a valid contract, resulting in damages.

▰▰◼

Asahi Kasei Pharma Corp. v. Actelion Ltd.

Pharmaceutical company (P) v. Competitor (D)

222 Cal. App. 4th 945 (2014).

NATURE OF CASE: Appeal from verdict awarding plaintiff compensatory and punitive damages in an action for, inter alia, wrongful interference with contract.

FACT SUMMARY: Actelion Ltd. (D) and some of its executives argued they could not be liable for wrongful interference with a license agreement (the License Agreement) between Asahi Kasei Pharma Corporation (Asahi) (P) and CoTherix, Inc. after Actelion (D) acquired CoTherix, since at that point Actelion (D) had an economic interest in the License Agreement and was not a third-party interloper, or complete stranger, to the contract.

RULE OF LAW

A corporate entity that acquires a controlling interest in a contracting party is not shielded from liability for wrongful interference with the contracting party's contract where the acquiring entity's interference is not justified because it has used unlawful means to interfere with the contract.

FACTS: Asahi Kasei Pharma Corporation (Asahi) (P), a Japanese pharmaceutical company, developed Fasudil, a drug that Asahi (P) sought to market in the United States for treatment of pulmonary arterial hypertension (PAH). To obtain regulatory approvals for Fasudil, and to develop and commercialize it in North America and Europe, Asahi (P) entered into a licensing and development agreement (the License Agreement) with CoTherix, Inc., a U.S.-based biopharmaceutical company. Asahi (P), which sought expeditious development of Fasudil, had turned to CoTherix because it had a proven track record of bringing similar drugs to market quickly. Asahi (P) considered CoTherix's ability to move quickly in clinical development of Fasudil to be particularly important to preservation of Fasudil's market exclusivity before facing generic competition. When the License Agreement was entered into, Asahi's (P) competitor, Actelion Ltd. (D), a Swiss company, held the dominant share of the U.S. pulmonary arterial hypertension (PAH) drug market. Actelion (D) subsequently acquired all of the stock of CoTherix, and concurrently notified Asahi (P) CoTherix would discontinue development of Fasudil. Asahi (P) sued Actelion (D) and three of its executives asserting claims, inter alia, of intentional interference with the License Agreement, alleging the defendants had acted with malice, oppression, or fraud. Asahi (P) presented evidence Actelion (D) acquired CoTherix specifically because it saw Fasudil as a significant threat to its market dominance and the defendants used unlawful means to stop the development of Fasudil, there-

by interfering with the License Agreement. Specifically, Asahi (P) argued the Actelion (D) defendants used extortion and fraud to kill Fasudil as a competitive product. The jury was instructed a person cannot be liable for interference with a person's own contract, if that person was a party to the contract at the time of the interference. The jury was also instructed on the justification defense, that in certain situations, a particular defendant could not be liable for intentional interference with contract if that defendant's conduct was justified, but that this affirmative defense of justification was inapplicable if the particular defendant used unlawful means to interfere with the License Agreement, including intentional misrepresentation, concealment, and extortion. The jury returned a verdict in Asahi's (P) favor, awarding around $550 million in compensatory damages, and $30 million in punitive damages. The Actelion (D) defendants appealed, arguing they could not be held liable for wrongful interference with the License Agreement, since Actelion (D) was not a third party to the agreement after it acquired CoTherix, and Actelion (D) stood in the shoes of CoTherix in determining how to proceed with the contract. Asahi (P) countered by noting the applicable law recognizes corporate owners, officers and directors may be liable for interfering with corporate contracts; claims of privilege or justification are defenses that must be pleaded and proved; and to prevail on such defenses, defendants must show they did not "use improper means." The state's intermediate appellate court granted review.

ISSUE: Is a corporate entity that acquires a controlling interest in a contracting party shielded from liability for wrongful interference with the contracting party's contract where the acquiring entity's interference is not justified because it has used unlawful means to interfere with the contract?

HOLDING AND DECISION: (Bruiniers, J.) No. A corporate entity that acquires a controlling interest in a contracting party is not shielded from liability for wrongful interference with the contracting party's contract where the acquiring entity's interference is not justified because it has used unlawful means to interfere with the contract. To recover in tort for intentional interference with the performance of a contract, a plaintiff must prove: (1) a valid contract between plaintiff and another party; (2) defendant's knowledge of the contract; (3) defendant's intentional acts designed to induce a breach or disruption of the contractual relationship; (4) actual breach or disruption

Continued on next page.

of the contractual relationship; and (5) resulting damage. In this way, the expectation the parties will honor the terms of the contract is protected against officious inter-meddlers. Actelion (D) contends it cannot be liable for tortious interference with the License Agreement because the tort duty not to interfere with a contract falls only on strangers—interlopers who have no legitimate interest in the scope or course of the contract's performance. Although Actelion (D) does not contend it was a party to the License Agreement at any point, it urges the state's precedents on wrongful interference with contract should be read broadly so as to limit liability for intentional interference to complete "strangers" to the contract, not nonparties to the contract who have an interest therein. However, the state's courts have not recognized a corporate owner's absolute privilege to interfere with its subsidiary's contract. A "stranger," as used in the applicable precedent, means one who is not a party to the contract or an agent of a party to the contract. Thus, Actelion (D), by virtue of its ownership interest, is not automatically immune from liability for tortious interference with the License Agreement. Here, there was no evidence Actelion (D) had been authorized to act as CoTherix's agent with respect to the License Agreement. Because the jury was properly instructed on the elements of the tort of wrongful interference with contract, and was properly charged with considering whether the defendants used unlawful means to interfere with the License Agreement, the verdicts are affirmed. Moreover, because the Actelion (D) executives had actively participated in Actelion's (D) tortious conduct, they can be held personally liable for such intentional conduct. Finally, in this case the manager's privilege—which in certain instances can protect managers from personal liability when they counsel their principal to breach a contract when doing so is in the principal's interest—is inapplicable because manager's privilege does not exempt a manager from liability when he or she tortiously interferes with a contract or relationship between third parties. Affirmed.

▶ ANALYSIS

Some have argued this case should have been resolved as a contracts case, and, in fact, Asahi (P) won a $91 million contract claim in arbitration against CoTherix for breach of contract prior to bringing its wrongful interference action. Companies, such as those in the technology sector, which have grown through numerous acquisitions, argue the decision in this case could open them up to open-ended tort liability, as well as punitive damages, that are difficult to calculate prior to acquiring another company whenever the acquired subsidiary incurs contract liability. It was also argued this decision sidestepped the issue of whether a parent corporation has a duty not to interfere with its subsidiary's contracts by resting its holding on whether the Actelion (D) defendants had a qualified affirmative defense, which it was argued is a separate and logically subsequent question that arises only if a tort duty applies

in the first place. The California Supreme Court rejected similar arguments, and declined to review this decision (No. S216123 (review denied Mar. 12, 2014)).

◼◼◼

Quicknotes

AFFIRMATIVE DEFENSE A manner of defending oneself against a claim not by denying the truth of the charge, but by the introduction of some evidence challenging the plaintiff's right to bring the claim.

EXTORTION The unlawful taking of property of another by threats of force.

INTERFERENCE WITH CONTRACT RIGHTS An intentional tort whereby a defendant intentionally elicits the breach of a valid contract resulting in damages.

INTERFERENCE WITH CONTRACTUAL RELATIONS An intentional tort whereby a defendant intentionally elicits the breach of a valid contract resulting in damages.

MALICE The intention to commit an unlawful act with the intent to inflict injury without justification or excuse.

◼◼◼

Tarleton v. M'Gawley

Trading ship (P) v. Rival ship's master (D)

K.B., 170 Eng. Rep. 153 (1793).

NATURE OF CASE: Action for damages for interference with a prospective advantage.

FACT SUMMARY: Thomas Smith (P) sued M'Gawley (D) for maliciously preventing him from trading with natives on the coast of Africa.

RULE OF LAW

A person is liable for damage caused by his malicious interference with the prospective economic advantage of another.

FACTS: The Tarleton (P) was a ship docked at Calabar, on the coast of Africa. The ship's captain sent a smaller vessel led by Smith loaded with goods to trade with natives on another part of the coast in Cameroon. While docked there, a canoe of natives came up to trade and returned to their home for the purpose of further trade. While canoeing back, the natives were fired upon by M'Gawley (D) and thereafter were deterred from trading with the Tarleton (P) ship. Smith (P) sued, contending M'Gawley (D) had maliciously interfered with his continued trade, depriving him of an economic advantage. M'Gawley (D) defended, contending he shot at the natives, intending to stop any trade, because the natives were in debt to him. He contended, however, that no action could be brought by Smith (P) because Smith (P) violated the law of the natives by failing to pay a duty prior to engaging in trade, and interference with illicit commerce was not a wrongful action.

ISSUE: Is a person liable for malicious interference with the prospective economic advantage of another?

HOLDING AND DECISION: (Lord Kenyon, J.) Yes. A person is liable for damages caused by his malicious interference with the prospective economic advantage of another. In this case, Tarleton's (P) violation was of a local law. It is the responsibility of the local authority to enforce the law. It is not within M'Gawley's (D) power to take it upon himself to enforce the law. Therefore, his defense is ineffective. He clearly intentionally prevented the natives from trading with The Tarleton (P), which resulted in the deprivation of an economic advantage. Consequently, M'Gawley (D) is liable to Smith (P) in damages. Judgment for Tarleton (P).

▌ ANALYSIS

The tort illustrated in this case is closely linked to the tort of interference with contractual relations. A defendant will be allowed greater leeway in interfering with the rights of the plaintiff in a case where no contract exists. Traditionally, recovery for interference with prospective advantage was limited to commercial prospects; however, the trend has been away from this limitation.

Quicknotes

MALICE The intention to commit an unlawful act without justification or excuse.

People Express Airlines, Inc. v. Consolidated Rail Corp.

Airline (P) v. Railroad with chemical leak (D)

N.J. Sup. Ct., 495 A.2d 107 (1985).

NATURE OF CASE: Appeal from denial of summary judgment in negligence case.

FACT SUMMARY: In People Express Airlines Inc.'s (People Express) (P) case against Consolidated Rail Corp. (Conrail) (D), People Express (P) contended that it suffered business interruption losses as a result of an ethylene oxide leak in Conrail's (D) freight yard which forced People Express (P) to evacuate its premises.

🏛 **RULE OF LAW**
A defendant, who has breached its duty of care to avoid the risk of economic injury to particularly foreseeable plaintiffs, may be held liable for actual economic losses that are proximately caused by its breach of duty.

FACTS: An ethylene oxide leak occurred in the Consolidated Rail Corp. (Conrail) (D) freight yard when a railroad tank car carrying the chemical was punctured and ignited. Municipal authorities evacuated the area within a one-mile radius of the freight yard to lessen the risk to persons within the area should the car explode. The evacuation included the terminal building of Newark International Airport where People Express Airlines, Inc. (People Express) (P) operated. People Express (P) employees were prohibited from using the terminal for 12 hours. People Express (P) contended that it suffered business-interruption losses as a result of the evacuation. No physical damages to airline property or physical injury occurred. Conrail (D) entered a motion for summary judgment, which was granted by the trial court. The appellate division reversed, holding that recovery of negligently caused economic loss was not automatically barred where no property damage or personal injury has occurred. Conrail (D) appealed.

ISSUE: May a defendant, who has breached its duty of care to avoid the risk of economic injury to particularly foreseeable plaintiffs, be held liable for actual economic losses that are proximately caused by its breach of duty?

HOLDING AND DECISION: (Handler, J.) Yes. A defendant, who has breached its duty of care to avoid the risk of economic injury to particularly foreseeable plaintiffs, may be held liable for actual economic losses that are proximately caused by its breach of duty. Economic losses may be recovered as damages when they are the natural and probable consequence of a defendant's negligence in the sense they are reasonably to be anticipated in view of defendant's capacity to have foreseen that the particular plaintiff or identifiable class of plaintiffs is demonstrably

within the risk created by defendant's negligence. Here, People Express (P) was in close proximity to Conrail's (D) freight yard; its operations and particular foreseeability of economic loss resulting from an accident or evacuation were obvious; Conrail (D) had actual or constructive knowledge of the volatile properties of ethylene oxide. Actual knowledge of eventual economic loss is not necessary; rather, particular foreseeability will suffice. People Express (P) should have the chance to prove damages because of Conrail's (D) capacity to have foreseen that this particular plaintiff was within the risk created by their negligence. Affirmed as modified, and remanded.

▎ *ANALYSIS*

At early common law, a master was allowed an action for the damages he suffered as the result of injury to a servant. This was based on the philosophy of the era of the cottage industry, but the action has long survived in some jurisdictions for servants generally and in others for servants who were members of the master's household. The general trend is to treat servant cases like other cases.

━━■■━━

Quicknotes

INTERFERENCE WITH PROSPECTIVE ADVANTAGE An intentional tort whereby a defendant intentionally interferes with a valid business expectancy, resulting in the termination of the expectancy and damages.

NEGLIGENCE Conduct falling below the standard of care that a reasonable person would demonstrate under similar conditions.

PROXIMATE CAUSE The natural sequence of events without which an injury would not have been sustained.

532 Madison Avenue Gourmet Foods, Inc. v. Finlandia Center, Inc.

Businesses within city closures (P) v. Building owner, ground lessee and managing agent (D)

N.Y. Ct. App., 750 N.E.2d 1097 (2001).

NATURE OF CASE: Appeal of one dismissed and one allowed action for economic loss based on negligence and public nuisance.

FACT SUMMARY: Many business entities, including 532 Madison Ave. Gourmet Foods, Inc. (532 Madison) (P), 5th Ave. Chocolatiere (P) and Goldberg Weprin & Ustin (Goldberg Weprin) (P), were harmed when two separate buildings partially collapsed at separate times, and they sued to recover for their losses.

🏛 RULE OF LAW
(1) A landowner has no duty in negligence to protect an entire urban neighborhood against purely economic loss.
(2) When businesses are forced to close their establishments because of the collapse of nearby structures, and incur damages as a result, if the businesses do not incur special damages beyond those suffered by the public, they do not have a valid cause of action for public nuisance.

FACTS: A construction project on a 39-story office tower known as 540 Madison Avenue aggravated existing structural defects on the property causing a section of its south wall to partially collapse. As a result, bricks and mortar fell onto Madison Avenue, which is a heavily occupied prime commercial location. New York City officials (the City) closed 15 blocks of Madison Avenue for about two weeks. As a result of the accident, 532 Madison Ave. Gourmet Foods, Inc. (532 Madison) (P) had to close its 24-hour delicatessen for five weeks and it subsequently sued Finlandia Center, Inc. (D), collectively the building owner, ground lessee and managing agent, for damages. In a companion case, 5th Ave. Chocolatiere (5th Ave. Chocolatiere) (P), collectively a group of business entities, also sued alleging that shoppers were unable to gain access to their stores. In another case, three actions involving the collapse of a 48-story construction elevator tower on West 43rd Street, near Times Square, were consolidated. In that case, the City prohibited all traffic in a wide area of midtown Manhattan. Goldberg Weprin & Ustin (Goldberg Weprin) (P), collectively a law firm, a public relations firm and a clothing manufacturer, sought damages for economic loss based on gross negligence, strict liability and public and private nuisance. Both complaints were dismissed at trial. The appellate division affirmed the dismissal of *Goldberg Weprin,* but reinstated the public nuisance and negligence claims in *532 Madison* and *5th Ave. Chocolatiere,* for eco-

nomic loss. Goldberg Weprin (P) and Finlandia (D) appealed.

ISSUE:
(1) What is a landlord's duty in negligence when the sole injury is lost income?
(2) Do 532 Madison (P), 5th Ave. Chocolatiere (P) and Goldberg Weprin (P) have a valid claim for public nuisance based on the collapses forcing closure of their establishments, and thereby causing special damages beyond those suffered by the public?

HOLDING AND DECISION: (Kaye, C.J.)
(1) None. A landlord has no duty in negligence when the sole injury is lost income. We have never held that a landowner owes a duty to protect an entire urban neighborhood against purely economic loss.
(2) No. 532 Madison (P), 5th Ave. Chocolatiere (P) and Goldberg Weprin (P) do not have a valid claim for public nuisance based on the collapses forcing closure of their establishments, and thereby causing special damages beyond those suffered by the public. A public nuisance occurs when conduct substantially interferes with common rights of the public. Such a nuisance is a violation against the State, and is remedied by the proper governmental authority. A private person only has a public nuisance action when that person suffers a special injury beyond that suffered by the community at large. A nuisance is the invasion of interests in land. In the present case, the right to use the public space around Madison Ave. and Times Square was invaded by the building collapses and the City's decision to close off those areas and, therefore, a public nuisance occurred. However, there was no special loss sustained. The closures of the subject areas caused widespread economic loss to the businesses in the areas and therefore 532 Madison (P), 5th Ave. Chocolatiere (P) and Goldberg Weprin (P) claimed injuries no different from the injuries suffered by the public at large. Reversed as to *532 Madison* and *5th Ave. Chocolatiere* and affirmed as to *Goldberg Weprin.* All of plaintiffs' counts dismissed.

▶ ANALYSIS

As in *Anonymous,* Y.B. Mich. 27 Hen. 8, f. 27, pl. 10 (1536), the plaintiff's remedy in the present case is to be sought

Continued on next page.

through a governmental authority, and not via a private action in the courts.

━■━

Quicknotes

PUBLIC NUISANCE An activity that unreasonably interferes with a right common to the overall public.

━■━

Mogul Steamship Co. v. McGregor, Gow & Co.

Tea shipper (P) v. Tea shipper association (D)

Q.B.D., 23 Q.B.D. 598 (1889); *aff'd*, A.C. 25 (1892).

NATURE OF CASE: Appeal from dismissal of action for unfair competition.

FACT SUMMARY: Mogul Steamship Co. (Mogul) (P) contended McGregor, Gow & Co. (D) and other members of an association of shippers were liable in damages for unfairly attempting to lure Mogul's (P) customers from him.

🏛 RULE OF LAW
Competition, regardless of severity, does not give rise to a cause of action unless attended by elements of dishonesty, intimidation, or illegality.

FACTS: McGregor, Gow & Co. (McGregor) (D) and others formed an association of shippers in order to monopolize the control of tea carriage from Chinese ports and to drive Mogul Steamship Co. (Mogul) (P) out of this business. The association offered local shippers low freight rates and rebates in return for their not dealing with Mogul (P) or any nonassociation members. Mogul (P) sued, contending the association was liable in damages for unfairly competing with him. He contended that even if the tactics used would be permissible if done by one competitor, the activity became prohibited by its combined nature. The trial court granted McGregor's (D) motion to dismiss, and Mogul (P) appealed.

ISSUE: Is there a cause of action for unfair competition in the absence of dishonesty, intimidation, or illegality?

HOLDING AND DECISION: (Lord Bowen, J.) No. Competition, regardless of severity, does not give rise to cause of action unless attended by elements of dishonesty, intimidation, or illegality. McGregor (D) and other members of the association did nothing more than compete with Mogul (P) with no intent to any greater harm than was necessary to attract shippers away from him and into their business. There is no authority for the proposition that at some point rigorous competition becomes "unfair" and therefore contrary to law. It would be impracticable to attempt within the variegated world of commerce to judicially determine what level of competition would be "fair" in a given context. Further, merely because the association members act in concert does not render their activities unlawful. This would expand the concept of conspiracy beyond its proper scope. As a result, because the association acted in absence of dishonesty, intimidation, or illegality, their actions were not tortious. Affirmed.

DISSENT: (Lord Esher, M.R.) The actions of the association clearly were designed to interfere with Mogul's (P) right to carry on free trade and were therefore actionable.

▎ANALYSIS

The techniques employed by the association in this case are termed in modern times as predatory pricing. This is the endeavor to sell products very low for a short period of time in hopes of recovering the loss later when a monopoly is achieved. This case has been criticized for its narrow view of the harm of predatory prices in its characterization of the problem as a private dispute.

■■■■

Quicknotes

PREDATORY PRICING Pricing below the cost of production of a product with the intent of driving competitors out of business.

UNFAIR COMPETITION Any dishonest or fraudulent rivalry in trade and commerce, particularly imitation and counterfeiting.

■■■■

International News Service v. Associated Press

News wire service (D) v. Rival news wire service (P)

248 U.S. 215 (1918).

NATURE OF CASE: Appeal from denial of injunction against unfair competition.

FACT SUMMARY: Associated Press (P) contended International News Service (D) was liable for copying news from early editions of Associated Press (P) newspapers and subsequently selling it to its own customers.

🏛 RULE OF LAW
News, once reduced to a concrete form, is property, and it is unfair competition to appropriate it for one's own commercial use prior to its fair exploitation by the gatherer.

FACTS: Associated Press (AP) (P) and International News Service (INS) (D) were both news gathering services that were made up of several independent newspapers which combined to form a network of news-gathering power. Each made large annual expenditures in gathering news and selling it to their membership. INS (D) began copying news appearing in AP (P) member newspapers and selling it to its own customers in other parts of the world prior to the time AP (P) could get it to its own customers in those time zones. AP (P) sued, contending INS (D) had committed unfair competition by misappropriating AP's (P) property rights in the news. INS (D) defended, contending AP's (P) property right ended upon the first publication of the news. The district court refused to enjoin INS (D) from doing this, yet it did enjoin INS (D) from other forms of pirating, and both parties appealed.

ISSUE: Is it unfair competition to appropriate news for commercial use prior to its fair exploitation by its gatherer?

HOLDING AND DECISION: (Pitney, J.) Yes. News, once reduced to a concrete form, is property. A party who expends money to gather news intending to sell it has a right to fairly exploit it prior to its general dissemination. INS (D), in appropriating news that AP (P) has acquired through expenditures of time and money, is selling it as its own without comparable expenditures. This is an authorized interference with AP's (P) business and constitutes unfair competition. The printing of the news in selected newspapers does not constitute general dissemination. Therefore, until it is fairly exploited, the news retains its property value. As a result, INS's (D) actions should be enjoined. Affirmed.

DISSENT: (Brandeis, J.) Knowledge of public events cannot properly be termed property, and, therefore, no traditional property concept of the right to exclude exists in such knowledge. Therefore, AP (P) could not enjoin the publication of news by INS (D).

▶ ANALYSIS

This case has not commanded universal acceptance. In *Cheney Bros. v. Doris Silk Corp.*, 35 F. 2d 279 (2d Cir. 1929), it was held that no cause of action existed to protect the dissemination of clothing design patterns. The court read the present case narrowly and refused to extend principles of unfair competition to create a common law patent or copyright.

▬▬

Quicknotes

MISAPPROPRIATION The unlawful use of another's property or funds.

UNFAIR COMPETITION Any dishonest or fraudulent rivalry in trade and commerce, particularly imitation and counterfeiting.

▬▬

The National Basketball Association v. Motorola, Inc.

Professional sports organization (P) v. Manufacturer (D)

105 F.3d 841 (2d Cir. 1997).

NATURE OF CASE: Appeal from permanent injunction in misappropriation and copyright infringement action.

FACT SUMMARY: The National Basketball Association (NBA) (P) sued Motorola, Inc. (D) and the Sports Teams Analysis and Tracking System (STATS) (D) to prevent them (D) from transmitting scores and other data about NBA (P) games in progress via pagers known as "SportsTrax."

RULE OF LAW
Although a narrow "hot-news" misappropriation claim does survive preemption, the transmission of real-time NBA (P) games' scores and information tabulated from television and radio broadcasts of games in progress does not constitute a misappropriation of "hot-news" that is the property of the NBA (P).

FACTS: The National Basketball Association (NBA) (P) moved for a permanent injunction against Motorola, Inc. (D) and the STATS (D) to prevent them (D) from transmitting scores and other data about NBA (P) games in progress via pagers known as "SportsTrax." The SportsTrax is a handheld pager that displays updated information of professional basketball games in progress. The information includes the teams playing; score changes; the team in possession of the ball; whether the team is in the free-throw bonus; the quarter of the game; and the time remaining in the quarter. Motorola (D) manufactures and markets the SportsTrax paging device while STATS supplies the game information, via data feed from reporters who are watching the game on television or listening to them on the radio. The injunction was granted and it prohibited Motorola (D) and STATS (D) from transmitting data about NBA (P) games in progress without the permission of the NBA (P). Motorola (D) and STATS (D) appealed.

ISSUE:

(1) Does a state law "hot-news" misappropriation claim based on *International News Service v. Associated Press* (*INS*), 248 U.S. 215 (1918), survive preemption by the federal Copyright Act?

(2) Do the NBA's (P) claims fit within the surviving claims?

HOLDING AND DECISION: (Winter, J.)

(1) Yes. A state law "hot-news" misappropriation claim based on *International News Service v. Associated Press* (*INS*), 248 U.S. 215 (1918), is not preempted by the federal Copyright Act. Misappropriation law seeks to apply ethical standards to the use by one party of another's transmissions of events. The Copyright Act gives protection to simultaneously recorded broadcasts of live performances such as sports events. It also preempts state law claims that enforce rights equivalent to exclusive copyright protections when the work to which the state claim is being applied falls within an area of copyright protection. Although legislative history indicates that a "hot-news" *INS*-like claim survives preemption, much of New York misappropriation laws after *INS* goes well beyond "hot-news" claims and is preempted. The theory of the misappropriation cases relied upon by the lower court is considerably broader than that of *INS*. Such broad misappropriation doctrine based on amorphous concepts such as commercial immorality and society ethics is preempted because such concepts are synonymous with wrongful copying. Those cases were decided at a time when simultaneously recorded broadcasts were not protected under the Copyright Act and when state law claims they fashioned were not subject to preemption. Thus, only a narrow "hot-news" misappropriation claim survives preemption for actions concerning material within the realm of copyright. The surviving "hot-news" *INS*-like claim is limited to cases where a plaintiff generates or gathers information at a cost, the information is time-sensitive, a defendant's use of the information constitutes free-riding on the plaintiff's efforts, the defendant is in direct competition with a product or service offered by the plaintiffs, and the ability of other parties to free-ride on the efforts of the plaintiff or others would so reduce the incentive to produce the product or service that its existence or quality would be substantially threatened.

(2) No. The NBA's (P) claims do not fit within the surviving claims. SportsTrax, however, does not meet those criteria. Motorola (D) and STATS (D) have not engaged in unlawful misappropriation under the "hot-news" test. Although, the information transmitted to SportsTrax is time-sensitive and the NBA (P), via their upcoming product Gamestats, will be directly competing with SportsTrax, there are still critical elements missing in the NBA's (P) attempt to assert a "hot-news" *INS*-type claim. The NBA (P) has failed to show any competitive effect whatsoever from SportsTrax on generating the information by playing the games and transmitting live, full descriptions of those games. In addition, the NBA (P) has failed to show any free-riding by SportsTrax in the collecting and

Continued on next page.

retransmitting of strictly factual information about the games. SportsTrax is not a substitute for attending the games or watching them on television. Motorola (D) and STATS (D) are in no way free-riding on Gamestates because they (D) expend their own resources to collect purely factual-information generated by the NBA (P) games to transmit to SportsTrax pagers through their own network and assemble and transmit data themselves. Injunction denied.

► ANALYSIS

This case would have come out differently if SportsTrax got its information directly from a Gamestats pager.

━━■■■━━

Quicknotes

COPYRIGHT INFRINGEMENT A violation of one of the exclusive rights granted to an artist pursuant to Article I, section 8, clause 8 of the United States Constitution over the reproduction, display, performance, distribution, and adaptation of his work for a period prescribed by statute.

MISAPPROPRIATION The unlawful use of another's property or funds.

PERMANENT INJUNCTION A remedy imposed by the court ordering a party to cease the conduct of a specific activity until the final disposition of the cause of action.

━━■■■━━

Ely-Norris Safe Co. v. Mosler Safe Co.

Quality safe manufacturer (P) v. Inferior safe manufacturer (D)

7 F.2d 603 (2d Cir. 1925).

NATURE OF CASE: Appeal from dismissal of action for unfair competition.

FACT SUMMARY: Ely-Norris Safe Co. (Ely-Norris) (P) contended Mosler Safe Co. (D) was liable for unfair competition for selling substandard quality safes that resembled and led consumers to believe they were the same quality as Ely-Norris (P) safes.

> ## ⚖ RULE OF LAW
> A competitor cannot take away customers from another through the use of deceit.

FACTS: Ely-Norris Safe Co. (Ely-Norris) (P) manufactured a high-quality safe containing an explosion chamber that protected it against burglary. Mosler Safe Co. (Mosler) (D) subsequently produced a safe, under its own name, which physically resembled the Ely-Norris's (P) safe but did not contain an explosion chamber. Consumers, believing the safe to be of comparable quality, bought Mosler (D) safes. Ely-Norris (P) sued on the basis of unfair competition. Mosler (D) defended on the basis that its safes were not palmed off as Ely-Norris (P) safes, as they were sold under Mosler's (D) name, and, therefore, no action was presented.

ISSUE: Can a competitor be allowed to lure away customers from another through the use of deceit?

HOLDING AND DECISION: (Hand, J.) No. A competitor cannot take away customers from another through the use of deceit. The use of a competitor's name is only one way of showing palming off. In this case, Mosler (D) manufactured his safes to resemble Ely-Norris (P) safes in order to draw customers away. The safe was of a lower quality, yet this information was not communicated to the customer. Clearly this action is as deceitful as using Ely-Norris's (P) name. Therefore, the dismissal of the action was error. Reversed.

▶ ANALYSIS

The typical palming off of action accrues to the buyer of the product who has made his purchase based on deceitful practices. However, the costs of litigation often force the wrongful merchant to prosecute the action in order to recover his rightful profit.

▬▬

Quicknotes

DECEIT A false statement made either knowingly or with reckless disregard as to its truth and which is intended to induce the plaintiff to act in reliance thereon to his detriment.

PALMING OFF/PASSING OFF Conducting business or selling goods in a manner so as to mislead potential clients or consumers into believing they are doing business with, or purchasing goods from, another entity.

UNFAIR COMPETITION Any dishonest or fraudulent rivalry in trade and commerce, particularly imitation and counterfeiting.

▬▬

Mosler Safe Co. v. Ely-Norris Safe Co.

Inferior safe manufacturer (D) v. Quality safe manufacturer (P)

273 U.S. 132 (1926).

NATURE OF CASE: Appeal from reversal of denial of injunction for unfair competition.

FACT SUMMARY: The court of appeals reversed the trial court and enjoined Mosler Safe Co. (D) from producing safes that led consumers to believe they were of the same quality as Ely-Norris Co. (P) safes.

RULE OF LAW
In order to recover for palming off, a plaintiff must show he actually lost customers as a result of the defendant's action.

FACTS: Ely-Norris Co. (P) held a patent on safes containing explosion chambers. It sued Mosler Safe Co. (Mosler) (D), who manufactured a safe which resembled Ely-Norris's (P) safes but did not contain an explosion chamber, contending the resemblance was a form of palming off Mosler (D) safes as Ely-Norris (P) safes. Other safe manufacturers also employed explosion chambers, and Ely-Norris (P) did not specify any lost sales. The trial court refused to enjoin Mosler (D) from selling its safes, and the court of appeals reversed. Mosler (D) appealed.

ISSUE: Must a plaintiff show he actually lost customers in order to recover for palming off?

HOLDING AND DECISION: (Holmes, J.) Yes. In order to recover for palming off, a plaintiff must show he actually lost customers as a result of the defendant's actions. In this case, other manufacturers also infringed on Ely-Norris's (P) patent and sold safes with explosion chambers. Therefore, it cannot be shown that any customers were lost due exclusively to Mosler's (D) palming off. As a result, the injunction was improper. Reversed.

ANALYSIS

Palming off is the common law action codified by trademark and copyright statutes for infringement of distinctive property rights. Where no protected copyright or patent exists, a party may resort to state unfair competition actions. In some cases, federal copyright laws may preempt such state actions.

Quicknotes

PALMING OFF/PASSING OFF Conducting business or selling goods in a manner so as to mislead potential clients or consumers into believing they are doing business with, or purchasing goods from, another entity.

UNFAIR COMPETITION Any dishonest or fraudulent rivalry in trade and commerce, particularly imitation and counterfeiting.

Tort Immunities

Quick Reference Rules of Law

PAGE

1. *Berkovitz v. United States.* The discretionary function exemption in government torts actions insulates the government from liability if the action challenged in the case involves the permissible exercise of policy judgment. — 238

2. *Clinton v. Jones.* The doctrine of separation of powers does not require federal courts to stay all private actions against the President until he leaves office. — 239

Berkovitz v. United States

Paralyzed infant (P) v. Federal government (D)

486 U.S. 531 (1988).

NATURE OF CASE: Appeal from dismissal of action for damages for negligence.

FACT SUMMARY: Berkovitz (P), then a two-month-old infant, ingested defective oral polio vaccine and contracted a severe case of polio.

RULE OF LAW

The discretionary function exemption in government torts actions insulates the government from liability if the action challenged in the case involves the permissible exercise of policy judgment.

FACTS: Kevan Berkovitz (P), as an infant, ingested a dose of oral polio vaccine manufactured by Lederle Laboratories. Within one month, he contracted a severe case of polio that left Berkovitz (P) paralyzed and unable to breathe without the aid of a respirator. It was determined that Berkovitz (P) contracted the disease from the vaccine. Berkovitz (P) filed a suit against the Government (D) on the grounds that it had wrongfully licensed Lederle Laboratories to produce the vaccine and had wrongfully approved release of the particular lot of the vaccine containing Berkovitz's (P) dose. The Government (D) filed a motion to dismiss for lack of subject-matter jurisdiction on the ground that the licensing and release of the vaccine fell within the discretionary function exception of the Federal Tort Claims Act (FTCA). The district court denied the motion, and the court of appeals reversed. Berkovitz (P) appealed.

ISSUE: Does the discretionary function exemption in government torts actions insulate the government from liability if the action challenged in the case doesn't involve the permissible exercise of policy judgment?

HOLDING AND DECISION: (Marshall, J.) No. The discretionary function exemption in government torts actions only insulates the government from liability if the action challenged in the case involves the permissible exercise of policy judgment. Berkovitz's (P) first allegation with regard to the vaccine's licensing is that the Government (D) issued a product license without first receiving data the manufacturer must submit, showing how the product matches up against regulatory safety standards. The Government (D) had no discretion to issue a license without first receiving the required data; to have done so violated a specific statutory and regulatory directive. The regulatory scheme governing the release of vaccine is distinct from that governing the issuance of licenses. There is no regulatory duty requiring the government to examine all vaccine lots and prevent the distribution of noncomplying lots.

However, the Government (D) had adopted a policy of testing all vaccine lots for compliance with safety standards and preventing distribution of any lots failing to comply. This left no room for the implementing officials to exercise independent policy judgment. Thus, the Berkovitz (P) complaint is directed at a governmental action that involved no policy discretion. Reversed and remanded.

ANALYSIS

The discretionary exception has been invoked by the Government successfully in a variety of situations. For example, in *Ford v. American Motors Corp.*, 770 F.2d 465 (5th Cir. 1985), the court held that the governmental decision to sell used postal office Jeeps to the public was protected by the discretionary exemption, even though the government did not warn the public of the jeep's propensity to roll over.

Quicknotes

DISCRETIONARY FUNCTION The power conferred upon a person, entity, or governing body, to exercise personal judgment when discharging their duties.

NEGLIGENCE Conduct falling below the standard of care that a reasonable person would demonstrate under similar conditions.

SOVEREIGN IMMUNITY Immunity of government from suit without its consent.

Clinton v. Jones

President of the United States (D) v. State employee (P)

520 U.S. 681 (1997).

NATURE OF CASE: Appeal of order reinstating trial in suit for damages against the President.

FACT SUMMARY: President Clinton (D), who was sued by Jones (P) following an alleged incident that occurred in 1991 before his election to the office of President, sought to have all litigation on the matter suspended until after his term had concluded.

🏛 **RULE OF LAW**
The doctrine of separation of powers does not require federal courts to stay all private actions against the President until he leaves office.

FACTS: Clinton (D) was elected to the presidency in 1992, and re-elected in 1996, with his term of office expiring on January 20, 2001. In May 1991, while serving as the Governor of Arkansas, he delivered a speech at an official conference held at the Excelsior Hotel in Little Rock, Arkansas. Paula Jones (P), a state employee working at the registration desk of the conference, alleged that she was persuaded to leave her desk and visit Clinton (D) in a business suite at the hotel where he made "abhorrent" sexual advances that she vehemently rejected. In May 1994, Jones (P) filed suit against Clinton (D), seeking damages and alleging deprivation and conspiracy to deprive her of federal civil rights under color of state law, and state-law torts of intentional infliction of emotional distress and defamation. Clinton (D) filed a motion to dismiss on grounds of Presidential immunity, and requested the court to defer all other pleadings and motions until after the immunity issue was resolved. The district court denied the motion to dismiss on immunity grounds and ruled that discovery could proceed, but ordered any trial stayed until the end of Clinton's (D) presidency. Jones (P) and Clinton (D) appealed, and the appellate court affirmed the denial of the motion to dismiss, but reversed the order postponing the trial. The U.S. Supreme Court granted certiorari.

ISSUE: Does the doctrine of separation of powers require federal courts to stay all private actions against the President until he leaves office?

HOLDING AND DECISION: (Stevens, J.) No. The doctrine of separation of powers does not require federal courts to stay all private actions against the President until he leaves office. The principal rationale for affording certain public officials immunity from suits for money damages arising out of their official acts is inapplicable to unofficial conduct. Although Clinton (D) argues that the doctrine of separation of powers places limits on the authority of the Judiciary to interfere with the Executive Branch, it does not follow that these principles would be violated by allowing Jones's (P) action to proceed. There is no suggestion that the Judiciary is being asked to perform any function that might in some way be described as executive, or that this decision will curtail the scope of official powers of the Executive Branch. Furthermore, only three sitting Presidents have been subjected to suits for their private actions, and it is unlikely that this decision will result in a deluge of such litigation. If Congress deems it appropriate to afford the President stronger protection, it may respond with appropriate legislation. Affirmed.

▌**ANALYSIS**

The President is absolutely immune from civil damages liability for his official acts in office. *Nixon v. Fitzgerald*, 457 U.S. 731 (1982). In *Fitzgerald*, the Court noted that because of the singular importance of the President's duties, diverting his energies by concern about private lawsuits would raise unique risks to the effective functioning of the government. Clinton argued, albeit unsuccessfully, that he too would be distracted from his public duties by participation in Jones's (P) lawsuit. But the *Fitzgerald* court's central concern was not the distraction of participating in a trial, but the worry and caution attendant to the possibility of damages actions stemming from any particular official decision.

■■■

Quicknotes

CERTIORARI A discretionary writ issued by a superior court to an inferior court in order to review the lower court's decisions; the Supreme Court's writ ordering such review.

DEFAMATION An intentional false publication, communicated publicly in either oral or written form, subjecting a person to scorn, hatred or ridicule, or injuring him or her in relation to his or her occupation or business.

INTENTIONAL INFLICTION OF EMOTIONAL DISTRESS Intentional and extreme behavior on the part of the wrongdoer with the intent to cause the victim to suffer from severe emotional distress, or with reckless indifference, resulting in the victim's suffering from severe emotional distress.

SEPARATION OF POWERS The system of checks and balances preventing one branch of government from infringing upon exercising the powers of another branch of government.

■■■

Glossary

Common Latin Words and Phrases Encountered in the Law

A FORTIORI: Because one fact exists or has been proven, therefore a second fact that is related to the first fact must also exist.

A PRIORI: From the cause to the effect. A term of logic used to denote that when one generally accepted truth is shown to be a cause, another particular effect must necessarily follow.

AB INITIO: From the beginning; a condition which has existed throughout, as in a marriage which was void ab initio.

ACTUS REUS: The wrongful act; in criminal law, such action sufficient to trigger criminal liability.

AD VALOREM: According to value; an ad valorem tax is imposed upon an item located within the taxing jurisdiction calculated by the value of such item.

AMICUS CURIAE: Friend of the court. Its most common usage takes the form of an amicus curiae brief, filed by a person who is not a party to an action but is nonetheless allowed to offer an argument supporting his legal interests.

ARGUENDO: In arguing. A statement, possibly hypothetical, made for the purpose of argument, is one made arguendo.

BILL QUIA TIMET: A bill to quiet title (establish ownership) to real property.

BONA FIDE: True, honest, or genuine. May refer to a person's legal position based on good faith or lacking notice of fraud (such as a bona fide purchaser for value) or to the authenticity of a particular document (such as a bona fide last will and testament).

CAUSA MORTIS: With approaching death in mind. A gift causa mortis is a gift given by a party who feels certain that death is imminent.

CAVEAT EMPTOR: Let the buyer beware. This maxim is reflected in the rule of law that a buyer purchases at his own risk because it is his responsibility to examine, judge, test, and otherwise inspect what he is buying.

CERTIORARI: A writ of review. Petitions for review of a case by the United States Supreme Court are most often done by means of a writ of certiorari.

CONTRA: On the other hand. Opposite. Contrary to.

CORAM NOBIS: Before us; writs of error directed to the court that originally rendered the judgment.

CORAM VOBIS: Before you; writs of error directed by an appellate court to a lower court to correct a factual error.

CORPUS DELICTI: The body of the crime; the requisite elements of a crime amounting to objective proof that a crime has been committed.

CUM TESTAMENTO ANNEXO, ADMINISTRATOR (ADMINISTRATOR C.T.A.): With will annexed; an administrator c.t.a. settles an estate pursuant to a will in which he is not appointed.

DE BONIS NON, ADMINISTRATOR (ADMINISTRATOR D.B.N.): Of goods not administered; an administrator d.b.n. settles a partially settled estate.

DE FACTO: In fact; in reality; actually. Existing in fact but not officially approved or engendered.

DE JURE: By right; lawful. Describes a condition that is legitimate "as a matter of law," in contrast to the term "de facto," which connotes something existing in fact but not legally sanctioned or authorized. For example, de facto segregation refers to segregation brought about by housing patterns, etc., whereas de jure segregation refers to segregation created by law.

DE MINIMIS: Of minimal importance; insignificant; a trifle; not worth bothering about.

DE NOVO: Anew; a second time; afresh. A trial de novo is a new trial held at the appellate level as if the case originated there and the trial at a lower level had not taken place.

DICTA: Generally used as an abbreviated form of obiter dicta, a term describing those portions of a judicial opinion incidental or not necessary to resolution of the specific question before the court. Such nonessential statements and remarks are not considered to be binding precedent.

DUCES TECUM: Refers to a particular type of writ or subpoena requesting a party or organization to produce certain documents in their possession.

EN BANC: Full bench. Where a court sits with all justices present rather than the usual quorum.

EX PARTE: For one side or one party only. An ex parte proceeding is one undertaken for the benefit of only one party, without notice to, or an appearance by, an adverse party.

EX POST FACTO: After the fact. An ex post facto law is a law that retroactively changes the consequences of a prior act.

EX REL.: Abbreviated form of the term "ex relatione," meaning upon relation or information. When the state brings an action in which it has no interest against an individual at the instigation of one who has a private interest in the matter.

FORUM NON CONVENIENS: Inconvenient forum. Although a court may have jurisdiction over the case, the action should be tried in a more conveniently located court, one to which parties and witnesses may more easily travel, for example.

GUARDIAN AD LITEM: A guardian of an infant as to litigation, appointed to represent the infant and pursue his/her rights.

HABEAS CORPUS: You have the body. The modern writ of habeas corpus is a writ directing that a person (body) being detained (such as a prisoner) be brought before the court so that the legality of his detention can be judicially ascertained.

IN CAMERA: In private, in chambers. When a hearing is held before a judge in his chambers or when all spectators are excluded from the courtroom.

IN FORMA PAUPERIS: In the manner of a pauper. A party who proceeds in forma pauperis because of his poverty is one who is allowed to bring suit without liability for costs.

INFRA: Below, under. A word referring the reader to a later part of a book. (The opposite of supra.)

IN LOCO PARENTIS: In the place of a parent.

IN PARI DELICTO: Equally wrong; a court of equity will not grant requested relief to an applicant who is in pari delicto, or as much at fault in the transactions giving rise to the controversy as is the opponent of the applicant.

IN PARI MATERIA: On like subject matter or upon the same matter. Statutes relating to the same person or things are said to be in pari materia. It is a general rule of statutory construction that such statutes should be construed together, i.e., looked at as if they together constituted one law.

IN PERSONAM: Against the person. Jurisdiction over the person of an individual.

IN RE: In the matter of. Used to designate a proceeding involving an estate or other property.

IN REM: A term that signifies an action against the res, or thing. An action in rem is basically one that is taken directly against property, as distinguished from an action in personam, i.e., against the person.

INTER ALIA: Among other things. Used to show that the whole of a statement, pleading, list, statute, etc., has not been set forth in its entirety.

INTER PARTES: Between the parties. May refer to contracts, conveyances or other transactions having legal significance.

INTER VIVOS: Between the living. An inter vivos gift is a gift made by a living grantor, as distinguished from bequests contained in a will, which pass upon the death of the testator.

IPSO FACTO: By the mere fact itself.

JUS: Law or the entire body of law.

LEX LOCI: The law of the place; the notion that the rights of parties to a legal proceeding are governed by the law of the place where those rights arose.

MALUM IN SE: Evil or wrong in and of itself; inherently wrong. This term describes an act that is wrong by its very nature, as opposed to one which would not be wrong but for the fact that there is a specific legal prohibition against it (malum prohibitum).

MALUM PROHIBITUM: Wrong because prohibited, but not inherently evil. Used to describe something that is wrong because it is expressly forbidden by law but that is not in and of itself evil, e.g., speeding.

MANDAMUS: We command. A writ directing an official to take a certain action.

MENS REA: A guilty mind; a criminal intent. A term used to signify the mental state that accompanies a crime or other prohibited act. Some crimes require only a general mens rea (general intent to do the prohibited act), but others, like assault with intent to murder, require the existence of a specific mens rea.

MODUS OPERANDI: Method of operating; generally refers to the manner or style of a criminal in committing crimes, admissible in appropriate cases as evidence of the identity of a defendant.

NEXUS: A connection to.

NISI PRIUS: A court of first impression. A nisi prius court is one where issues of fact are tried before a judge or jury.

N.O.V. (NON OBSTANTE VEREDICTO): Notwithstanding the verdict. A judgment n.o.v. is a judgment given in favor of one party despite the fact that a verdict was returned in favor of the other party, the justification being that the verdict either had no reasonable support in fact or was contrary to law.

NUNC PRO TUNC: Now for then. This phrase refers to actions that may be taken and will then have full retroactive effect.

PENDENTE LITE: Pending the suit; pending litigation under way.

PER CAPITA: By head; beneficiaries of an estate, if they take in equal shares, take per capita.

PER CURIAM: By the court; signifies an opinion ostensibly written "by the whole court" and with no identified author.

PER SE: By itself, in itself; inherently.

PER STIRPES: By representation. Used primarily in the law of wills to describe the method of distribution where a person, generally because of death, is unable to take that which is left to him by the will of another, and therefore his heirs divide such property between them rather than take under the will individually.

PRIMA FACIE: On its face, at first sight. A prima facie case is one that is sufficient on its face, meaning that the evidence supporting it is adequate to establish the case until contradicted or overcome by other evidence.

PRO TANTO: For so much; as far as it goes. Often used in eminent domain cases when a property owner receives partial payment for his land without prejudice to his right to bring suit for the full amount he claims his land to be worth.

QUANTUM MERUIT: As much as he deserves. Refers to recovery based on the doctrine of unjust enrichment in those cases in which a party has rendered valuable services or furnished materials that were accepted and enjoyed by another under circumstances that would reasonably notify the recipient that the rendering party expected to be paid. In essence, the law implies a contract to pay the reasonable value of the services or materials furnished.

QUASI: Almost like; as if; nearly. This term is essentially used to signify that one subject or thing is almost analogous to another but that material differences between them do exist. For example, a quasi-criminal proceeding is one that is not strictly criminal but shares enough of the same characteristics to require some of the same safeguards (e.g., procedural due process must be followed in a parole hearing).

QUID PRO QUO: Something for something. In contract law, the consideration, something of value, passed between the parties to render the contract binding.

RES GESTAE: Things done; in evidence law, this principle justifies the admission of a statement that would otherwise be hearsay when it is made so closely to the event in question as to be said to be a part of it, or with such spontaneity as not to have the possibility of falsehood.

RES IPSA LOQUITUR: The thing speaks for itself. This doctrine gives rise to a rebuttable presumption of negligence when the instrumentality causing the injury was within the exclusive control of the defendant, and the injury was one that does not normally occur unless a person has been negligent.

RES JUDICATA: A matter adjudged. Doctrine which provides that once a court of competent jurisdiction has rendered a final judgment or decree on the merits, that judgment or decree is conclusive upon the parties to the case and prevents them from engaging in any other litigation on the points and issues determined therein.

RESPONDEAT SUPERIOR: Let the master reply. This doctrine holds the master liable for the wrongful acts of his servant (or the principal for his agent) in those cases in which the servant (or agent) was acting within the scope of his authority at the time of the injury.

STARE DECISIS: To stand by or adhere to that which has been decided. The common law doctrine of stare decisis attempts to give security and certainty to the law by following the policy that once a principle of law as applicable to a certain set of facts has been set forth in a decision, it forms a precedent which will subsequently be followed, even though a different decision might be made were it the first time the question had arisen. Of course, stare decisis is not an inviolable principle and is departed from in instances where there is good cause (e.g., considerations of public policy led the Supreme Court to disregard prior decisions sanctioning segregation).

SUPRA: Above. A word referring a reader to an earlier part of a book.

ULTRA VIRES: Beyond the power. This phrase is most commonly used to refer to actions taken by a corporation that are beyond the power or legal authority of the corporation.

Addendum of French Derivatives

IN PAIS: Not pursuant to legal proceedings.

CHATTEL: Tangible personal property.

CY PRES: Doctrine permitting courts to apply trust funds to purposes not expressed in the trust but necessary to carry out the settlor's intent.

PER AUTRE VIE: For another's life; during another's life. In property law, an estate may be granted that will terminate upon the death of someone other than the grantee.

PROFIT A PRENDRE: A license to remove minerals or other produce from land.

VOIR DIRE: Process of questioning jurors as to their predispositions about the case or parties to a proceeding in order to identify those jurors displaying bias or prejudice.